The Republican Army in the Spanish Civil War, 1936–1939

This is a long-awaited translation of a definitive account of the Republican Army in the Spanish Civil War. Michael Alpert examines the origins, formation and performance of the Republican Army and sets the Spanish Civil War in its broader military context. He explores the conflicts between communists and Spanish anarchists about how the war should be fought as well as the experience of individual conscripts, problems of food, clothing, arms and the role of women in the new army. The book contains extensive discussion of international aspects, particularly the role of the International Brigades and of the Soviet Russian advisers. Lastly, it discusses the final uprising of professional Republican officers against the Government and the almost unconditional surrender to Franco. Professor Alpert also provides detailed statistics for the military forces available to Franco and to the Republic and biographies of the key figures on both sides.

MICHAEL ALPERT is Emeritus Professor of the History of Spain at the University of Westminster.

Other works on the Spanish Civil War by the author

La guerra civil española en el mar, Madrid: Siglo Veintiuno, 1987; rev. edn Barcelona: Editorial Crítica, 2008

A New International History of the Spanish Civil War, Houndmills: Palgrave Macmillan, 1994; rev. edn 2004. Translated as *Aguas Peligrosas: Nueva Historia Internacional de la Guerra Civil Española*, Madrid: Akal, 1998

The Republican Army in the Spanish Civil War, 1936–1939

Michael Alpert

CAMBRIDGE
UNIVERSITY PRESS

CAMBRIDGE UNIVERSITY PRESS
Cambridge, New York, Melbourne, Madrid, Cape Town,
Singapore, São Paulo, Delhi, Mexico City

Cambridge University Press
The Edinburgh Building, Cambridge CB2 8RU, UK

Published in the United States of America by Cambridge University Press, New York

www.cambridge.org
Information on this title: www.cambridge.org/9781107028739

Original title: El Ejército Popular de la República, 1936–1939

First published in Spanish by Editorial Critica, S. L. 2007
First published in English by Cambridge University Press 2013

Printed by MPG Printgroup, UK

A catalogue record for this publication is available from the British Library

Library of Congress Cataloguing in Publication data
Alpert, Michael, 1936– author.
[Ejército Popular de la República, 1936–1939. English]
The Republican Army in the Spanish Civil War, 1936–1939 / Michael Alpert.
p. cm.
Includes bibliographical references and index.
ISBN 978-1-107-02873-9 (hardback)
1. Spain–History–Civil War, 1936–1939. 2. Spain. Ejército Popular de la República. I. Title.
DP269.23.A47 2013
946.081'42–dc23
2012035322

ISBN 978-1-107-02873-9 Hardback

Contents

Maps

Tables

Preface

On 18 July 1936 military insurgents in Spain declared a State of War without the consent of the Government, with the aim of overthrowing the Popular Front Government of the Spanish Republic. The uprising was successfully resisted in many parts of Spain, and thus developed into the Civil War of 1936–9, ending with the victory of General Franco on 1 April 1939. The Republic constructed what was in effect a new army, which it called the Popular Army of the Republic (*Ejército Popular de la República*). In the Republican press the Popular Army (the Spanish adjective *popular* means 'of the people' but to call it 'People's Army' would suggest a similarity to forces which did not exist at the time, as well as begging the question of communist influence) was also often called the *Spanish* Army, to underline the fact that Franco's forces were foreign, as indeed they were to a greater extent than those of the Republic. Its opponents generally called it the 'Red' Army or *Ejército Rojo*. Here it is called the Republican Army.

The Republican Army consisted of the remainder of those parts of the Spanish Army, of its war material and of its professional and non-commissioned officers who had not rebelled and in some cases had taken part in the crushing of the rebellion of their fellow officers in the week of 18–25 July 1936. From these the Republic created a military force which fought the war arising from the coup launched by the larger part of the officers and the garrisons. The Republican Army became a full-size force of several hundred thousand men, who fought for two years and eight months in particular conditions of inferiority.

Its interest for historians and military specialists lies in the issues that arose during the war from arguments about the nature of the army, from the political tensions suffered at the time as they affected the character of a national army fighting a civil war, together with questions of armament and politico-military issues regarding appropriate strategy. For military, social and political historians the significant questions lie in the area of the extent to which an army can be 'revolutionary', how this term is interpreted and how far discussion of the nature of the Republican Army can be understood and assessed against the criteria of successful forces created in comparable situations elsewhere. The Spanish Communist Party and the Soviet Russian advisers of the Republican Army inevitably thought in terms of their experience of the Russian Civil War of 1918–20. In historical terms, references were made to the Red Army of the Russian Revolution, the armies of the French Revolution of the late eighteenth century and even to the New Model Army in the English Civil War of the seventeenth century. In their turn, the experience of the Spanish Civil War was important for the Soviet Army, and for the anti-Nazi guerrilla forces of the Second World War, for the Cuban revolutionaries under Castro and for the armies of communist China and Vietnam.

While in the immediate aftermath of the Spanish 'transition to democracy', as it came to be called, which followed General Franco's death in November 1975, interest in the Civil War of 1936–9 which had brought him to power seemed to wane, in recent years the volume of doctoral theses, scholarly work, academic and more popular books, television programmes, websites, Web forums and similar reflections of interest has swelled. This book, which had two earlier Spanish editions in 1978 and 1989, though it has never before appeared in English, joined a number of major works on the Second Republic and the Civil War when another revised and much extended Spanish edition came out in 2007. This edition took into account the work which had appeared since its first edition, in particular research based on archival material made available in the USSR, dealing with international participation and arms supply. Furthermore, in recent years many local histories, personal accounts and biographies have enabled historians to stand back and see the Republican Army in a wider context.

Spain is a member of NATO and the European Community. It has successfully navigated the shoals of establishing democracy. The Civil War of 1936–9 is an essential part of its history. The aim of this English edition, which incorporates information taken from very recent work by scholars on the individual experiences of conscripts in the Republican Army and reflects new views, is to make an account of the Army, its international volunteers and its Soviet advisers, its political and organisational difficulties and solutions, available to the non-Spanish-reading public and to readers interested in military questions in general as well as in Spain.

It would be impossible to name all those people who, beginning with Hugh Thomas, the supervisor of the doctoral thesis which was the original form of this book, have contributed to it. Many of them, veterans of both sides of the Spanish war, whom I came to know when researching in Madrid in 1971, are no longer with us. Professional Spanish officers were of enormous help in interpreting procedures and the vocabulary of Spanish military matters. The regular seminars on contemporary Spain at the Cañada Blanch foundation in London were a constant stimulus, as have been the communications from descendants of participants in the war and students of it who frequently send me emails with valuable information or usefully challenge me on what they have read in the Spanish editions of this book. Lastly, I must thank Christopher Feeney, who put so much effort into the copy editing of the book.

I have occasionally been accused of a certain 'aseptic' neutrality. I plead guilty, because I have tried to deal with facts with as little prejudice as possible. In any case, foreigners who deal with '*cosas de España*', as Richard Ford's book *Gatherings from Spain* of 1830 was called in Spanish, must tread warily and with respect.

Archival sources

Official publications consulted include the *Gaceta de Madrid*, known during the Civil War as *Gaceta de la República*, and cited as *Gaceta*, and the *Diario Oficial del Ministerio de la Guerra*, later *de Defensa Nacional*, or daily bulletin of the Army, later National Defence, Ministry, cited as *DO* or *Diario Oficial*.

British documents are taken from the Foreign Office General Correspondence series (FO 371) with prefix W (Western) and suffix 41 (corresponding to Spain).

References to the frequently cited diary of President Azaña are from the 1968 Mexico City edition of his complete works (*Memorias de Guerra* in his *Obras Completas*).

The following abbreviations are used:

C	*carpeta*, folder
CGG	*Cuartel General del Generalísimo*, material archived in General Franco's HQ
DN	*Documentación Nacional*, Documents of the Nationalist or Insurgent Army
DR	*Documentación Roja*, Documents of the Republican Army
L	*legajo*, file
n.d.	No date of publication
n.p.	No place of publication
SHM	*Servicio Histórico Militar*, Civil War section, now called *Archivo Militar de la Guerra*

Notes on the text

NAMES

Spanish people put their father's name first, followed by their mother's. For example, Juan Hernández Saravia. Sometimes only the patronymic is used; sometimes both surnames, as in the Pérez Salas family. Sometimes the matronymic is used, as in the case of the poet Lorca (really Federico García Lorca), or that of the Prime Minister Caballero (really Francisco Largo Caballero), though he may sometimes be found referred to both as Largo and as Largo Caballero

ARMY BRANCHES AND RANKS

The officers who fought in the Spanish Civil War are usually referred to by the branch to which they belonged (infantry, artillery, cavalry, engineers, supply, carabineers, civil guard and others). Air Force and *Guardia de Asalto* (armed police) officers were seconded from their original Arms.

Abbreviations

CEDA	*Confederación Española de Derechas Autónomas*, electoral grouping of right-wing parties, led by José María Gil-Robles
CNT	*Confederación Nacional del Trabajo*, very large, decentralised and broadly based anarchist trade-union organisation
FAI	*Federación Anarquista Ibérica*, leaders of the CNT and anarchist revolutionaries
JSU	*Juventudes Socialistas Unificadas*, United Socialist and Communist Youth
MAOC	*Milicias Antifascistas Obreras y Campesinas*, Workers' and Peasants' Antifascist Militias
PCE	*Partido Comunista de España*, Spanish Communist Party
POUM	*Partido Obrero de Unificación Marxista*, left-wing, anti-Stalinist communist party
PSOE	*Partido Socialista Obrero Español*, Spanish Socialist Party, divided between revolutionary and reformist wings
PSUC	*Partido Socialista Unificado de Cataluña*, United Catalan Socialist and Communist Party
UGT	*Unión General de Trabajadores*, Federation of Socialist Trade Unions
UMRA	*Unión Militar Republicana y Antifascista*, Association of Republican and Antifascist Military Officers

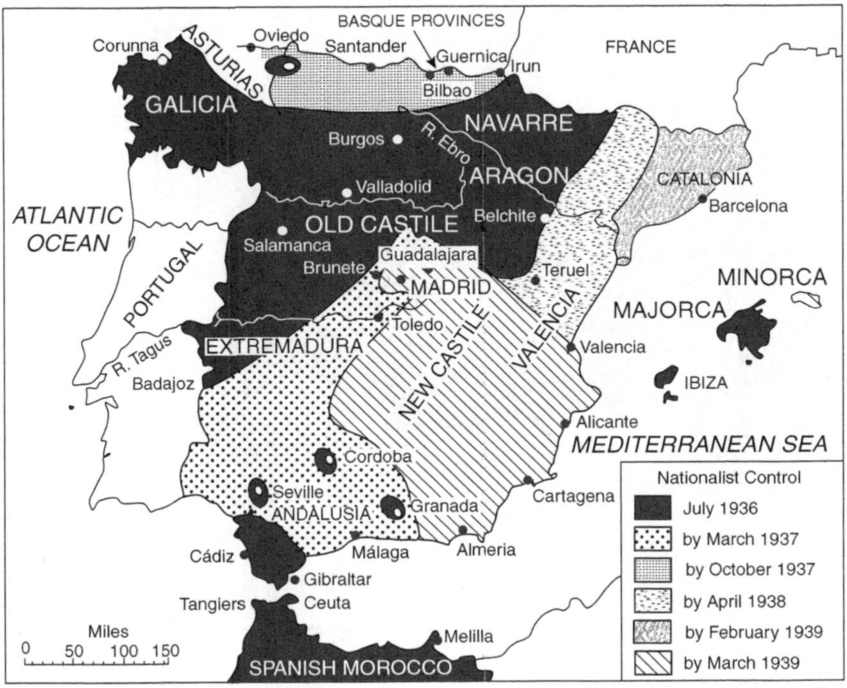

Map 1 Franco's control of Spain, 1936–9

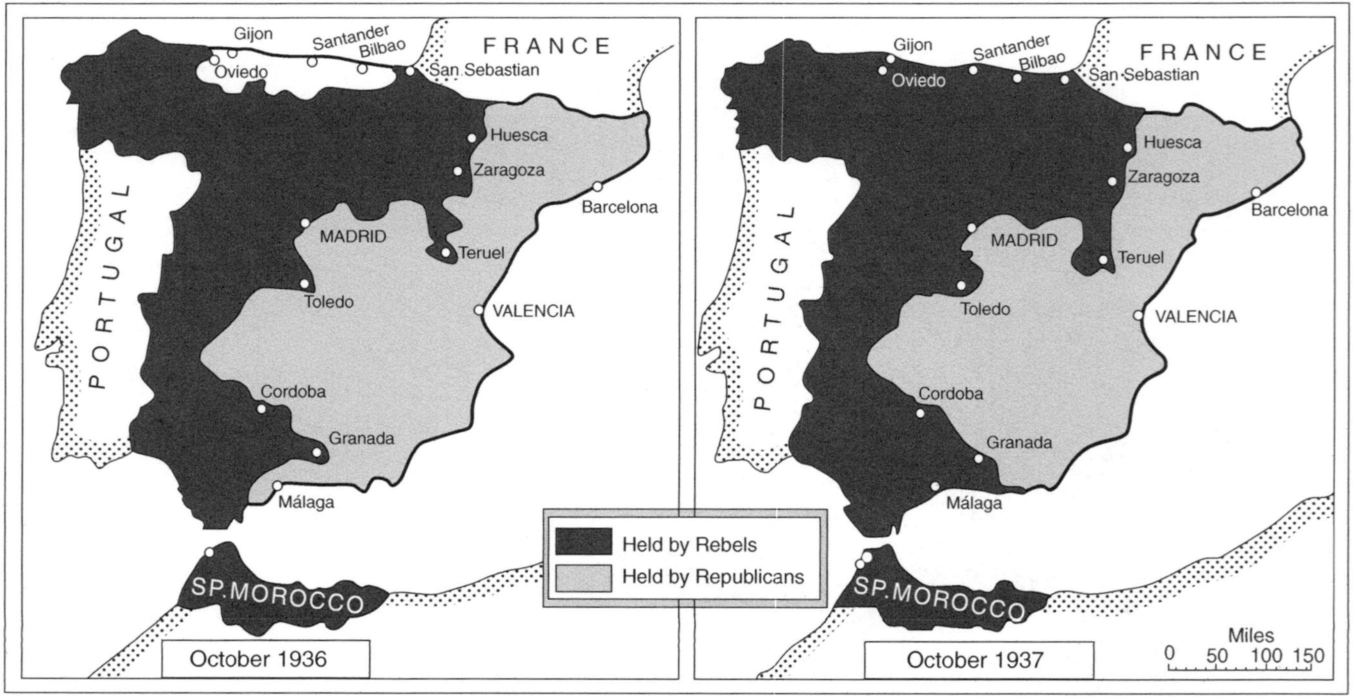

Map 2 One year of the rebel conquest

Map 3 Spain in the summer of 1938

1 The Spanish Army in 1936

The two armies of the Spanish Civil War of 1936–9 were essentially Spanish, though the one commanded by General Franco, known at the time as 'Nationalist',[1] included significant Italian infantry forces, while the Republican, 'Red' (an adjective used by both sides), 'Popular' or 'People's' Army contained brigades of international volunteers. Despite the presence on Franco's side of battalions recruited by the Spanish *Falange* or Fascist Party, and the institution of political commissars in the Republican Army, both armies were based on traditional Spanish models, and were offshoots of the existing pre-war Army. Before examining the formation and characteristics of the Republican Army, then, some description of the pre-war Army is required.[2]

The establishment of the pre-war Army was 101,455 men on the Peninsula, the Canary Islands and the Balearics, together with 30,383 in the Spanish zone of the Moroccan Protectorate. Most were conscripts. Since 1930, compulsory service had effectively lasted for one year. Taking into consideration deserters and exemptions, plus the so-called *cuotas*, such as university students, who served a shorter period, as well as the medically unfit, the actual number of conscripts was considerably smaller than the establishment. At the outset of the Civil War, then, most of the troops in barracks, including a significant

[1] The adjective 'Nationalist', used commonly for Franco's army in English-language sources during the Civil War, is better avoided, because in Spain it evokes regional and separatist concepts to which the victors in the Spanish Civil War were hostile. 'Insurgent' is probably more appropriate.

[2] Among other works, the following are enlightening: M. Aguilar, *El ejército español durante la Segunda República*, Madrid, 1986; M. Alpert, *La reforma militar de Azaña*, 2nd edn, Granada, 2008; Carolyn Boyd, *Praetorian Politics in Liberal Spain*, Chapel Hill, NC, 1979; G. Cardona, *El poder militar en la España contemporánea hasta la guerra civil*, Madrid, 1983; S. Payne, *Politics and the Military in Modern Spain*, Stanford, CA, 1967, rev. as *Ejército y sociedad en la España liberal*, Madrid, 1977; R. Salas Larrazábal, *Historia del Ejército Popular de la República*, Madrid, 1973; C. Seco Serrano, *Militarismo y civilismo en la España contemporánea*, Madrid, 1984.

number of those in Morocco, were young men completing their term of compulsory service, who had very little training in military skills.

Despite the reforms of the Second Republic, which had come into power in April 1931, military equipment and training were deficient. The technical level was low given that many of those recruits who came from the educated classes of society or had qualifications served no more than a short period, leaving, as had always been the case, working-class conscripts, often illiterate, to constitute the majority.

With the final pacification in 1927 of the Spanish zone of Morocco, which had cost large loss of life and huge amounts of money ever since the process had begun in 1909, and given the lack of funds for realistic and extensive manoeuvres, the Army had not had war experience. However, the *Tercio de Extranjeros*, or Foreign Legion (though it was mostly Spanish in composition), an elite force of volunteers, and the native Moroccan regiments – known as *Regulares* – benefited from more intensive training. These units would double and treble in size during the Civil War and would form the nucleus of the Franco's Insurgents against the Republic.

The Army also lacked modern equipment. While the artillery had some relatively modern pieces, in general its material was antiquated and heterogeneous. In general, the Spanish Army was not in sympathy with modernising ideas current in Europe between the two World Wars. Although artillery and engineer officers were undoubtedly highly trained, military technology was in general backward. In any case, resources were lacking to motorise or mechanise the army. At the beginning of the Civil War, Spain had only two small tank units equipped with outmoded machines. Spanish military writers described and commented on tank experiments carried out abroad, but their reaction was almost always hostile. Infantry methods developed in Germany to solve the problem of advancing against a deep defence line were not practised and hardly considered in Spain. In brief, with the exceptional use of troops to maintain order during strikes (for lack of a sufficiently trained and equipped public order force until the Republic created the *Guardia de Asalto*, and because the officers expected to be called on to keep order), life for officers and troops was routine and boring.

While conscripts saw their time in military service as a mere interval in their lives, for officers the Army represented their career and their personal ideals. The swollen number of officers – in 1932, the year which reflected the maximum effect of the reductions imposed by the Republic, there were 12,968 officers on the active list, not counting the 58 generals (since the latter figure includes generals of brigade, as well as divisional commanders, the figure for generals is quite small) – echoed a certain backwardness in social vision which did not insist on early retirement for officers once they had reached the limit of their professional effectiveness. Only 26 of the 217 colonels in the main branches (infantry, cavalry, artillery and engineers) of the Army in 1936 were under 55 years old. Most of the generals were over this age and even majors of under 40 were rare. The absence in Spain of an adequate reserve officer class meant that, during the Moroccan wars, very large numbers of new second lieutenants (*alféreces*) had been commissioned annually, and were now creating severe promotion blocks. Thus the most competent and ambitious officers were frustrated by the strict seniority required for promotion, while there had been dissatisfaction with the very rapid battlefield promotions (*ascensos por mérito en campaña*) made during the Moroccan campaigns and which placed some officers high up on the seniority lists at every stage in their careers. Many people insisted that these promotions were a result of favouritism, and confused personal valour with the ability to run and lead military units.

In contrast with their colleagues in Great Britain, France or Germany, countries which either recruited their officers from an upper-class and often financially comfortable background, or which had a well-developed and universal social and educational structure, Spanish officers tended to come from a lower-middle class background, and one rarely concerned with social or intellectual matters. The military cadet was often one of many children of a minor civil servant or non-commissioned officer. Indeed, the level of recruitment of cadets with fathers in the service was very high. Nor was it rare for cadets to be admitted when very young, so that the military academy served in some ways as a secondary school and, given its discipline and the length of time spent there, a sort of military 'seminary', which inculcated a tendency to develop fixed attitudes.

Intervention in politics by means of coups d'état or the threat of them had been characteristic of the Spanish Army. From one aspect this might be considered as inevitable, given the chaos, civil wars and political vacuum of the nineteenth century. From another aspect the behaviour of the officers might be explained by the perceived absence in Spain of other ways of advancing in society. To some extent, the Army was a means of access to power and social status for the officer whose social background might be humble or who was himself an ex-sergeant promoted for his ability and long service into the list of officers, called the *Escala de Reserva Retribuída*, who held ranks of lieutenant, captain and sometimes higher but who were on a seniority list separate from that of their academy-trained colleagues.

In the nineteenth century military insurrections had had liberal tendencies, but in the period since the restoration, at the end of 1874, of the Bourbon monarchy, following the abortive First Republic, newer generations of officers had reacted in a hostile manner to working-class activism, especially in its peculiarly Spanish anarchist garb, whether violent or unionised, as well as to Catalan regionalism and to the anticlericalism typical of the gamut of most intellectual, dissident or republican attitudes. Furthermore, the catastrophic military and naval defeat of Spain by the United States in 1898 polarised ideas and emotions. The officers saw themselves as suffering death, sickness and wounds, and enduring defeat and the shame, while Spain, undermined by subversive ideas and governed by weak and venal politicians, had sent an army and a navy to a war for which they were inadequately prepared. For those who saw the military question as a microcosm of the problems of Spain, the loss of Cuba and the Philippines revealed the deficiencies of the Army and the consequences of an attitude which was mired in out-of-date traditions. The army needed reform as part of a wide change which would Europeanise and modernise the country as a whole.

Attitudes steadily polarised. The Army reacted to criticisms of it in the press by forcing the passing on 20 March 1906 of the *Ley de Jurisdicciones*, which would be used for the next 25 years to gag critics of the Army with threats of court martial.

In 1916 infantry officers had created unions or *Juntas de Defensa* to defend their promotion interests in the same way that artillery and engineers officers used to swear on being commissioned that they would accept promotion only by seniority. By threats to mount coups, the *Juntas* coerced a succession of Ministers of War, who were almost always generals. Yet, contrary to what had been, perhaps ingenuously, hoped in reformist circles, the *Juntas* did not rise to demand a reforming parliament and a new regime. On the contrary, the officers used force to repress strikes in 1917 and after.

The self-interest of Army officers was to an extent satisfied by the *Ley de Bases para la Organización del Ejército* of 10 March 1918, which was introduced into the *Cortes* – the Spanish parliament – by the civilian War Minister Juan de la Cierva. The law increased the size of the Army and created more posts for officers. To tackle the excess it removed a number of officers from the active list, but it did nothing to unblock promotions or to lower ages of retirement. Other measures, such as salary increases and the near abolition of battlefield merit promotions, did nothing to reform the real problems or to answer the question of what type of army was needed, how much should be spent on it and how the necessary changes should be introduced.

The military disaster in Morocco in August 1921 acted as a catalyst to officers' discontent. On one side, investigation into who was responsible for the catastrophe and officers' resentment about being unjustly blamed for it, added to fear of a far-reaching reform and even abandoning the Protectorate, played an important part in General Miguel Primo de Rivera's coup of 13 September 1923. On the other hand, military incompetence and corruption led to the rise of a younger group of officers who would be known as *africanistas*, which in turn led to a fresh way of waging war finally bringing about the defeat of the insurrectionary tribes of the Riff mountains. This campaign was marked by the emergence of the *africanistas* typified by Francisco Franco, who became a general of brigade at the age of 34.[3]

The *Juntas* crystallised hostility between officers who expected to spend their careers in Peninsula garrisons, and Africanists who volunteered for active service in Morocco, where there were more opportunities to put their training and skills into practice, although they were also more likely to be killed, suffer wounds or fall ill.

Public opinion about Africanists was split. Traditionalists saw them as heroes sacrificing life and health to the glory of Spain's civilising mission. Progressives considered them rapacious, bloodthirsty mercenaries, who protected commercial interests (in the valuable iron-ore mines of the Riff) against the repressed protests of the Moroccan people, and received medals and promotions thanks to royal favour.

As for working-class organisations, antimilitarism was an essential element in the fundamental concepts of Spanish anarchism, and this would lead to many problems in the Republican Army during the 1936–9 Spanish Civil War. Socialists were opposed less to the Army in principle than in practice, because the burden of military service fell heavily on the working class. For the Left in general, Morocco was a hotbed of corruption, favouritism and self-interested cliques.[4] It is interesting that a leading Africanist, Colonel José Asensio Torrado, appointed commander of the Central Operations Theatre by socialist Premier Largo Caballero in September 1936, and later Under-Secretary for War, was dismissed and heavily criticised for attitudes which his detractors claimed he had absorbed in his career in Morocco.[5]

[3] See Sebastian Balfour, *Deadly Embrace: Morocco and the Road to the Spanish Civil War*, Oxford University Press, 2002.

[4] For an exposé of the anti-*africanista* attitude and a picture of life in Moroccan garrisons, see Antonio Cordón, *Trayectoria: recuerdos de un artillero*, Paris, 1971, and Arturo Barea's autobiographical novel, *La ruta*, Buenos Aires, 1951.

[5] Cordón, *Trayectoria*, 262; Juan Modesto, *Soy del Quinto Regimiento*, Paris, 1969, 52ff.; Enrique Líster, *Nuestra guerra*, Paris, 1966, 56. These three authors were leading communists in the Republican Army.

The *Diario Oficial del Ministerio de la Guerra* of 31 January 1933 carried a list of typical Africanists, whose rapid battlefield promotions were under reconsideration by Manuel Azaña, Prime Minister and reforming Minister of War in the Second Republic. The several hundred officers on the list include men who would be among the leaders of the 1936 uprising. Franco himself, Alonso Vega, Asensio Cabanillas, García Escámez, Muñoz Grandes, Goded, Fanjul, Orgaz, Aranda, Alvarez-Arenas, Varela, Monasterio, Barrón, Delgado Serrano, Losas, Sáenz de Buruaga, Tella, Castejón, Barrera, García Valiño and Esteban-Infantes would all be generals or senior officers in the Insurgent army in 1936–9.[6] Nevertheless, in this list of Africanists who had been decorated or rapidly promoted others can be found some who would hold important posts in the forces of the Republic, among them Pozas and Llano de la Encomienda, Asensio Torrado, Otal and Villalba, Valcázar and del Rosal, together with the airmen Díaz Sandino, Camacho, Hidalgo de Cisneros and Riaño. But Sanjurjo, who had led the victorious campaign against the Riff insurgent Abd'el Krim, conspired against the Republic in 1932 and, had he not died in an air accident, would have led the Government which it was planned would follow the coup of July 1936, and Franco, who had spent almost all his career in Morocco and obtained nearly all his promotions on battlefield merit, were typical *africanistas*.[7]

Primo de Rivera (1923–1930)

The divisions in the Army over the promotion system were most evident in the hostility between the artillery and the engineer corps on one side, and the infantry on the other. The former swore, when they received their commissions, to accept promotion only by strict seniority, and thought that battlefield promotions were often unfair and due to pure luck.

The crisis came to a head during the dictatorship of General Primo de Rivera. He insisted on making abundant battlefield promotions during the Riff war, contravening the 1918 *Ley de Bases*, which allowed such promotions on a very restrictive basis. Consequently, the artillery officers declared a strike. As a result, some 2,000 of them were suspended without pay. The bitterness created by Primo de Rivera's promotions led to other protests and acts of indiscipline. The Artillery Academy at Segovia was closed and officers were punished with heavy

[6] Except Fanjul and Goded, who were executed by the Republic.

[7] On Franco see Paul Preston's impressive *Franco: A Biography*, HarperCollins, 1993.

fines. Primo de Rivera's reorganisation of the General Staff, including the conversion of the specialised Staff Corps into a mere Service, thus attacking its elitist character, also created bitterness; but possibly the greatest anger was caused by the policy of retiring officers more or less arbitrarily, and this affected not only the specialised Corps but also a number of prestigious infantry generals.

The culmination of the reforms of the Primo de Rivera dictatorship was the reopening in 1927 of the General Military Academy. This imposition of a common course for all cadets before they began their specialised artillery or engineer studies was accepted in principle,[8] but it created anger in the specialised corps, particularly when General Franco was appointed Director of the Academy in 1927 and proceeded to surround himself with a teaching staff of Africanists. The powerful influence of this nursery of young officers would become evident when the proportion of officer graduates of the new Academy who joined the Insurgents was overwhelming.

This description of splits within the Army between 1917 and 1931 must be taken into account in considering the origins of the Republican Army in the Civil War. It would certainly be wrong to describe the splits among the Spanish officers' corps at the outset of the war as a clear dividing line separating the *Juntas* from their opponents, the *africanistas* from the *peninsulares*, the specialised Corps from the infantry, or the supporters of Primo de Rivera from those who conspired and rebelled against him. Nevertheless, and to a certain degree, the Republican Army inherited the attitudes of the *Juntas*. Many of those who plotted against Primo de Rivera would find themselves in commands. Several of them were artillery and engineer officers, who would command large infantry units in the Civil War, in contrast to practice in Franco's army; Hernández Saravia, Moriones and Jurado, Republican Army commanders but not infantry men, are outstanding examples. In addition, links with politicians were maintained, partly because the Republican Army was highly politicised, while Francoist military leaders rejected politics, at least overtly.

The Second Republic (1931–1936)

Primo de Rivera fell in January 1930, and after a period of uncertainty and municipal elections which returned Republican majorities

[8] General Emilio Mola, 'Director' and brain of the uprising of 18 July 1936, wrote, 'Our peculiar organisation prevents us obtaining, from the specialised officer corps, generals who are suitable to command units including all three Arms [artillery, engineers and infantry]', *Obras Completas*, Valladolid, 1940, 1026.

in urban areas where voting was less subject to manipulation, King Alfonso XIII left the country and a Republican regime took power on 14 April 1931. From 1931 to 1933, when Minister of War and then Prime Minister, Manuel Azaña carried out a comprehensive reform of the Army, although much remained to be done when Azaña finally lost power in September 1933.[9]

Undoubtedly the reform created an atmosphere of resentment and intrigue, of hatred and envy, but it does not seem that the division among the officers in July 1936 had much to do with the reform of 1931–3. Whatever the hatreds that Azaña's reforms inspired among officers, no measure that Azaña took could have led anyone to fear for the very existence of the Army. Even if this had been so in 1931, when by some words taken out of their context some officers might have been justified, though mistaken, to think that Azaña intended to abolish the Army, this was impossible by the spring and summer of 1936 when the international situation was no longer one of permanent hope of peace and internationalism. Now there was a general fear of another war against Germany, led by a Hitler who was aggressive, revanchist and resolved to recreate German militarism, and against fascist Italy under a boastful and warlike Mussolini, whose fascist 'new man' had just crushed Abyssinia. While Spain would probably maintain its neutrality, as in the 1914–18 conflict, it needed to modernise its defence system.

Nevertheless, the speed with which Azaña legislated – or, rather, decreed, given that he did it with almost no parliamentary debate – his reform in 1931, together with his evident lack of tact and his scorn for the feelings and assumptions of Army officers, had the effect of creating among them not only bitterness but also disdain for left-wing Republicanism, and this would still be present in 1936 among officers for whom the feeling of belonging to 'the military family' was more important than any other social or political attitude.

The reforms

The reductions in numbers in all officer ranks in the active list took place swiftly, since the famous decree of 25 April 1931 made a vague threat of compulsory retirement on standard terms if sufficient officers did not voluntarily and almost immediately accept the advantageous terms offered in the decree of retirement on full pay according to rank (though generally speaking without the various supplements added for particularly responsibilities or posts). The result was the immediate

[9] Alpert, *La reforma militar.*

retirement of over 8,000 officers. The 190 generals in 1931 became 90 in 1932, while from 20,576 officers the lists were reduced to 12,373.

It would be difficult to analyse whether the friction and bitterness caused by this block to the careers of so many officers inclined them towards insurrection in 1936 against a Republic of which Manuel Azaña, author of the retirements decree, became President in May 1936. Nevertheless, it is worth stressing that left-wing opinion was convinced that too many officers with progressive views had accepted the retirement offer, among them several of those involved in the failed Republican uprising in Jaca in 1930. Franco himself believed that most monarchist officers had remained in the Army.[10] The main criticism of some authors is that the Republic did lose officers indiscriminately, given that Azaña refused to purge the Army politically. He thought that all those officers who were unhappy about serving the Republic had been granted retirement under favourable conditions. Indeed, many of the men who would hold high commands in the Republican Army during the war, for instance Antonio Cordón, Adolfo Prada and Francisco Galán, had taken advantage of Azaña's decree to take early retirement.

The decree did not include any reduction in the ages of normal retirement. One of the consequences was that it was mostly the most senior among the generals and colonels who remained in the service, while the younger ones took early retirement. Thus officers, particularly at senior ranks, were no younger than they had been before the mass retirements. In both armies during the Civil War many generals and senior officers had to be retired because their physical condition was unsuitable for the rigours of active service. In the Republican Army, few of those generals who could have been employed did in fact have commands, and age was an important factor.

Another one of the measures taken by Azaña, relevant to the Civil War of 1936–9, was his rationalisation of the regiments, where many units which existed merely in a skeletal form were disbanded. The result was an army of fewer but more complete regiments of cavalry, infantry and engineers. It was on the basis of this consolidation that José María Gil-Robles, CEDA Minister of War in 1935, could make a start in modernising equipment and weapons.

The decrees of 14 July 1931, which fused the two seniority lists of academy-trained and ex-ranker officers, the law of 4 December 1931,

[10] 'The Retirement Law ... was politically biased in that it wanted to rid the army of monarchist officers ... but those who wanted to retire did so and we became the majority.' F. Franco-Salgado-Araujo, *Mis conversaciones con Franco*, Barcelona, 1972, 397.

which established the corps of non-commissioned officers and thus by giving them status tried to attract them towards the Republic, and the Law of 12 September 1932 on recruitment and promotion within the officer corps probably had little influence in reinforcing any feeling of loyalty to the Republic when the officers and NCOs were faced with pressures and the circumstances of 18 July 1936. What is certain is that there was insufficient time for Azaña's hopes that his reforms would attract well-educated young men to a military career to bear fruit. His vision was that such recruits would be rapidly promoted and then proceed to the Military Academy, where the new law reserved 60 per cent of the places for them. As for boys who competed for direct entry, the reform required them to have completed a year of university science studies first, but the restriction on new Military Academy admissions was so extreme in 1931–6 that the measure had no significant effects. Only the closing of the General Military Academy of Zaragoza, commanded by Franco, necessary perhaps for urgent financial reasons, had the effect of politicising what was a mere technical issue. Closing the Academy would create the legend of an Azaña who was resentful and perverse, determined to destroy or 'triturate' – Azaña's somewhat unfortunate use of this verb in a speech came back over and over again to haunt him – the Army and thus leave Spain, in the words of his enemies, undefended against Bolshevism and Freemasonry, the *bêtes noires* of the Spanish Right.

The Republic's re-examination of battlefield promotions affected a number of officers who would occupy important commands in the Republican Army in the Civil War. Nevertheless, right-wing propaganda about these promotions, some of which were cancelled, helped to produce the image of a Republic which treated its gallant warriors badly while it favoured those officers who had the minister's ear, that is his military cabinet or private advisers. Certainly, the cabinet did not behave appropriately on the question of advising the minister about promotions, particularly in the important Madrid garrison.[11] In his diaries, Azaña refers to himself as prisoner of a camarilla. His problem was that he lacked confidence in those generals, among them Franco, whose gifts and qualities were respected by the officers in general. Azaña thought that those generals, mostly Africanists, and monarchists who had supported Primo de Rivera, could never share his view of a Republican Army which was suitable for the emergent bourgeois Republic.

[11] Manuel Azaña, *Obras Completas*, Mexico City, 1966–8, IV: 320. See also the tendentious work of J. Arrarás, *Historia de la Segunda República española*, Madrid, 1956, 141.

Gil-Robles and Franco

The period between November 1933 and February 1936, often called the 'Black Biennium' and characterised by Centre-Radical and Radical-CEDA governments, removed from their commands the generals whom Azaña had appointed, replacing them with others who had been supporters of Primo de Rivera or Africanists fundamentally hostile to the concept of a Republican Army. One of the first acts of the Radical administration which followed the elections of late 1933 was to amnesty General Emilio Mola, who had been subject to investigation for his actions as Director General of internal security in the months preceding the triumph of the Republic on 14 April 1931. Mola was now appointed military commander in Morocco. Likewise, General Sanjurjo and other officers, imprisoned in August 1932 after a failed uprising, were now amnestied. General Franco was promoted to the first vacancy in the seniority list of Generals of Division, and appointed special adviser to Diego Hidalgo, Minister of War during the repression of the socialist and anarchist rebellions in Asturias in October 1934, thus ignoring Carlos Masquelet, the Chief of Staff, who was considered politically unreliable.[12] When Gil-Robles was War Minister in 1935, he appointed Franco Chief of Staff. General Fanjul, who had attacked the Azaña reforms as a parliamentary deputy and would be shot after his failed attempt at rebellion in Madrid in 1936, became Under-Secretary for War. General Goded, whom Azaña had at first favoured and who would also be executed in 1936 in Barcelona, became Director of Air Services as well as Inspector-General of the Valencia military command.

The uprisings of October 1934 in Asturias and Catalonia led to the resignation or dismissal of a number of officers with progressive sympathies. Hernández Saravia resigned, as did Hidalgo de Cisneros from his post as military attaché in Rome. Federico Escofet and Enrique Pérez Farrás, officers with Catalan sympathies, received death sentences, later commuted, while Jesús Pérez Salas, Vicente Guarner, Fernando Condés and several others were tried by courts martial. These men would be well known in the Republican Army in the Civil War and, in some cases, occupy leading positions.

The Radical-CEDA administrations of 1933–6 left the Azaña reforms substantially untouched, but tackled the need to modernise equipment, whose deficiencies the Asturias campaign had revealed.

[12] According to Gil-Robles, leader of the CEDA, Masquelet 'did not inspire the least confidence', *No fue posible la paz*, Barcelona, 1968, 140.

By 1935, the Weimar Republic had disappeared, replaced by warlike Nazism, confined for the moment to Germany. But Mussolini's Italy was already testing the waters over Abyssinia, which in December 1935 would fall victim to fascist aggression. In November 1935 the Spanish *Cortes* approved an ambitious project put forward by Gil-Robles. He planned to buy modern aircraft at a cost of 400 million pesetas over five years, and announced contracts to manufacture 24 new 75 mm artillery batteries and the modernisation of older material, as well as the purchase of the long 155 mm Schneider gun. Plans to buy tanks were announced as well as a major reorganisation which would provide the army with mountain and mixed battle units. These ambitious plans were the result of Franco's spell in the General Staff.

Nevertheless, financial stringencies prevented most of those projects from becoming reality, even though the *Cortes* agreed to increase the military budget for 1936 by 40 per cent as part of a three-year rearmament programme with a special budget of 1,100 million pesetas. It is unlikely that any government, even one not dependent on a coalition, could have imposed such a tax burden on Spain.

The Popular Front Government elected in February 1936 did not proceed with the Gil-Robles programme, except in regard to strengthening defences in the Balearics and the Strait of Gibraltar, where artillery provision was increased. When the Civil War began in July, the delivery of the 24 75 mm batteries was almost complete.

Whether the attempted coup of 1936 which led to the Civil War was caused by the disorder and perceived threat of revolution caused by the Popular Front Government, or because of the latter's inaction in combating such a threat, it happened only because the Army was abnormally sensitive to unimportant changes and because its history conditioned officers to expect to be called on to act as protectors of public order by declaring a State of War. There was no real possibility that the Army or the paramilitary *Guardia Civil* might be dissolved.[13] The fears were perhaps real, but dissolving the army and creating an armed people's militia were no more than mere proposals by Madrid socialists as a change in the PSOE's stated policy.[14]

[13] The Popular Front reflected the decision of the Communist Party of the Soviet Union that communists should cease to attack parties on the Left or even in the Centre, and concentrate on defeating the threat of authoritarian right-wing groups to liberal and parliamentary regimes, paradigmatically France. While the Spanish communists accepted this, they did not participate in the centrist Republican Government which followed the victory of the Popular Front in elections in February 1936.

[14] R. de la Cierva, *Los documentos de la primavera trágica*, Madrid, Secretaría General Técnica del ministerio de Información y Turismo, 1967, No. 20

Given the history of the Spanish Army and its internal splits, even deeper after the conflicts of the Azaña years and the involvement of the Army in the social struggles of the 1933–6 epoch of reactionary government, it is hardly surprising that the triumph of the Popular Front should have created anxiety among army officers, though its manifesto contained nothing threatening to them. The Army's traditional role in maintaining public order in Spain was about to clash with the new and confident excitement of the street. Thus the military, rightly or wrongly, became obsessed with the fear not only that the society of traditional values which it defended was in peril, but also that Moscow and international Freemasonry would destroy that society by first destroying the army. That fear was at the root of military hostility towards the regime. When a newspaper as important as the clerico-conservative *El Debate* told the officers that 'In the Spanish army there is a reserve of moral values which are ever more lacking in the world', it is not strange that officers should have a view of their own role which was to a certain degree unreal.[15]

UME, UMRA and MAOC

The growing extremism in Spanish politics during the Second Republic led to the establishment of semi-secret organisations of Army officers that reflected the ideologies which they supported. There were two major ones: the UME or *Unión Militar Española*, by whose members in many garrisons the uprising of July 1936 was planned, and the UMRA or *Unión Militar Republicana y Antifascista*.

UMRA arose in 1935 when the *Unión Militar Antifascista*, founded by the Communist Party at the end of 1934,[16] and the *Asociación Militar Republicana*, which appears to have originated in Republican anti-Primo de Rivera circles in the 1920s, were merged at the end of 1935.[17]

UMRA's first meeting took place at the home of Captain Miguel Palacios, of the Medical Corps, who would command a division of the Republican Army in the Civil War. The manifesto was composed by Lieutenant-Colonel Carratalá, who was killed or perhaps assassinated when he refused to join the insurrection of the Madrid garrison in July 1936. Among the founders of UMRA were future leaders of the

[15] J. M. García Escudero, *El pensamiento de 'El Debate'*, Madrid, 1983, 343.
[16] Dolores Ibárruri *et al.*, *Guerra y Revolución en España*, Moscow, 1967–71, 66.
[17] Modesto, *Soy del Quinto Regimiento*, 13. See also M. Aroca Mohedano's biography of Azaña's loyal ally (*General Juan Hernández Saravia, el ayudante militar de Azaña*, Madrid, 2006, 95ff.).

Republican Army such as Enciso, Orad de la Torre, Fuentes, Barceló and Ristori de la Cuadra.[18]

UMRA was headed by Captain Eleuterio Díaz Tendido, later given responsibility for judging the loyalty of officers to the Republic.[19] In Barcelona, UMRA was favoured by the Catalan autonomous government, the *Generalitat*, which would appoint Colonel Antonio Escobar of the *Guardia Civil*, Lieutenant-Colonel Felipe Díaz Sandino, later Defence Counsellor, Major Vicente Guarner and a significant number of other UMRA officers to important positions during the war.[20]

In the spring and summer of 1936 UMRA's few hundred committed left-wing and Republican officers helped the antifascist cause by training militias of the United Communist and Socialist Youth Organisation, the *Juventudes Socialistas Unificadas*. One of the instructors was Captain of Engineers Carlos Faraudo, assassinated by rightist gunmen, and another was Lieutenant Castillo, whose murder was avenged by his *Guardia de Asalto* comrades with the killing of the right-wing political leader José Calvo Sotelo in the early hours of 13 July 1936.

Republican officers

The characteristic of many – though by no means all – the Army officers implicated in Republican activities was their anti-elitism. Some were frankly left wing, such as the Galán brothers. Others, like Segismundo Casado, had more general Republican sympathies. Several had taken part in abortive conspiracies and maintained links with politicians who aimed at a thorough reform of the Army. The Insurgent plotters, for their part, associated with politicians but never trusted them completely. The leaders of the Right during the Second Republic of 1931–6 disappeared into Republican prisons when the war began, or escaped abroad, but they do not appear in Franco's governments. In contrast, Republican military leaders lived the war in an atmosphere of political conflict. Most of them were obliged to identify and join one or another political grouping. This is not to criticise them, since they recognised that the fountain of authority had to be civilian government, to which most of them remained loyal until the end. But it is evident

[18] For biographies of these officers see Appendix 4.

[19] María Teresa Suero Roca, *Militares republicanos de la guerra de España*, Barcelona, 1981.

[20] *Ibid.*, 129. See V. Guarner, *Cataluña en la guerra de España*, Madrid, 1975, 64–5. For the appointments see *El Sol*, 17 September 1936.

that the inability to separate the Republican Army from politics was a permanent characteristic.

A document from the Information Section of the insurgent army during the war, based on the notorious 'documents' used by Insurgent propaganda to justify the military uprising,[21] stated that 150,000 trained militia were ready to carry out a revolution in Spain. Yet, as for the proletarian militias, the best-known of which are the MAOC or *Milicias Antifascistas Obreras y Campesinas* (Workers' and Peasants' Antifascist Militias), which trained on Sundays in the sierra to the north of Madrid, communist authors give figures of between 1,000 and 1,500 militants, but this is probably only the nucleus.[22] There is little reliable information on the MAOC. One source claims that its role was limited to protecting meetings with no more than a few revolvers.[23] The small number quoted by Juan Modesto, the leading communist militia commander in the Republican Army, may also indicate a communist and Soviet wish to minimise their activities before the war. Nevertheless, such figures are quite out of proportion with the 150,000 militia claimed in justification of the military uprising of 18 July 1936.

Finally, there seems to have been no military preparation on the part of the Left, apart from the cursory drilling of the MAOC and despite all the revolutionary verbiage, parades and red flags of the spring and summer of 1936, although such events undoubtedly fuelled fears of revolution. While Comintern delegates did visit Spain in 1936 they had no military role.[24]

The tension-filled history of the Second Republic had polarised military opinion, dividing it sufficiently to be to some degree the cause of the failure of the attempted *putsch* of 18 July 1936. Since there was a small group of officers

> who genuinely shared the ideal of a transformation of Spanish society by way of the implanting of the dictatorship of the proletariat, and since this

[21] *Servicio Histórico Militar*, Documentación nacional, legajo 91, carpeta 2 (hereafter DN, L, C). See also H. R. Southworth, *El mito de la cruzada de Franco*, Paris, 1963, 247–52, for a discussion of the 'documents'.

[22] Modesto, *Soy del Quinto Regimiento*, 14.

[23] Líster, *Nuestra guerra*, 27.

[24] Vittorio Vidali, alias 'Carlos Contreras', an Italian communist who was later political commissar of the Spanish communist militia regiment, the *Quinto Regimiento*, arrived in Spain in December 1934 with a fundamentally political mission. He did not take part in militia activities (personal communication from Vidali to the author, 2 February 1973).

> was strengthened by many Republicans who had been disgusted by the vile behaviour of the 'uncrowned monarchy', and who, though still dominated by bourgeois ideas, preferred to fight in favour of a socialist regime rather than continue to maintain ... the privileges of the old oligarchies[25]

it would be possible to create the Republican Army. It might be added that, for many of the officers who fought with the Republic, what they were fighting for was not a socialist regime but simply the Republican constitution which they had sworn to defend.

[25] Margarita Nelken, *Por qué hicimos la revolución*, Madrid, 1936, 148.

2 Military and paramilitary forces in Spain on 18 July 1936

Organisation

In the Peninsula, the Canaries and the Balearic Islands, the Spanish Army was organised in eight divisions and two independent commands. Divisional commands were located, in numerical order, in Madrid, Seville, Valencia, Barcelona, Zaragoza, Burgos, Valladolid and La Coruña. Within the divisions regiments and other units were distributed in smaller towns. For example, the Third Division had units in Alcoy, Alicante and Murcia as well as in Valencia, and although the 2nd Infantry Brigade was part of the Madrid division, its headquarters were in Badajoz. There were mountain brigades with command posts in Gerona, Bilbao and Oviedo and an independent command in Asturias. Each division had two infantry brigades, each of two regiments, each of which had a theoretical strength of 1,200 men. The division also had, at least on paper, two artillery regiments, a battalion of sappers and other auxiliary units. Some divisions had cavalry regiments.

In all the Army had 40 infantry regiments, 8 mountain battalions, 2 machine-gun battalions and 1 mounted on bicycles, 10 cavalry regiments, 1 of mounted artillery and a unit of self-propelled artillery. There were sixteen 16 light artillery regiments and 4 of heavy artillery, 4 regiments of large-calibre coastal artillery and units of mountain artillery and anti-aircraft guns. There was 1 regiment and 8 battalions of sappers and several other specialised engineers' units. Finally, there were 2 tank regiments.

In theory, after the military uprisings in many centres on 18–20 July 1936 had been crushed, and the area which the Republic held had been clearly demarcated, which took a few days more, the Republic retained a considerable portion of the Army: 36 battalions of infantry out of a total of 80 plus the 8 mountain units, 3 of the 10 cavalry regiments, 5 of the 8 engineer battalions, 1 of the 2 machine-gun battalions and 1 of the 2 tank regiments. Also at the disposal of the Republic were the cyclist battalion and a considerable number of smaller specialist units.

The Republic also held 2 of the coastal artillery regiments, 2 of the regiments of heavy artillery and 6 of the 16 of light artillery.

The data must be analysed and described statistically, for many of these units, while physically within what was to be known as the Government or Republican zone of Spain, were hardly usable in creating an army. The two cavalry regiments in Barcelona, for example, whose officers had risen but had been suppressed by the joint action of loyal paramilitary forces and working-class organisations, followed their officers and would require complete reorganisation. One of the battalions of the railway regiment was composed of university students completing their brief military service during the summer vacation and belonging to a social class which in general was unsympathetic to the Republic.[1] The signals regiment went over en masse to the Insurgents on 20 July 1936, carrying off with them the conscript son of the socialist leader Francisco Largo Caballero. Nor did the Republic retain much of the heavy artillery regiment stationed in San Sebastián when the Insurgents took it on 13 August 1936. These examples could be multiplied.

To what extent the Republic managed to make use of the military units which remained in its zone will be examined later. However, for a more accurate analysis, the numerical proportions of the forces available at the beginning of the war to both sides need to be calculated.[2]

There are several discordant versions of these statistics, some of which fail to mention their sources.[3] The returns from the various units, made

[1] J. Arrarás, ed., *Historia de la Cruzada española*, Madrid, 1939–43, XII: 336 (hereafter *Cruzada*).

[2] These are some calculations:

1 'Incidencias de la lucha', *Revista de Historia Militar* (Madrid), 17 (1964), 122, gives Republicans: 36,685, Insurgents: 23,595. The source is a document from the Nationalist Army Staff headquarters (DN (= *Documentación Nacional*), L91, C2). The letter heading the document states that it needs the information 'for propaganda purposes', which suggests that the figures should be accepted with caution.

2 Ricardo de la Cierva, *Historia de la guerra civil española*, Madrid, 1969, I: 69, quotes the following figures: Republicans: 32,365, Insurgents: 18,935. Once the locations of the units are scrutinised, it is difficult to accept these figures, which, in any case, have no stated source. Certainly, the units were reduced in size because of summer leave, but returns show that this was evenly balanced on both sides. There is no indication that any one garrison was particularly bereft of manpower.

3 The *Servicio Histórico Militar* carried out a careful analysis based on the returns corresponding to July 1936. Thus, by checking on places and the returns it is possible to obtain a result with a high level of reliability.

[3] See the unclassified report in the *Servicio Histórico Militar*, which includes testimonies of competent witnesses and describes how all the troops supported the insurrection of the officers. See also F. Lacruz, *El alzamiento, la revolución y el terror en Barcelona*, Barcelona, 1943, *passim*.

Table 2.1 *Number of men in barracks in July 1936*

Republican zone	
Total number of men in barracks in infantry, cavalry, artillery and engineers	27,135
Total in all branches	34,280
Total on summer leave	11,908
Total available if men on leave returned to their units	46,188
Nationalist zone	
Total number of men available in the main Arms	30,387
Total in all Arms	31,760
On leave	13,166
Total available if men on leave returned to their units	44,926

Table 2.2 *Initial manpower in the major Arms available to each side*

	Republicans	Nationalists
Infantry	14,595	18,181
Artillery	7,064	7,543
Cavalry	1,213	2,756
Engineers	3,996	1,659
Tanks	267	248

every ten days, provide a more acceptable view of the real situation. Table 2.1 lists figures for July 1936.

The total number of men in the main Arms has been altered slightly to correct obvious errors while estimates have been made for units which do not appear in the returns. However, the totals of all men available and of those on leave are those of the official periodic returns. Absolute totals are larger because they include auxiliary units of which Madrid had a considerable number. The Nationalist or Insurgent zone had more divisions and a larger number of men on leave. An accurate figure for men on leave who returned to their own units cannot be calculated, and indeed for some it was impossible to return to their units because they were now in the enemy zone.

The forces available to the two sides in the major Arms are shown in Table 2.2. In infantry, the most important arm, the Insurgents had a majority of troops. The Republic was preponderant only in engineers and in the few thousand men in non-combatant Arms in the capital.

Furthermore, in the Insurgent zone, no unit deserted en masse to the other side, as did the signals regiment. Only recently had the Republic War Ministry transferred two regiments out of the Madrid division, and these proved very useful to the Insurgents. The two cavalry regiments in Barcelona joined the rebellion. Indeed No. 3 was proposed for a collective medal after the war.

Figures for the paramilitary *Guardia Civil*, militarily better trained and disciplined than raw conscripts; for the *Carabineros*, utilised for frontier and general excise controls; and for the militarised and militarily officered *Guardia de Seguridad y Asalto*, a city police created by the Republic in order to safeguard public order without having to call in the army, are as follows:

Guardia Civil	32,869
Carabineros	14,113
Guardia de Seguridad y Asalto	17,660

To calculate the number of these forces which remained in the service of the Republic it is not enough to identify the 24 *tercios* and 10 *zonas*, each about the size of a regiment and commanded by a colonel, in which these forces were organised, because the lines dividing the Republican and the Insurgent zones often crossed them. In Córdoba, for example, most of the province was in Republican hands, but the city itself was in Insurgent hands from the outset. A better view can be obtained by analysing the *comandancias* or subdivisions, which were much smaller. The numbers for these are given in Table 2.3.

The maximum possible of *comandancias* has been attributed to the Republic, taking into account all the uprisings of the *Guardia Civil*, among many other places, in La Roda, in the province of Albacete, and Puente Genil in the province of Córdoba.[4] It had to be disarmed in Málaga.[5] All its officers were executed after their failed uprising in Murcia.[6] In Badajoz it joined the contingent from the neighbouring province of Cáceres and went over to the Insurgents, having disobeyed Government orders to go to Madrid.[7] In Asturias and Andalusia in general, the *Guardia Civil* rose.[8] Most of the *Guardia Civil* in the province of Jaén abandoned its posts and retired to the stronghold of

[4] DR, L473, C3.

[5] Luis Romero Basart, *Impresiones de un militar republicano*, Barcelona, 1937, 10.

[6] Arrarás, *Cruzada*, XXIV: 20.

[7] *Ibid.*, XV: 193.

[8] See J. M. Martínez Bande, *La guerra en el norte*, Madrid, 1969, 21 (hereafter *Norte*), and the same author's *La campaña de Andalucía*, Madrid, 1969, 13 (hereafter *Andalucía*).

Table 2.3 *Number of paramilitary* comandancias *available to both sides*

	Republican	Nationalist	Total
Guardia Civil	108	109	217
Carabineros	54	55	109
Grupos de Asalto	10	7	17

Santa María de la Cabeza, where it was besieged by Republican forces for several months. Finally, the best-known example of the *Guardia Civil*'s decision to join the insurrection is that of the 800-plus men who resisted Government forces from the shelter of the military academy in the Alcázar of Toledo. Furthermore, the loyalty of the 50 per cent of *Guardia Civil* posts which did not actually challenge the Government is also doubtful.

Even in Barcelona, where the crushing of the military uprising was due to a great extent to the loyalty of General Aranguren and Colonel Escobar, who commanded the *Guardia Civil* in Catalonia and Barcelona respectively, a well-informed observer commented that 40 per cent of the officers were later dismissed as untrustworthy by the Republican authorities.[9] It would be fair to conclude that only rarely could *Guardia Civil* units be considered entirely reliable pro-Republican forces, which is why it was greatly expanded and its title was changed to *Guardia Nacional Republicana*.

As for the *Carabineros*, a force under the Ministry of Finance (*Hacienda*) and responsible for excise and customs control rather than public order as was the *Guardia Civil*, it was not as valuable to the Insurgents as the latter. Some *Carabinero* posts, especially in the north-west province of Galicia, resisted the Insurgent officers' take-over. A thousand *Carabineros* took refuge in Portugal, whence a ship took them to a Republican port.[10] *Carabineros* in Asturias fought against Insurgent army forces advancing to relieve the siege of the Insurgent garrison of Oviedo.[11]

During the war the number of *Carabineros* increased to about 40,000 men. The decision to recruit another 14,000 was taken in October 1936.[12] Normally, *Carabineros* were considered crack troops and thus in

[9] Lacruz, *El alzamiento*, 213.
[10] L. Bazal, *¡Ay de los vencidos!*, Toulouse, 1966, 111.
[11] Martínez Bande, *Norte*, 115.
[12] See *El Sol* of 26 October 1936.

general they were well armed and trained. But several observers of different military and political views opinions judged their performance unsatisfactory. The corps was said to have been a demoralised body and a safe refuge for well-connected young men, suffering few losses.[13] Certainly the corps of *Carabineros* was attractive and well uniformed. Conditions of entry were: Spanish nationality, between 18 and 25 years of age, a minimum height of 1.75 m and possession of a good-conduct certificate as well as another indicating loyalty to a political party or union in the Popular Front.[14] The conditions were less demanding than those of peacetime, when they included a fearsome examination of a solid syllabus. Three times as many candidates applied as there were places. The old *Dirección General de Carabineros*, whose last head had been the rebel General Gonzalo Queipo de Llano, was abolished, and the corps would now come under the Under-Secretariat of the War Ministry, and be led by a loyal colonel, Rodríguez Mantecón, now promoted to general of brigade, thus making the *Carabineros* part of the new army. But although this elite corps might have been the nucleus of a group of crack assault divisions, it never was, although some of its units, especially the 40th Division, were of high quality. Furthermore, although the *Carabineros* were now under the War Ministry, in practice they still remained to a considerable degree under the control of Dr Juan Negrín, ex-Minister of Finance, and Prime Minister of the Republic from May 1937, and under the direct control of Dr Rafael Méndez, a professor of pharmacy who was a personal friend of Negrín.

The *Cuerpo de Seguridad y Asalto* does not seem to have opposed the military insurrection in those cities and towns where it succeeded but, in general, in the Republican zone its opposition seems to have contributed to the failure of the uprising, especially in Madrid and Barcelona.[15] As these two cities, together with Valencia and Bilbao, remained under the control of the Republican Government, it may well be that the latter had at its disposal more of these well-disciplined police, who were armed and ex-servicemen, than the Insurgents. *Grupos de Asalto*, highly trained for control of urban disorder, were equally distributed

[13] See R. Sanz, *Los que fuimos a Madrid*, Toulouse, 1969, 249, writing from a strongly CNT standpoint; J. Henríquez Caubín, *La batalla del Ebro: maniobras de una una división*, Mexico City, 1944, 345, who writes as a communist and Chief of Staff of the 35th Division, and the chief of the General Staff, Vicente Rojo, *¡Alerta los pueblos!*, Buenos Aires, 1939, 18 (hereafter *Alerta*).

[14] *Gaceta de Madrid*, 24 September 1936.

[15] See Arrarás, *Cruzada*, XI: 285; XII: 312, 406; XIV: 102; XV: 183, 200 for a description of the *Guardia de Asalto*'s passivity in Granada, Valladolid, Burgos, Seville and Zaragoza, all places where the uprising was successful.

between the Government and the Insurgents. Nevertheless the officers of this body, who came from the army and often had battle experience in Morocco, were not particularly loyal to the Republic. During the reaction of 1934–5 they had been purged by Colonel Agustín Muñoz Grandes, who would later command the Blue Division of Spanish volunteers against the USSR in the Second World War and was appointed Vice-President of the Spanish Government under Franco.[16] An indication of the unreliability of these officers is that throughout 1939 only 254 names appear in the *Boletín Oficial del Estado*, the official gazette of the Franco regime, as being dismissed the service for their activities during the war. And there are also other indications of the doubtful loyalty of the *Asalto* officers to the Republic.[17]

This corps also recruited widely at the beginning of the war.[18] Conditions were less exigent than pre-war, but it was essential to obtain a guarantee from an organisation which was part of the Popular Front. The corps was merged by decree of 27 December 1936 with the *Guardia Nacional Republicana* to form the new *Cuerpo de Seguridad Interior*. Sometimes the *Asaltos* were used as shock troops, for example in the struggle to preserve the integrity of the Catalan Front in 1938. In the same battle, in which the Republican zone was split in two and many units were left in complete chaos, the *Asaltos* captured deserters, helped reform units and took the role of military police. Like the *Carabineros*, the *Asaltos* came under a civilian ministry, in this case the Ministry of the Interior or *Gobernación*. Naturally the Chief of Staff, General Vicente Rojo, resented this removal of units from his command.[19] Julián Henríquez Caubín, a senior officer in the communist-dominated Army of the Ebro, claims to have observed an entire *Asalto* division cross into France in such excellent condition that it ought to have been used to offer a fierce resistance to the advancing Franco armies.[20] As with the *Carabineros*, it would seem that the Republican authorities lost the opportunity to be more decisive and imaginative and to use a relatively

[16] Julián Zugazagoitia, *Guerra y vicisitudes de los españoles*, Paris, 1968, I: 148. The author was Secretary of the Defence Ministry.

[17] Ricardo de la Cierva describes the activities of an *Asalto* lieutenant who was a secret agent of the Insurgents and in charge of the organisation of military transport in Madrid. R. de la Cierva, 'Feliciano Martín Villoria, el hombre que justificó la Quinta Columna', *Historia y Vida*, 3 (June 1968), 56–65. Mr Goodden, the British consul in Valencia, reported that at the time of the Republican surrender in late March 1939, a large number of officers of *Asaltos* had Nationalist sympathies (The National Archives, FO 371 series, W6704/8/41, of 11 April 1939).

[18] On 24 September 1936 the Minister of the Interior (*Gobernación*), Angel Galarza, told the press that 200 men were being recruited to the Corps daily.

[19] Rojo, *Alerta*, 31.

[20] Henríquez Caubín, *La batalla*, 346.

dependable nucleus of trained men as the hard nucleus of a new army. Yet the chaos of the first weeks of the war, which opened the way to the emergence of popular militias and then to the Republican Army, made all attempts to use existing forces useless.

Military and paramilitary forces in the Republican war effort

All available data tend to demonstrate that, with very few exceptions, the military units stationed in the Republican zone were of little use, mainly because to a variable extent their officers had rebelled, hesitated, had not demonstrated clear enough loyalty to the regime in the earliest skirmishes with the Insurgents, or done anything save place their fidelity to the Republic before their loyalty to their comrades or their political views. For this reason units of the Spanish army in one zone cannot be fairly compared with those in the other. For example, a battalion from the Castilian city of Valladolid, where opposition to the garrison's uprising was swiftly suppressed, could leave for the Front with its officers and non-commissioned officers (except for the few who had demurred and had been killed or arrested) and without a mob of suspicious revolutionary militia swarming round them. On the other hand, a company or battalion of troops which formed part of an early Republican column was usually no more than a few remains of sections and platoons, led perhaps by a subaltern officer or a sergeant who had been promoted on the spot, leaders whom the men might well not know, and which had merged with a militia. The consequences of such a situation for discipline and fighting ability were serious.

Before examining the Madrid division, which had the most troops available, a brief survey of the other divisions in the Republican zone is appropriate.[21]

In the area covered by the columns which marched out of Barcelona to attack the Insurgent Front along the Huesca–Zaragoza–Teruel line following the crushing of the military rebellion in the Barcelona garrison, the only traces of the army are the occasional companies and smaller units of the four mountain battalions garrisoned in Catalonia. Their presence was due to the loyalty of Colonel Villalba, commander

[21] Most details are taken from Colonel Martínez Bande's series (see Bibliography), which was founded on this senior officer's thorough and competent scrutiny of available records in the archives of both sides of the Spanish Civil War, and is in general free of political prejudice. I benefited from long conversations with him.

of the brigade half-mountain stationed at Barbastro. No military insurrection took place here, but there were only 382 men. The other battalions of the brigade were also at very low strength. There were also a few hundred men from Infantry Regiment No. 16 who advanced from their base at Lérida towards Huesca merged with the militia column led by the anarchists Ascaso and Jover. It is unlikely that the columns attacking the Huesca–Zaragoza line included as many as a thousand troops. The rest were untrained and undisciplined militia.

In the Valencia division, about 2,250 troops accompanied columns commanded by officers (see Peire, Benedito and Manuel Pérez Salas in Appendix 4). A column of almost 400 *Guardia Civil* was sent to reduce the Insurgents in the provincial capital of Teruel, but went over to them.[22]

In Andalusia, in General Miaja's Republican column attacking Córdoba in August 1936, there were about 250 *Guardia Civil* and *Carabineros* and a machine-gun section (equivalent to a platoon in the British Army) from the battalion stationed in Castellón. Here and there in the documents there are imprecise references to troops from regiments in Alcoy, Almería and Málaga.

In the north of Spain, the garrisons in Galicia and Asturias had rebelled against the Government, except for the mountain battalion stationed in Bilbao, which was operational for some time though its officers were untrustworthy and later faced courts martial.

In short, the Republican authorities had to find troops where they could in order to give some poor semblance of military order to heterogeneous columns of militia which were trying to resist the Insurgents. However, most units in the Republican zone had had to be dissolved and the troops – mostly conscripts with scarce training – had been sent home. In the Madrid division, however, fewest units had needed to be dissolved, yet even here, once the troops had been sent home and the officers who had taken part in the rebellion had been arrested, calculations showed that there were no more than 70 officers and 1,313 NCOs and men available.[23] It was impossible to create a coherent force with these men, previously belonging to different units stationed all over the area of the division, which in the last pre-war return on 1 July 1936

[22] J. M. Martínez Bande, *La invasión de Aragón y el desembarco en Mallorca*, Madrid, Editorial San Martín, 1970, 92, reports that the civil guards were outraged by the behaviour of the militia towards the civilian population. This may well have been a factor, but it seems more likely that the move was premeditated.

[23] DR, L954, C12. The date on the document is 1936, without day or month, but presumably refers to the situation following the crushing of the insurrection on Monday 20 July 1936.

had numbered 828 officers and 10,425 other ranks.[24] A document of 3 September 1936 offers a vivid description of just how difficult it was to put together even a battalion of a few hundred troops. The three companies mentioned, which had about half their establishment, were commanded by officers brought from a cavalry remount depot, from Army driving schools and a motor-cycle unit. As for the troops, the original four regiments of infantry, of which the division was comprised, were so scattered that sappers and other specialised troops were included in the battalion, which had to be thrown together. Even to obtain rifles – for the arsenals had been looted by the militias – many telegrams had to be sent and weapons collected in dribs and drabs from many towns.[25]

To some extent, the Madrid garrison had been subverted by the Spanish Communist Party (PCE).[26] How significant this was cannot be stated for certain, although the British military attaché reported twice in April 1936 that there was a 'subversive minority' of NCOs. He also remarked that the younger officers were less politicised, which was significant given that it was precisely those officers who participated in the uprising in most of the other garrisons of Spain.[27]

Even in Madrid, it would be mistaken to suppose that the Republican authorities could use the military units to any coherent extent. Manuel Azaña, who was President of the Republic when the war began, comments that it had been difficult to find six companies and a battalion of sappers to go out to the sierra, north of Madrid, to which the Insurgents had advanced, in the days after the outset of the war.[28] The picture would have been like the description that one militiaman was to give, years after:

> Early every morning the Madrid militiamen, organised by parties, trade unions and local groups, left the capital and returned late in the evening from their day spent in the Guadarrama mountains ... They set off for the sierra as though they were going on a Sunday outing ... accompanied by some political women but also by that particular type of Madrid prostitute of the time with enormous breasts and buttocks.[29]

Both the President of the Republic and the British military attaché were repeating what people, probably officers of varying rank, had told them. They were unlikely to have gone deeply into the question themselves

[24] DR, L1, C3. [25] DR, L955, C4.
[26] Líster, *Nuestra guerra*, 26.
[27] FO 371 W3042 and W3268/190/41.
[28] Azaña, *Obras Completas*, III: 487.
[29] R. Fraser, *Blood of Spain: The Experience of Civil War 1936–1939*, Allen Lane, 1979, 117.

at that moment. Nevertheless, all the evidence points to sheer military chaos as compared with the order and discipline in garrisons where the Insurgents had prevailed.

Some archival material was preserved from the reports concerning the primitive columns fighting around the capital in the first weeks of the war, and they provide a general view.[30] So, for example, the column commanded by Captain Francisco Giménez Orge was composed of militia, 142 *Guardias Civiles*, almost two companies of *Guardias de Asalto* and small units of artillery and signals. On 24 October 1936, Captain López Tienda's column had 519 troops out of 5,073 men altogether, while the retired Lieutenant-Colonel Mangada, on 10 October 1936, had 825 soldiers out of a total of 4,789. For some days, the archives have complete records of the columns, and they show that, on 16 October 1936, there were 12,492 troops and paramilitaries fighting around Madrid out of a total of 52,131, that is about 25 per cent.

However, many of these 12,492 troops and paramilitaries may have been militia listed in military units but who were not troops but drivers, radio-telegraphists and similar auxiliaries. Furthermore, the figures for paramilitary are probably maxima. Yet even if the number of men with some military training was as small as 9,000, it was still a force sufficient to tackle the Insurgents. It was this balance that led to the successful defence of the northern approaches to Madrid. If the Government's columns, which were probably as large as those of the Insurgents, failed to drive the latter back, it was almost certainly because of their indiscipline and their lack of officers. When, however, the professional Moroccan and Legionary forces of General Franco's African army came into contact with the Republican conscripts and militia who were defending the southern and western approaches of Madrid, their far superior training and discipline enabled them easily to overcome their heterogeneous and unruly opponents.

The question remains whether the José Giral Government, which took power on 19 July 1936 and would stay in office until 4 September, would have done better not to distribute arms to the militias but to wage war with the military forces remaining to it, augmented by calling up the reserves and recruiting paramilitaries. This point is frequently made by commentators and historians of the Spanish Civil War but is disputed by others who believe ideologically in the efficiency of a mass people's army. It is true that the militias fought poorly, antagonised loyal officers and obstructed the Republic's military efforts. Even most anarchists, members of or sympathisers with the immense CNT,

[30] DR, L966 and L967.

opposed on principle to State authority and military discipline, finally accepted that their militias should be militarised, uniformed and disciplined under the code of military law. It could also be said, however, that the building of a large army by the Republic itself provoked the calling-up by the Insurgents of reservists, prolonging and intensifying the war and adding to the bitterness of defeat. But this argument ignores the fact that the military forces available to the Republic in the emergency of the summer and autumn of 1936, in terms of infantry battalions and officers to command them, were much fewer than those of the Insurgents. Moreover, it ignores the fact that if the Popular Front regime, which had come into power as a result of the elections of February 1936, had been sufficiently strong to refuse to distribute weapons to the militias in July 1936, then it would have been strong enough to overcome a military rebellion which broke out when it was half-planned and which failed where its leaders assumed it would be successful and triumphed where it was feared to fail. By the time the Government of the Second Republic had succeeded in dominating the militias and channelling their strength, the moment had passed when the war could have been fought by the purely military forces which were present in July 1936.

3 The militia months: July–December 1936

Origins of the militias

The immediate reaction of the population of Madrid to the military uprising which was taking place in their midst was observed by Major Segismundo Casado, commander of the Presidential cavalry escort. He wrote later, from exile in Britain after the war:

> When Franco's rebellion broke out on the 18th of July 1936, the people reacted in an astonishing manner. All the political parties and the syndicalist organisations of the Popular Front began to recruit volunteers to repel the aggression. They did not need to use artifice or propaganda for this, because the masses, both of workmen and peasants, came out in their thousands and very promptly, to enrol in different units of the militia. Groups and battalions of militiamen were formed rapidly, and this was the basis of the People's Republican Army.[1]

While the following is a simplified view of a complicated circumstance, the memories of a militiaman are emblematic of the general atmosphere and complete military unpreparedness among those who would actively oppose the Insurgents:

> All we Republicans remember how we began to fight. A group of friends would meet, climb on to a lorry, a private or requisitioned car; some had pistols, others rifles and a few cartridges. We went to look for Fascists. When we came up against resistance we fought. Most times, once the ammunition was fired off, we came back, not to a defensive position or anything like that, but to the place where we had started.[2]

Another observer of the amateur nature of the resistance to the coup, observed, thinking of his experiences in 1914–18: 'How obvious it is that Spaniards haven't fought in a real war!'[3]

[1] Colonel S. Casado, *The Last Days of Madrid*, trans. R. Croft-Cooke, Peter Davies, 1939, 46.
[2] A. Vilanova, *La defensa del Alcázar de Toledo*, Mexico City, 1963, 122–3.
[3] J.-R. Bloch, *España en armas*, Santiago de Chile, 1937, 19.

If this writer had been with the Insurgents, however, he would have realised that it was not the absence of war experience that created the chaos but the lack of direction and the breakdown of social order.

Another interesting point of view from which to observe the militias is that of a professional officer in the Ministry of War, to which the militias had to apply for supplies. José Martín Blázquez, a captain in the Supply Corps or *Intendencia*, was one of the small group of loyal officers who ran the Ministry immediately after the insurrection. He describes the difficult conditions in which he had to work, interrupted by constant demands for chits for supplies from militiamen[4] Madrid was being sacked for weapons and food. According to Martín Blázquez, the only people who were being helpful to him were the socialist parliamentary deputies and the occasional communist militiamen who tried to reason with those who were making constant demands.

Professional officers were in the difficult position of being accused of complicity with the Insurgents if they objected to the demands of the militia, even if they were outrageous, as an unproven but not unlikely story recounts. An anarchist militia column demanded several hundred fountain pens. When the responsible officer in the War Ministry refused, the militia leader asked whether his *compañeros* did not have the right to write home. This may explain the officers' haste to place themselves under the protection of some political party, especially the Spanish Communist Party, which shared the professional officers' view of how to fight the war.

The question of supplies would have to be solved before wastefulness led to surrender through complete exhaustion. The problem was solved by abolishing by decree the People's Supply Committee (*Comité Popular de Abastecimientos*), a militia body, which was replaced by a similar-sounding entity (without the word *Popular*) called the Provincial Supply Committee, followed by a decree insisting that an order from the Services Section of the ministerial staff was required before supplies could be obtained from the Ministry's stores.[5]

The order limiting the demands for supplies was fiercely resisted, with the result that a further decree with the same intention was issued on 4 August 1936, but irregular issue of supplies did not cease until the Government, in its struggle to regain control, created the *Inspección General de Milicias*.

[4] José Martín Blázquez, *I Helped to Build an Army*, trans. F. Borkenau, Secker and Warburg, 1939, 125ff.

[5] *Gaceta*, 26 July 1936.

Barracks, stormed by the militia, in some cases with the help of *Guardia Civil* and professional officers, had been looted and taken over as mobilisation centres. Almost daily, the press carried proclamations calling on men to join the militias which were being organised by the parties, the major trade union organisations – UGT and CNT – individual unions and other groups and associations. Refugees who had fled from the military repression which the Insurgents were systematically carrying out in the provinces of Old and New Castile included the *Milicias burgalesas* from Burgos and *Los Comuneros*, echoing a popular uprising of the sixteenth century in the towns of Castile, and a choice of title perhaps as eloquent as the medieval imagery favoured by the Insurgents under Franco. The political heroes of the various parties were represented in the titles of the militia columns. Aida Lafuente, a young female communist who was killed in the Asturias revolution in October 1934, an event which had terrified those who feared social upheaval as well as those who were alarmed at the danger of a sort of clerico-fascism similar to the authoritarian regime imposed in the same year in Austria, gave her name posthumously to a battalion, as did Captain Condés, the *Guardia de Asalto* officer who, a week before the military uprising, had been involved in the murder of José Calvo Sotelo, leader of the right-wing *Frente Nacional*. And there were at least three militias which bore the name of the German anti-Nazi martyr Ernst Thaelman. Other colourful titles of militia groups referred to their aims and slogans, including the Steel Companies (*compañías de acero*), Union of the Sons of the Proletariat (*Unión de Hijos del Proletariado*) or *UHP* and the anarchist column using the slogan of the Mexican revolutionary Emiliano Zapata, Bread and Freedom (*Tierra y Libertad*).

The first days of one of these variously named battalions or columns were described by Victor de Frutos, a militia leader who rose to command the 10th Division of the Republican Army. The May the First (*Primero de Mayo*) Battalion was recruited from the working-class Madrid district of Carabanchel. It was based in the *Escuela de Tiro* or Musketry School and enjoyed the services of the band of the Carabanchel bullring. Soon 350 men had joined, sufficient for the authorities to consider it viable. Only 50 had completed their military service but they found 6 regular corporals to put them through some basic training. Some of the men, especially if they were of the anarchist CNT, saw no point in barrack-square drill, and among other disciplinary problems it was hard to convince the men to stay in barracks after dark or at least not to take their rifles home with them. The unit was commanded by a captain of *Carabineros*. After one week's training and the election of junior officers, the first company went up to the Front, though most of the others enjoyed a generous entire month of training.[6]

From the first day of the military uprising, the Government had striven to solve the problem of how to find a substitute for the old Army, of which only disorganised remains were left. The beginning of the Republican Army can be dated to 3 August 1936, when a decree was issued establishing battalions of volunteers to be recruited from among members of militia in their twenties, who would be commanded by professional officers and NCOs, would wear uniforms and indications of rank and would serve for two months or the duration of the war.[7] Such a brief contract of service demonstrates the Giral Government's perhaps short-sighted view of the problem that the insurrection posed, although it could not have foreseen that Franco would be able to transport the Moroccans and Legionaries of his professional African army over the Strait of Gibraltar.

The volunteers called for in the decree of 3 August would enjoy the same food and accommodation terms as conscripts completing their year of military service. Additionally, they would be given preference for entry to the police and low-level public service posts. Their jobs would be kept for them and they would have the privilege of naming their own substitutes. On 18 August, recruitment of volunteers was opened to Army reservists, provided they could show a certificate of loyalty from an organisation which supported the Popular Front. These would serve for six months or the duration of the war, and would be paid the quite high sum of 10 pesetas per day but would have to pay for their food. Following these decrees, on 4 September the first volunteer battalion invited militiamen to enrol in what was to be the beginning of a new army. The 1st Battalion paraded through the provincial capital of Albacete, where it had trained, on 17 September. The 2nd Battalion was inspected on 24 September while a further two were ready by 17 October. Altogether, 31 battalions were formed.

Recruitment was entrusted to the Central Recruitment Board (*Junta Central de Reclutamiento*) under Diego Martínez Barrio, leader of the Unión Republicana party and Government delegate for the Levante or provinces of the south-east, the Minister of Agriculture, Mariano Ruiz Funes, and General Fernando Martínez Monje, who had commanded the Valencia military region. The *Junta Central de Reclutamiento* was granted full powers; any obstruction from uncontrolled militia would be considered treason. The *Junta* was based in the south-eastern city of

[6] Victor de Frutos, *Los que no perdieron la guerra*, Buenos Aires, 1967.
[7] *Gaceta*, 4 August 1936.

Albacete, which had been selected, though it lacked military installations, probably because it was a major railway junction and was far away from the overheated atmosphere of Madrid. The later development of the city as a base for the International Brigades of volunteers was probably due to these factors.

The area of the *Junta Central de Reclutamiento* would cover the entire Republican zone, except for Catalonia, the Basque Country, Santander and Asturias. The centrifugal forces of the revolution, provoked by the military insurrection which had taken over in Galicia, Old Castile and large parts of Aragon and Andalusia, had impelled regions where the insurrections had failed to act independently of Madrid, where central government and thus military direction were struggling to assert themselves.

The volunteer battalions were not universally well received. Among others, the left-wing socialist newspaper *Claridad* proclaimed on 20 August 1936: 'To think of any other type of army which would replace the militias in order to control in some way their revolutionary action is to think in a counter-revolutionary way.'

This encapsulates the issue. While the Insurgents were bringing their sizeable *Falange* and Traditionalist militias under army command, the Republicans, at least their more left-wing sectors, were seeing the militias as a symbol of the revolution which they thought or hoped was in progress. Indeed, hostility to formal militarisation, generally associated with the CNT, was not limited to the anarchists. In fact, and as will be seen later, it was only the communists who demanded formal militarisation from the beginning. It is not easy to understand the opposition. Other countries at war had understood that even a citizen army must conform to the lines of military organisation traditional to that country. In those parts of Spain where the insurrection had triumphed, militarisation was not even discussed. The *Falange* and other political militias were brought under military control by simple order. However, in the areas of Spain where the insurrection had failed, among a broad sector of progressive opinion it had crystallised the hostility to militarism which was expressed in the belief that the system had to be ended. It was believed, mistakenly, that the Insurgents could not be more than a few officers leading some unwilling young men doing their military service, and was merely one more of the series of military coups or *pronunciamientos* characteristic of Spanish history, and that it was menaced by a hostile population and was totally incapable of resisting for long the industrial and financial power of Republican Spain, as Indalecio Prieto, later Minister of Defence and leading socialist, claimed in a speech on 8 August 1936.

Despite the volunteer battalions, numerically it was clearly the militias which were bearing the brunt of the fighting. And so the Government decided to bring them under its control. It began this by establishing, on 6 August 1936, the *Inspección General de Milicias*, under Major Luis Barceló, a prominent officer belonging to the PCE, whose policy was militarisation.[8] The role of the *Inspección* was to channel funds, supplies and military orders to the militia columns, dissolve those which were too small to be viable and direct their militarisation. On 20 October the *Inspección* was put directly under the orders of Colonel José Asensio Torrado, Chief of Operations in the Central Zone, that is the fronts around Madrid, and changed its title to *Comandancia de Milicias*, administered by Servando Marenco, an officer from the *Cuerpo de Intervención Militar*, which dealt with questions of budgets and accounting. The new Republican Army owed him a great deal, because the battalions of militia were later to be formed relatively smoothly into the brigades of the new army.

The *Comandancia de Milicias* expanded so swiftly that it left the volunteer battalions behind, and recruitment to them was abandoned by decree in the *Gaceta* on 28 August. The same decree referred to the militias as being the army, ordering the promotion of suitable men to NCO ranks, which would be recognised after the war, that is to say that the militias would be the new post-war army. Significantly, this is the first indication that 'after the war' an entirely new military establishment would be needed. Militia officers would have to attend new emergency courses, which were set up for infantry, artillery and engineers. Unfortunately, these were not very successful because to enter them a high level of education was required in an atmosphere where '*señoritismo*' or preference for 'young gentlemen', as the militia called it, was out of fashion. On 16 August 1936 the *Gaceta* had decreed that militias which were now militarised had a right to daily rations and 10 pesetas a day (the volunteers had had to pay for their own food). This high daily rate of pay was frequently criticised. It was, after all, more than many militiamen could earn in civilian life.[9] It is difficult to understand why it was fixed so high except perhaps to encourage men with family responsibilities to join the militias. Battalion paymasters would continue in their posts but each column would be accompanied by an officer from the Supply Corps (*Intendencia*).

Initially, 10 million pesetas were assigned to finance militia pay. The Government was resolved not to tolerate claims based on exaggerated

[8] *Gaceta*, 6 August 1936.

[9] The exchange rate was approximately 50 pesetas to the pound sterling.

returns of men, and a *Gaceta* decree of 1 September 1936 threatened to withhold funds unless full lists of names were sent to the Ministry for verification.

In the chaotic circumstances of the early weeks of the war, the distribution of pay was at times erratic. Lieutenant-Colonel Juan Hernández Sarabia, Minister of War, spoke of 'insuperable difficulties' in paying the militia. There were complaints from 'Carlos Contreras' (the Italian communist Vittorio Vidali), political commissar of the communist-organised Fifth Regiment, who wrote in the unit's daily paper: 'The militiaman never knows for sure when he is going to get his pay. Nor does he know who he gets it from, his regiment, his union, his party or the Ministry of War.'[10] As for the appointment of commanders, one officer who went over to the Insurgents reported about the Republican forces: 'They have absolutely no efficient leaders, because the junior officers have been chosen from among the NCOs, who are now commanding companies. The sergeants and corporals have been appointed in the same way and have no control.'[11] According to this report, there was widespread dissatisfaction among the militia.

The *Comandancia Militar de Milicias* had its own structure, announced on 21 October 1936 in the *Diario Oficial del Ministerio de la Guerra*. Under Servando Marenco, who was given full autonomy, was a secretary and five sections: recruitment, organisation and personnel, weapons and uniforms, food and medical services. There would be an end to the channelling of money through political parties.

The *Comandancia* had an enormous task before it. Marenco sent out circular after circular striving to forge the beginnings of an army from the undisciplined crowds of militia who had filled the streets of Madrid after the Insurgents had been crushed. Marenco's orders have extensive introductory preambles, explaining and justifying his orders. This was necessary because the militias resisted discipline and orders on principle. A series of letters in September 1936 reminded party and union committees that the *Comandancia* was in charge now.

Payments were closely controlled. Some letters contained a refusal to pay unarmed men whose responsibilities could not be considered strictly military. A *Comandancia* meeting on 9 October 1936 concluded: 'Counting from the 11th of this month, no pay lists will be considered unless presented by properly formed, armed and militarised battalions.'

[10] *Milicia Popular*, 6 September 1936.
[11] CGG, L147, C2.

So punctiliously were the accounts kept that the *Comandancia* decided to pay only 80 instead of 170 pesetas for the days between 18 July and 5 August, because the militia had received subsidies from their local municipalities and had made unauthorised requisitions of foodstuffs.[12]

On 21 May 1937, the Pay Section of the *Comandancia de Milicias* returned the tiny sum of 3,768 pesetas and 19 céntimos to the public funds. Its scrupulous accounting displays how seriously it meant to spend public money only on those militias who accepted national authority. The Government had almost complete control of spending and excellent book-keeping records.

The records of the *Comandancia de Milicias* contain details about the number and political identity of militiamen, their ages, places of birth, previous incomes and the proportion who suffered wounds. The typical militiaman did not belong to a party, earned between 5 and 10 pesetas per day in civilian life, was aged in his twenties and worked as an agricultural labourer or in the building industry.

To calculate the number of militiamen, the method which allows for fewest errors is to divide the sum of money spent in a given period by the 10 pesetas pay received by each man. There is a risk of overstating the numbers because the units tended to exaggerate their numbers. However, on the other had, at the beginning some CNT militia refused to accept pay because this implied accepting the principle of militarisation.[13]

The total spent by the *Comandancia Militar de Milicias* between 15 August 1936 and 28 February 1937 is close to 179 million pesetas. The average number of men is thus close to 90,000, which corresponds closely to the figure of 89,391 men on the Central Front for October 1936, obtained by totalling the returns of men sent in by the militia columns.

In July and August 1936 very few militias had proper military organisation but by September there were at least 46 units each comprising a basic battalion of 300 men, which was taken as an acceptable figure while the formal establishment of a militia battalion had not yet been laid down. By September, most of the militias had battalions of this size. The largest were the numbered volunteer battalions, the *Joven Guardia* (Young Guard), *Juventud Campesina* (Peasant Youth) and the battalion named *El Terrible*. While there was a taste for violent-sounding titles, with units called *Terror Rojo* (Red Terror) and *Drácula*, *El Terrible*

[12] For these orders see DR, L1, C344.

[13] According to Miguel González Inestal, a sub-commissar general nominated by the CNT.

had probably been recruited from men who worked in the mine of that name in Peñarroya in the province of Córdoba.

The militias were now an embryonic army. As will be seen below, it was in that month that some of the militia battalions began to be formed into the first mixed brigades of the new army.

The militias of Aragon

The *Comandancia Militar de Milicias* covered central, southern and eastern Spain. In Catalonia the situation was different. The militia columns which marched into Aragon against the Jaca–Huesca–Zaragoza–Teruel line, held by the Insurgents, answered to the Defence Council, headed by Colonel Felipe Díaz Sandino, of the Catalan autonomous government, the *Generalitat*. The Catalan Statute of Autonomy did not, however, include the devolution of defence responsibilities, which rendered the Defence Council unconstitutional. However, the official 4th Division of the Army, based in Barcelona, headed by General Francisco Llano de la Encomienda, had failed to act decisively against the Insurgents and had been sidelined.

The Barcelona garrison had been decimated when the officers' uprising had been defeated, which made it impossible to exercise any authority similar to that of Madrid with its framework of government and military command. Luis Companys, President of the Generalitat, had called together the leaders of the anarchist CNT and FAI, suggesting that they form a militias committee and appoint as military adviser Major Enrique Pérez Farrás, a professional officer of separatist and left-wing sympathies who had been expelled from the Army after taking part in the Catalan uprising in October 1934. This *Comité de Milicias Antifascistas* included prominent CNT and FAI leaders.[14] The composition of the committee varied and included at different times members from smaller groups such as the dissident Marxist POUM or *Partido Obrero de Unificación Marxista* and the autonomist *Estat Catalá*.[15]

[14] The committee was formed first of Aurelio Fernández of the CNT in charge of security, José Asens (CNT), Rafael Vidella (PSUC), Tomás Fábregas (Republican), Diego Abad de Santillán (FAI), who had charge of organising the militias, Juan García Oliver (FAI), Head of Operations, Jaume Miravitlles (Esquerra de Catalunya), José Torrents (PSUC), supplies and Marcos Alcón, transport.

[15] Sanz, *Los que fuimos*, 71–2. The author was a prominent pre-war anarchist who would command the 26th Division of the Republican Army. Other sources include Diego Abad de Santillán, *Por qué perdimos la guerra*, Buenos Aires, 1940, and José Peirats, *La CNT en la revolución española*, Toulouse, 1951–3 (hereafter *CNT*), and *Los anarquistas en la crisis política española*, Buenos Aires, 1964. Also *De julio a julio*, a special number of the newspaper *Fragua Social*, Valencia, 19 July 1937. The somewhat skimpy archives of the Generalitat on military matters are in DR, L556, C3.

The barracks of the Barcelona garrison were occupied by the militias and renamed *Lenin*, *Marx*, *Bakunin*, *Carlos Marx* and *Vorochilov*. However, there was virtually no time for military training when news came that Zaragoza, a large city with a powerful anarchist tradition, had been taken by the Insurgents, although it had been hoped that General Cabanellas, commander of the 5th Division, would resist calls to join the insurrection. Catalonia was now directly threatened.

On Friday, 24 July 1936 a large column, with some 3,000 militiamen from all parts of the left-wing political spectrum, was organised and set off at about midday in a huge convoy of coaches, lorries, taxis and cars from the Paseo de Gracia in Barcelona.[16] President Companys insisted that the column should be commanded by men of recognised military and professional prestige, in the hopes that their orders would be obeyed. If not, the column would be anarchic in nature as well as mostly anarchist in ideology. The choice fell on Pérez Farrás and the legendary Buenaventura Durruti, a charismatic CNT/FAI leader, who were accepted by the militia and led the column from a Hispano-Suiza limousine. Huge numbers of volunteers had come forward and a selection had to be made in order to arm them all. After panicking when an aircraft bombed the column, it regrouped at Bujaraloz and finally got within 14 km of Zaragoza. The Durruti column was organised on an anarchist basis, with ten men forming a group, ten groups a *centuria*, all electing their leaders, and five groups an *agrupación*. The leaders of these bodies formed the war committee of the column,[17] which had to approve the decisions of the Technical Military Council, consisting of the few officers who accompanied the militia. Pérez Farrás was unhappy with the unmilitary way the column was organised, so Durruti gave Sergeant Manzana, a professional soldier who had absorbed libertarian ideas, the task of obtaining stocks of ammunition, artillery, machine-guns and of organising medical services.[18] Other columns, including the POUM and the PSUC militias, left on the following days. There were some troops from the 10th Regiment and a small number of other military units. How many men there were is difficult to estimate. Abad de Santillán and Peirats speak of 150,000 in the first days and the former mentions 30,000 at the Front in September.[19] Ricardo Sanz, a militia leader, declares that 18,000 passed through the Bakunin barracks in one month. In order to reach a conclusion within possible

[16] For a description, see Pelai Pagés, *Cataluña en guerra y en revolución*, Seville, 2007, 81.
[17] Abel Paz, *Buenaventura Durruti 1896–1936*, Paris, 2000, 283.
[18] *Ibid.*
[19] Abad de Santillán, *Por qué perdimos*, 64; Peirats, *CNT*, II: 135.

orders of magnitude each column would have to be examined, but there were unfortunately no accounts of pay recorded with the minute detail of the Madrid *Comandancia de Milicias*. In his *La invasión de Aragón*, the military historian Colonel Martínez Bande uses Insurgent sources based presumably on prisoners and deserters, whose information would be both partial and unreliable.

Colonel Vicente Guarner produced a post-war memorandum[20] which tends to give lower figures. However, he was in charge of the *Sección Técnica* of the *Comité de Milicias* and would have had more reliable figures than most. Going from north to south there were three broadly identifiable columns:

1 The *Columna Pirenaica* under Major Mariano Bueno, advancing on Huesca with 1,500 militia and two 105 mm batteries, each of 6 or 8 guns.
2 The Villalba column, with possibly a thousand militia under Colonel Villalba, was also advancing on Huesca with the POUM columns *Lenin* and *Maurin*. The whole column had about 4,500 men. The POUM columns had also had a surplus of volunteers. Among them were some groups formed from athletes who had come to Barcelona for the abortive Popular Olympics in rivalry with the coetaneous Berlin celebrations. They had few professional officers. Neither José Rovira nor Jordi Arquer, who led these columns, had military experience, though Rovira's capacity soon became evident, according to Bob Edwards, captain in the POUM's international militias and later a British Member of Parliament.
3 The *Los Aguiluchos* under García Oliver, a CNT militant, had about 2,000 militia. García Oliver soon returned to his administrative responsibilities in Barcelona (he would be Minister of Justice in the Republican Government of Largo Caballero from early September onwards), leaving command to Luis Escobar and Miguel García Vivancos, who later commanded the 25th Division of the Republican Army. This column, and the *Columna Roja y Negra* (Black and Red), would join the Ascaso column commanded by Domingo Ascaso and Gregorio Jover, and by September may have totalled 7,000 men.
4 The PSUC column had 2,000 men and three artillery batteries and was commanded by José del Barrio, later an army corps commander of the Republican Army.
5 The Durruti column was probably the largest of all. Figures given vary from those of *The Times* of London, which estimated 6,000, to

[20] Lent to me kindly by Professor Hugh Thomas.

> Mikhail Koltsov of *Pravda*, who, as might be expected from a man considered Stalin's personal representative in Spain and who would disapprove of anarchist lack of seriousness, reduced the figure to 1,200.[21] It should also be said that the column grew rapidly and that the correspondent of *The Times* made his calculations after the Russian. Certainly, by November the Durruti column sent 3,000 men to Madrid, though this may or may not have been the entire column.[22]

South of the River Ebro was the *Columna Hilario* with 1,000 men, including some soldiers from the Tarragona garrison, the column commanded by Colonel Martínez Peñalver with 600, the Macia-Companys Catalan nationalist column and the Ortiz column, these latter two with 4,500 men between them.

These were the major columns in Aragon in 1936. It seems unlikely that the number of men at the Front at any time was more than 35,000.[23] They faced a smaller number among the Insurgents but given that the militia were attacking they clearly ought to have been more numerous. They were indeed weak and fighting against troops and militia who were properly disciplined and led by experienced officers.

In the Valencia area there were two columns of importance, the *Columna de Hierro* and the *Columna Uribarri*.[24] The *Columna de Hierro* or Iron column, named from its origin in the steel mills of Sagunto, was undoubtedly problematic. One of its principal apologists accepts that it left the Front and returned to Valencia in September demanding that the police forces should be disbanded and replaced by militia vigilantes.[25] It also destroyed police and judicial records. To what point it can fairly be accused of terrorising the region depends on the value of the evidence of its critics. It may be that the Iron column became the scapegoat for the depredations and outrages of other militias and that possibly groups of looters and robbers claimed to be part of the column.[26]

21 M. Koltsov, *Diario de la guerra de España*, Paris, 1963, 32.

22 A description of the Durruti column can be found in *Indice biográfico de la 26 división*, n.p., 1938.

23 Slightly smaller figures are given by J. Camps and E. Olcina, *Les milícies catalanes al front d'Aragó*, Barcelona, 2006, 67ff.

24 Most of the accusations against the *Columna de Hierro* are from B. Bolloten, *The Spanish Revolution: The Left and the Struggle for Power during the Civil War*, Chapel Hill, NC, 1979, ch. 23. On the *Columna Uribarri* see F. Llovera, *La Columna Fantasma*, Valencia, n.d. (1937?).

25 Peirats, *CNT*, I: 272

26 E. Manzanera, *The Iron Column: Testament of a Revolutionary*, Kate Sharpley Library, 2006, 15.

At a meeting held in Valencia on 22 March 1937, before its members disappeared into the anonymous mixed brigades, the Iron Column's budget was opened to public view, though how these large sums had been obtained was not revealed. The money had been spent thus:

100,000 pesetas on 'rationalist' (that is irreligious) schools
100,000 pesetas on military hospitals
100,000 pesetas spent on foreign anarchists
200,000 pesetas on food for Madrid
1,000,000 pesetas on publications, a library and the international anarchist press.[27]

A proportion of this 1,500,000 pesetas (£30,000) would have had to be provided by the State in any case, but the column had no right to make expropriations or to decide to spend money on some of these purposes. If the accounting was correct, and the CNT had a reputation for rectitude in financial matters, nothing was spent on building private empires and maintaining leaders in luxury. Yet the spending raises a major question about the activities of anarchist columns in eastern Spain. Could they take advantage of the near absence of social control and law enforcement which the military uprising had brought about to try to carry out the libertarian revolution when what was needed, in the view of other people, was to construct a reliable form of resistance and attack the Insurgents? The column would, in reply to such a question, have quoted from the few numbers which remain of its newspaper *Línea de Fuego* (Front Line), published in Valencia every two days. At a meeting in October 1936 two men had been expelled for 'immorality' and five new rules for militia discipline were quoted from *Frente Libertario*, published by the CNT's *Comité de Defensa*.

1 Everybody must obey the battalion committees and elected delegates.
2 The militiaman cannot do what he wants but must go where he is ordered.
3 Men who disobey will be punished.
4 Serious offences include desertion, abandoning one's post, pillage and making demoralising comments.
5 Although enrolment was voluntary, militiamen are soldiers of the revolution and must obey orders.

[27] Peirats, *CNT*, II: 39.

The tone in which this list of commandments was repeated in *Línea de Fuego* indicates that the leaders of the column were aiming to instil discipline. The words themselves could have come from any of the many manuals for militia, even a communist one.

The *Columna de Hierro* was militarised at the end of March 1937 and became the 82nd and 83rd Mixed Brigades of the new Republican Army. The '*incontrolables*' had been imprisoned, as President Azaña noted.[28]

The *Columna Uribarri* or *Columna Fantasma* was led by Manuel Uribarri, a *Guardia Civil* officer of marked left-wing views, noisy and quarrelsome, who had severe differences with Captain Alberto Bayo during the failed expedition to retake Majorca led by the latter in August 1936 and later with the communist militia leader and army corps commander Enrique Líster. Bayo complains about Uribarri's conduct and there is evidence to suggest that he was a person of considerable self-importance.[29] The *Columna Fantasma* had discipline problems and published lists of rules, but its chronicler describes it as almost perfect: signals worked without interruption, with direct lines to Madrid, Valencia and all the airfields(!). As for education, there were schools, film shows, lectures and a circulating library and a small orchestra. The column had a postal system under a post office official, a section in charge of rooting out 'fascists' in the villages the column occupied, two warehouses full of provisions in Valencia, a clothing factory (presumably confiscated from its owner) employing a hundred women, three arms workshops and a complete operating theatre.

The importance of all this is that those who wrote praising the militia columns before they were militarised and became part of the Republican Army, obeying a military hierarchy and thus the General Staff and the Minister of War, aimed to demonstrate that excellent organisation could be achieved without militarisation, which was itself something that was characteristic of the enemy. It was not merely the immediate foe who needed to be defeated, but the ideals behind the military uprising. Unfortunately, the Uribarri column was unsuccessful in the expedition to retake Majorca for the Republic and, furthermore, the enemy forced it to retreat continuously.

[28] Azaña, *Obras Completas*, IV: 744, diary entry of 21 August 1937.

[29] Alberto Bayo, *Mi desembarco en Mallorca*, Guadalajara (Mexico), 1944, 72. Uribarri orated from the balcony of the Valencia Provincial Assembly building, promising to suppress the uprising in a few days using rhetoric such as 'Tonight victory will be our bride'. See J. Cirre, *De Espejo a Madrid*, Granada, 1938, 14, and Llovera, *La Columna*, *passim*.

Militias in the north

Bilbao and San Sebastián, in the Basque Provinces, which remained loyal to the Republic, witnessed militia concentrations as soon as the rebel regiments were defeated. The formal creation of the Basque militia dates from 8 August 1936, when the leaders of the Defence Junta, the Basque nationalists Irujo, Monzón and Lasarte, guided by Captain Saseta, an officer sympathetic to Basque nationalism, assembled their militants and created the *Eusko Gudarostea*, the Basque title for the Basque militias. By the end of 1936 there would be 70 battalions of these militia, 32 of them Basque nationalist and the others a mixture of anarchists, communists and socialists.

The discipline of the Basques was in general better than that of the other militias, though there were very few professional officers to lead them.[30] So was their military organisation. When the UGT in the Basque Country constructed their three battalions of militia, the first two were for men who had completed their military service or knew how to handle a firearm. Their aim was not to carry out a social revolution but to keep their political autonomy, granted by the Statute approved on 1 October 1936, even though this did not permit the Basque region to run its own military forces. Furthermore, in large areas of the rest of Republican Spain, murder, the burning of churches, the killing of clergy and widespread pillage was sometimes the work of individual criminals taking advantage of the breakdown of public order, but often carried out by militias who could not be brought to justice in the chaos which Republican leaders were struggling to dominate (gangs of a different political hue also carried out widespread murder in the Insurgent zone, but this was tolerated and even encouraged by the military, whose authority and power were unchallenged). In the Basque Provinces, however, outrages of the sort were far less common, for the Basques were profoundly Catholic and their clergy tended to support Basque autonomy. Indeed, the militia battalions of the *Partido Nacionalista Vasco* were accompanied by chaplains who celebrated open-air Mass.[31]

Not having professional officers, however, meant that essential aspects of war, such as digging trenches and posting guards, might be neglected, while weapons, including the Colt machine-guns, notorious for their slack belts, with which the UGT battalions had been supplied,

30 For a rather less favourable view see Pelai Pagés, *Cataluña*. See also the socialist M. de Amilibia's view in his *Los batallones de Euskadi*, San Sebastián, 1978.

31 A. Montero, *Historia de la persecución religiosa en España*, Madrid, 1961, 357. Some priests were imprisoned in Bilbao and executed by revolutionary sailors, who were not Basques, after insurgent bombing in 1937.

were poorly maintained.[32] The six months between the beginning of the war and the launch of General Mola's assault on Bilbao at the end of March 1937 do not seem to have been occupied in creating an army to the same extent as in central Spain,[33] possibly because of the differences of opinion between the Basque President, Aguirre, and the Madrid Government. Political officers or commissars, for example, were not introduced into the Basque forces until 17 May 1937, and were not given any specific training for their role.

The Fifth Regiment

The two major and significant militia groups preceding the construction of the Republican Army were the Fifth Regiment or *Quinto Regimiento*, organised by the PCE, and the CNT's Confederate Militia of the Central Region or *Milicias Confederales de la Región Central.*

Enrique Líster, who replaced Enrique Castro Delgado, first leader of the *Quinto Regimiento*,[34] recalled that the regiment sprang from the pre-war MAOC and from the fifth of the five volunteer battalions that were called for as soon as the uprising was suppressed in Madrid.[35] His information coincides with that of Major Fernández Navarro, the officer who had been ordered to create the battalions.[36] Juan Guilloto León, alias 'Modesto' and the only militia officer who rose to the rank of general in the Civil War, recalls that the MAOC were concentrated in a convent in the Calle Francos Rodríguez, which is where the Fifth Regiment based itself.

The suggestion that the Fifth Regiment was so-called because the pre-war Madrid garrison had four infantry regiments can thus be discounted. The fifth of the five volunteer battalions which Major Fernández Navarro had been ordered to form joined some embryonic formations of the MAOC from the working-class Cuatro Caminos district of Madrid and used the convent as a barracks. PCE leaders

32 F. Uribe Gallejones, *Un miliciano de la UGT*, Bilbao, 2007, 53.

33 *Ibid.*, ch. 4.

34 Modesto, *Soy del Quinto Regimiento*, 25. Castro Delgado was the first leader of the *Quinto Regimiento.* Líster denies this, but Castro Delgado's rupture with the PCE discredits anything said about him by communist authors. Vittorio Vidali (alias Carlos Contreras), the political commissar of the *Quinto Regimiento*, confirmed to me privately (personal communication, 2 February 1973) that Castro Delgado was appointed leader of the regiment by the PCE.

35 Líster, *Nuestra guerra*, 61–2.

36 In a letter located in the municipal archives of Alicante (my thanks to Francisco Fúster).

learnt of this and a PCE meeting on 20 July decided to form communist militias which would serve as an example to other groups.

The question of how many men were in the Fifth Regiment is important insofar as it provides some order of magnitude of the communist contribution to the militias in general. The difficulty in calculating the numbers arises from the nature of the Fifth Regiment, which was a training centre and not a fighting unit. Thus one cannot always be sure which battalions had belonged to it. All the communist authors claim 70,000 men, which comes from the last issue of the Fifth Regiment's newspaper *Milicia Popular*, and that half of them were communists. However, it would have been hard to find 35,000 young enough card-holding communists in 1936 Spain. The figure must include members of the United Socialist and Communist Youth, the *Juventudes Socialists Unificadas* or JSU.

The registers of the *Comandancia Militar de Milicias* and a further two lists in the archives suggest between 22,500 and 25,000 men in the Fifth Regiment.[37] A return signed by Líster, probably in October 1936, refers to 50 battalions.[38] Even if each battalion had numbered 500 men, which is improbable, the total would not have passed 25,000. According to 'Carlos Contreras', the figure of 70,000 refers only to recruitment in Madrid and that a further 50,000 joined from the provinces.[39]

Furthermore, there are some interesting comments from the Pay Office of the *Comandancia de Milicias*. The Pay Office had refused to recognise one of the regiment's battalions as properly constituted to receive pay. The following complaint, expressed in general terms, appears in the records:

> The Fifth Regiment presents one single payroll and does not distinguish between the battalions for which pay is claimed. In other words, the claim made under the heading of Fifth Regiment is merely a long list of names. This creates serious problems for the proper conduct of the task of the *Comandancia*.[40]

The sums involved were very large. In December 1936 and January 1937 almost 2 million pesetas were spent on the *Quinto Regimiento*, which demanded a million and a half more to compensate for sums spent on other battalions 'which were born from us'.

Many competent militia officers and political commissars emerged from the Fifth Regiment, among them Ascanio, Leal, Modesto, Líster, Merino, Aguado, Pertegás, Barcia, Delage, Santiago Alvarez, José del

[37] DR, L1334, C10 and L1335.
[38] DR, L1334, C10.
[39] V. Vidali, *Il Quinto Reggimento*, Milan, 1973, 20.
[40] DR, L1334, C16.

Campo, Daniel Ortega and Gustavo Durán (see Appendix 4). Another was Valentín González, known as 'El Campesino', who had notorious disagreements with the PCE militia leaders and was imprisoned in the Soviet Union, where he took refuge after the war.[41] Others, such as Modesto, would have emerged as leaders even without the Fifth Regiment.

What was original and significant about the *Quinto Regimiento* was its realistic attitude towards the war. While the euphoria of the early days seemed to be reflected among the other militias by the conviction that a few lorries full of brave men, armed with rifles and small arms taken from looted barracks, could easily put to flight a handful of rebellious officers and *Falangistas*, especially because the young conscripts who had been marched out of Insurgent garrisons were unwilling and because the civilian population was hostile, the *Quinto Regimiento*, in contrast, knew that it had to tackle a formidable enemy. The other militias did not understand the importance of professional officers and of discipline, and were often openly hostile to both, but the attitude of the *Quinto Regimiento* was different. This explains why the relative short-sightedness of CNT leaders such as Cipriano Mera and Buenaventura Durruti – at least at the outset of the war – would give way to the revolutionary awareness and experience of 'Carlos Contreras', pseudonym of the Italian communist Vittorio Vidali and principal military adviser delegated by the Communist International in Spain until the arrival of the Russians.

In a series of articles in *Milicia Popular*, the skilfully edited newspaper of the Fifth Regiment, Contreras analysed the meaning of the war and how it should be waged. These articles contain the essence of the PCE's attitude towards the military aspects of the war and are thus enormously significant in clarifying the views of the party about the appropriate character of the new Republican Army which the PCE saw as essential. He remarks on the surprise that many people expressed at the victories of the people over the professional officers in Madrid and other cities. It is erroneous, he stresses, to think that those successes prove that military professionalism is useless and that mere heroism is sufficient for victory. Heroism in itself may even be counter-productive when not accompanied by suitable military technique. Command is vital and competent leaders should be given full authority. Furthermore the concept of the military 'technician' subordinate to the political leader, prevalent in the CNT militias, is totally incorrect, in a revolutionary

[41] His memoirs, ghost-written by the dissident *poumista* Julián Gorkín, were published in English as *Listen Comrades*, Heinemann, 1952.

war, writes Contreras. It is even less right for decisions to be taken by committee votes. The error of antimilitarism lies in confusing the word 'officer' with the role of officers in the pre-war Army. The difference between an officer, even a professional one, in a revolutionary army, and the Insurgent officers, lies in their attitude towards their men. But there must be authority and respect for military principles.[42]

The attractiveness of this communist posture was understandably very great for professional officers who had not joined the insurrection against the Popular Front Government but who were nevertheless uncomfortable leading undisciplined militias.

Although the Fifth Regiment was a training base, it did create its own combat units, known as the Steel Companies or *Compañías de Acero* and the *Brigada de la Victoria*. Given that these formations were directly associated with the Fifth Regiment and hence to the PCE, they were assumed to be unlikely to behave in the undisciplined manner of other militias. Recruitment was carefully supervised. Men had to be in good physical condition, have had some basic military training and swear to obey the strict discipline of the Fifth Regiment. The Steel Companies were autonomous, with their own services of signals, ambulance sections and so on. This is significant, because the fighting unit complete with services would constitute the essence of the *Brigada Mixta*, the basic unit of the Republican Army.

Towards the end of August the Steel Companies merged with the *Brigada de la Victoria*, returning from the Front on 15 September. It was met with the customary propagandistic spectacle, accompanied by speeches by Spanish and foreign activists. But its achievements had not been spectacular. Granted, no militia was more than mediocre at the time, but the determination of the editors of *Milicia Popular* to glorify the non-existent triumphs of troops trained by the PCE is such an evident example of propaganda that it can easily lead to the minimisation of the real achievements of the *Quinto Regimiento*.

Apart from laying such emphasis on discipline, the principal success of the Fifth Regiment was to include in its organisations the entire apparatus of military infrastructure: administration, a Staff, an officers' training school, guerrilla units, supplies, transport and signals, a nurses' school and women's organisations to help the families of the fighting men. It developed loudspeaker broadcasts to try to demoralise the raw conscripts on the other side and it launched the first literacy campaigns among the militia. It adopted factories and, in the words of one of its early leaders, the later Colonel Líster, it

[42] Carlos Contreras (Vittorio Vidali) in *Milicia Popular*, 20 August 1936.

cooperated enthusiastically and loyally with the authorities, maintained close links with all the political parties and unions, helped other battalions … maintained uninterrupted contact with the civilian population by means of its publications, newspapers, meetings, lectures, cinema, band, artistes, exhibitions, posters, etc.[43]

The Fifth Regiment's major publication was its daily *Milicia Popular*, which appeared from 26 July 1936 until 29 January 1937. Well written, it served the party as mouthpiece for its ideas about how the Republican Army should be. There was also a publishing house which put out works by writers such as Ramón Sénder and Rafael Alberti. There were courses provided for a new brief baccalaureate, while the radio station of the regiment began its broadcasts with talks by Líster, Sénder and foreign communists such as the Italian socialist Pietro Nenni. Extraordinary efforts were made to drill the minds of the men. There were daily visits by Popular Front personalities and foreign correspondents, who left greatly impressed by the organisation and morale of the Fifth Regiment, where nothing was left to chance and where a nursery for combatants' children enjoyed the service of two refugee German psychoanalysts. This torrent of energy was unleashed by the *Comisión de Trabajo Social* or Social Work Committee, which was an interesting precursor for the system of commissars that would be used by the Republican Army. As well as the *agitprop* already described, the committee set up art exhibitions (on strictly realistic and revolutionary subjects) and showed the well-known films about the Russian Revolution *Chapaiev*, *Kronstadt* and the world-famous *Battleship Potemkin* in rough-and-ready cinemas, not only in Madrid but also in villages up and down the Front. The feverish activity of the committee can be measured by the 47 cinema performances which took place in 44 days in a tour of the Teruel and Andalusian fronts with a lorry and a projector. On 27 December 1936 there were six cinema showings of these films in Madrid alone.

The same day, *Milicia Popular* announced that 70 per cent of the *Quinto Regimiento* was now fully militarised and enrolled in the first mixed brigades of the new Republican Army. No more enrolments into the Fifth Regiment would be accepted. Barracks would be evacuated and all equipment and material would be handed over to the commands of the new brigades. Barracks would become *Casas del Combatiente* or rest and relaxation centres for troops, thus anticipating the *Hogar del Soldado* or 'Soldier's Home' of the Republican Army. Lastly, on 27 January 1937 the *Quinto Regimiento* was officially dissolved, having completed its task.

[43] Líster, *Nuestra guerra*, 65

Careful examination of what remains of the records of the Fifth Regiment leads to the conclusion that there was a massive propaganda effort to underline its importance and thus that of the Spanish Communist Party in stimulating a 'correct' stance towards how to create a new army and fight the war against the Insurgents. Yet the importance of the Fifth Regiment, for all that, should not be underestimated. To have trained 25,000 men was an astonishing achievement for a minority group, and the attempt to achieve respect for military values against the general atmosphere of the militia in the Republican zone in the early weeks of the war was highly positive. The influence of the Fifth Regiment would be seen clearly in the institution of the Political Commissariat and in many other aspects of the Republican Army, especially the proliferation of propaganda. If the *Quinto Regimiento* was not quite as important in the Spanish Civil War and in the formation of the Republican Army as the PCE has claimed, it nevertheless had enormous significance in the history of what might be termed the 'taming' of the revolution.

The anarchist militias

The militias of the CNT in central Spain lack the publicity which the Fifth Regiment has received.[44] The CNT's Defence Committee investigated applications to join militia in order to remove Insurgent sympathisers and others who, frightened for their lives, were trying to hide in the militias (on the other side, so many anarchists joined the fascist *Falange* that it became known as the '*FAIlange*'). Next, it called men to the militia as they were required. Every 20 men elected a delegate, every hundred or *centuria* another delegate. The *centuria* delegates formed the battalion committee.[45]

The anarchists of the CNT were searching for the most democratic system possible consistent with military organisation, but contradiction between theory and practice was evident. Units might well be called *grupos* or *centurias*, but in fact they were sections, platoons[46] and

[44] Sources for the CNT militias in the Centre of Spain are in DR, L1334, C11 of the *Comandancia Militar de Milicias*, and in E. de Guzmán, *Madrid Rojo y Negro*, Madrid, 1937. The author edited the newspaper *Castilla Libre* during the war, was sentenced to death by court martial after the Francoist victory, but was amnestied in 1941. See also the memoirs of a leading CNT militia and later corps commander, Cipriano Mera, *Guerra, exilio y cárcel de un anarcosindicalista*, Paris, 1976.

[45] Guzmán, *Madrid Rojo*, 78.

[46] The Spanish *sección* is equivalent to the British and American platoon, commanded by a junior officer, while the *pelotón* is a smaller unit, like the British section, commanded by a sergeant.

companies. Theories apart, organisation and hierarchy are inherent to armies, and the CNT had in the end to accept and accustom itself to them.

In four days 4,000 men joined the anarchist column, armed with what they had been able to seize from military installations at Alcalá de Henares, some miles east of Madrid, the birthplace of Cervantes, which had been seized by CNT groups from the Insurgents. Their leader was an officer, Lieutenant-Colonel Francisco del Rosal Rico, who would go on to command the IV Army Corps of the Republican Army, and who shared command with the ascetic Cipriano Mera, the building worker who would follow del Rosal in command of the IV Corps. The 'Staff' of the column consisted of a civil engineer and three journalists. The del Rosal column, with 835 militiamen in August 1936, was the largest CNT unit.[47]

By September 1936, CNT militia in the central war theatre had grown to a total of 5,591 militiamen. Pay and supplies could be obtained only by proper accounting and returns. By October pay was being issued to 12,151 militiamen in anarchist columns such as the *Columna de Andalucía*, the *Columna España Libre*, the *Milicias Confederales* and others. The figure increased rapidly and in December the two major CNT militia columns, the *Columna de Andalucía* and the *Milicias Confederales*, counted over 23,000 men in their ranks.

Much less propaganda was made about them than about the Fifth Regiment, but the anarchist militia units would appear to have had a structured organisation of equal amplitude. The same committees – for supplies, recruitment and pay – appear; recruits underwent a medical examination and were lodged in barracks.

Nevertheless, most of the extant information about the early militia comes from the great anarcho-syndicalist organisation, the CNT itself, which was eager not to fall behind in showing that its adherents had been among the first to fight the Insurgents. Thus the information cannot be seen as totally accurate in all aspects, although a comparison between anarchist memoirs and what is in the archives show that the reports are not too wide of the mark.

As for more personal issues, the archives hold many documents and letters about the fate of the militiamen, who did not wear identification tags. Nor did the Insurgents communicate names of dead militia through any agency, such as the Red Cross, to the Republican authorities. Many militiamen were fugitives from the Insurgent zone, where

[47] These and following figures are all taken from the records of the *Comandancia Militar de Milicias*. Ultimately they all depend on returns from the units concerned.

their lives had been at risk if they had been politically active on the Left. Moreover, the level of illiteracy among them was high, given that the average militiaman was an uneducated agricultural day-labourer or worked on a building site. This latter factor explains the importance laid on basic education by all political group militias, and this would be a marked aspect of the Republican Army.

The achievements of the militias

Another subject where the facts have been obscured by authors who have been concerned to write apologia for their own political groupings is that of the discipline and military achievements of the militias. Communists praise the heroism of their militia, while anarchists condemn the militarisation which was imposed from late 1936 to the summer of 1937 for having stifled the true revolutionary spirit of the militia.[48]

Furthermore, reports from professional officers are generally critical of the militia. Mainly they refer to the panic which led to unnecessary retreats. One particularly interesting and lengthy report was drawn up by Colonel Mariano Salafranca about the *Columna de Oropesa*, which was defending the main highway into Madrid from the south-west. Salafranca had been ordered to take command of the column on the night of 28–29 August 1936 although, as he writes, his military colleagues had warned him that the situation was very difficult. When Salafranca wrote this he was of course defending himself by claiming that most professional officers would have refused the order because if they failed they might be accused of treasonably betraying the inexperienced militia to the enemy. He is even boasting about how he has fulfilled his duty. Yet merely to mention that he might not have obeyed the order to take over command of the militia column is indicative of the atmosphere of the moment.

Salafranca had no information and had had no previous briefings on the situation; nor was there any formal take-over of command. Morale was low and a militia officer had been murdered while trying to stem a rout. Salafranca's headquarters was a roadmenders' hut from which he tried to organise the column, spread over 15 km of highway. On 30 August he laid down proper channels, 'in order to exercise some control over the tiresome and pernicious militia habit of interfering with command'.

[48] One of many examples could be Abad de Santillán, *Por qué perdimos*.

Salafranca reported that at least one group of militia left its post to go and eat in the nearest town. His general comments are pointed.

> The retreats are caused by the general structure and heterogeneous character of the militia. They are a formless mass which contain noble spirits, valiant and passionate for the cause they are defending, together with completely opposite types ... and ... an amorphous mass, ready, according to the situation, to follow their leaders, without ideas of their own and, when things become difficult and dangerous, seeking egoistically the easiest way to save their lives.[49]

Salafranca continues that all this is well known, and criticises the General Staff for having entrusted a flat, open area to a militia column, when it was common knowledge that the militia could fight in open country only if it consisted of rough terrain with trees or other cover.

Even this relatively local report suggests that if the militia had been employed in terrain where they could have used cover, if they had been provided with appropriate officers and NCOs and if the logistics of ammunition supply had been better, and if, in general, the authorities of the Republic had been able to use their militia as the Insurgents did with the Carlist *Requetés* and the Falangists, less would have been demanded of men who simply did not have the training or discipline which would have corrected the faults which, as Colonel Salafranca so eloquently wrote, were endemic.

In such circumstances, poor morale was excusable. Certain execution was the fate which awaited militia captured by the rapidly advancing columns of Moroccan *Regulares* and *Legionarios*. Whether all captured militiamen were executed, as was the case after the fall of Badajoz to the Insurgents on 15 August 1936, which is the best-documented example of the savagery of Franco's forces, in the early days of the war prisoners were not usually taken. The Insurgents saw the militia not as soldiers but as *francs-tireurs*, mere rebels against the declaration of the State of War which had constituted the uprising. Franco's forces were also in the numerical minority, and could afford to leave behind only a handful as garrisons as they passed through towns and villages. Furthermore, in many of the places they captured they found evidence of murders and other crimes committed either by militia or local activists against priests, landowners and the middle and upper socio-economic class in general. They had no compunction and even a sense of justice in taking no prisoners.

Yet it would be an error to assume that the militias never fought valiantly. Examples of courageous resistance can be found in the reports

[49] DR, L967, C12.

of Insurgent commanders on the taking of Espejo (Córdoba), the mining region of Río Tinto (Huelva), Mérida and Sigüenza (Guadalajara), where the militia resisted until the end.[50]

The comment of Vicente Rojo, later Chief of the Republican Army's Staff, is the most measured:

> Militia units could resist sporadically in some places where some leaders could impose their will, but this does not change the fact that in general the militias were rolled back incessantly and that the retreat lacked the slightest orderliness, even though there might be many acts of bravery in the struggle.[51]

The militias were ignorant of the most basic military rules, which suggests that even those who had completed their military service had not been minimally trained. They went forward in long, wide lines and then bunched up, offering excellent targets. They stuck to the roads, so that a single aircraft with a machine-gun could put an entire column to flight. They did not obey orders, which had to be accompanied with threats.[52] Their fire discipline was poor. Thousands of cartridges were wasted trying to down aircraft, which only contributed to revealing their position, assuming they were camouflaged, which is unlikely. Frequently they refused to dig trenches. Understandably, they had little resistance to physical privations and they suffered greatly from the summer heat.[53]

On the Aragon Front these militia characteristics were even more pronounced, but were less obvious because the Insurgents were too weak to do anything but maintain their own lines. The Republican militias would return to Barcelona for the weekend, argue about the orders, refuse to hand over captured war material to militia of other political hues or fortify positions.[54]

[50] See J. M. Martínez Bande, *La marcha sobre Madrid*, Madrid, 1968, 32n., quoting the Insurgent General Asensio Cabanillas, and the same author's *La campaña de Andalucía*, Madrid, 1969, 70, citing the Insurgent commander Sáenz de Buruaga, 110n., and cables to Franco from the military governor of Huelva.

[51] V. Rojo, *Así fue la defensa de Madrid*, Mexico City, 1967, 56.

[52] DR, L967, C14 contains an order of 23 November 1936 from Lieutenant-Colonel Ortega, with a statement that his orders must be obeyed without excuse or pretext of any sort ('sin pretexto ni excusa de ninguna clase'), which suggests that such disobedience was common.

[53] DR, L966, C14 contains a report from a battalion commander that headquarters considered so important that it reproduced it and distributed it to column commanders on 7 October 1936. It enumerates all the characteristics of the militias and suggests possible remedies, among them better basic training.

[54] Despite its tendentious character, the memoir of Rafael Miralles Bravo, *Memorias de un comandante Rojo*, Madrid, 1975, gives vivid descriptions of the disorder among the anarchist columns.

If the British writer George Orwell's experience of the POUM barracks in Barcelona was at all typical, the poor results at the Front were hardly surprising:

> On my second day in the barracks, there began what was comically called 'instruction'. At the beginning there were the most frightful scenes of chaos. The recruits were mostly boys of sixteen and seventeen from the back streets of Barcelona, full of revolutionary ardour but completely ignorant of the meaning of war. It was impossible even to get them to stand in line. Discipline did not exist; if a man disliked an order he would step out of the ranks and argue fiercely with the officer ... the so-called 'instruction' was simply parade-ground drill ... that useless nonsense which I had learned when I was fifteen years old ... Obviously, if you have only a few days in which to train a soldier, you must teach him the things he will most need ... Yet this mob of eager children, who were going to be thrown into the front line in a few days time, were not even taught how to fire a rifle or pull the pin out of a bomb.[55]

The leaders of the militia knew that something had to be done. The Intelligence officer attached to the del Rosal column told the General Staff that the CNT had decided to reinforce discipline.[56] Most of the militias published instructions about military order and discipline. Federica Montseny, anarchist Minister of Health in Francisco Largo Caballero's broad-based Government, which took over from the Giral administration in early September 1936, demanded better discipline in her speech at the funeral of Buenaventura Durruti, killed, probably by the accidental discharge of a firearm, on the Madrid Front, as did other anarchist leaders such as the Minister of Industry, Juan Peiró.[57] After the defeats of September 1936, few would have disagreed with demands for discipline. But anarchist ideas of discipline were limited to the men obeying their elected delegates, whom they could change if they disagreed with them. Changing officers from below is not the way to fight wars. It would not be long before the CNT had to undergo a massive change in its attitude.

In such a situation of chaos and indiscipline, the situation of those professional military men who had remained loyal to the Republic was not at all enviable. Both General Riquelme and General Asensio Torrado failed as Commanders-in-Chief in central Spain, largely because they could not adapt to the militia manner of behaviour.

Riquelme, however, like a number of other generals – on both sides – had enjoyed no active command for several years and does not seem

[55] George Orwell, *Homage to Catalonia*, Penguin, 1966, 12–13.
[56] DR, L967, C26.
[57] Peiró cited in Peirats, *CNT*, I: 253. See also Federica Montseny, *In Memoriam of Comrade Durruti*, Barcelona, 1937.

to have been capable of commanding a force on active service. In a report he asks for a long list of essential and basic supplies, such as plates, writing materials and tents. In Barcelona, where hardly any military infrastructure was left after the suppression of the uprising, it was understandable that the militiamen had been told to come equipped with sheets, soap and towels to join the columns marching into Aragon, and that groups which had machine-guns had been assured that they would be allowed to stay together.[58] But criticism of the militias in the central region demands an answer to the question of why the large number of officers in Madrid did not act with the efficiency of their Insurgent brother-officers in Burgos, Valladolid and La Coruña. Why had they not apparently concerned themselves to ensure that the men went to the Front with at least the minimum regulation kit? It is not surprising that the militias distrusted the officers and that consequently the militia sometimes forced officers to lead from the front and in this way some irreplaceable potential leaders were killed.

The communists and the professional officers

The valour and value of career officers was first understood by the communists of the Fifth Regiment. Among the professionals praised in early issues of *Milicia Popular* were Manuel Márquez, Miguel Gallo, the Galán brothers, Mangada and Barceló (see Appendix 4). Asensio Torrado would lose his post through communist pressure, but he had been generously praised by the communists when Largo Caballero promoted him to general and, as one of the acts of his administration, gave him command of the Central Zone at the beginning of September 1936. On 16 September 1936, *Milicia Popular* published Asensio's reply thanking the Fifth Regiment and its political commissar 'Carlos Contreras' for appointing him its honorary commander. Whether the communists turned against Asensio because he refused to join the party or whether they thought that his methods would not lead to victory is uncertain. The communists saw clearly that the attitude of professional officers had to be adapted to the needs of the situation, whether or not they accepted a party card. Dolores Ibárruri, the PCE deputy known as 'La Pasionaria', praised the career officers in these words: '[L]oyal officers, who sided with the Republic, who deserve our complete respect, who fight with the People and the People have the duty to trust them!'

[58] *Solidaridad Obrera* (the leading anarchist newspaper), 26 July 1936.

The tone was different a month later, when *Milicia Popular* published a piece by Contreras referring to '[s]o many defeats of loyal troops, defeats caused by the incapacity and ineptitude of a few generals'. The only generals who could be meant were Asensio and José Miaja in Madrid. And Contreras continues: 'If the generals of retirement keep ordering retirements, they should be retired themselves. Let them go with their pensions and goodbye.'

It would be hard to try to prove that this displayed a PCE attempt, instigated by the Comintern advisers, to take power, when this would have been against Soviet policy at the time. The attack on Asensio reflected a sincere belief that professional officers should be replaced by competent and younger militia leaders. And whatever their opinion about General Miaja, the communists would back him to the hilt during the battle for Madrid.

Conclusions

Some conclusions can be extracted from this study of the militia period before the creation of the Republican Army. Firstly, the uprising and the revolution exacerbated the centrifugal tendency which has so often appeared at critical moment in Spanish history. This phenomenon can be seen in Catalonia and in the Basque Provinces. There was no common effort to launch an offensive in Aragon, where the enemy was relatively weak, which might have forced the Insurgents to try to relieve it and thus slowed down the drive of Franco's African Expeditionary Force as it moved up from Seville through Extremadura before turning north-east to relieve the siege of the Alcázar of Toledo in early September. It would also have been advisable to dispatch a number of officers to the Basque Country, a move which would have paid dividends, given that the Basque militias were more amenable to discipline than the others. But the quiet Insurgent fronts were left unattacked while the Legion and the *Regulares* stormed northwards.

Secondly, the militias were not 'the nation in arms'. In the entire area overseen by the *Comandancia Militar de Milicias*, the greatest figure for militia than can be stated is 92,000 men, to which can be added the 25,000–35,000 men in the militias in Aragon and Valencia, a relatively small figure given the density of population in those areas and their level of politicisation. Only in the Basque Provinces was participation really high, but even so many of the militia were conscripts called to service in the autumn of 1936.

Thirdly, the Government probably erred in not using the forces which remained to it as a skeleton for the immediate call-up of reservists. However, it was the weakness of the Giral Government, which took over on Sunday 19 July 1936, once the Insurgents refused to talk peace, which forced it to allow the militias to run themselves. The attempt to form battalions of volunteers recruited from the militia but subject to military law failed. The militia phenomenon was an inevitable consequence of the political and social situation of Republican Spain.

Fourthly, this was the period when the PCE crystallised its concepts and introduced many of the characteristics of the Republican Army, in particular, the system of political commissars. It was the communists who had the clearest vision of the situation, but they hid it for many decades after the war under a barrage of propaganda which fought and refought the ideological battles of the Spanish Civil War without really clarifying the problems.

Fifthly, the militias demoralised the professional officers who had dealings with them. Thus few of the professionals who tried to direct the efforts of the militias were still in post at the end of the war. Of the leaders of the Republican Army in 1939, only Escobar, colonel in command of the *Guardia Civil* in Barcelona in 1936, had been a senior officer. Rojo, Casado, Menéndez, Matallana and Prada, the Chief of Staff and the army commanders at the end of the war, were almost unknown mere majors at the outset of the conflict.

Lastly, the militias in general were of little military value. The best they could do was to halt the advance of the skeleton Insurgent forces moving on Madrid from the north, and to prevent the Insurgents moving eastwards from their Huesca–Zaragoza–Teruel line. They were not badly armed, as is proved by the long lists of material captured by the Insurgents. These lists also demonstrate that they were incapable of destroying their weapons before retreating, which is an elementary rule of war.

This last is a conclusion which has general validity. A revolutionary force without discipline is effective only if it has sufficient time and space to build the necessary military structure and if the enemy lacks efficiency. The *Falange* leader, Manuel Hedilla, however, ordered all his militia to put themselves under the command of professional officers, to respect them and obey their orders. They did not have much alternative, given the overall domination of Insurgent Spain by the military. The parallels drawn at the time with the French and Russian revolutions are not really valid. As so often, in this Spain was also *sui generis*.

The militias frequently accused the officers of treason, though often the officer in question was simply doing his best to pass over to the Insurgents either because he sympathised with them, or because loyalty to his comrades was more important in his view than to the Republic, or because he was afraid for his own safety or because the excesses of the revolution disgusted him. Yet often the demands of the militias were impossible to satisfy.[59]

[59] Examples can be found in Martín Blázquez, *I Helped to Build*, 100, and General Mariano Gámir Ulíbarri, *De mis memorias*, Paris, 1939, 17. The anarchist Cipriano Mera's account, criticising the professionals from some aspects, is enlightening here (*Guerra*, 43).

4 Militarisation

> To bring those masses under discipline and into a military structure controlled by the State, with commanders who take their orders from the Government, in order to wage war in accordance with plans drawn up by a General Staff, that has been the Republic's major problem.
>
> Azaña, *Obras Completas*, III: 487

The military situation

By September 1936 it was clear that Spain had been plunged into a civil war and was not facing merely a military rebellion with scattered foci. The euphoria of July and August had disappeared. Painful reality had imposed agonising reconsideration on many who had opposed the militarisation of the militias, among them the Prime Minister himself, the socialist leader Francisco Largo Caballero. He had formed a broad-based administration on 4 September including, for the first time, two communist ministers, Jesús Hernández and Vicente Uribe, as well as a Basque nationalist, Manuel de Irujo. In November they would be joined by that contradiction in terms, four anarchist ministers. Caballero would put a vast project into motion: to restore the integrity of the Republic. One aspect of this was to recreate the Army and put an end to disorderly and inefficient militias.

The Insurgents, who now called themselves *nacionales*, and were known in the British press as Nationalists, had envisaged a swift coup, which had become a war. Although on some fronts they had made little advance, the Republican militias had been able to do little more than detain them. In contrast, the militias constantly broke and retreated in the face of General Franco's expeditionary force from Morocco, as it advanced from Andalusia towards Madrid.

Circumstances had forced the leaders of the CNT's militias and many others to reconsider their attitude. It was evident that 'the discipline of indiscipline', to use the anarchist expression, had not functioned. The militia had retreated in the face of the superior military ability of far smaller numbers. Insurgent troops on most fronts, but particularly along the line of march of the Moroccan *Regulares* and the professional *Legionarios*, had recovered large amounts of abandoned weaponry which the new Republican Army would seriously lack in the following months. North and east of the capital, the Insurgents had established positions which would be remain until the end of the war. Furthermore, they had succeeded in linking Franco's army, marching northwards from Seville, with General's Mola's forces advancing south from the cities of Castile and Galicia. In eastern Spain, a line stretched from Huesca through Zaragoza to Teruel, which the Insurgents defended with little difficulty, having thrown back the early attempts by the militias moving west from Barcelona and Valencia. General Queipo de Llano had consolidated the land within the lines around his territories in Andalusia, which included the large cities of Seville, Granada and Córdoba, and the coastline from the friendly Portuguese frontier as far as Málaga. Although the Insurgent Nationalists were thinly spread, no militia force managed to dislodge them. In the north, while Asturias (except for the city of Oviedo), Santander and the Basque Country remained in Republican hands, the capture of Irún on 5 September by the Insurgents cut off communications between Republican territory in northern Spain and France, except by sea.

Major military reorganisation was thus the most urgent task for the Republic's new Government, as it steadily took back the reins of power from local committees, and strove to put an end to the murders and other outrages which had horrified its leaders.

Reorganisation and appointments

Caballero's first act was to replace General Riquelme in command of the Republican forces in the Central Region with José Asensio Torrado,[1] the most senior colonel of the Staff Corps retained by the Republic and, having been promoted to that rank at the early age of 35, an officer of singular ability. He believed in the efficiency of discipline as well as in its external manifestations, disdaining to wear the working-men's overalls (*mono*) which some officers had preferred to the uniform which they feared was provocative in those early days of emotional antimilitarism.[2]

[1] *Gaceta*, 5 September 1936.
[2] See Henry Buckley (British journalist in Madrid), *Life and Death of the Spanish Republic*, Hamish Hamilton, 1940, 248.

Both as commander of the Central Region and later as Under-Secretary for War, Asensio was to a considerable extent responsible for the efficient impulse towards Republican military organisation and, to this extent, Caballero's confidence in him was justified. Asensio's later fall came about because he was unable to control the chaotic situation in Málaga, which was taken, undefended, by the Insurgents in February 1937, and after a two-month-long communist campaign against him, whose reasons are not totally clear.

On 22 October 1936, as enemy forces approached the capital, Caballero appointed General of Brigade José Miaja to command in Madrid. Before the uprising Miaja had commanded one of the two brigades in the Madrid division. He had been unsuccessful in his attempts to take Córdoba with the exiguous forces which could be scraped up after the suppression of the military uprising. Since then he had been unemployed, perhaps not completely trusted, especially since it was probably known that the 'Director' of the uprising, General Emilio Mola, had counted on his support.[3]

The reasons Caballero appointed Miaja to Madrid, where he would later head the semi-autonomous *Junta Delegada*, are complicated and unclear. His military career had not been particularly distinguished. He had spent long years in bureaucratic posts and in charge of recruits' depots. The Republic had favoured him (there was little choice because so many generals had taken early retirement, and Miaja was not distrusted, as were Africanist officers). He had commanded various infantry brigades. He was briefly Minister of War in the Popular Front Cabinet of February 1936. Yet he had also been invited to join the ephemeral government put together on 19 July 1936 by the *Unión Republicana* politician Diego Martínez Barrio to replace the administration which had resigned in the face of the uprising and to try, unsuccessfully, to reach an agreement with the Insurgents.

Possibly it was Miaja's very conservatism which attracted the favour of Caballero and his advisers. He was also on good terms with the professional officers whom it was necessary to attract to the new army. Miaja had no history of planned plots or coups and he was known to have been opposed to handing arms over to the militias and to have protested repeatedly at summary killings of captured rebel officers.[4]

[3] Mola wrote to a friend, 'I don't believe that Miaja is as bad as they say.' Arrarás, *Cruzada*, XVII: 385.

[4] See Bolloten, *Spanish Revolution*, 30; Arrarás, *Cruzada*, XVII: 393; M. Gámir Ulíbarri, *De mis memorias*, Paris, 1939, II: 16.

A general who was known not to have particularly left-wing sympathies was needed. Later communist sources claim that he was to be a symbol. In Líster's words: 'We needed a general. He was a general ... we all strove to surround him with the prestige which he hardly deserved.'[5]

Another of Caballero's appointments was General Sebastián Pozas as commander of the Central Region, relieving Asensio, who became Under-Secretary for War.[6] As Director-General of the paramilitary *Guardia Civil*, Pozas had rejected Franco's suggestion that he should take over the situation after the contested victory of the Popular Front in the elections of February 1936.[7] During the Giral Government, from 19 July until 4 September, Pozas had been Minister of the Interior (*Gobernación*). The PCE ministers in Caballero's Cabinet approved his appointment as commander in the Central Region because they favoured any measure which would impose the discipline of military hierarchy on anarchist chaos. *Milicia Popular* proclaimed that the Fifth Regiment would put 'all our strength, our enthusiasm, our energy at his service'.

The Basque President, Aguirre, asked repeatedly for Asensio or Pozas to be sent to Bilbao to organise the shaky Basque Staff.[8] In particular he wanted a replacement for General Francisco Llano de la Encomienda, who had been sent to Bilbao on 15 November 1936. Llano de la Encomienda had the confidence of the Republic and had been appointed by the Popular Front Government of February 1936 to command the Barcelona division, even though as a general of brigade he did not have the appropriate rank. However, he had been dispatched hurriedly to the north and the lack of clear orders about his role had created friction with the Basque leader.[9]

Among other appointments made by Caballero, probably on the advice of Asensio, was that of General Carlos Bernal to command the base at Albacete, approximately half-way between Madrid and the Mediterranean coast,[10] and recently organised to administer the several military units which were taking shape in the south-east of the country. Bernal would not take any field commands during the war. Later he was made Director-General of Transport and ended the war in command of the land installations of the Cartagena naval base.[11] Another general

[5] Líster, *Nuestra guerra*, 288.

[6] *Gaceta*, 14 and 23 October 1936.

[7] J. Arrarás, *Francisco Franco*, Valladolid, 1939, 231–3.

[8] José Antonio de Aguirre, *Informe al Gobierno Central*, and telegram to Ministry of War in DR, L54, C4.

[9] DR, L853, C2.

[10] *Gaceta*, 23 October 1936.

[11] *Gaceta*, 14 February 1938 and 21 January 1939.

of brigade, Fernando Martínez Monje, in command of the Valencia division, was appointed to lead the newly created Army of the South (*Ejército del Sur*), in November 1936. He would be dismissed following the loss of Málaga in February 1937, a disaster which would cast him and other Caballero appointees into the wilderness.

The high command and the General Staff

Soon after he became Prime Minister, Caballero reformed the Higher War Council (*Consejo Superior de Guerra*), the senior consultative body created in 1931 to advise the War Minister, at that time Manuel Azaña. Its members were the Chief of Staff and the three inspector-generals, of whom only one, General García Gómez-Caminero, was in late 1936 still in the service of the Republic. The post of Chief of Staff did not regain its pre-war prestige until Vicente Rojo, a mere newly promoted major when the war began in July 1936, occupied the position in May 1937 and was promoted to the rank of general in November 1937. The *Gaceta* announced on 9 November 1936 that the Higher War Council would become a political body, to include the Minister (in this case Caballero himself) and Indalecio Prieto, the socialist Minister for the Air Force and the Navy, Julio Just of Republican Left (*Izquierda Republicana*), Minister of Public Works, Vicente Uribe of the PCE, Minister of Agriculture, Juan García Oliver (FAI), Minister of Justice, and the Minister for Foreign Affairs, Julio Alvarez del Vayo. The reorganisation thus placed the direction of the war ultimately in the hands of the widely based Caballero Government. It was reformed just after the entry of four CNT/FAI leaders into the Government and probably at their suggestion, after the proposal by the CNT plenum of regional organisations that military operations should be directed by a National Council of Defence on which the unions and the political parties should be represented.[12] Nevertheless, the Higher Council does not appear to have had much influence on the organisation of the Republican Army, which during that autumn was being rapidly constructed under the leadership of the newly reformed General Staff.

The General Staff had been reorganised as part of the Azaña reforms in 1931 but retained its traditional basis of a general of division (the highest rank of general after the Azaña reforms) at its head, and with sections denominated: (1) Organisation and Mobilisation; (2) Information; (3) Operations; (4) Services and Supplies; (5) Cartography. In 1936,

[12] See *El Sol*, 18 December 1936.

once the chaos caused by the defeat of the attempted military coup in the capital had died down, the General Staff in the War Ministry, a large building set back in gardens on the corner of the Calle de Alcalá and the Paseo de Recoletos, was taken over by a group of Republican officers who took on the huge task of satisfying the demands of the militias and guiding them and their operations. One of them, Major Segismundo Casado, commander of the Presidential cavalry guard, writes that there were only 25 Staff officers.[13] Overwork and anxiety about their families' and their own safety led to the physical and mental collapse of some. It must have been hard to find officers who were capable and who would agree to take on such demanding tasks as planning operations, organising and supplying the militias and finding officers for them. Those who did so were already known as fervently loyal to the Republic: Juan Hernández Sarabia, Antonio Cordón, Leopoldo Menéndez, Manuel Estrada, Segismundo Casado, José Fontán and Manuel Fe (see Appendix 4).

Staff officers who had thrown in their lot with the rebels and joined them in the various barracks and other centres which had been reduced by loyal forces and the crowds, had left the Staff in chaos. The disorder was magnified by the depredations of militia who had surged through the offices in an apotheosis of triumphant antimilitarism. Many officers who had not joined the insurrection had had to be sent home or had fled either for fear that they were not reliable or for their own protection. Some sort of order had not been restored until September. For a few weeks a shadow Staff, called *Secretariado Técnico*, had been led by Antonio Cordón, later Under-Secretary for Defence, with José Martín Blázquez and José Cerón as secretaries and with embryonic pay and supply sections.[14]

Caballero and General Asensio, his Under-Secretary, worked tirelessly to bring some order to the chaos in the Ministry and the Staff, and managed at last to put a stop to the incessant coming and going of the 'minor and self-important persons who claimed that they were of key importance in resisting the enemy' (*'personajes y personajillos que aseguraban ser piezas claves de la resistencia'*).[15]

On his first day in power, Caballero announced his new General Staff.[16] It was headed by a Staff major, Manuel Estrada, with other

[13] S. Casado, 'The Republican Command in the Spanish Civil War', *National Review* (London), July, 1939.

[14] *El Sol* of 22 August 1936 reported the dismissal of a colonel, 18 lieutenant-colonels and 25 other Staff officers. See Martín Blázquez, *I Helped to Build*, 279, for his account of this period.

[15] Cordón, *Trayectoria*, 258.

[16] DO, No. 176.

majors heading the sections. Few came from the old Staff Corps though many had Staff diplomas. Segismundo Casado, Vicente Rojo and Antonio Cordón were appointed to the Operations Section: José Luis Fuentes was entrusted with the organisation of artillery, an important responsibility later raised to an Inspectorate-General.

A few weeks later, on 20 October 1936, Rojo, whose outstanding capacity had become evident, was appointed deputy Chief of Staff. Other changes included the appearance of civilian advisers to facilitate military organisation. These included the political commissar of the Fifth Regiment, Vittorio Vidali, alias 'Carlos Contreras', the PCE Minister of Agriculture, Vicente Uribe, the CNT/FAI Minister of Justice, Juan García Oliver, and Julio Alvarez del Vayo, socialist Foreign Minister, all members of the Higher Defence Council. For the first time, a non-Spaniard would sit on the Staff. This was 'Emil Kléber', an ex-officer of the Austro-Hungarian Army who had received military training in the USSR. He would command the first of the International Brigades until a dispute with Rojo, Chief of Staff of the defence of Madrid, led to his dismissal. Also on the Staff were Angel Gil Roldán and Miguel González Inestal of the CNT, who would become sub-commissars-general, Daniel Ortega of the PCE and several others, probably in order to reassure the militia that the political and union leaders were happily collaborating with the military in directing the war. This General Staff seems to have turned out to be unworkable, because yet another list appeared on 30 November 1936. Unlike the previous Staff, while the civilian organisations were granted one member in each section, no specific civilian appointees were named, while Estrada was replaced as Chief of Staff by the much more senior General Toribio Martínez Cabrera, who was at the time in command of the Cartagena naval base and had held important Staff posts in the past.

None of these three Staffs lacked ability. Most of their members were Staff Corps officers on the active list or had attended courses and received diplomas in Staff work. The Insurgent General Staff was no more distinguished. In February 1937 the latter consisted of a general, a Staff Corps colonel and six field-grade officers, all on the active list and, and two retired officers and five others with appropriate Staff qualifications. However, the roles of the two Staffs were dissimilar. The Insurgents always had clear directions from their military leadership and were free of any political pressure. All that can be said is that the Republican General Staff was at least potentially as able as the Insurgent one.

The problem of setting up a Staff was linked with the question of authority. From all sides came calls for *Mando Unico* or unity of command, even from autonomous Catalonia, where on 26 September 1936 the parliament or *Generalitat* officially demanded 'Single command, coordination of all forces, obligatory militias and strengthening of discipline' ('*Mando único, coordinación de todas las unidades combatientes, creación de las milicias obligatorias y refuerzo de la disciplina*'), though, interestingly, it used the word '*milicias*' and not '*ejército*', that is, army.

Demands for unity of command had been made early on in the war. Caballero's newspaper *Claridad* had earlier been opposed to militarisation, but came out in favour on 27 August 1936 as did the right-wing socialist Indalecio Prieto on the same day in *El Sol*. Now in power, on 16 September 1936, Caballero insisted that without exception all forces fighting the Insurgents should put themselves under the orders of the Minister of War, that is himself. 'The Staff and the Ministry of War are constructing and perfecting a concrete plan in order to create a Popular Army on a new basis', quoted *El Sol*. Perhaps this was the first time that the words *Ejército Popular* had been used.

Finally, even the anarchist CNT, traditionally so opposed to authority, demanded a single command when Juan Peiró, the anarchist Minister of Industry, spoke in Valencia on 27 November 1936.[17] That anarchists had joined a government was in any case a reversal of their principles.

Unity of command, which was far from the reality of the situation, was officially proclaimed in the *Gaceta* on 16 October 1936, in a decree which announced that the Ministry of War had assumed all command through the General Staff, which would act not as the executive branch of command, but as a consultative and auxiliary body under the supreme commander ('*no como órgano ejecutivo del Mando, sino como cuerpo consultivo y auxiliar de quien lo ejerce, o sea, del jefe superior*').

This peculiar statement seems to have been intended to assure the antimilitarists that the General Staff was not going to direct operations independently of the Government.

The militarisation of the militias

The General Staff and the leading politicians were in agreement: it was vital to militarise the militias completely and to create a properly organised army.

One of the first tasks of the Government was to get better control over the militias. In particular, the large number of men who had appointed themselves to act as vigilantes, breaking into people's dwellings, arresting

[17] Quoted in Peirats, *CNT*, II: 254.

and often murdering them without government authority (this was happening on the other side also, but with government, that is, military authority), was contributing to the breakdown of public order and hindering the war effort. The *Gaceta* decree of 17 September 1936 tackled the problem by setting up an official vigilante body called the *Milicias de Vigilancia de la Retaguardia* or Rearguard Vigilance Militias, and declaring any other similar body illegal. One reason for establishing this body was that many enemies of the Republic had found their way into the now illegal groups. This is not surprising, because many people, aware of the suspicion with which they were regarded for their political opinions, may well have sought refuge or to demonstrate their loyalty by joining what were little better than gangs. However, it seems more likely that it was the free hand given to criminals of all sorts which was leading to the outrages that had appalled the leaders of the Republic and had been widely publicised in the foreign press as the precursors of a complete social revolution. On the Franco side, the strict censorship and the smaller number of foreign consulates, as well as the sympathy that many consuls felt for the Insurgents, seem to have led to far less foreign press publicity for the killings which took place in their part of Spain.

Next, Caballero directed his attention to the principal militia body. It has been claimed that he was opposed to militarisation and that only the Soviet advisers who were now in Spain who convinced him to the contrary.[18] Nevertheless, Caballero appointed Asensio to command the Central Region as soon as he took power, which shows that he wanted to provide the militias with an adequate military structure. Caballero had a long history of combative public activity. To 'convince' him against his will was hardly possible. What probably happened was that what the loyal generals themselves told him agreed with what was obvious, even to the anarchists.

On 30 September 1936, at the end of his first month in office Caballero published two further significant decrees in the *Gaceta*. The preamble to the first recognised that an efficient army was required and that it would be formed out of the existing militias. All officers and NCOs who could be vouched for politically would become part of the Spanish army ('*pasarán a las escalas activas del ejército*'). The General Staff would direct them towards the branches and corps as required. The second decree proclaimed grandly: 'Thus begins the creation of the future army

[18] See Louis Fischer, *Men and Politics*, Cape, 1941, 336. Fischer was a journalist with communist sympathies who was a trusted confidant of the Soviet military advisers. See the collection of Soviet documents in S. Radosh, M. Habeck and G. Sevostianov (eds.), *Spain Betrayed: The Soviet Union in the Spanish Civil War*, New Haven, CT, 2001.

of the People.' ('*Se inicia así la formación del futuro ejército del Pueblo.*') From 10 October in central Spain and 20 October elsewhere, the militia would be brought under the Code of Military Law. Militiamen who were unwilling should send up their names to the *Comandancia de Milicias*, which would erase them from the rolls. Ages for enlistment were 20–35, which was an essential limitation, given that many boys of little more than 16 and many middle-aged men had enrolled in the militia.

With militia units very scattered and the poor level of communications, it was very difficult to impose order. As late as 13 December 1936 an order was circulated that the militia columns should immediately list all their members, in order to achieve 'the real militarisation of the militias, which all of us have been demanding for so long' ('*la verdadera militarización de las milicias, que tantas veces hemos pedido todos*'). Furthermore, as late as January 1937 the *Comandancia* was still having to prohibit militia columns from admitting new recruits directly.[19]

Wearing uniform, saluting militarily and such examples of militarisation had to be justified frequently and in detail. The explanations prefacing each order are highly prolix, as for example a circular letter of December 1936 which requests that, as far as possible, the men should wear dark lumber jackets and trousers because 'uniformity of dress was always the external sign indicating that an army was disciplined' ('*la uniformidad en el vestido fue siempre el signo exterior que marcó el grado de disciplina de un ejército*'). Other items of clothing were 'at odds with the gravity of the moment we are living and the ideal which unites us' ('*reñidas con la seriedad del momento que vivimos y del ideal que nos une a todos*'). The salute was recommended, and the superior in rank should return it, because 'the salute is not humiliating; it strengthens mutual affection and awakens currents of fellow-feeling' ('*el saludo no humilla, sino que estrecha lazos de afecto y despierta corrientes de simpatía*').[20] Such verbosity contrasts with the military terseness of the Insurgent Francoists, whose orders normally began 'Kindly carry out ...' ('*Sírvase cumplir ...*'), without any attempt at explaining the reason for the order. There was no need to remind Falangist or Traditionalist militia that they had to salute. Yet in the documents of the Republican Army there are many examples of extensive preambles to simple orders, such was the deep-rooted dislike of anything which had to do with military tradition, a hatred which the attempted coup had crystallised. So true was this, especially among the anarchist militias, that a CNT activist, who later held a superior position as sub-commissar general, recounted that he had to visit one unit after the next because the supply officers were

[19] DR, L1334, C1 and C16. [20] DR, L1334, C1.

refusing to issue war material and other supplies so long as the militias were not properly militarised. The CNT activist had to go wherever militarisation, that is military procedures, uniforms, rank badges and saluting, was being resisted and sometimes speak as far down as company level. If they wanted weapons, ammunition, medical supplies and so forth, they had to accept militarisation. If they did not, the CNT would not survive. Sometimes he had to convince the men one by one. Generally, he was successful. He encountered the greatest opposition in the anarchist militias which later became the builder Cipriano Mera's IV Army Corps.[21]

As they were formed into the anonymous mixed brigades of the Republican Army, the militias had to abandon the picturesque titles which they had adopted in the heady revolutionary days of the summer. Likewise, units which had nuclei of pre-war regiments were ordered not to use the previous names and numbers. As might have been expected, it took time to eradicate these uses and as late as April 1937 it was felt necessary to circulate an order reminding political commissars and battalions that no document was valid if it referred to names rather than numbers.[22] Yet even the communists, such great opponents of the anarchist revolutionary spirit and enthusiasts for grey disciplined monotony, often referred to units by the names of their leaders.

On 27 December 1936, the *Gaceta* published a prototype for a militia battalion, a model for the new army.[23] It consisted of four rifle companies and one machine-gun company commanded by captains. Each company had three platoons, each platoon two sections and each section three squads. What is striking is the total fidelity to tradition. There is no sign that the authorities understood that the lack of trained officers and NCOs and the huge number of untrained and relatively unbiddable men required a more flexible structure. The weight of traditional bureaucracy in the Ministry of War was evident. The details are minutely described, down to which particular man carried the Verey or flare-signalling pistol and which corporal in the squad should be armed with a revolver. This prototype made it clear that this was not going to be a revolutionary army, and that its organisers were not considering the gross shortage of career leaders. The bureaucratic mind would not be able to adjust to the urgency of the situation.

So far, militarisation had affected the battalions of militia, but it was by now obvious that a more permanent structure was needed. That is to say, it was 'evident' at the time. Nevertheless, the defeat of the

[21] Interview with Miguel González Inestal.

[22] DR, L480, C6. [23] See Appendix 1 for details.

Republican Army led to much writing of the 'why we lost the war' kind. Anarchist opinion tended to protest that the formally structured Republican Army crushed the revolutionary spirit of the early weeks. The Spanish genius, as seen in the Peninsular War, known in Spain as the War of Independence (1808–13), was for irregular, guerrilla war.[24]

Guerrillas

In view of the Spanish guerrilla tradition, as exemplified in the Peninsular and Carlist wars of the nineteenth century, together with the persistence of rural banditry until a comparatively late date and the armed opposition to the Franco regime until the early 1950s, widespread guerrilla activity might have been expected by forces loyal to the Republic against Franco's Nationalist Insurgents.

In the view of Enrique Líster, the communist activist and later corps commander, the excellent possibilities for guerrilla warfare were not taken advantage of by the Government. He claims that Largo Caballero and Prieto, Ministers of War and Defence until early 1938, systematically refused to provide suitable support for guerrillas.[25] Captain Alberto Bayo, who would later advise Fidel Castro in his campaign in Cuba and had led the ill-fated expedition to Majorca to try to take back that island in August 1936, wrote that he was given a force of 500 men to harass the enemy in the mountains of Toledo, but that Generals Pozas and Miaja had found their attempts to help him thwarted by Prieto, who, as Minister of National Defence from May 1937, cancelled the project.[26] It is certainly true that, despite the PCE's advocacy of the formally organised army as opposed to militias, there was communist support for guerrillas. *Milicia Popular* published a trenchant article on their formation and possibilities on 8 October 1936.

Nevertheless, evidence on their activities in 1936 is scarce. There were frequent attacks on the lightly guarded railway between Jaca and Huesca in the Aragonese Pyrenees and in Andalusia.[27] These were probably by unofficial bands of desperate men who had managed to flee from their home areas before what was often a murderous occupation by the Insurgents. In view of the general absence of control by the Republican Government over militia in those areas, attacks on the Insurgents were organised only on a very local basis. This is not to

[24] See in particular Abad de Santillán, *Por qué perdimos*, especially pp. 261ff.
[25] Líster, *Nuestra guerra*, 277.
[26] Bayo, *Mi desembarco*, 214, whose hostility to Prieto, who, as Minister for the Navy had refused to support the Majorca expedition, is patent.
[27] Martínez Bande, *Aragón*, 77, and *Andalucía*, 65.

say that they were not effective. They caused a great deal of trouble. Franco's Chief of Staff in southern Spain remarked that one small group operating behind Nationalist lines on the Granada Front required the attentions of an entire regiment.[28]

The first mention of official guerrilla formation came on 19 December 1936 when Vicente Rojo, Chief of Staff of the defence of Madrid, ordered guerrilla units to be formed within the XII International Brigade and the Fifth Regiment. The use of the particular units suggests some communist pressure. There were to be 2 groups of 50 men each.[29] The Information or Intelligence Section of the General Staff, Major Manuel Estrada Manchón, encouraged the use of guerrillas. Nevertheless, organisation was very slow. There is no evidence of guerrilla activity by a 'Maquis' of people living in the Insurgent zone, although the latter included relatively large populations in poverty-stricken depressed agricultural areas with a guerrilla tradition. The efficiency and ruthlessness of the repression probably discouraged such activity. Nevertheless, plans to launch an attack to the west, with the idea of cutting off Andalusia from the rest of the Insurgent zone, included the use of guerrillas for gathering intelligence and carrying out railway and bridge destructions. Caballero approved a project to formalise guerrilla activity within the Republican Army and to establish special intensive courses. On 17 April 1937 10 groups of 125 men each, composed of volunteers, led mostly by commissars, were formalised to carry out sabotage in areas close to the Insurgent lines in Extremadura, Andalusia, around Madrid and in Aragon. The Russian advisers took some responsibility for the preparation of guerrilla units. Artur Sproguis was an adviser to guerrillas on the Málaga Front. Another was Ilya Starinov.[30] The Spanish commander was Alberto Calderón.[31] The NKVD *rezident*, Orlov, claimed to have, by July 1937, 1,600 guerrillas trained in 6 camps and about 14,000 men trained, supplied and led by Soviet instructors in Nationalist-occupied territory.[32] Insurgent reports on guerrilla activity do not mention Russians although in November 1938 a German listening station in Spain reported a radio message from guerrillas sent in Russian. Most Russians had withdrawn by this date, which might

[28] J. Cuesta Monereo, 'La guerra en los frentes del sur', in *La Guerra de Liberación Nacional*, Zaragoza, 1961, 232.

[29] DR, L968, C21.

[30] See Paulina and Adelina Abramson, *Mosaico Roto*, Madrid, 1994, 228.

[31] See the article by Rodríguez Velasco referenced in note 35, below. Was this Infantry Captain Alberto Calderón Martínez (*Anuario Militar 1936*)?

[32] MS quoted by S. Payne, *The Spanish Revolution*, Weidenfeld and Nicolson, 1970, 345n.

indicate that Soviet advisers had taken an active part in guerrilla warfare earlier in the Spanish Civil War.[33]

In later 1937 activity increased. Prisoners reported to Insurgent interrogators that José Coello de Portugal, a retired officer who reappeared on Staff lists in late 1936, was in charge of 200,000 pesetas per month (£905,000 at the then rate of exchange of the depreciated Republican peseta) to foment activity behind the Insurgent lines.[34]

Most of the surviving records about guerrilla activity come from Insurgent military records and have to be judged accordingly.[35] References in memoir literature are rare and incoherent. For example, Rojo mentions that he planned a coup with 60 guerrillas during the battle of Belchite in August 1937, but General Pozas, in ultimate charge of the operation, decided against using the guerrillas.[36]

Nationalist Intelligence produced a report on the guerrillas of the Republican Army on 23 October 1937.[37] Ten companies of guerrillas had been formed, each composed of three platoons. The companies were of about 75 men only, who were mostly escapees from the Insurgent zone. They operated along weakly held parts of the lines and their activities were causing some concern. Perhaps this Nationalist report was based on activities referred to by 'La Pasionaria' when she boasted of them at the Plenary Session of the Central Committee of the PCE on 13 November 1937. However, she gave few examples of their feats. While referring to December 1936 as the starting date, she gave examples from August 1937 only,[38] none of which seems to have been particularly vital in hampering the enemy war effort: a couple of bridges, the odd supply train and isolated motor-cars. Things, however, would change in late 1937 (see Chapter 11).

[33] CGG, L281, C8. However, the Soviet historian Colonel Rybalkin says nothing about guerrillas, even in his chapter about the lessons drawn from Spain by the Russian military. D. Kowalsky, *La Unión Soviética y la guerra civil española, una revisión crítica*, Barcelona, 2004. Furthermore, the editors of *Spain Betrayed* say little about guerrillas in their respective indexes. Nor do they mention Starinov.

[34] CGG, L281, C7.

[35] Recently Hernán Rodríguez Velasco published an article with the title 'Las guerrillas en el Ejército Popular de la República (1936–1939)', *Cuadernos de Historia Contemporánea*, 33 (2011), 235–54, using documents deposited in Spain by the late Colonel Manuel Estrada Manchón, who was Chief of Staff from 4 September 1936 until 27 November 1936, later head of the Information Section of the General Staff, followed by Staff appointments in different corps before returning to the Information Section of the General Staff.

[36] V. Rojo, *España heroica*, Buenos Aires, 1942, 119.

[37] CGG, L281, C3.

[38] D. Ibárruri, *En la lucha*, Moscow, 1968, 205–6.

The mixed brigades

The mixed brigade was the basic fighting unit into which the militia battalions were organised. 'Mixed' meant that other Arms, which traditionally were attached only to divisions or army corps, such as cavalry, artillery, signals, sappers and other second-echelon troops, were added to the infantry brigade in order to make it into an autonomous unit.

It is unlikely that the mixed brigade was introduced at the behest of the Soviet military advisers who began to arrive in Spain in September 1936.[39] Nor was it a totally unknown military formation in Spain. The term appeared in a *Gaceta* decree of 26 April 1931 reorganising mountain troops into a unit called the *Brigada Mixta*. Even more significantly, the *Revista de Estudios Militares*, a journal devoted to scholarly study of military matters, published a series of articles in October and November 1933, after a report on Swiss manoeuvres in 1933, by Staff officers who in general advocated the mixed brigade.

José Martín Blázquez, one of the few career officers at the heart of organisation in the early days of the war, recalls that mixed brigades had been formed during the Riff war of the 1920s, and that the Russian advisers and the Spanish Staff had advocated them independently as the Republican Army was being created.[40] This was probably so, because the mixed brigade resembled the improvised Spanish columns which had fought in Morocco, while to some extent Russian infantry regiments were already supplied with artillery, engineers and other auxiliaries.[41] Soviet sources on the Spanish Civil War do not claim paternity for the system as introduced in Spain. Koltsov, for example, the *Pravda* correspondent, claims that the prototype, though not the idea of the mixed brigade, was adopted at the insistence of the Fifth Regiment,[42] while the Soviet senior artillery adviser, Voronov, claims that the Spanish General Staff agreed to introduce the mixed brigade because the PCE and 'other democratic organisations' insisted.[43] Finally, Vicente Rojo, Chief of Staff of the Republican Army, writes that the mixed brigade was ideal for the situation.[44] The likelihood is that the Soviet advisers

[39] The *locus classicus* for this view is Casado, *Last Days of Madrid*, 59, who refers to the mixed brigade as 'exotic', although the sub-commissar-general who worked with Casado on the rapid organisation of brigades in Albacete could not recall any criticism on his part at the time (interview with Serafín González Inestal, October 1971).

[40] Martín Blázquez, *I Helped to Build*, 293–4.

[41] M. Garder, *History of the Soviet Army*, Pall Mall Press, 1966, 74.

[42] Koltsov, *Diario*, 291.

[43] R. Malinovski *et al.*, *Bajo la bandera de la España republicana* (hereafter *BLB*), Moscow, n.d. [1968?], 73–4.

[44] Rojo, *Madrid*, 137.

and the PCE, in the wings or in the Higher War Council, encouraged the Army Staff, who were already interested, to adopt the mixed brigade as the basic independent fighting unit in which to incorporate the militia battalions.

The structure of the mixed brigade is variously described, because the model changed as the war continued.[45] While it was probably the best way to incorporate the militia battalions, a cursory study of the mixed brigade shows its limitations. Four infantry battalions, even if they were up to strength, would be insufficient to justify the support of so many second-echelon troops. There would also be a tendency towards imbalance between combat troops and service units. Yet, in reality, the brigades often lacked some of their accompanying artillery and much of their services, thus becoming not particularly useful columns and little different from militia.[46]

The first order to create a mixed brigade came on 18 October 1936. Six brigades were to be formed, based for training at Alcalá de Henares, Ciudad Real, Albacete, Alcoy, Murcia and Villena, towns in the Republican rearguard in New Castile and the Levante.[47] It proved a very difficult task to complete the brigades according to the establishment laid down. As an example of the sort of improvisation that was required, a later brigade was created by ordering a *Guardia Civil* officer to go to Málaga, take two battalions of the regiment normally stationed there, add a group of recently recruited *Carabineros* battalions and, on the way, pick up whatever weapons he could from Almería, a port 126 miles along the coast. All this would have to be done without the aid of experienced NCOs and overcoming the resistance of local committees which were unwilling to surrender men or weapons.

Barely two weeks later, an urgent teletype summoned these untrained brigades to Madrid, which was under threat of occupation by Franco's African Expeditionary Force. Indeed General Martínez Monje protested from Albacete that the troops were not ready. He proposed sending two battalions from each brigade and leaving the other two as a reserve and base depot, a system used in other armies, and one which would have helped in training subsequent recruits.[48]

[45] See Appendix 1 for models of the mixed brigade.

[46] Captain Basil Liddell Hart, the British military expert, concluded that an independent brigade required five infantry battalions. Moreover, he probably had in mind the British battalion, with its minimum of 800 infantry, rather than the considerably smaller Spanish equivalent. See his *Defence of the West*, New York, 1950, 252.

[47] DR, L1334, C10. Letter from the Organisation Section of the General Staff to the Inspector-General of Militia.

[48] DR, L482, C1.

The commanders of the first six mixed brigades were:

1st Enrique Líster, transferred from command of the Fifth Regiment;
2nd Jesús Martínez de Aragón, a lawyer;[49]
3rd José María Galán, captain of *Carabineros* and brother of Fermín, shot for his part in the Republican insurrection at Jaca in December 1930, and of Francisco (see Appendix 4);
4th Arturo (another source gives Eutiquio) Arellano, a retired officer;
5th Fernando Sabio, a retired officer;[50]
6th Miguel Gallo, infantry captain on Staff of the President of the Republic.

Líster, Galán and Gallo were members of the PCE. They and Jesús Martínez de Aragón had played an important part in the communist-inspired Fifth Regiment.

All had fought with the earliest militias, but the Staff sought career officers whose political record was unimpeachable and to whom the important task of creating militarised militia could be confided. Their appointments, while approved by the increasingly important PCE, were not due to communist pressure, but correct in the particular circumstances.

The pace quickened as more and more militia battalions, four at a time, were formed into numbered mixed brigades. In central Spain, by spring 1937, mixed brigades 1–50 had been formed. Numbers 51–82 were being organised in the Levante and that part of Andalusia controlled by the Republic, from reservists called to the colours. By May 1937 there were 153 mixed brigades in the central, south and Aragon regions. Numbering of mixed brigades in the north (Basque Country, Santander and Asturias) continued until number 189 was reached.

Given the circumstances, the shortages of kit and the lack of trained NCOs and career officers, these brigades were by no means ready for combat, and were superior to the enemy only in volume. The Republican Army lacked professional and trained troops, unlike Franco's Moroccan *Regulares* and *Legionarios*. To take one example, Juan Modesto's 4th Division, part of the defence of Madrid, had three brigades, Nos 36, 41 and one as yet unnumbered because it was

[49] The history of this brigade is in Appendix 2.
[50] Retired officers were not necessarily of pensionable age. In most cases they had left the service following the April 1931 Azaña decree granting retirement on full pay.

unarmed. Of the eight battalions of the two numbered brigades, two had no arms.[51]

The picturesquely named 'Red Lions' (*Leones Rojos*), 'Steel' (*Acero*), 'Spartacus' (*Espártaco*) and others on the lists of the *Comandancia de Milicias* now disappeared into the anonymity of the mixed brigades of the Republican Army. The remains of the pre-war regiments were distributed among the brigades, together with those officers who were available and approved. With bureaucratic nicety, the daily gazette of the Ministry of War required the flags of the old, pre-war regiments to be sent to the Army Museum.[52]

Many pathetic letters from militiamen's wives and parents are preserved in the documents, usually enquiring where they are. Sometimes it took a long time to locate them, since militia battalions had often been distributed among several brigades. Political and trade-union bodies also tried to trace their members through the militias in which they had combatted the insurrection, but the inevitable reply from the Ministry of War was that the militia could no longer be identified and certainly could not be described in political terms.

Further organisation: an army takes shape

It is not possible to know for certain if the creators of the mixed brigades intended them to be used as independent units which could be brought together as needed for specific actions, or as the first phase in building an army according to the traditional model, with brigades, divisions and army corps. If the former was the case, the latter soon became the reality, because in November 1936 the authorities decided to create divisions on the traditional basis of three brigades per division.

The first three divisions were numbered on 27 November 1936, composed of brigades encamped to the north and west of Madrid. As commanding officers, the Ministry of War appointed Lieutenant-Colonel Domingo Moriones, of the railway regiment, Major Enrique Fernández Herrera, an artillery officer, and a retired officer, Infantry Captain Adolfo Prada. These appointments exemplify the problem of command in the Republican Army. One had retired, while the other two came from technical branches of the service and were inexperienced in leading large bodies of infantry, yet both Moriones and Prada would be in command of entire armies before the war ended.

[51] DR, L971, C4 of 22 January 1937.
[52] *DO*, 30 July 1937.

A further five divisions were formed on the Madrid Front before the end of 1936, all under career officers save the fourth, commanded by Juan Modesto, who was by now well advanced in his meteoric military career. These divisions were heterogeneous in numbers, organisation and armament. The 6th Division is a good example.[53] Its commander, Colonel Mena, was a retired officer of left-wing views. His three brigade commanders, Lieutenant-Colonel Romero, *Carabineros* Major Rovira and Lieutenant-Colonel Arce, had taken decisive roles in the defence of Madrid in November after Franco's forces had reached its western suburbs.[54] The headquarters of the brigades and divisions were in various places within the city. The brigades were composed of eight, six and six battalions. While two of them were at strength or close, at just over 4,000 men, the third had only 3,025. Even by incorporating 20 militia battalions into the division it had not been possible to make up the 12 regulation infantry battalions. A report dated 19 January 1937 noted that each brigade was equipped with rifles of five or six different calibres.[55] This was a persistent problem even in small units of the Republican Army and indicates the administrative chaos it suffered. There was certainly a shortage of rifles, mainly because of the large numbers in the hands of men in the rearguard but also because so many had been abandoned in the catastrophic retreats of the militia when faced with the Moorish *Regulares* and the *Legión*; yet better organisation ought to have been able to ensure that at least at battalion level all infantrymen were armed with the same calibre rifle, thus easing the supply of cartridges.[56]

Surviving documents indicate that these first divisions were no more than agglomerations of battalions. In no way, whether number of men, level of armament or structure, did they have the power of a division in the usual sense of the term. Yet very soon, divisions were formed into army corps, beginning with the Madrid Corps (*Cuerpo de Ejército de Madrid*) on 31 December 1936. This became I Corps, with Lieutenant-Colonel Moriones in command, and was composed of the 1st, 2nd and 3rd Divisions. Remaining divisions formed the II Corps.[57]

More units were rapidly established. In June 1937, a month before the first great trial of the new army at Brunete, there were 72 divisions in the Republican Army, articulated in 17 army corps.

[53] DR, L971, C22. [54] DR, L953, C9. [55] DR, L971, C22.

[56] The point was made in DR, L968, C10, minutes of the *Junta Delegada de Madrid*, where General Miaja complains that brigades were arriving from the Levante without arms.

[57] DR, L955, C4.

As for larger masses of men, some documents dating from the end of 1936 refer to the 'First' and 'Second' Armies on the Madrid Front,[58] but no more was heard of the term until later. However, the beginnings of a form of army-level organisation can be seen in the orders of the War Ministry issued on the night of 6–7 November 1936. The Government was evacuated to Valencia because it was feared that Franco's forces were about to invade Madrid. General Miaja was ordered to defend the city, with complete authority as head of the Delegated Junta, but the other forces on the Central Front were entrusted to General Pozas.[59] These would be the nucleus of the Army of the Centre (*Ejército del Centro*).

On 15 December 1936 the development of brigades and divisions in the Government-controlled parts of Córdoba and Granada provinces was such that General Martínez Monje, who had been in charge of forming brigades in Albacete, was able to take command of the newly formed Army of the South (*Ejército del Sur*). Later in 1937, three further armies would be created, of the East, of Extremadura and of the Levante; the Army of the South would be renamed Army of Andalusia and a new Army of Operations (*Ejército de Maniobras*) would come into being. For the battle of the River Ebro, which began on 25 July 1938, the Republican General Staff would assemble three corps into the Army of the Ebro. Lastly, after the territory of the Republic had been split in two when Franco's forces reached the sea at Vinaroz on the Mediterranean coast, in April 1938, there would be two army groups, of the Centre and of the East.

L'Exèrcit de Catalunya

The military model adopted for the rest of Republican Spain was resisted in the autonomous region of Catalonia, where the *Conselleria de Defensa*, the unconstitutional equivalent of the Ministry of War, published, on 24 October 1936, a decree militarising the militias, dissolving the Antifascist Militias Committee (*Comité de Milicies Antifeixistes*) and calling up men between the ages of 20 and 30. Colonel Vicente Guarner had been the 'technical adviser', as anarchist ideology insisted on calling him, of the militias. He was now given the post of Chief of Staff. That is to say he had the same role as previously but with more

[58] DR, L482, C1.

[59] The text of the order, signed by Largo Caballero, can be found in the memoirs of Miaja's military secretary Antonio López Fernández, *General Miaja, defensor de Madrid*, Madrid, 1975, 58–9.

authority, at least in theory. On 6 December 1936, along the Aragon Front, from Huesca to Teruel, all the militias were renamed *L'Exèrcit de Catalunya* or Army of Catalonia.[60] The army had three divisions, with headquarters in Barcelona, Tarragona and Gerona, headed by career officers: Colonel Guillermo de la Peña, who had been in command of a recruiting depot and had been a judge in the court martial which had sentenced the rebel generals Goded and Fernández Burriel to death and was thus irrevocably committed to the anti-Insurgent cause; Colonel Villalba, who was already at the head of a militia column; and the retired Major Eduardo Medrano. The Catalan government considered that these three divisions, together with a fourth which would be formed in January 1937, should be under its control and not under that of the General Staff of the Republic, a view counter to the Constitution and the Statute of Autonomy itself, which reserved matters of defence to the Government of the Republic. Thus the Catalan divisions were not numbered but conserved the names of the columns which had formed them: *Ascaso*, *Carlos Marx* and *Durruti*. Nor did the Catalan Staff accept the brigade system until this was imposed after the central government recovered its authority in Barcelona in May 1937. The short-lived Army of Catalonia was abolished and the *Conselleria de Defensa* replaced by General Pozas as commander of the Army of the East, whilst internal security services were taken over by officers sent from other parts of Republican Spain.[61] The Catalan divisions were then numbered from 26th (ex-Durruti) to 30th ((ex Macia-Companys). The great illusion of a free Catalonia defending itself had faded.

Militarisation in the north: *Eusko Gudarostea*

Militarisation in the northern Republican zone was carried out swiftly, though not exactly as prescribed. The Basque militias, which had been controlled by various political bodies, were militarised on 26 October 1936. Difficulties arose, however, when General Francisco Llano de la Encomienda, sent by the Government, ordered the battalions to adopt numbers and to be formed into brigades. None of this was done until April 1937 in the midst of the Insurgent campaign against Bilbao. The Basques tried to form an army, called *Eusko Gudarostea* in the Basque language, which was as unconstitutional as the Catalan attempt to do likewise.[62] The Basque units, unlike the Republican Army in general,

[60] *Diari Oficial de la Generalitat* (quoted in Martínez Bande, *Aragón*, 197).
[61] *Gaceta*, 4 May 1937.
[62] For a description of the Basque military effort see Martínez Bande, *Norte, passim*.

did not have political commissars. As a senior officer commented in his report dated 21 November 1937 on the collapse of the Front in the north, there was no political friction and mutual tolerance was the rule, but the lack of commissars led to distrust of the officers.[63] The Basque President, Aguirre, brought war industries under military control, and created a General Staff which he headed. The call-up of reservists had created abundant forces. On 26 November there were 25,000 men under arms, with an artillery regiment and supply, medical and other services. All this was an admirable achievement considering the relative scarcity of military personnel in the region.[64]

As the Insurgents advanced towards Bilbao, Aguirre grew more desperate. In April 1937 he cabled the Republican Government in Valencia, asking for General José Asensio to be sent to Bilbao, even though he was in disgrace, blamed for ultimate responsibility for the loss of Málaga. At the end of the month Aguirre asked for Pozas, complaining that Llano de la Encomienda was incapable of leading the 60,000 men which the Basque forces now totalled. His petition was not attended to until 27 May, and only partially, when Llano de la Encomienda was replaced by General Mariano Gámir Ulíbarri, who had been without a role since the beginning of the conflict. Aguirre expressed himself satisfied with Gámir, who stayed in the northern zone until almost the end of the campaign and the Insurgent victory, managing to get out and returning to Republican Spain through France (given that the Spanish Civil War was not an international conflict, international neutrality law did not apply, and Spanish military personnel finding themselves in neutral territory, such as France or Gibraltar, were returned to Spain).

Aguirre's report to the Government about the way the war had been waged in the north contains lengthy complaints about interferences in the Basque armed forces. He speaks of attempts to enforce the system of political commissars, for which he blames communists. He accuses the military advisers of General Llano de la Encomienda of plotting to undermine the Basque Staff.[65] The Government, however, had before it another report from a senior officer, Lieutenant-Colonel Francisco Buzón Llanes, dated 21 November 1937. This officer had served on

[63] Quoted *ibid.*, document 5.

[64] For a description of the Basque military effort, and personal characterisations of the few officers available, see the essential work of George Steer, *The Tree of Gernika*, Hodder and Stoughton, 1938. As a journalist in Bilbao, Steer's classic article on the destruction of Guernica by German aircraft in Franco's service appeared in *The Times* on 28 April 1937 with immense public impact. Steer died accidentally in Burma in the Second World War.

[65] Aguirre, *Informe al Gobierno Central*, quoted *passim* in Martínez Bande, *Norte*.

the Staff of the Army of the North.[66] While Buzón praised the Basque authorities' control of public order, he criticised the Basque military for not consenting to political commissars and the consequent lack of trust between officers and men. He also underlined negatively Aguirre's refusal to introduce the brigade and division structure, and a strange dual command system by operational and supply officers. He was also critical about the Basque senior officers' capacities.

Santander and Asturias, the other two northern areas loyal to the Republic, suffered difficulties also. The commanding officer in Santander was José García Vayas, who had led the infantry battalion stationed in the port of Santoña. In Asturias, the garrison had rebelled in its entirety. In both areas the militias had accepted militarisation, numbered their battalions and had introduced brigades and divisions. (These were numbers 52–63. When the Basque units fighting in Santander and Asturias finally adopted the divisional system, they were numbered 48–51.) The divisions were grouped in Army Corps XIV, XV and XVI.

Militarisation and bringing these forces into the Republican Army did not, however, solve some insuperable difficulties. Few career officers were available to lead 16 divisions of troops. Parochialism, or 'cantonalism' as it is known in Spanish history, the fissiparous and centrifugal tendency at times of crisis, appeared at once. From the beginning of the war Asturias, a mining area of strong revolutionary character, where troops had been required to put down an uprising as recently as October 1934, a repression directed from Madrid by Franco, had been governed by a Popular Front committee headed by Belarmino Tomás, who took charge of military matters. The Chief of Operations was Ramón González Peña, one of the leaders of the miners' uprising of October 1934.

Santander kept itself separate from the rest of the northern zone to the extent that General Llano de la Encomienda, commander at the time of the Army of the North, had to submit to a customs inspection on crossing the 'frontier'.[67] Colonel Buzón's report condemned the time and effort spent on petty bureaucracy, as well as the frivolity of officers' behaviour in Santander. They spent their time in cafés or the elegant beach facilities of this resort instead of using the opportunity to train men.

At the end of 1936 and in early 1937 Republican forces in the north were numerically superior to those of the Insurgents. The figures

[66] The Buzón Llanes report is in DR, L853, C8.
[67] *Ibid.*

quoted by Martínez Bande indicate that they did not lack arms.[68] This is confirmed by the Chief of Staff of the Republican Army of the North, Francisco Ciutat, who blames the failure to resist on the lack of a concerted effort, 'which explains why the Army could not profit from its material and numerical advantage during the winter of 1936'.[69]

Ciutat was, however, a communist who would be inclined to blame the defeat principally on the lack of military unity so strongly demanded by the PCE. However, there may well have been other reasons, among them the overwhelming Insurgent superiority in aircraft and in the technique of close air–ground support which had been introduced by the German Condor Legion, a force of about a hundred aircraft, ever more modern as the war progressed, sent to aid Franco but also to train German flyers in new ways of war. Furthermore, the Republican Navy, despite its numerical superiority, had failed to contest the Insurgent blockade of the Cantabrian coast.[70]

Conclusions

By June 1937 the militarisation of the new Republican Army had been largely completed. Those remaining vestiges of the militias in Aragon were being extirpated. The forces in the north had broadly the same organisation as the rest of the army. Big strides had been made in creating a new officer corps; military training was progressing; large quantities of war material had arrived. The Republican Army was about to embark on its first great test: the battle of Brunete.

It was a large army with over half a million men, possibly more than the enemy had at that time. Nevertheless, any return of the men actually present in any Republican mixed brigade shows that the model, as laid down in the *Gaceta*, was largely illusory.

Prime Minister and War Minister Francisco Largo Caballero, together with the General Staff, had built what was probably the largest army in the history of Spain, with a classic structure. Yet very few men in the Republican Army had experience of such a structure in the battlefield. On the other side, the Insurgents did not use the brigade as a permanent unit, but merely created brigades where necessary and then dissolved them. They did not establish permanent army divisions until their battalions were ready, with sufficient officers and

[68] Martínez Bande, *Norte*, *passim*.

[69] DR, L853, C18.

[70] For a detailed study of the war at sea, see Michael Alpert, *La guerra civil española en el mar*, Barcelona, 2008.

war material. Army corps were created whenever it was decided to accumulate several divisions for an offensive. In the Republican Army, the General Staff imposed the formal hierarchy of divisions, corps and armies on the basis of the mixed brigades, but these had not been properly put together, were ramshackle and insufficiently armed as well as poorly led.

Despite these faults, to the Staff's credit must be placed the tremendous energy it invested in constructing this army; the number of officers hospitalised with cardiac and gastric illnesses is not surprising, given the overwork and the strain they suffered.[71] Consequently, the achievements of the Organisation Section of the General Staff must be compared not only with their enemy but also in the context of the ferocious opposition to formal militarisation from most of the parties of the Popular Front from the beginning of the war as well as from the mighty CNT during many months, and indeed from very many of the conscripts called to the colours throughout the conflict.

It is easy to criticise the errors of the Republican military leaders, but their training and their difficult personal positions as career officers meant that it was hard and sometimes dangerous for them to point out the mistakes in the political decisions which were being made by powerful political forces which no officer could defy.

The military situation in July 1937

In the months while the Republican Army was taking shape, the Insurgents had broken through the defences of Bilbao, on the northern coast, which fell to Franco on 19 June 1937. In central Spain, Madrid had been successfully defended in November and December 1936, and the attempts of the Insurgents to besiege and isolate it from its rearguard and source of reinforcements in the Levante had failed, though the Republic had lost territory.

The International Brigades (see below) had arrived and taken part in the battles around Madrid, and the Italian forces (the *Corpo di Truppe Volontarie* or *CTV*) sent to participate on Franco's side had taken Málaga in early 1937, but had suffered a severe defeat at Guadalajara in March 1937. This last battle had been used as propaganda to suggest that Fascism was not invincible, nor was mechanisation a military panacea. Though these affirmations were correct, Guadalajara was not a good example to prove it. Republican optimism was unfounded, because the Italians had advanced much further than they had been obliged to

[71] DR, L954, C2, patients admitted to the Carabanchel (Madrid) military hospital.

retreat, while the weather and logistics had given the Republicans considerable advantages. The Republican Army's attempts to take the initiative had been unsuccessful. To the east, the city of Teruel, an Insurgent salient, was still unconquered and there was no significant military activity along the Huesca–Zaragoza line in Aragon. The Republican brigades along the lines in Extremadura and Andalusia were having no impact on the scattered Insurgent units formed mostly of new recruits, *Falange* militia and *Guardia Civil* which made up the Insurgent forces. The loss of Málaga was a catastrophe which led to an investigation into the role played by Generals Asensio Torrado, the Under-Secretary for War, Martínez Monje, commander of the Army of the South, and Martínez Cabrera, Chief of Staff. Although the case against them was dropped, those generals would never occupy significant posts again. Indirectly, the loss of Málaga would lead, three months later, to the fall of Caballero, the crushing of the POUM and the CNT in Barcelona, and the establishment of the Government of Dr Juan Negrín.

5 Professional officers in the Republican Army

Left-wing writers underline how few professional military men served the Republic. They claim that few of those who did so were convinced of the justice of the Republican cause and that most of them found themselves accidentally in those parts of Spain where the military uprising failed, such as Madrid, Barcelona and Valencia. For these authors, the small number, lack of enthusiasm and even the treason of the professionals contributed to the defeat of the Republic. One typical comment, from Julio Alvarez del Vayo, the Republic's Foreign Minister, made in exile immediately after the war, was:

> The majority of officers had made common cause with the rebels. Of 15,000 officers, barely 500 remained in the service of the Republic. Many of these 500 were Republicans by conviction; the rest stayed with the Government out of fear or in order to perpetuate acts of sabotage within the army ranks.[1]

Francoist historians did not want to draw readers' attention to the number of conservative and Catholic officers, such as Vicente Rojo, Chief of Staff of the Republican Army, and Antonio Escobar, *Guardia Civil* commander in Barcelona, who refused to join the insurrection of 18 July 1936 and who served the Republic, but could hardly be described as communists or 'sold to the Popular Front'.[2] It was not until towards the end of the Franco regime that the figure of only 500 loyal officers was questioned by revisionist historians who had access to military sources. Five thousand was one figure quoted, though this included 1,500 who came out of retirement.[3] Until recently, it was not possible to have access to the military justice records which recorded the courts martial of officers in the Republican Army who remained in

[1] J. Alvarez del Vayo, *Freedom's Battle*, Heinemann, 1940, 120.

[2] J. Arrarás, in the multi-volume *Historia de la Cruzada española*, refers in such terms to loyal officers, that is, when he does not use the all-embracing pejorative description of them as Freemasons (Freemasonry, Communism and Judaism were the habitual *bêtes noires* of the Spanish traditional right wing).

[3] Colonel R. Salas Larrazábal, 'The Role and Growth of the Republican Popular Army', in Raymond Carr (ed.), *The Republic and the Civil War in Spain*, Macmillan, 1971.

Spain after its defeat. A lengthy process of reading each one, in order to separate career officers from promoted private soldiers and NCOs, and also from many who simply hid, together with those who escaped from Spain, would, if the records were complete, allow a calculation to be made.[4]

The generals

In 1936 there were three lieutenant-generals, the highest Spanish Army rank.[5] No promotions to that rank had been made since 1931. All three, López Pozas, Castro Girona and Rodríguez Casademunt, were investigated and expelled from the Army after the failure of the July 1936 coup. The first was imprisoned and murdered in the notorious killings at Paracuellos del Jarama, where prisoners were evacuated from Madrid in the face of the imminent Insurgent occupation of the city.

Of the 24 generals of division, most of the 8 commanders of the military regions refused to rebel. Some, including Salcedo in La Coruña, Batet in Burgos, Villa-Abrille in Seville, Molero in Valladolid and Gómez Morato, High Commissioner in Spanish Morocco, were arrested by the Insurgents. In Zaragoza, Miguel Cabanellas joined the insurrection, as did Goded in the Balearics and Franco in the Canaries. López Ochoa, considered responsible for the atrocities committed during the suppression of the Asturias mini-revolution of October 1934, was murdered by a mob in the military hospital in Madrid.[6] Of other generals of division, Losada, Villegas, Gonzalez Carrasco, Virgilio Cabanellas and Sánchez Ocaña were dismissed by the Republican authorities. Rodríguez del Barrio died just before the uprising. Núñez del Prado, Director-General of the Air Force, was shot by the rebels. In all, only

[4] Among recent discussions of Republican officers are: C. Zaragoza, *Ejército Popular y militares de la República*, Barcelona, 1983; M. T. Suero Roca, *Militares republicanos de la guerra de España*, Barcelona, 1981. C. Navajas Zubeldía, *Leales y rebeldes: la tragedia de los militares republicanos*, Madrid, 2011, usefully summarises recent studies. Julius Ruiz, *Franco's Justice. Repression in Madrid after the Spanish Civil War*, Clarendon Press, 2005, offers some useful data as does P. M. Egea Bruno, 'La represión franquista en Cartagena (1939–1945)', unpublished manuscript, Murcia, 1987, though this is mainly about the Navy and Marines (my thanks to the author for sending me this unpublished research). The most recent study is J. García Fernández (ed.), *25 militares de la República*, published by the Ministry of Defence, Madrid, 2011.

[5] Ranks and locations of officers in 1936 are taken from the *Anuario Militar de España* and are valid for 30 April of that year, though a few important subsequent changes are indicated in an insert.

[6] See Purificación Celeiro and Libertad López Ochoa, *Memoria familiar. Memorias de un soldado*, with introduction and notes by Michael Alpert, Barcelona, 2007, 30–3 and 335.

a minority of the generals of division took part in the uprising. This is not surprising, given that promotion to this highest rank in the Army was largely determined by political considerations and that the Popular Front Government of February 1936 had appointed many generals to posts precisely because they were thought to be trustworthy. Although the Government distrusted Franco, posting him to the Canaries, as far away as possible (so they thought) from the Peninsula, the rebellions of Queipo de Llano, Inspector-General of *Carabineros*, and of Miguel Cabanellas were unexpected, since both were Freemasons and had Republican antecedents. Queipo in particular had been a conspirator against the dictatorship of Primo de Rivera.

Among the divisional generals who remained loyal to the regime were Pedro La Cerda, José Riquelme, Cristóbal Peña Abuín, Juan García Gómez-Caminero and Carlos Masquelet. All were close on 65 years of age, save Riquelme, and all had more or less honorific posts. None took any active part in the war after the first few weeks.

The situation was little different in the Insurgent army because only Franco and Queipo, of the divisional generals, took an active part in operations. Franco, at 44, was exceptionally young for his rank. Two other younger divisional generals, Fanjul and Goded, were executed when their attempts to rebel in Madrid and Barcelona were thwarted. Gil Yuste, Ponte, Orgaz and Dávila, divisional generals who served under Franco, came from the Reserve.

As for the 57 brigadier-generals, the following remained loyal and served in the Republican Army: Pozas, Director-General of the *Guardia Civil*, Aranguren, commander of the *Guardia Civil* in Catalonia, Llano de la Encomienda, commander of the Barcelona division, Martínez Monje, commander of the Valencia division, Castelló, commander of the 2nd Infantry Brigade (Badajoz), Miaja of the 1st Infantry Brigade (Madrid), Martínez Cabrera, of the Cartagena naval base, Gámir Ulíbarri and San Pedro Aymat, commanders of infantry brigades in Valencia, Cavanna del Val and Cardenal, commanders of artillery brigades, Cruz Boullosa, Under-Secretary for War, and Bernal, temporarily without post. Only Gámir, Miaja, Martínez Cabrera, Pozas, Bernal, Llano de la Encomienda and Martínez Monje were employed actively in the Republican Army. The average age of these generals was, however, over 60. A certain number of brigadier-generals were arrested by the Insurgents. Of these, Caridad Pita in La Coruña, Romerales in Morocco and Campins in Granada were court-martialled and shot. Of the others, most were dismissed without pension by the Republic, either because they were known to have thrown in their lot with the Insurgents or because an examination of their political record concluded that they were not sufficiently reliable to be employed. Some were shot for active participation in the uprising, including Fernández Burriel in Barcelona and García La Herrán in Madrid. Some few were retired.

Thus, of the just over 80 divisional and brigadier-generals on the active list in the Spanish Army of 1936, few played an active role during the war. Few of these were loyal to the Republic, or rather to the Popular Front Government of 1936. A number, however, were distrusted by the Insurgents, arrested and sometimes shot. Many were just too old to take active commands in war. Though most of the brigadier-generals in what would become the Republican zone did not take part in the uprising, they were distrusted and dismissed, while others remained unposted, or given only rearguard responsibilities.

Of the few who served in the Republican Army, Castelló suffered a nervous breakdown and went to France, while at the end Miaja rebelled against the Negrín Government. Martínez Monje and Martínez Cabrera, respectively commander of the Army of the South and Chief of Staff, were subjected to investigation after the loss of Málaga in January 1937, until their release, after which they were put under the direct orders of the Minister of National Defence.[7] After the loss of Bilbao in June 1937 Llano de la Encomienda and Gámir do not appear until much later, as Inspector-General of Infantry and in charge of training respectively.[8] The collapse of the Aragon Front in April 1938 saw Pozas disappear until close to the end of the war when he was appointed military governor of the frontier town of Figueras.[9]

Thus, with the exception of Miaja, no pre-war general played a significant part in command of fighting troops in the Republican Army for any length of time. And, although few pre-war generals, except for Mola, Varela, Saliquet, Queipo de Llano and Franco, had significant responsibilities in the Insurgent army either, Mola at 49 and Varela at 45 were two of the youngest generals of brigade and consequently took field command. Franco's corps commanders would be the younger *africanista* lieutenant-colonels and colonels, but the Republican Army would be led by men of often junior rank and, as will be seen, often by militia officers.

Officers

The establishment or *plantilla* of officers, that is those who had posts rather than the larger number (15,401) on the active list, was 8,851

[7] *DO*, 18 May 1938. [8] *DO*, 15 October 1938.
[9] *DO*, 24 January 1939.

in the Peninsula, Canaries and Balearics, plus 1,683 in the Spanish zone of the Moroccan Protectorate. To these must be added *Guardia Civil* and *Carabinero* officers. A number in Morocco were almost immediately arrested and some shot for opposing the uprising. These included some senior officers of the Legion and Moroccan *Regulares*, a number of Staff officers and Franco's cousin, who was Head of the Air Force in the Spanish zone of the Protectorate. General Gómez Morato, Commander-in-Chief of the armed forces in Morocco, was arrested and General Romerales, High Commissioner of the zone, was court-martialled and executed.[10] Altogether, there may have been several hundred arrests in the areas of Morocco and the Peninsula where the uprising was successful. Some officers may have been released and served in the Insurgent forces.

According to the returns of regiments on 1 July 1936, there were 2,271 officers occupying posts of command in the main branches of the service (infantry, cavalry, artillery and engineers) in what became the Government zone, and 2,655 in the Insurgent area.[11] The latter figure is the greater because it corresponds to the larger number of units in the five (out of eight) administrative military divisions where the insurrection was successful (Seville, Zaragoza, Valladolid, Burgos and La Coruña). As for the paramilitary forces, their officers seem to have been equally divided though, as has been seen, in most places, save Madrid and Barcelona, *Guardia Civil* rebelled, while *Guardia de Asalto* officers tended to support whichever side had been victorious.

The Army Yearbook (*Anuario Militar*) shows that 423 officers were in service with the Air Force, approximately equally divided between the two zones. There were also a considerable number of officers without posts (*disponibles*) or seconded to posts in the civil administration.

Thus it would be reasonable to suppose that the number of military officers on the active list was approximately equivalent on each side once the two zones were more clearly delineated, for, although Madrid was held by the Republican Government, the majority of the other divisions were held by the Insurgents.

Furthermore, a large number of the over 8,000 officers who had accepted the favourable terms for early retirement granted by the Azaña law of 25 April 1931 were still of military age. Thus, broadly speaking, there were perhaps as many as 10,000 career officers living in what

[10] See Navajas Zubeldia, *Leales y rebeldes*, 164–7. As yet, more detailed studies have not emerged, but my earlier calculation of 150–300 officers arrested by the Insurgents was probably under-estimated.

[11] DN, L1, C3.

became the Government zone. These men would be available for service in an international war. This conflict was, however, a civil war and the question of who was loyal and even suitable for the particular circumstances became important.

Given that the war had been provoked by a military insurrection, all officers resident or stationed in the Republican zone, save those whose political views were clearly loyal to the Republic, were suspected of at least potential disloyalty. A large number were arrested or went into hiding. At least 250 officers were killed or arrested in the suppression of the insurrection in Madrid alone, while figures for other towns and cities suggest that 1,200 at least were known to be disloyal from the outset. During the war, there would be a special body (see below) set up to investigate the background and conduct of each career officer in the Republican zone, while the daily bulletin or *Diario Oficial* of the Ministry of War periodically published long lists of dismissals. Sometimes a name was listed with the explanation that the officer concerned was in the service of the Insurgents (‘*por encontrarse prestando servicio en terreno faccioso*’), at other times that his whereabouts was unknown (‘*por encontrarse en ignorado paradero*’), but there were also long lists of officers living in the Republican zone but who were judged not to be trustworthy enough to have commands in the Republican Army and were thus dismissed the service. The *Diario* of 27 and 31 January, 2, 3, 9 and 24 February and 3, 22 and 30 March 1938 listed 3,668 names of officers, and 129 on 17 and 19 May of the same year. Earlier, on 23 August 1936, *El Sol* announced the dismissal of 23 colonels and another 50 officers. Such news appeared regularly. On 27 August 1936 the *Gaceta* announced the dismissal of 700 *Guardia Civil* officers. A striking statistic of younger officers is that of the 700 officers who had graduated from the General Military Academy while under Franco’s command between 1927 and 1931, only 37 were dismissed after the Civil War, presumably for having served the Republic, while 84 had been shot in the Republican zone. The overwhelming majority had been imprisoned in the Government zone or had served in the Insurgent army.[12]

Other non-official statistics include 3,000 officers arrested, quoted by the *Pravda* correspondent Koltsov, who was close to centres of power, and a figure of 1,100, including 700 of field rank (major and above) held in the Model Prison of Madrid alone on 11 August 1936.[13]

[12] J. Busquets, *El militar de carrera en España*, Barcelona, 1967, 57

[13] J. de Aralar, *La rebelión militar española y el pueblo vasco*, Buenos Aires, 1937, 17.

These figures suggest that an order of magnitude of about 4,000 career officers were arrested and/or executed or murdered in the Government zone within a few days of the uprising. However, there is post-war evidence to suggest that many officers simply hid. The *Gaceta* of 26 July 1936, a few days after the insurrections had been suppressed, invited all retired career officers and NCOs of 65 and under to apply to be reinstated in the service. Special mention was made of Francisco Galán, of the *Guardia Civil*, who had done this. However, officers who had taken early retirement were not likely to possess the same skills as those on the active list. One reserve officer was so incompetent that he wounded a militiaman when firing a cannon.[14] This man may have belonged to the *escala de reserva retribuída*, that is he was a promoted NCO, as well as retired, but the Republic had little choice.

All these limitations on the actual number of active list officers who were available and trustworthy become clearly evident in the official provisional Republican Army List that the Ministry of National Defence published in September 1938.[15] It is incomplete and has to be interpreted side by side with the last pre-war Army List of April 1936, but it shows that of the career officers on the active list in 1936 only about 2,000, that is 14 per cent, were still in the Republican Army in 1938, which corresponds to the figure quoted by the Chief of Staff, General Rojo, who would have had access to the information.[16]

Commanders of the Republican Army

Whatever the actual numbers of career officers in Republican Spain, a survey of commanders at different levels in both the Popular and Insurgent armies reveals the marked insufficiency of professional military officers in the former.

In the Insurgent army – the *Ejército Nacional* as it styled itself, led by General Franco – according to a command list dated January 1938, all the army commanders, Dávila, Saliquet, Queipo de Llano and the *generalísimo*, Franco, had been of general rank in 1936 (though Dávila had been in the Reserve). The army corps commanders had all been the youngest infantry colonels (Pablo Martín Alonso was 41, Sáenz de Buruaga and García Escámez 44). Most of the divisional commanders had been lieutenant-colonels. All commanders of infantry units came from the infantry and almost all were on the active list in 1936. Even in 1939, at the end of the Civil War, when lower-rank officers might

[14] Gámir, *De mis memorias*, II: 17. [15] DR, L506.
[16] Rojo, *España heroica*, 42.

have been expected to be commanding larger formations, a list of the 36 brigade commanders in the Insurgent army shows that, save 2, all had been majors, lieutenant-colonels and in the odd case colonels. They had all been infantrymen and all on the active list. Very few of the close on 23,000 war-temporary second-lieutenants (*alféreces provisionales*) ever commanded more than a platoon, while only 497 took a course to become company commanders. It is doubtful if any non-career officer ever rose to lead a battalion.

A revealing contrast, however, is displayed by the command lists in the Republican Army at roughly the same time. On 18 December 1937 the army commands were held by Juan Hernández Sarabia, who in 1936 was a retired lieutenant-colonel of artillery and personal adviser to President Azaña; Adolfo Prada, who had retired as a major in 1931; Ricardo Burillo, whose battle experience in Morocco was limited to command of a company and who had been a major of the *Guardia de Asalto*; José Miaja; and Sebastián Pozas, generals of brigade. Miaja's last command in the field had been as a colonel in 1925, while Pozas had achieved that rank through battlefield merit the same year. Neither had commanded more than a regiment in the field. Pozas, in addition, was from the cavalry. Of the army corps, six were commanded by militia officers. The rest were under professional officers, but most of these had been relatively junior before the war. Moriones had been a lieutenant-colonel of engineers, Vidal a colonel of infantry and Sánchez Plaza a lieutenant-colonel of cavalry. These three had at least commanded battalions and regiments, but Perea and Romero were not even on the active list in 1936 and had retired as captain and major respectively. Antonio Ortega had been a second-lieutenant of *Carabineros*, following 30 years in the ranks.

As for the commanders of the 59 divisions, the most senior rank held in 1936 was that of lieutenant-colonel; 4 had been majors and 18 captains of infantry. The only other career officers were a reserve cavalry lieutenant, an infantry lieutenant, an engineers officer, topographer by profession and pilot, a long-service NCO recently promoted to second lieutenant, and a number of retired captains and majors. While some career military men might have had exceptional talents, none had experience of handling a division or even a brigade in the field before the Civil War. Their ranks were almost always lower than those of Insurgent divisional commanders. The lack of experience in Morocco, or even on peacetime manoeuvres, is significant. Furthermore, seventeen divisional commanders of the Republican Army emerged from the militias, only one of whom, Enrique Líster, had received some brief military instruction in the USSR.[17]

[17] Líster, *Nuestra guerra*, 22.

At brigade level in the Republican Army, there were 49 career officers who had command or were Chiefs of Staff of the 188 mixed brigades mentioned in the command tables of December 1937. These brigades were composed of four infantry battalions and a complement of artillery and other services with the aim of making the mixed brigade, as it was called, autonomous. In this sense it was different from the brigade in Franco's army, which consisted merely of half a division and had no structure laid down for it. Indeed, the Insurgent division itself could vary, according to needs, between 10 and 24 battalions.[18] Therefore, the small Republican Army brigades needed leadership and Staff of high calibre, but in 1936 the 49 professionals who led them had been in most cases officers with scarce military experience at more than subaltern level.

At higher levels there were insufficient Staff officers, for not all the heads of section, even at army corps level, were career officers or even new officers who had undergone rigorous and intensive Staff training. At divisional level, most Staff officers were infantry officers, but in one case he was a second-lieutenant recently promoted from the rank of senior NCO in the *Guardia Civil*. At brigade level, Staff-trained officers were virtually unknown.

Whatever the theoretical number of officers available in the Republican zone, very few were employed to command fighting units. A number of authorities have expressed the view that this constituted a political error, and that the services of a large number of officers who could have been used were disdained. Nevertheless, it was unlikely that Spanish officers, accustomed as they were to seeing themselves as a corporate body, would take arms against their comrades to defend a cause towards which they felt lukewarm. It was considered imprudent to entrust leadership to many officers and if, in some cases, the Republic was mistaken, in others the contrary was true.

Loyal to the people's cause. *Leales geográficos:* hostile to the republic

Generalisation about career officers who served in the Republican Army is unreliable because each officer acted for personal reasons. Nevertheless, some classification may aid description, and some prominent personalities can be looked at individually.

To begin with, there was a small group of officers whose loyalty was undoubted. They were members of UMRA or of Left and Republican

[18] Divisions of the Insurgent forces in January 1938 are listed in DN, L439, C40.

parties, associated with Catalan nationalism or in some way identified with political attitudes that guaranteed their fidelity.

The Galán brothers, for example, were members of the PCE (see Appendix 4). Both rose to lead army corps, although José María was only a lieutenant of *Carabineros* and Francisco a retired captain of the *Guardia Civil*. Another, Miguel Gallo, who had taken part in the failed Republican uprising at Jaca in December 1930, was also a communist and had served in the Presidential military household. In 1936 he was a 32-year-old captain who two years later commanded an army corps. Another member of the PCE, Luis Barceló, was a leader of UMRA and perhaps had had a hand in planning the assassination of the Rightist leader José Calvo Sotelo.[19] He is also thought to have taken an active part in the drumhead courts martial of captured rebel officers in Madrid.[20] He was the first Inspector of Militia. He rose to command an army corps, but was executed during the Casado coup at the end of the war, suspected of involvement in the shooting of *casadista* officers.[21] Enrique Pérez Farrás was one of the few officers associated with Catalan nationalism. Sentenced to a long term of imprisonment for his involvement in the Barcelona Catalanist uprising in 1934, he was amnestied by the Popular Front regime elected in February 1936. He rose to the rank of colonel.[22] However, his appointment to direct the Catalan militias had been made by the Catalan Government, which had no constitutional competence to do so, and, when the militias were militarised in 1937, he was shunted into rearguard posts, ending the war as military governor of Gerona.[23]

There were other officers whose political stances were not dictated by their party membership but rather by close relationships with politicians and conspirators against the monarchy and the Primo de Rivera dictatorship during the 1920s. Some of them reached high positions in the Republican Army. Juan Perea Capulino, for example, a retired infantry captain, had collaborated with the CNT in the 1920s.[24] Reincorporated into the army by decree in the *Gaceta* of 6 August 1936, and having led militia in the battle for Madrid, he led a division and soon was promoted to lieutenant-colonel. In 1938 he was entrusted with the Army of the East until the collapse of the front in Catalonia in early 1939. Two others, Leopoldo Menéndez and Juan Hernández Sarabia, were

19 Modesto, *Soy del Quinto Regimiento*, 17.
20 Arrarás, *Cruzada*, XVIII: 493.
21 Casado, *Last Days of Madrid*, 179.
22 *DO*, 5 May 1938. 23 *DO*, 24 January 1939.
24 Personal information from CNT leader Miguel González Inestal. See J. Perea Capulino, *Los culpables. Recuerdos de la guerra 1936–1939*, Barcelona, 2007.

close associates of the President of the Republic, Manuel Azaña. They became generals and headed the Army of the Levante and the Eastern Army Group (*Grupo de Ejércitos de la Región Oriental*) respectively.

Lastly there were a number of career officers who had not been associated with left-wing or even Republican politics before the war. Some presented themselves for duty at the very outset of hostilities, led militia columns or grappled with logistic problems. Others remained in the background for a while, but gradually came forward as the Government seemed to be getting a grip on the chaos and lawlessness of its zone.

Among the former are José Fontán, a Staff Corps major who remained at his post in the War Ministry and fulfilled important roles in the General Staff throughout the war; José Cerón, another Staff major, described in different sources as apolitical, Catholic (in a Spain where all public religious activity had ceased, churches had been converted into garages and thousands of clergy murdered) and conservative;[25] Antonio Escobar, *Guardia Civil* colonel in Barcelona, whose Catholicism was well known,[26] and to whom is attributed the loyalty of the *Guardia Civil* and its attack on the rebellious officers of the garrison, an offence for which he was executed by the victors. Escobar commanded columns in Madrid and was sent to Barcelona in May 1937 to take over police services. He reached the rank of general and led the Army of Extremadura.[27]

There were many other men of this conservative and traditional hue who nevertheless served in the Republican Army of the Republic at times when officers frequently risked being killed by their own men. In their defence when they were court-martialled by the victors they said that they had sworn to defend the constitutional order and had done no more than their duty.

Next, there were those officers who were described as '*leales geográficos*', that is, they were loyal to the Republic because the uprising found them in that part of Spain. Had they been in the zone where the uprising was successful they would have been content to serve in that army. Yet many of these men gave the best they could, and did not hesitate to assume grave responsibilities, for which they suffered greatly after the war. Others strove to remain in the background, hoping, in vain, that a negative attitude would save their career and even perhaps their rank if the Insurgents won.

[25] Cordón, *Trayectoria*, 275, and, from Franco's headquarters, CGG, L292.
[26] Lacruz, *El alzamiento*, 99.
[27] *DO*, 28 June 1938.

Lastly there were those who acted as enemy agents and saboteurs, such as Colonel Centaño, in charge of an artillery repair workshop in Madrid, who revealed his role to Colonel Casado.[28] Yet there were officers who played duel roles. Major Mota, for example, who taught on the officers' course at the *Carlos Marx* school and then in *Escuela Popular de Guerra No.1*, was an efficient teacher of gunnery and at the same time an agent of the *Socorro Blanco* or 'White Aid', rescuing suspected people from the hands of the military police.[29]

A '*leal geográfico*' who took on the greatest responsibility was Vicente Rojo. His father, an NCO, had retired and died before Vicente was born and the latter was educated in the military orphans' school. Selected to be a lecturer at the Toledo Infantry Academy, he and Captain Emilio Alamán founded a collection of books of military doctrine in which the new theories on tank warfare, advocated in the 1920s in Britain by Liddell Hart and in Germany by Heinz Guderian, were described.[30] He took the Staff diploma and in February 1936 was promoted to major, serving on the General Staff. He belonged to no political party or military organisation, referring in one of his books to 'my intentional and absolute separation from political and economic matters'. His principal concern was to maintain the hierarchical structure of the army ('I have always believed that rank and seniority should be strictly respected'[31]). When the Civil War began, while in Madrid Rojo protected family members of his colleagues besieged in the Military Academy in the Alcázar of Toledo; he himself declined to remain in the Alcázar, which he visited to try to persuade the besieged officers and civil guards to surrender. He saw his duty as being to the elected government.

In the Caballero administration's first General Staff Rojo appears in the Operations Section.[32] By the following month he was deputy Chief of Staff.[33] When Madrid was threatened and left in the charge of General Miaja, Rojo was selected as Chief of Staff for the battle to defend the city.

Rojo is thought of as 'ambivalent' and 'enigmatic'.[34] When he returned to Spain and was court-martialled for 'military rebellion', he was asked whether he had thought of crossing the lines during the war. He said he had thought of doing so, because his feelings urged him in that direction ('*razones de orden sentimental*') but he saw his duty as remaining

[28] Casado, *Last Days of Madrid*, 207.
[29] Miralles Bravo, *Memorias*, 121.
[30] Jesús I. Martínez Paricio *et al.* (eds.), *Los papeles del general Rojo*, Madrid, 1989, 25.
[31] Rojo, *Madrid*, 213 and 28.
[32] *DO*, 5 September 1936. [33] *DO*, 10 October 1936.
[34] Martínez Paricio *et al.*, *Los papeles*, 75.

with the Republic.[35] It is true that he had to consider his family, but many officers had family in the contrary zone. He had never taken part in politics on either side.[36]

Rojo made a favourable impression on the influential *Pravda* correspondent Koltsov,[37] fitting as he did the communist image of the apolitical professional officer. Rojo himself, as would be expected, denies the importance of Soviet advisers in the battle for Madrid.[38] Soon after he was appointed Chief of Staff in the defence of Madrid he made a formal complaint about the self-aggrandisement of Kléber, commander of the XI International Brigade, which was 'frankly harmful' ('*francamente perjudicial*'),[39] as indeed Rojo considered the exaggerated accounts of the military feats of the Internationals. It was Kléber, rather than Rojo, who was dismissed. Indeed, the Soviet advisers (see below) had been ordered to avoid giving any impression of superiority in their dealings with the Spanish professional officers.[40] As one reporter wrote to Moscow, 'The adviser to the Spanish Chief of Staff sees Rojo from time to time and is absolutely uninterested [this would seem to mean 'uninvolved': MA] in the staff's current work.'[41] These denials may be taken as a partial rejection of Caballero's careless statement that Rojo was 'communist' and the accusation by authors of anarchist sympathies that he was too detached and Olympian to know what was really going on at the Front.[42] When the CNT protested about the appointment of communists to command brigades, Rojo, in a letter to Hernández Sarabia, commander of the Eastern Army Group, disassociated himself from the problem, asking only that it be solved as soon as possible.[43]

Unfortunately, the Republican Army was inevitably politicised. The political and ideological divisions of the rear were present and indeed magnified at the Front. Rojo's detachment was admirable but unrealistic. Sometimes he should have acted more firmly, for example when Líster took his forces out of Teruel against orders.[44] The accusation of detachment is frequently made about military Staff officers, but

[35] *Ibid.*, 76. [36] Cordón, *Trayectoria*, 429.

[37] M. Koltsov, *Diario de la guerra de España*, Paris, 1963, 220 and 276ff.

[38] Rojo, *Madrid*, 69, 87, 139–51.

[39] Martínez Paricio *et al.*, *Los papeles*, 86.

[40] Radosh *et al.*, *Spain Betrayed*, 495, report from Colonel Sverchevsky criticising behaviour of Soviet military advisers, and 432, on 'Kleberism'.

[41] *Ibid.*, 291.

[42] F. Largo Caballero, *Mis memorias*, Mexico City, 1954, 195. The communist minister Jesús Hernández claims that Rojo refused to accept a PCE membership card, in his *La grande trahison*, Paris, 1971. The anarchist view was expressed to me by the González Inestal brothers, who were sub-commissars general.

[43] DR, L69, C11. [44] DR, L1064, C2.

Rojo's self-imposed isolation seems to have been part of his character, as may be seen by the brevity of his communications to Indalecio Prieto, Minister of National Defence from May 1937 until April 1938.[45] Juan Negrín, Prime Minister and Minister of Defence from April 1938 until the end of the war, considered Rojo to possess all the qualities of competence and discipline required by a Chief of Staff, but to lack qualities of command, and to be unable to communicate enthusiasm and determination to the troops.[46] Yet the Republic had no military Commander-in-Chief, a fact which Rojo himself lamented,[47] nobody to play a role such as Franco's, which was both political and military, or, to look further afield, to be like Montgomery, Alexander or Eisenhower, and many other British and United States senior commanders in the Second World War who had the necessary charisma. Only in Madrid had the State of War been declared, and Miaja did indeed have the gifts that Rojo was judged to lack. This was, nevertheless, unfair because Rojo's duty was to direct Staff work in compliance with the decisions of the Minister.

Rojo's clarity of vision led him to pessimism, particularly during the disastrous collapse in spring of 1938, while he had little confidence in the ability of what was left of Republican Spain to resist once Catalonia had been lost in January and February 1939.[48]

The detached professionalism of Rojo led him to appear to lack empathy with the men he commanded, which at times could be close to disdain. He told Prieto once that he could not understand the retreats of terrified Republican recruits. 'It is something psychological that is difficult to understand.' ('*Esto es algo de tipo psicológico, que resulta difícil de comprender.*')[49] After two weeks of the exhausting battle of Brunete, fought in the heat and thirst of July 1937, he wrote using terms such as 'lack of decision and energy … reveal an attitude of passivity which is inappropriate for the tactical situation' ('*falta de decisión y energia … ponen de relieve una actitud de pasividad inconveniente a la situación táctica*').[50] And when asked for reinforcements during the bitterly cold days of the battle of Teruel in 1937–8, he wrote, 'The Command thinks it unnecessary to recall that to refer to suffering, which is the nature of all war, is contrary to the spirit of self-sacrifice that must colour all military activity.' ('*No cree el Mando necesario recordar que es contrario al espíritu de*

45 See some of these in DR, L461 and L462.
46 According to Arrarás, *Cruzada*, IV: 678.
47 Rojo, *Alerta*, 25.
48 See *ibid.*, 230, 239, 249, where he defends himself against the accusation of defeatism.
49 DR, L461, C7. 50 DR, L665 bis, C7.

abnegación que debe presidir toda actividad militar el hacer alusión a fatigas o a penalidades pasadas, propias de toda guerra.')[51]

Yet Rojo was fully aware of the limitations of the Republican Army. Inexperienced and untrained troops, lacking confidence in their leaders, who were also inexperienced for the commands they held, could panic sometimes, as could their officers. As Rojo wrote to Prieto after the Republican Army had been forced out of Teruel: 'I need to persuade you that it will be a long time before our commanders act as they should, and this applies to both militia and professional officers, and to the commissars.' ('*Quiero llevar a su ánimo una convicción de que tardaremos aún mucho tiempo para que los jefes de nuestro ejército se comporten como es debido, tanto los de milicias como los profesionales y los comisarios.*')[52]

Yet criticisms of Rojo are few and far between. Abad de Santillán, expressing a CNT view, claims that Rojo was subordinate to the Soviet advisers,[53] whereas Jesús Pérez Salas expresses the career soldier's view that Rojo was promoted over the heads of other more competent officers.[54] Lieutenant-General Barroso, Franco's Chief of Staff, however, considered Rojo to be the best Staff officer in Spain.[55] A Chief of Staff must to a certain extent be detached, in order to be able to carry out his duties. Yet, given this, it might be asked how a Chief of Staff should issue operational orders to units, commanders and troops whose capacity to execute them he doubts. It might also be argued that Rojo's greatest success was in the defence of Madrid, where he was in direct contact with a Commander-in-Chief, General José Miaja.

In 1954, Rojo applied to return to Spain from exile. The request was refused with the words 'refuse him bread and salt' ('*negadle el pan y la sal*').[56] His return was authorised at last in 1956, perhaps with the support of his old colleague at Toledo, the now General Emilio Alamán. When Rojo returned the following year he was tried and condemned to 30 years' imprisonment for the crime of 'military rebellion'. Nevertheless, an immediate pardon was issued without Rojo applying for it. Yet he did suffer the associated penalties of loss of career and of pension rights.

Turning to General José Miaja, his earliest biographer did his best to construct a working-class and progressive background for him. Miaja's father was a master armourer in the Asturias weapons industry. Miaja himself was abstemious and adopted vegetarianism for some

[51] DR, L1064, C2. [52] DR, L461, C5.
[53] Abad de Santillán, *Por qué perdimos*, 258.
[54] Jesús Pérez Salas, *Guerra en España 1936–1939*, Mexico City, 1947, 147.
[55] Personal information from the late Dr George Hills.
[56] Martínez Paricio *et al.*, *Los papeles*, 179–84, describes Rojo's return.

time, progressive characteristics which would not usually be shared by Spanish officers. He read books on history and social issues and was dismissed for his 'liberal' stance from the bench of judges who court-martialled strikers in 1917 (one of whom was Francisco Largo Caballero, who would be his direct superior as Minister of War in 1936–7).[57] Apart from this last point, which is not confirmed elsewhere, nothing indicates that Miaja's views were significantly different from those of other officers.

His military career was not undistinguished. He was promoted to major on battlefield merit in Morocco, and reached the rank of lieutenant-colonel by the age of 41 and colonel at 47. Promoted to general of brigade on 4 July 1932 (together with some other colonels who in 1936 would join the insurrection), he was removed from his command during the *bienio negro*, the years from November 1933 until February 1936 which were characterised by a conservative reaction to the Republic's reforms of 1931–3. According to his biographer he had 'blown the whistle' on a military conspiracy in Madrid.[58]

Did his appointment as interim Minister of War in the Popular Front Government which took power after the elections of February 1936 indicate that he sympathised with revolutionary ideals? Certainly he regained his command in Madrid. His attitude during the following months is referred to in a letter from the 'Director' and chief planner of the military insurrection which would lead to the Civil War, General Emilio Mola: 'Despite what I say about Mola, I don't have a bad view of him and so I don't agree with the bad qualities which are generally attributed to him.' ('*Pese a lo que digo de Miaja, no tengo mal concepto de él y me resisto por ello a creer las malas cualidades que generalmete se le atribuyen.*')[59] This, despite Mola's charitable view, does indicate that the Director's associates did consider Miaja to be at least not in favour of any coup. Yet Miaja was invited to be Minister of War in the Martínez Barrio Cabinet which tried in vain to negotiate with Mola during the night of 18–19 July 1936 and to save the country from the consequences of a military insurrection. One might speculate that he was invited in the hopes that his presence would be seen as a gesture to conciliate the Insurgent officers. It was not the first time that Miaja had been used to calm tense situations. On 17 May 1936 he had been sent to Alcalá de

[57] L. Somoza Silva, *El general Miaja*, Mexico City, 1944. The more recent work by Miaja's military secretary, López Fernández, *General Miaja*, provides some valuable details. I have not seen a recent work on Miaja published in Asturias by Juan José Menéndez.

[58] López Fernández, *General Miaja*, 27.

[59] Arrarás, *Cruzada*, XVII: 385.

Henares, some 25 miles north-east of Madrid, to investigate disputes between officers of the garrison and groups of left-wing civilians. In June a similar matter took him to Toledo. In both cases the garrisons were transferred. A transfer meant serious upheaval for the families of officers and career non-commissioned officers. Miaja's task was to try to smooth matters over.

However, once the Insurgents had rejected the conciliatory attempts of the Martínez Barrio Cabinet and José Giral had formed his Government, Miaja declined to continue as Minister of War, probably because he did not want to take responsibility for distributing weapons to the militias which were being formed.[60] This was why General Castelló, who had left the Badajoz garrison thinking he was to take over command in Madrid *vice* Miaja, found on arrival that he was to take over the War portfolio, a responsibility which would cause him to suffer a nervous breakdown.

Even the semi-official *Historia de la Cruzada española*, normally so fierce in condemnation or praise, was unable to take a firm position on Miaja. It may be that the position of his family, at the time living in Morocco and arrested by the Insurgents, was the most important of his concerns. While Miaja blamed the failure of his assault on Córdoba immediately after the insurrection on the absence of air cover,[61] an early Insurgent military historian claims that the general was simply incompetent.[62] Whatever the reason, Miaja was sent to command the division in Valencia while its titular head, General Martínez Monje, was busy organising the new army in Albacete. However, as the Insurgent forces approached Madrid, on 24 October 1936 Miaja was entrusted once more with command in the capital, and no more doubts about his loyalty were expressed.

The metamorphosis of a general with no particularly great military reputation or clear political identity to becoming the 'Saviour of Madrid' began on the night of 6/7 November 1936, when the Government, preparing for its hurried evacuation to Valencia in face of the imminent Insurgent assault on Madrid, ordered Miaja to take charge of the defence of the city. Yet even here there is some doubt, because Miaja's

[60] The differences in historians' opinions themselves suggest that Miaja was prevaricating. See Bolloten, *Spanish Revolution*, 30. Somoza, *El general*, 125, claims that Miaja was angry at bureaucratic procrastination in arming the crowds, while Arrarás, *Cruzada*, XVII: 406, describes him as relieved at the delay. Luis Romero, *Tres días de julio*, Barcelona, 1967, 433, quotes a cable from Miaja: 'Do not hand ammunition to anyone without a written order over my signature.' ('*Absténgase de entregar municiones al que no lleve una orden escrita y firmada por mí: general Miaja*.')

[61] DR, L966, C1.

[62] J. Cirre Jiménez, *De Espejo a Madrid*, Granada, 1938, 172.

appointment and that of General Pozas to command the central region were placed in each other's envelopes. This was almost certainly a result of the haste of the evacuation, but it could have had grave consequences if both generals had not disobeyed their orders and opened the letters at once.[63] How did Miaja react to his appointment? Did he think he was being given an impossible task?

What is certain is that the PCE and the Soviet advisers who had arrived gave Miaja their full support. Later, they claimed that they thought that he was an incompetent, but they needed a general as a figurehead, and they also hoped that Miaja's politically neutral history and his protests at the killings of rebel officers by the mob would help to attract the large number of professional officers living in Madrid to its defence.[64]

Indeed, Miaja's competence was in doubt. The later Prime Minister, Juan Negrín, told President Azaña, who confided his words to his diary, that Miaja 'doesn't know where the Front is and can't hold more than four soldiers in his mind at once' ('*no sabe por dónde va el frente, no le caben en la cabeza cuatro soldados*'). This is followed by the comment that if Rojo, Miaja's Chief of Staff, had personal gifts of leadership, he would be in command, which implies that Miaja did indeed have that magical charisma.[65] His gift was to know how to bring together the disparate forces in Madrid and succeed in making the city resist for 28 months.

The surviving minutes of meetings of the *Junta Delegada de Defensa*, the cabinet in miniature which governed Madrid, composed of two members from the PSOE, two from the UGT, two from the PCE, two from the JSU, two from the CNT and two from the anarchist *Juventudes Libertarias*, two from the Republican Left and two from the Syndicalist Party, show that Miaja rarely spoke and generally accepted the majority decision.[66] His skill lay in making useful suggestions, especially the appointment of Rojo and the other members of the Staff. To select an efficient Staff and leave it to get on with the task is arguably an aspect of efficient leadership.[67]

[63] Rojo, *Madrid*, 47–8. López Fernández, *General Miaja*, 58, thinks the mistake was intentional, a sabotage on the part of a bureaucrat or officer in the Ministry of War. This was presumably Miaja's own view, conveyed to López Fernández, who was his military secretary.

[64] For the communist opinion see Koltsov, *Diario*, 189, Líster, *Nuestra guerra*, 258, and Malinovski *et al.*, *BLB*, 20. 'From the point of view of military knowledge, he was the prototype of backwardness.'

[65] Azaña, *Obras Completas*, IV: 678.

[66] DR, L968, C10. See J. Aróstegui and J. Martínez, *La Junta de Defensa de Madrid*, Madrid, 1984.

[67] Rojo, *Madrid*, 32.

Personally, Miaja was particularly jovial, possessing that highly regarded 'Hail fellow, well met!' quality called in Spanish *campechanía*. He was the opposite of the retiring and even distant Rojo, and enjoyed the adulation he received. Caballero's complaints to President Azaña about Miaja's superficial irresponsibility arose, in the President's opinion, from personal differences between the austere Caballero and the sociable Miaja.[68]

Azaña notes how difficult it was to pin him down: 'Talkative ... he jumps from one thing to another, like a bird.' ('*Locuaz ... salta de una cosa a otra, como un pájaro.*')[69] Azaña's references to Miaja's observations about new recruits, militia commanders, arguments with the Staff and other questions are, however, irritatingly vague when they could have cast interesting light on Miaja's opinions, which, with the exception of a few official documents, are preserved only in secondary sources.

If Miaja had kept his dominating position in Madrid merely because of political convenience, popular scorn would have soon become evident. Miaja was valiant and resourceful. He harangued the militia when they fled from the enemy and sent blank ammunition to one position which was about to be abandoned for lack of cartridges.[70] He was successful in creating a sort of 'Ourselves alone' spirit which led Caballero to remind him that he was the head of a mere 'delegated' administration. Arturo Barea, who worked in the censorship in the Madrid telephone building, quotes him saying, 'For them [presumably the Government and General Staff in Valencia] we here in Madrid are just s—t.' ('*Nosotros ... los de Madrid, no somos para ellos más que mierda.*')[71] It was precisely his popularity which made Prieto, Minister of Defence, propose him as Supreme Commander in the central-south zone when the enemy split the Republic in two in April 1938.[72]

Miaja caused irritation in high places by his refusal to detach troops from his command for operations planned for other fronts. The most important of these episodes was the attack planned on the Extremadura Front in May 1937.[73] The General Staff intended to launch an offensive to capture Mérida and isolate the Insurgents in Andalusia. The Central

[68] Azaña, *Obras Completas*, IV: 591.
[69] *Ibid.*, 732
[70] López Fernández, *General Miaja*, 123–4.
[71] Somoza, *El general*, 210. Quotation from Arturo Barea, *La forja de un rebelde*, vol. III, *La llama*, Buenos Aires, 1951, 292.
[72] Indalecio Prieto, *Cómo y por qué salí del Ministerio de Defensa Nacional: intrigas de los rusos en España*, Mexico City, 1940.
[73] See Casado, *Last Days of Madrid*, 69–73; Casado was Head of Operations at this time.

Army, under Miaja's command, proposed an attack at Brunete, to the north-west of Madrid, which was later carried out, and resisted the order of the General Staff to detach units for the planned campaign in Extremadura. The operation in Extremadura reflected daring and strategic vision. Certainly the risks were great, and the Soviet advisers may have had good cause to be unwilling to detach the high-quality aircraft which were being sent from Russia to Spain. However, it is less likely that Miaja was urged by his Russian advisers to refuse to move his troops than that he wanted to retain a powerful army in central Spain and around Madrid, where he thought the greatest danger was. On 13 February 1937 he was complaining that his units were being taken away as soon as they were formed: 'It seems they are determined to have another Málaga, but as I want to defend Madrid properly, as is my duty and as I think I have done, I cannot go on like this.'[74]

Nevertheless, Miaja's letter to Caballero was not a frank refusal, but a grave warning and a series of counter-proposals from a general to a Minister of War who was being advised by a General Staff of officers who were well junior to Miaja. In other armies, Miaja would have been dismissed and replaced, but Caballero did not have this luxury.

Miaja again objected to detaching units for a projected operation as part of an amphibious operation against Motril (Granada) at the end of 1938, in order to relieve enemy pressure on Catalonia.[75] However, security had been so lax that the Motril landings might well have been disastrous.[76]

Miaja's 'communism', of which Caballero complained to Azaña, was that of a senior officer who found that communists were efficient and disciplined. Azaña was shrewd enough to note in his diary that Miaja was no communist. In fact, his politics were unknown. In 1932 he had told the President that socialist should be shot![77] Naturally, given the peculiar situation of the Republic, Miaja found himself at times in conflict with the Government and the General Staff. It is true that Miaja showed a degree of independence which, as Casado complained, was a court-martial offence.[78] However, it was also true that Miaja thought, possibly correctly, that he had been left holding the baby on the night

[74] DR, L968, C10, *Actas de la Junta Delegada de Defensa de Madrid.* See Miaja's answer to Caballero in López Fernández, *General Miaja*, 235–9, who believes that the episode was used by the communist ministers in their campaign against Caballero.

[75] Rojo, *Alerta*, 98

[76] Azaña, *Obras Completas*, IV: 903, repeating what Negrín or a senior officer had told him.

[77] *Ibid.*, 589.

[78] Casado, *Last Days of Madrid*, 71.

of 6–7 November 1936, when Franco's forces appeared to be about to launch their attack on Madrid, and that this gave him the right – he would have called it duty – to make his own decisions. It was pride, prudence and a degree of obstinacy rather than obedience to Soviet advisers which made Miaja refuse to detach troops for the Aragon Front in 1938, when such a transfer would probably have been approved by the Russian advisers.[79]

How loyal was Miaja to the Republican cause? Some sources accuse him of allowing his Staff to be infiltrated by agents and sympathisers of the Insurgents, some of who were suspected to have been negotiating with the enemy months before the end of the war.[80] But this could not have been known two years earlier. Miaja had to keep an uncertain balance between communist militia officers and professional officers. He had to run a city swollen with tens of thousands of refugees and suffering bombing from the air and shelling from the nearby enemy-occupied Casa de Campo and University City, and he had to endeavour to maintain agreement between the different political forces represented on the *Junta de Defensa*.

The Republic had been split in two when Franco reached the Mediterranean at Vinaroz. Almost at once, on 16 April 1938, the *Diario Oficial* announced Miaja's appointment as Commander-in-Chief of the Army Group of the Centre, the Levante, Andalusia and Extremadura, abbreviated to GERC. Did Miaja believe that the Republic was already defeated? A knowledgeable source later reported that he was rumoured to have secured a diplomatic passport in October 1938.[81] On 3 January 1939, as two Republican armies retreated towards the French frontier in Catalonia, the State of War was at last declared. Miaja was granted complete powers in what was left of the Republic, while General Matallana, whose desire to end the war was better known, became head of the army group. Once the Government left Spain in early February, Miaja found himself in a situation of supremacy that no leader of the Republican Army had known. His military secretary recalls that Miaja communicated with Prime Minister Negrín and Chief of Staff Rojo, who were in Toulouse, on 9 February, having crossed into France with 400,000 civilian and military refugees.[82] Miaja wanted to negotiate a peace, given the catastrophic weakness of his forces and their lack of ammunition, aircraft and weapons in good condition.

[79] See comments by Franco's Staff in CGG L277, C11.
[80] Casado, *Last Days of Madrid*, 71.
[81] Letter to the Foreign Office from British consul in Valencia in FO 371, W6704/8/41 of 11 April 1939.
[82] López Fernández, *General Miaja*, ch. 22.

When on 5 March 1939 Colonel Casado carried out his insurrection against the Negrín Government, establishing the National Defence Council (*Consejo Nacional de Defensa*), Miaja's acceptance of the presidency of this body must have contributed to the authority of the Council being accepted by the professional officers all over Madrid, New Castile, the Levante and those other parts of central, southern and south-eastern Spain which were still in Republican territory. By that time, given that on 13 February 1939 Franco had published his Law of Political Responsibilities (*Ley de Responsabilidades Políticas*), Miaja knew that unless he fled Spain his own future was bleak. He must also have been physically and mentally exhausted. The communist militia colonel, Líster, found him '*idiotizado*' and, although Líster never seems to have thought much of Miaja and was diametrically opposed to the latter's desire for surrender, one wonders what the myopic 61-year-old general and the energetic young communist who had risen from the Fifth Regiment to command an army corps, had to talk to each other about. The less harsh Modesto, the only militiaman to become a general, calls him 'simple'.[83] To accept the Presidency of the National Defence Council displayed either extreme vanity or courage, for he would be no more than a straw man. Perhaps it was his vanity, for the Council did not cancel his promotion, decreed by Negrín, to lieutenant-general as it had Rojo's.[84] In the event, Casado's attempt at a conditional surrender failed. Miaja abandoned Spain for Oran, Marseilles and Paris. With his family, previously exchanged, he sailed for Mexico in May 1939. Had the Insurgents captured him he would probably have faced the firing squad. Under the Law of Political Responsibilities he was sentenced to 15 years' exile, the loss of valuable property in Morocco and of his nationality. His wife was fined 1 million pesetas (£20,000).[85] In Mexico he gave some lectures, dying in 1958.

Despite the attempts of his biographer to give him a firmly Republican and progressive background, Miaja was probably only 'geographically loyal'. He was pushed into a situation from which he was unable to extract himself and which his vanity found pleasant. Had he refused to serve the Republic, his membership of the right-wing UME and perhaps other activities which an investigation could have revealed might have cost him his life. He did not know how the war would end and, like so many others, his family was living in the enemy zone.

[83] Líster, *Nuestra guerra*, 252; Modesto, *Soy del Quinto Regimiento*, 278.
[84] *DO* of 15 March 1939.
[85] *Boletín Oficial del Estado*, 20 September 1939.

The great majority of the professional officers who served in the Republican Army must have been 'geographically loyal', with little sympathy, if any, for the revolution which took place in those areas where the military uprising had been suppressed. It would be absurd to call them 'communists' or 'Marxists' merely because they served the Republic and because the communists had some respect for them. An Argentine journalist painted a vivid picture of their coldness towards revolutionary excitement. He entered the headquarters of Colonel Villalba at Barbastro in Aragon and gave the regulation salute with his clenched fist. No officer responded and all looked coldly at him.[86] Yet to use the expression 'geographically loyal' in a pejorative manner would not be justified, if only because the term could also been applied to a large number of officers on the other side who merely obeyed their superiors' orders. In 1936, officers were less concerned with politics than how to survive on their poor pay. The only common preoccupation of all of them was public order.[87] Thus it is reasonable to consider that, once the initial chaos of the revolution which took place in the Republican zone was over, officers who had had nothing to do with the insurrection thought that the best thing was to accept a post in the new army. They probably thought that, in the worst of cases, if the Insurgents won, they would not in a worse position than before and would be able to return to pre-war routine. Despite Franco's executions of captured officers during the campaigns, the hundreds of career soldiers did not seem aware that at the very least they would be expelled from the Army. And, if the Republic was victorious, as seemed likely in 1936, the road to promotions seemed open, given that the rebels would certainly be dismissed from the service.

It is very difficult to analyse this group of officers and discover to what extent lack of enthusiasm, discomfort at the politicisation of the Republican Army or unhappiness about its inefficiency, once they had had to give up pre-war routine and deal with masses of men who were not easily amenable to discipline, were more characteristic of these officers than mere treason.

Yet some Republican officers have been accused of treason. Sometimes this refers to events at the beginning of the war, when the situation was fluid. Here 'treason' is a relative term. Sometimes 'treason' meant no more than a refusal to undertake a militarily mistaken action. Some officers agreed to lead militias in exchange for their lives (see Colonel

86 J. Gabriel, *La vida y la muerte en Aragón*, Buenos Aires, 1938, 89.

87 Casado, *Last Days of Madrid*, 47–9, and Pérez Salas, *Guerra en España*, 80. Both had progressive views and their opinions about most of their colleagues are probably accurate.

Salafranca's report in Chapter 3). In some cases they tried and succeeded in crossing the lines. How early in the war an officer went over to the Insurgents was significant after the war, when officers of the Republican army were court-martialled by the victors. That Vicente Rojo did not cross over was evidently significant in the harsh sentence he received in 1957 and the fact that, even though amnestied, he was denied his civil and pension rights.

Though there may well have been clear indications of treasonable acts later in the war, it is not always evident that these were anything more than inefficiency. The Soviet advisers tended to use the word 'sabotage' when what seems to be meant is idleness and inability to change the habits of routine behaviour.[88] Maidanik, for example, accuses most Spanish Staff officers of formally obeying orders but trying to hinder them being fully effective and sabotaging supplies.[89] While the accusations may be genuine, they do not seem to have led to the obvious conclusion of a court martial. They tend to refer to confusion, disorder, lost documents, lack of information (perhaps concealed from the Soviet advisers) and unnecessary transfers of troops, none of which is unknown in war in general.

On the other hand, many career officers showed great loyalty and valour. The Argentinian communist Córdova Itúrburu observed that professional officers suffered great losses while leading untrained militias. Political commissars often had to persuade the militias that Staff officers at least had to stay in the rear.[90] Forty-five career officers lost their lives in the defence of Madrid up to 12 January 1937.[91]

In some rare cases there may have been acts of treason. The best known of these is the passing of information about points designed to be weak in the Iron Belt or *Cinturón de Hierro* around Bilbao. The traitor was Major Goicoechea, who designed the fortifications. Indeed, the Basque forces did suffer the consequences of treason by officers, not discovered perhaps because of the refusal to appoint political commissars,[92] who would have kept a careful eye on the officers. Another two officers concerned with the Iron Belt, Murga and Anglada, were shot

[88] See Radosh *et al.*, *Spain Betrayed*, *passim*.

[89] K. Maidanik, *Ispanskii proletariat b nasionalsno-revolutionnoi voine*, Moscow, 1960, 216; see also N. Voronov, in Malinovski *et al.*, *BLB*, 75–6, and Koltsov, *Diario*, 303. For the 'confession' of a Staff officer see Angel Lamas, *Unos ... y otros*, Barcelona, 1972.

[90] C. Córdova Itúrburu, *España bajo el comando del pueblo*, Buenos Aires, 1938, 51.

[91] DR, L954, C5 and L968, C1.

[92] According to the Basque President, Aguirre, in his report to the government of the Republic (cited Martínez Bande, *Norte*, document 2)

when discovered to be part of a spy ring.[93] Other members of the Staff did not return to the Republican zone after the collapse of the Northern Front, and in consequence were dismissed from the army.[94]

The major accusation of treason refers to Colonel Casado's uprising on 5 March 1939 against the Negrín Government, which Casado considered constitutionally illegal, given that the Republic was without a President once Azaña had resigned and refused to return to Spain from the Spanish embassy in Paris. Casado's stated intention was to seek peace and prevent the take-over of the leadership of the Republican Army by communist militia leaders. Probably the majority of professional officers in the central-south zone to which Republican territory had been reduced supported the Casado coup (the other armies had crossed into France with Rojo and the General Staff). A later chapter will discuss the Casado episode in detail, but whether the word 'treason' is appropriate is relevant in this discussion of the role of the professional officers. Specific accusations were made post-war against two senior Staff officers, Antonio Garijo and Felix Muedra, while the communist units which fought the *casadistas* in the streets of Madrid in the middle weeks of March 1939 executed three Staff officers, whom they accused of treason.[95]

Antonio Garijo led the Information Section of the GERC. He may have left himself open to suspicions because of a lack of discretion, according to the communist accusation.[96] Yet it is difficult to accept that he would have remained in his post if his actions were so well known. He was one of the officers who tried to negotiate with Insurgent officers late in March at Gamonal aerodrome near Burgos. The minutes of the conversations do not justify any suspicion that Garijo was passing information.[97] Of course he was concerned with the fate that awaited officers of the Republican Army. Antonio Cordón, the communist Under-Secretary for War, effectively in charge of the army given Negrín's other preoccupations, excuses himself for not having acted against Garijo by claiming that Miaja and Rojo doubted that Garijo had communicated information to the enemy.[98] The defence of Garijo by the anarchist García Pradas reinforces the view that the communists,

[93] Murga was executed on 14 November 1936. See Steer, *Tree of Gernika*, 108 and *passim*, for unfavourable comments on most of the officers in the Basque campaign. For Goicoechea see J. M. Martínez Bande, *Vizcaya*, Madrid, 1971, document 3.

[94] Montaud, Aguirre's Chief of Staff, was dismissed in *DO* of 8 August 1937.

[95] Casado, *Last Days of Madrid*, 172.

[96] Líster, *Nuestra guerra*, 99, who had not been in the zone.

[97] CGG, L277, C10. [98] Cordón, *Trayectoria*, 415.

for one reason or another, detested Garijo, who, if he was a traitor, was extremely circumspect.[99]

As for the other frequently accused Staff officer, Lieutenant-Colonel Muedra, the fact that he was to be found supporting his family by running a little shop nearly 20 years after the war hardly indicates that if he did provide an Intelligence service for the enemy, the latter were grateful (see below).

The Control and Information Bureau

To some unclear extent, the reliability and loyalty of professional officers was verified by the *Gabinete de Información y Control* (Classifying Committee) set up at the beginning of the war in order to classify the career soldiers. Uncertainty and distrust of officers required some check on their backgrounds. With the troops released from their oaths and deserting, with arms in the possession of uncontrolled militias, that majority of officers who did not have undoubted left-wing antecedents was felt almost by definition not to be trusted. However, if an officer's trustworthiness was confirmed by an official body, he would have the confidence to command a militia battalion or one of the new mixed brigades of the Republican Army, and his guaranteed loyalty would oblige his political commissar to back him up.

A large number of officers in the Republican zone were put into the category of 'unposted' while investigations took place. Such lists of *disponibles* appeared almost daily. At a court martial of captured Insurgents, General Miaja informed the Ministry of War that the loyalty of 60 per cent of officers stationed or living in the Government zone was doubtful.[100]

The first classifying committee was established in late September 1936. Its task was to examine applications of militiamen to be accepted as officers in the new army.[101] Its members were Captain Eleuterio Díaz Tendero, who had been commissioned from the ranks, founder of the UMRA, representing the Ministry of War, Captain Luis Barceló, Inspector-General of Militias, and Lieutenant-Colonel Gonzalo de

[99] J. García Pradas, *Cómo terminó la guerra de España*, Buenos Aires, 1940, 120. Jesús Hernández's accusation in *La grande trahison*, 153, that Garijo was decorated by Franco has no foundation and is exceptionally unlikely. Manuel Tagüeña, later a corps commander, met Garijo in 1937 and was favourably impressed, but his break with the PCE would possibly incline him to defend an officer whom the communists distrusted. See his *Testimonio de dos guerras*, Mexico City, 1973, 159.

[100] *El Sol*, 4 September 1936.

[101] *Junta clasificadora para el ingreso en el ejército del Personal de Milicias* (*Gaceta*, 30 September 1936).

Benito of the General Staff. Despite the latter's seniority, one may assume that he played a minor part in the judgement of applicants because the other two had well-known antecedents. Díaz Tendero had been compiling lists of officers disloyal to the Republic since before the war.[102]

Shortly afterwards, the authorities established the *Gabinete de Información y Control*, which investigated career officers, classifying them as F (fascists), A (antifascists) or I (indifferent). Díaz Tendero compiled an important report, dated 25 November 1936, on his work.[103] After fierce condemnation of the inefficiency and disorder of the early weeks of the Civil War, he claims that the Republic had sufficient officers and non-commissioned officers for subordinate positions, and a large number of retired personnel still of military age. The problem was at company level. He recommended promoting all lieutenants and senior sergeants (*brigadas* in the Spanish Army). His advice was followed. Nevertheless, went on the report, there was no shortage at the level of major and above (field officers or *jefes*), and he asked why they were not being employed. His answer was that confusion and indiscipline was preventing the appointments of *jefes*. He quoted an artillery battery which had 4 officers and 22 NCOs, while another was led only by a single sergeant. Personal influences, added to the general breakdown of organisation and discipline, almost certainly did lead to uneven distribution of commands. Díaz Tendero also criticised the situation where militia officers boasted about having professionals under their orders. Furthermore, many officers were in hiding and others had found posts for themselves in the military bureaucracy when they could have been required to take field commands.

The report does not confirm Díaz Tendero's reputation as a firebrand of the Left, who wanted to have none but known progressives officering the new army. On the contrary, he complains that, while the Ministry of War employed officers whom the *Gabinete* thought of doubtful loyalty, it often left others, recommended by the *Gabinete*, cooling their heels. A typical case was Major Carlos García Vallejo, whom the *Gabinete* describes, somewhat mysteriously, as 'provisionally loyal' (*leal provisional*) but who led militias and later commanded the XVII Army Corps. Antonio Cordón, who might have been justifiably hostile to García Vallejo because he supported the Casado coup in 1939, nevertheless considered the classification of this officer as unjust.[104] Cordón

[102] Suero Roca, *Militares republicanos*, 148. See Salas Larrazábal, *Historia del Ejército Popular*, 493–4, for the errors of the *Gabinete*.

[103] DR, L477, C6. [104] Cordón, *Trayectoria*, 307.

recalls the contrary case of a highly regarded cavalry officer who went over to the other side with the plans of Republican positions, accompanied by his orderly, who turned out to be his disguised wife.

During the first weeks of the war, the *Gabinete de Información y Control* received the data collected by local and largely self-appointed committees who strove to check up on the backgrounds and opinions of officers. Early in 1937 the *Gabinete* was brought under the control of the Ministry of War.[105] It was to be the only organisation with the right to decide on the loyalty of an officer. It was to be consulted before a man was promoted or when a retired officer applied to be reinstated. Its committees were to be composed of between three and seven members, half minus one of whom were to be elected from among political commissars. In Madrid, Barcelona, Valencia, Albacete and Mahón (Minorca) there would be regional committees which would in their turn elect the national *Gabinete*. The new head would be a junior cavalry officer promoted from the ranks, Antonio Fernández Gaizarín. Evidently the aim was to bring classification of officers under control. As for Díaz Tendero, he was posted to the Northern Front on 23 February 1937. The change may have been part of Largo Caballero's campaign against what he considered overmuch communist influence, for Díaz Tendero, while not a member, was in close contact with the PCE.[106] The 'default position' of Spanish communists, was, however, favourable to neutral and even conservative officers, so they could not be totally supportive of Díaz Tendero's more extreme views. Officers favoured by the PCE and the Fifth Regiment had not had difficulty in achieving posts and promotions. Yet Díaz Tendero may have been sent to the north to investigate the suspicions of disloyalty among officers there.

All through 1937 and 1938, the *Gabinete* investigated career officers and NCOs serving in the Republican Army. If their loyalty was confirmed, they were promoted to the next rank with effect from 19 July 1936.[107] Others, described as disloyal (*desafectos al Régimen*), were dismissed the service, losing their pension rights and becoming liable to trial and criminal penalties. Meanwhile, a large number of men were simply left without postings. The situation attracted the attention of the correspondent of *The Times*, who wrote on 9 January 1937: 'Apart from a few ancient dugouts, who cut rather pathetic figures, the old type of army officer has disappeared.' Given the circumstances, it was only to be expected.

105 *DO*, 8 January 1937.
106 Bolloten, *Spanish Revolution*, 277; Cordón, *Trayectoria*, 288.
107 *DO*, 13 October 1936.

Of course, most of the career officers would have happily served in the Republican Army in other circumstances, if, for example, the structure of the pre-war Army had not been destroyed by freeing the conscripts from their oath of loyalty and encouraging the conscripts to desert; but Republican Spain was in a revolutionary situation and those who were not trusted had to be kept apart.

Officers who had taken early retirement under the conditions of the Decree of 25 April 1931 were looked at suspiciously, except those who were well known to be loyal. They were judged to have retired because they did not want to serve the new Republic. This was untrue, for it was notorious that quite a number of officers of progressive views, including the communist Cordón, later Under-Secretary of War, had taken early retirement, while others whose political views were clearly monarchist and highly traditional stayed on. In most cases a decision based on personal, family and financial considerations, rather than a political view, had led to an officer applying to leave the service. A later scholar's study of judicial processes during the war concludes that 57 per cent of the officers who were investigated were declared loyal.[108] Nevertheless, this figure implies that 43 percent were of doubtful loyalty. Nor does the figure include those who escaped investigation. At the time, however, there was strong feeling that the officers were being wrongly treated. Vicente Rojo, the Chief of Staff, wrote a long letter to Prieto, Minister of National Defence, on 11 August 1937, complaining of the 'general distrust of those who have unselfishly and with self-sacrifice served loyally' ('*la general desconfianza hacia los que han prestado de manera desinteresada y abnegadamente un leal concurso*').[109]

It is certainly striking that the organisation and basic training of the new mixed brigades of the Republican Army were often entrusted to a career officer, whereas usually once the brigade was allocated to a division and became, in theory, ready for active service, command was entrusted to a militia officer.[110] Yet this may have been no more than a matter of relative ages and physical fitness for field service.

Officers were still being dismissed at the end of 1937. The Ministry of National Defence, presumably under some pressure, recognised that some of the dismissals may have been unjust, and asked those officers who had not been confirmed in their posts to come forward to do so to avoid their expulsion from the service because their whereabouts was

[108] Cervera, *Madrid en guerra: la ciudad clandestina 1936–1939*, Madrid, 1998, 154–5 and 186–7.

[109] Quoted in Martínez Paricio *et al.*, *Los papeles*, 92–3.

[110] See the useful tabulations in Carlos Engel, *Historia de las brigadas mixtas del Ejército Popular de la República*, Madrid, 1999.

unknown.[111] That an officer could be occupying a post without being confirmed in it, and then be dismissed because his existence was unrecognised, indicates to what degree traditional bureaucracy held sway.

When Antonio Cordón became Under-Secretary for War on 8 April 1938, he linked the *Gabinete* to the Personnel Section of his own office and on 14 April appointed Eleuterio Díaz Tendero, founder of the Office for Information and Control of Career Officers, as head of Personnel. Thus Cordón, as was proper for his post, had full access to officers' personal records and so did the PCE, of which Cordón was a member. One consequence of this was a complaint from the FAI later that year that first-class officers of proven loyalty were not being appropriately employed.[112]

Officers' competence

The competence of professional officers in the Republican Army is frequently decried in literature on the Spanish Civil War. Such criticism is not surprising in respect of *Guardia Civil*, *Carabineros* and artillery officers when they acted as infantry brigade or division commanders, or when lieutenants were Chiefs of Staff and sergeants commanded battalions. As always, Azaña expressed his mordant vision of the situation. Speaking of Juan Cueto, commander of a Basque militia column, he wrote: 'A *Carabinero* officer, getting on in years [he was 55], totally removed from any professional field operational training, hardly seemed appropriate for his post.' ('*Un jefe de Carabineros, ya entrado en años, apartado profesionalmente de toda instrucción de campaña, no parecía el más indicado para el caso.*')[113] However, what alternative was there? There was a severe lack of professionals in the Basque Country and in other parts of Republican territory to command companies and battalions, a lack masked only by massive promotions and appointments of sergeants and lieutenants, many of whom, in the Spanish system, were themselves promoted long-term NCOs. For example, between April and September 1938, 4,208 sergeants were promoted lieutenants (the rank of *alférez* or second-lieutenant was abolished), while 3,388 lieutenants were made up to the rank of captain.[114]

At the summit, for reasons which have been seen, few generals and senior officers had remained in the Republic's service. In 1937 the

111 *DO*, 13 December 1937.
112 Abad de Santillán, *Por qué perdimos*, 272.
113 Azaña, *Obras Completas*, IV: 752.
114 Calculated by *Nueva España*, the newspaper of the 49th Division, 12 December 1938.

Insurgents confirmed that 74 infantry colonels were in their service.[115] Of the 49 others in the 1936 list, once the killed, executed, arrested, fled and dismissed colonels have been subtracted, very few were left. In any case, the future Soviet Marshal Malinovski fustigates the 'survival of aged traditions, bureaucracy, indifference, backwardness and incapacity at the highest levels, often dominated by career officers on the active list, trained in the routine of the monarchist [that is, pre-Second Republic of 1931] army'.[116]

Lest this statement be thought pure communist propaganda, Rojo himself, who perhaps suffered more than any one the failure of Republican Army commanders to carry out his plans, writes: 'The commanders, in a word ... know how to fight from fixed positions but not how to manoeuvre' (*'se sabe combatir en posiciones pero no maniobrar'*).[117] This also helps to explain the prolix orders of Republican Staffs, observed and criticised by the Soviet advisers.[118]

Soviet criticisms, however, have to be used cautiously, because there is always a political background to them. Malinovski, for example, refers to bureaucratic mentality and incompetence of high-ranking Republican officers, but he relates it to the predominance at the highest levels of career officers 'hostile to the interests of the people'.[119] He means, of course, that more opportunities ought to have been given to militia officers. Yet, as will be seen, though a few militia officers performed extremely well, others were poor and Malinovski's implicit assumptions do not bear close analysis.

The military commanders of the Republican Army also criticised their subordinate career officers. Lieutenant-Colonel Manuel Matallana, for example, in his report on the battle of Brunete in July 1937 where he held the post of Chief of Staff of the Army of the Centre, criticised the commander of the XVIII Corps, Enrique Fernández Heredia, for failing to cooperate with his own Chief of Staff and not knowing the units under his command well. Other commanders did not know how to use the resources they had and how to coordinate artillery fire with the advance of their infantry. Consequently, Matallana recommended that every brigade, division and corps commander should undergo an advanced, specialised course.[120]

115 CGG, L93, C10. 116 Malinovski *et al.*, *BLB*, 19.
117 Rojo, *España heroica*, 95.
118 C. Liubarskii, *Nekotorie Operativno-Lakticheskie vivodi iz opita voini v Ispanii*, Moscow, 1939, quoted by Payne, *Spanish Revolution*, 347.
119 Malinovski *et al.*, *BLB*, 19.
120 These reports can be found in various places in the Republican Army archives. Reports on Brunete can be read in J. M. Martínez Bande, *La ofensiva sobre Segovia*

Insurgent reports often throw light on the subject. One professional officer who went over to the enemy wrote a report on the VIII and IX Corps of the Army of the South. In it, he remarks on the inappropriateness of giving Joaquín Pérez Salas, an artillery officer, excellent in his own field, command of an infantry corps. He was unable to cooperate with his Staff and the result was that normal military operations could not be undertaken and the distribution of his forces left much to be desired.[121]

Conclusions

The various opinions about the professional military men who served in the Republican Army can be exemplified in the memoirs of the career officer Jesús Pérez Salas and the communist militia leader Enrique Líster.

Pérez Salas, one of three brothers in the Republican Army and one who fought with Franco, had a history of conspiracy against the monarchy. For a short time he was posted to President Azaña's military household and as police chief in Barcelona. After the failed left-wing and Catalanist uprising of October 1934 he left Spain, returning with the Popular Front victory of February 1936.

His opinions, which coincide more or less with those expressed by Colonel Casado, can perhaps be considered to be those of most professional officers of generally progressive sympathies. They thought that most officers were not closely allied with the oligarchy or the Church and that their real concern was public order. The militias should not have been armed. The existing military structure could have been used, while professional officers should have been protected from political interference and treated with more respect, especially in relation to officers of the militias, together with whom a new officer corps could have been formed.

These views, however, are disputable. Even before the failed coup of General Sanjurjo in 1932, Army officers tended to be distrusted. When war came it took many months to persuade militia to accept formal militarisation. And, besides, whatever the interests of most career officers, in reality they had risen against the Government or at least joined the rebels.

y la batalla de Brunete, Madrid, 1972, documents 9–13, and in R. Casas, *Brunete*, Madrid, 1967, appendix 1. See also a contemporary description and analysis in Severiano Montero, *Brunete*, Madrid, 2009.

[121] CGG, *Estado Mayor Central*, Information Section, 30 November 1937.

The militia officer and corps commander Enrique Líster saw that there were truly loyal officers, as well as incompetent ones and others who were enemies of the Republic. Many officers simply did not understand the political nature of the war and of the new Republican Army. This was more or less true, but it is Líster's words which are doubtful. There were different ways of seeing the 'political nature' of the Civil War. The term 'Popular Army' itself will be considered later when wider aspects of communism in the army are investigated, but it may already be evident that the terms 'People's' or 'Popular' Army (the literal translation of *Ejército Popular*) are not fully applicable to it.

Criticisms of the professional competence of career officers were so frequent, and are to be found in such varied sources, that it would seem that inefficiency, caused by the great shortage of experienced officers at almost all levels, was a primary factor in the defeat of the Republican Army.

6 A new officer corps

Promotions

The grave shortage of professional army officers led the Government of the Republic to introduce a series of measures in order to provide the earliest militia columns with leaders who had a least some knowledge of military technique. Thus, in the *Diario Oficial del Ministerio de la Guerra* of 18 August, 3, 16 and 22 September and 10 October 1936, the Government promoted all sergeants and warrant officers (*brigadas*) to the next higher rank, though warning them that they would need to undergo some tests. The *brigadas* became second lieutenants or *alféreces*, and all the *alféreces* and lieutenants were promoted to the next rank. One immediate result of this was the long lists of promotions to the rank of corporal and sergeant in the paramilitary *Guardia Civil* (now renamed National Republican Guard or *Guardia Nacional Republicana*), the *Carabineros* and the *Guardia de Asalto*.[1]

On 22 September 1936 all these promotions were backdated to 19 July 1936, the day that the military uprisings had taken place in most of the peninsular garrisons. A decree of 21 October promoted all loyal officers to the next higher rank as far as colonel, though this had to be approved individually by the Information and Control Office. As has been seen, by 27 March 1937 these promotions had not all been approved, and an order was issued that all officers whom the *Gabinete de Información y Control* had labelled '*leales provisionales*', and so had not been promoted, should send in their details for their cases to be reconsidered. In fact, relatively few officers had received the complete approval of the *Gabinete*: the promotions of 50 captains, 270 lieutenants and 1,080 *alféreces* and non-commissioned officers had been announced in the *Diario Oficial* of 30 November 1936, together with a further 792 *alféreces* and NCOs on 11, 12 and 13 January 1937. The formal announcements of promotions continued into 1937 until on

[1] See, in particular, *Gaceta*, 14 September 1936.

22 October, as the new militia officers came on stream, the Ministry decided that newly promoted officers should occupy their posts for six months before actually displaying their new rank badges. Nevertheless, 'loyalty' promotions, as they were called, went on. As late as 1938, the *Diario Oficial* was continuing to list promotions, backdated to 19 July 1936, often at the same time as it was announcing a further promotion earned since then. On 3 June 1938, for example, 505 NCOs were made up to lieutenants with effect from the beginning of the war and were immediately promoted to captain.

Generals and senior officers (majors and above)

The Azaña reform of 1931–3 had abolished the rank of lieutenant-general, the most senior one in the Spanish Army,[2] leaving only the categories of general of brigade and general of division. The *Diario Oficial* of 18 February 1937 merged the two ranks, allowing the generals of brigade to wear the insignia of lieutenant-generals: three gold stars outlined in red, placed in the angles between a crossed sword and baton. However, they would be known simply as 'generals'. They would enjoy the privileges of a divisional general but only half the corresponding salary if the *Gabinete de Información y Control* did not authorise them to have command of troops. This was presumably the case with Generals San Pedro Aymat and Cavanna del Val, who were not dismissed the service but not given posts of command either. It would seem that the Prime Minister and Minister of War, Francisco Largo Caballero, accepted this measure unwillingly because later that year he complained in public that '*compañeros socialistas*', referring probably to Prieto, who held the portfolio of Air and Navy, and Negrín, later Minister of National Defence, had given a substantial annual salary increase of 4,000 pesetas to the generals of brigade.[3] The only pre-war generals of division serving in the Republican Army were La Cerda, Riquelme, Peña Abuín, García Gómez-Caminero and Masquelet. Except for the last-named, all were very close to retirement age. The unification of the ranks of general officers was a means of promoting generals of brigade for their loyalty.

Officers' salaries according to their rank remained as they had been before the war, that is 5,000 pesetas per year for a lieutenant and 22,000 for a general. Given that the pay for private soldiers was now a very high

[2] Captain-general was not a rank but an office or '*dignidad*'. Today it is reserved for the king.

[3] Peirats, *CNT*, II: 385, citing Caballero's speech in Madrid's Pardiñas cinema on 17 October 1937.

10 pesetas a day (in the Insurgent army the pay was only 50 céntimos), the income difference between the ranks was reduced considerably.

However, on 27 October 1938 the *Diario Oficial* announced that the different grades of general officer were to be reintroduced, with sizeable salary differences. Generals of brigade would receive 20,000 pesetas annually, generals of division 25,000 and the restored lieutenant-generals 30,000. The reason stated was that the army had grown. Proper consideration for military hierarchy would be needed in a later and non-revolutionary Spain. The decree signalled the end of the egalitarian trend of the heady early days of the Spanish Civil War, when generals donned workingmen's blue overalls and when Carlos Bernal, the most recently promoted general of brigade, was made equal in rank to Riquelme, who had been a general of division since 1929.

By late 1938, of course, there were many more generals. Escobar (28 June 1937), Rojo (22 October 1937) and Hernández Saravia (28 December 1937) had had the crossed sword and baton sewn on to their uniform sleeves. The major reorganisation of the Republican Army after the great disaster of April 1938, when the Republic had been split in two, brought in its wake the promotion of Leopoldo Menéndez, commander of the Army of the Levante and close friend of President Azaña. The difficult position of military professionals is exemplified in his case. The communist Under-Secretary for War, Cordón, praises him for his energy and technical capacity, yet criticises him for not understanding the nature of a people's army.[4] A CNT report, on the other hand, abuses him as a communist and adds that he should be shot ('*elemento fusilable*').[5] How can this be explained? Menéndez was respected by Cordón and other PCE-associated officers, which was enough to provoke whoever wrote the CNT report, but he did not have particular sympathies for the politically correct pieties of a 'people's' army. In March 1939 he would ally himself with the Casado coup against the communist determination to continue to resist Franco until the expected European war broke out.

Other officers promoted to general rank were Matallana, Chief of Staff of the Central Army Group, and Jurado, Head of Anti-Aircraft Defence, who were promoted in the *Diario Oficial* of 19 August 1938. Casado was made a general in 1939, but refused to accept the promotion because he rejected the legality of the Negrín Government.[6]

[4] Cordón, *Trayectoria*, 240.
[5] Peirats, *CNT*, III: 231.
[6] Casado, *Last Days of Madrid*, 149, and *DO*, 15 March 1939.

The only army commanders not raised to general rank were Moriones of the Army of Andalusia, Perea, of the Army of the East, and Prada, who had led the Army of the North after Santander fell in August 1937, the Army of Andalusia from October 1937 until April 1938, and the Army of Extremadura until Casado summoned him after his own coup to head the Army of the Centre in March 1939.

Given the politicised nature of the Republican Army, there were political considerations implicit in these promotions and in the blocking of others. Perea, for example, was very much appreciated by the anarchist divisions under his command. Ricardo Sanz, one of the early militia leaders in Barcelona and a divisional commander in the Army of the East, refers to

> his truly ennobling labour ... Thanks to him, vulgar political considerations, introduced into most of the units of the other armies, found no echo in the Army of the East, nor could they develop in the face of the wall which the new commander represented.
>
> (*su labor ... verdaderamente enaltecedora. Gracias a su actuación, las cuestiones políticas ramplonas, introducidas en la mayor parte de las unidades de los demás ejércitos, no encontraron eco en el Ejército del Este, ni pudieron desarrollarse ante el muro de contención que representaba su nuevo jefe.*)[7]

Prada was accused by anarchists of having tried to put CNT members before firing squads and to be at least a PCE sympathiser.[8] This was the information which reached Azaña, who was sufficiently wise to despise ill-informed gossip.[9] 'Prada', noted the President sarcastically, 'who is now a communist', was elected to command in the north by the Council of Asturias, over the head of the Government appointee, General Mariano Gámir Ulíbarri. Similarly, Prada was condemned for draconian severity, having executed three brigade commanders.[10] Yet Casado was sufficiently convinced that he was not a PCE sympathiser to invite him to take over Casado's own post in command of the Army of the Centre in March 1939.

Thus it would seem that Perea and Prada, two army commanders who might have expected promotion to general and did not receive it, were certainly anti-communists. Does this mean that Matallana and Jurado were pro-communists? Certainly Cordón, the communist artillery officer who was Under-Secretary for War for the last year of the conflict, considered Jurado to be honourable, energetic and resolute,

[7] Sanz, *Los que fuimos*, 258.
[8] Peirats, *CNT*, III: 105.
[9] Azaña, *Obras Completas*, IV: 784.
[10] *Ibid.*, 84.

and thus willing to continue the war after Catalonia had been lost in early 1939.[11] Julián Zugazagoitia, who for some time was Secretary to the Minister of Defence, thought that Matallana was ostensibly loyal to Negrín but secretly encouraged the Casado coup.[12] Casado also thought that Negrín was suspicious of Matallana's loyalty.[13]

Jurado's rise followed a different path. He did not command an army but, as Inspector of Anti-Aircraft Defence (*Defensa contra Aeronaves* or *DCA*), he had the same status as General Bernal, the transport chief. Bernal, however, had been a general before the war when Jurado was a mere major. Jurado's family was in the Insurgent zone, which tended to lead to suspicion. Neither of the two leading PCE militia commanders, Enrique Líster and Juan Modesto, has much good to say of Jurado, whom they saw as a very traditional officer, unable to accept the new Republican Army.[14] Yet Rojo recommended his appointment to head the Eastern Army Group. This may have been a last-minute emergency appointment following the dismissal, for unclear reasons, of Hernández Saravia.[15] Having crossed into France after the loss of Catalonia in January 1939, Jurado declined to return to Spain. Thus promotions to general rank do not seem to have had political significance.

The immediate promotion of all loyal officers was followed by a number of promotions for battlefield merit (*méritos de campaña*). In the *Diario Oficial* of 28 December 1937, which registered Hernández Saravia's promotion to general, Federico de la Iglesia, Chief of Staff of the Mobile Army or *Ejército de Maniobras*, became a colonel, as did José Fontán, Head of Operations in the Army of the Centre; Sáez Aranaz, Chief of Staff of the Army of the Levante; Menéndez, at the time commander of the XX Army Corps; Fernández Heredia, commander of the XVIII Corps; and Gallego, commander of the artillery at the battle of Teruel. On 5 May 1938, a further number of senior professional officers received battlefield promotions, among them Joaquín Pérez Salas, commander of the VIII Corps, and his brother Jesús, an ex-Under-Secretary for War, Casado, commander of the Army of Andalusia, Cordón, Under-Secretary for War, José Luis Fuentes, Inspector-General of Artillery, Gerardo Armentia, commander of artillery in the Army of Andalusia, Pérez Farrás, ex-adviser to the anarchist Durruti column, Balcázar, commander of artillery in the Army of Extremadura, Casado Veiga, who occupied the same post in the

[11] Cordón, *Trayectoria*, 470.
[12] J. Zugazagoitia, *Guerra y vicisitudes de los españoles*, Paris, 1968, II: 258.
[13] Casado, *Last Days of Madrid*, 154.
[14] Modesto, *Soy del Quinto Regimiento*, 112; Líster, *Nuestra guerra*, 110, 252.
[15] Rojo, *Alerta*, 183.

Army of the Centre, and de los Mozos, in charge of fortifications in the Eastern Army Group. All these officers, save Cordón, who had retired as a captain in 1931, had been majors when the Civil War began, with varying seniority. But the prestige of their posts demanded recognition by the appropriate rank. With the exception of Pérez Farrás, for whose promotion the CNT may have pressed, these promotions seem reasonable both from the point of view of their seniority and their important posts. Cordón's rise would be meteoric, from retired captain to general,[16] as was Rojo's, from just-promoted major to lieutenant-general, but few officers obtained more than one promotion on merit as well as their 'loyalty' one. It does not seem that the army, had the Republic triumphed, would have been exceptionally heavily loaded with generals. If those who had reached that rank are added to the 12 who were still on the active list in 1939, the total is by no means excessive, given that many of the latter were on the point of retirement. Despite this, Azaña noted in his diary on 15 August 1938: 'Rivalry and disputes about promotions; there's no end to it.' (*'Rivalidades y disputas por los ascensos. Esto no tiene remedio.'*)[17]

In later entries, the President remarked sharply about the prodigal use of promotions, especially those granted in his view to satisfy communist demands. An Air Force colonel, Riaño, had told him that there were already eight Air Force colonels though there were insufficient posts for the four already in that rank, and that the result was to create a pretext for more generals. This was not true, however, and reflects what others told Azaña. The only Air Force generals were Ignacio Hidalgo de Cisneros, head of the service, and Emilio Herrera, Director-General of Technical Aeronautical Services.[18] In that year Azaña wrote that Negrín had admitted to him that too many men were being promoted and that it would cause problems after the war. Nevertheless, despite pressure to do so, Negrín had refused to merge the seniority lists of career officers, militia officers and war-temporary officers, known as officers '*en campaña*'. As will be seen, it was rare for a militia officer to rise above the rank of major. If, counterfactually, the Republic had won the war, Azaña's predictions about the excess of officers, that burden on Spain which he had tackled so boldly in 1931, would not have come true, simply because the vast majority of career officers were on the other side and most, if not all, would have been dismissed.

[16] His was one of the last promotions, appearing in the *DO* on 26 January 1939.
[17] Azaña, *Obras Completas*, IV: 889.
[18] *DO* of 15 September and 19 August 1938.

Junior officers

A number of external changes were made, in general simplifying and abolishing ranks. On 15 September 1938, while the new mixed brigades of the Republican Army were being formed, the *Diario Oficial* published a decree abolishing the ranks of *brigada* (senior sergeant or warrant officer) and of *alférez* (second lieutenant or ensign). By mid 1936, almost all holders of the latter rank had been ex-*brigadas* and had now been granted a 'loyalty' promotion to lieutenant. It probably seemed unnecessary to maintain the abolished ranks in the new army, but the result of promoting senior non-commissioned officers to officers' rank was that the Republican Army suffered a dearth of experienced senior non-commissioned officers. This did not happen in the Insurgent army, and the difference would count. As a rule, in mass, conscripted armies war-temporary junior officers can be improvised. Consequently, as in the First World War, they tend to become casualties soon (the expectation of life for a British subaltern in 1914–18 was ten days, while the Insurgents' *alférez provisional* was grimly called '*cadáver efectivo*'). The real backbone of an army are the experienced non-commissioned officers, of whom the Republican Army had few. This led to a general inefficiency of leadership at squad and section level. In his report on the attack at La Granja (Segovia) in June 1937, José María Galán, a well-known progressive officer, reported that the junior officers were not up to the job and thus that the commanders had lost contact with their smaller units.[19] Lieutenant-Colonel Menéndez, later commander of the Army of the Levante, in conversation with Azaña about the battle of Brunete in July 1937, told the President that the officers were '*nulos*' or useless at all levels, especially the battalion commanders.[20] During the battle itself Azaña, informed by his military advisers, wrote in his diary that, given that the night approach had taken the village of Brunete from the Insurgents and that the latter were thinly spread,

> in Brunete there was nobody who understood the situation and was determined to take advantage of the unexpected ease of the advance. Nevertheless, to take advantage of the unforeseen is a definition of military skill.
>
> (*en Brunete … no hubo nadie que se diese cuenta de la situación y resolviese aprovechar la improvista facilidad del avance. Sin embargo, en esto consiste el talento militar: en sacar parte de lo imprevisto.*)[21]

19 DR, L669, C3, quoted by Martínez Bande, *Brunete*, document 1.
20 Azaña, *Obras Completas*, IV: 712–13.
21 *Ibid.*, 691.

Rojo wrote to his personal friend Manuel Matallana, who was on the Staff of the Army of the Centre, summarising the position with military brevity:

> [T]his is the problem always with our advances. The troops lose élan ... they move forward indecisively ... I blame it on the lack of initiative among the officers, who can ... fulfil the first part of their task ... but when they are on their own in the field and they have to take decisions ... using their initiative, they seem to have nothing in reserve and they lack self-confidence.

> (*[S]e ha producido el problema de siempre en nuestras ofensivas, y es que la gente se desinfla ... hay poca decisión en el momento de echarse adelante ... lo achaco a la falta de iniciativa de los mandos que son capaces de ... desarrollar con acierto la primera parte de las papeletas ... pero cuando llegan a verse solos en el campo y al tener que actuar ... haciendo uso de su iniciativa, se les nota que no tienen nada dentro y carecen de confianza en sí mismos.*)[22]

A report from the commissar-general on the battle of Teruel, which lasted from November 1937 until February 1938, and in which the Republican Army occupied the city, only to lose it finally to an Insurgent counter-offensive, also bemoaned the shortage of capable officers.[23]

Such reports had become commonplace and may be exemplified in comments by the Chief of Staff, Vicente Rojo, who complains that incorrect information was sent back to Staffs.[24] He orders that careless talk must be stopped, orders must be obeyed, there must be confidence in the General Staff and less reliance on outdated ideas about an unbroken line and protection of the flanks. Officers must stay close to their units, retain the smallest possible number of troops in the front line, together with many other recommendations which were so basic that any officer would be expected to obey them without needing a reminder. A week after this circular letter had been sent out, a senior officer in the Army of the Levante wrote the following minute of a Staff meeting. Severe sanctions would be imposed on officers for 'lack of enthusiasm, abandoning one's post, avoiding danger, feigning illness, pessimism, disrespect for seniors and political favouritism' ('*falta de entusiasmo, abandono del puesto, evitar el peligro, fingir enfermedad, pesimismo, falta de respeto por los jefes, y parcialidad política*').[25]

Lastly, and at a lower level, a brigade circular, typical of many, instructed officers not to complain about their pay or ranks, to write

[22] Quoted by J. Martínez Reverte, *La batalla del Ebro*, Barcelona, 2003, 151.

[23] DR, L481, C4.

[24] V. Rojo, '*Instrucciones generales para el desarrollo de la maniobra ofensiva de conjunto*' ('General instructions for the development of joint offensive action'), 21 September 1937.

[25] DR, L462, C1.

honest and unambiguous reports and to be punctual.[26] All theses criticisms referred to career officers and promoted NCOs.

Militia officers

It became apparent very shortly after the outset that promoting professional soldiers would not solve the problem of officering the new army, especially considering how the NCOs and officers of the pre-war Army had been decimated. Consequently Caballero, presumably advised by Asensio Torrado and his new General Staff, signed a decree in the *Gaceta* of 16 September 1936 containing instructions about the training of officers *de complemento*, that is men with higher education and who had completed a very short period of compulsory military service pre-war, sometimes living at home and coming to barracks for half a day. These men were then commissioned as 'complementary' to their regiments or other Arms when required. They would then undergo a two-week course and become full officers. Likewise professional NCOs who had joined a paramilitary force after leaving the Army could take a 25-days course and be commissioned as subalterns. Men with degrees in science, engineering students and men holding the baccalaureate could also become officers after short courses. Broadly speaking, this is what would be done in any rapidly assembled mass army. Yet, only three weeks later, on 5 October 1936, the *Gaceta* issued a decree contradicting the assumptions of the decree of 16 September, beginning, 'Since the recruitment of officers according to the decree of … is not urgent …' ('*No siendo de urgente necesidad el reclutamiento de la oficialidad dispuesto por el decreto* …'). How could this be, given that the new mixed brigades were in the process of being formed and the *Gabinete de Información y Control* was underlining the shortage of officers and specifically recommending short courses to provide them?[27] One of the reasons for the change of policy may have been the hostility of the militias towards officers of higher social classes or 'young gentlemen' ('*señoritos*') emerging from short courses. Reserve and retired officers also seem to have been resented, unless they were known progressives, such as Francisco Galán, whose reinstatement was praised officially in the *Gaceta* of 23 September, which said that Galán 'was fighting for the people with loyalty and enthusiasm ' ('*con lealtad y entusiasmo lucha por las libertades del pueblo*').

[26] 42nd Mixed Brigade, *Instrucciones Generales para oficiales*, n.p., n.d.
[27] DR, L477, C6.

Within a week of the insurrection all retired officers under 65 had been authorised to re-enter the Army, but few seem to have done so.[28] Many secondary sources recall the incapacity of these men and of the reserve officers. Here is one example:

> This artillery group was commanded by a reserve lieutenant, already getting on in years and almost illiterate. The war had brought him promotion to major ... This was the general rule for all the '*patatas*' [long-service NCOs promoted to officer rank]. He knew how to order 'Fire!' 'Cease fire!' 'Clean the barrel!', and with this and the occasional curse, like a carter, he did his duty.[29]

Far more important was the increasing number and the influence of the militia officers. Generally speaking, they had acquired their authority because they had founded and recruited the columns, because they had been trade union leaders or, in the communist case, because they had been selected and trained previously by the political party or group which had identified their leadership potential.

When the militias had been militarised by *Gaceta* decree in September 1936 all militia NCOs and officers were formally appointed officers. The NCOs were invited to apply to be included in the official Army Lists. However, a few months later, the War Ministry complained that of 1,412 cases considered, 1,042 had not sent in their full details. Therefore a new order allowed all militia officers to enter the Army. Their details would be examined later. Existing ranks were respected, but the militia officers would be listed after the professional officers. There would be a permanent office in the Personnel Section of the Ministry whose task it would be to decide which men would be allowed to remain in the service after the war. It does seem that the concern of the Ministry was about who would have the privilege of remaining in the Army and with what status, rather than the immediate one of how to overcome the insurrection.

It is not surprising that Ministry functionaries had difficulty in checking the details of militia officers. Appointments and promotions had been made as required, and almost literally 'on the march'. Vittorio Vidali, alias 'Carlos Contreras', commissar of the Fifth Regiment, told the American journalist Anna Louise Strong that anybody who seemed intelligent was made an officer.[30] The official history of the PCE in the

[28] Salas Larrazábal, 'The Role and Growth', 162, calculates that there were about 1,500 retired officers in the Republican Army. This figure should be considered a maximum and may very well include retired NCOs. Specifically in the North, very few presented themselves for reinstatement (DR, L853, C3, and Arrarás, *Cruzada*, XXVI: 261, on San Sebastián).

[29] Bazal, *¡Ay de los vencidos!*, 163.

[30] Anna L. Strong, *Spain at Arms*, New York, 1937, 41.

Civil War states: 'Not infrequently they went to war as sergeants and returned as majors.' ('*No pocas veces iban al combate con el grado de sargentos y regresaban como comandantes.*')[31] Enrique Líster recalls that Colonel Asensio himself pinned the eight-pointed star of a major on his tunic on 20 August 1936 after a successful attack in the Sierra de Guadarrama to the north of Madrid.[32] There was pressure from the political parties and the powerful unions which formed the militias that their officers should have parity with promoted NCOs and officers of the active and reserve lists of the Army. Indeed, considerable administrative chaos was caused by military personnel serving in the militia with higher ranks than their substantive military ones. For example, Santiago Aguado Calvo, a professional *brigada* or warrant officer of *Carabineros*, became commander of the 100th Mixed Brigade with the rank of major. While the Provisional Army List for the Army in 1938 was being compiled (see below) the Ministry insisted that these men opt for the militia, with higher ranks but no guarantee that they would return to their substantive army rank after the war. Alternatively, they should opt to return to the Army List, with their 'loyalty' promotion and perhaps one more if the *Gabinete de Información y Control* approved.[33]

Senior militia officers

Major or *comandante* (changed to *mayor* in the decree of 30 November 1936) was the highest rank to which militia officers could aspire. It corresponded to the senior major in a traditional battalion. The academy-trained career officers did not want any militiaman to be able to reach a higher rank; even so, by November 1936 some militiamen were in command of the new mixed brigades and it would not be long before some were leading divisions. Since there would be a severe shortage of academy-trained officers after the war, militia officers would, it was thought, want to make a full-time career in the Army. Nevertheless, admitting such officers at high ranks would cause chaos in the carefully regulated promotions system. In its context, the issue was related to the matter of battlefield merit promotions which had caused such recriminations in the 1920s, had led to the phenomenon of the *Juntas de Defensa* of 1917, the problems with artillery officers that had faced Primo de Rivera and the discontent under Azaña. The Insurgents did not have this problem because their militia officers became only

[31] Ibárruri *et al.*, *Guerra y Revolución*, II: 185.
[32] In *Milicia Popular*, 4 September 1936.
[33] *DO*, 25 May 1937.

temporary *alféreces*, while their academy-trained officers were assigned higher *pro tempore* ranks or '*estampillados*' but only for the duration of the war.

However, at the end of 1937, with the growth of the Republican Army and the dismissal of such a vast number of career officers, militia officers often found themselves commanding brigades, sometimes divisions and even army corps. So, despite the objections of the military hierarchy, a decree appeared on 5 January 1938 preceded by a preamble referring to another of February 1937 which had restricted militia officers to the rank of major, and stating:

Such a limitation does not seem just, though measures should be adopted which, while relaxing this limitation, will prevent access to the highest posts in the army of those who have not displayed their military skill, together with personal valour on the battlefield.

(*No parece justa una limitación tan rígida, si bien procede adoptar medidas que, al levantar ese tope, impidan el acceso a los altos cargos del ejército a quienes no han probado en el campo de batalla una suficiencia militar, que se acredita conjuntamente por el valor personal.*)[34]

The meaning of these lines may be weighed by the negative nature of the expression, which contained not the slightest reference to the achievements of militia officers. A promotion would be allowed grudgingly only to those of proven ability in the field of battle. The detailed regulations insisted that such promotions above major for militia officers were to be granted only by Cabinet decree on the proposal of the Minister of National Defence, at the time the socialist Indalecio Prieto. The decision to concede such promotions to outstanding militia officers was taken under pressure, as Prieto indicated to the PSOE after his dismissal. Prieto was convinced that the communists, who wanted promotions for their leading militia officers, were plotting against him.[35]

As was to be expected, Líster was the first to be promoted to the rank of lieutenant-colonel. His promotion appeared in the same number of the *Diario Oficial* as the decree authorising such promotions. The announcement specifically mentioned his achievements during the battle for Teruel. However, Líster had refused to obey the orders of his superior, Lieutenant-Colonel Ibarrola, to send some of his units back to the city on the true grounds that they were badly knocked about. Yet

[34] *DO*, 5 January, 1938.

[35] Prieto, *Cómo y por qué*, *passim*. See on the opposite side Fischer, *Men and Politics*, 431, in whose opinion Prieto did not want to promote Líster and Modesto because of 'regulations'.

Rojo, the Chief of Staff, proposed his promotion in recognition of his record and as an encouragement.[36]

That politics entered into the thorny question of whom to promote is evident, for the first four promotions of militia officers were carefully balanced between communists and anarchists. After Líster came the turn of Cipriano Mera, commander of the IV Corps, who had been recommended for promotion after the triumph against Franco's Italian fascist allies at Guadalajara in March 1937.[37] Next came Antonio Beltrán, a protégé of Prieto's who was in command of the 43rd Division and described as an 'independent anarchist'.[38] Buenaventuri Durruti, the most famous of the anarchist column leaders, killed in Madrid in November 1936, was promoted posthumously.[39] In the *Diario Oficial* of 5 May 1938, promotions were granted also to Juan Modesto, Valentín González ('El Campesino'), Gustavo Durán, Nilamón Toral, José del Barrio and Manuel Tagüeña, all communists, to the anarchists Gregorio Jover and García Vivancos, to Recalde, commander of the 19th Division, and to Juan José Gallego Pérez, who, though previously an NCO and thus a professional, was still on the militia officers list.

In September 1938, 13 more such promotions were announced. The best-known militia leaders among them were Pedro Martínez Cartón, the parliamentary deputy whose 16th Mixed Brigade had occupied the Insurgent strongpoint of Santa María de la Cabeza, Manuel Cristóbal Errandonea, who had shown his capacity in the defence of San Sebastián, and Daniel Ortega, the communist deputy for Cadiz and Head of Services in Madrid. All three were communists.[40] Of CNT militia commanders, only Ricardo Sanz of the 26th Division (ex-Durruti column) and Victoriano Castán, of the 118th Brigade of the 25th Division (ex-Ortiz column), received promotion.[41] There was evidently an interval of months between the promotion of Líster and the others, which might have arisen from the unwillingness of ministers to agree to the proposals, though it may well have been a result of the pressure of other business, since the *Diario Oficial* published a decree on 24 April 1938

[36] Documents about Líster's refusal to obey orders are in DR, L1064, C2. See Salas Larrazábal, *Historia del Ejército Popular*, 1654ff., where the teletype exchanges between Rojo and Prieto are reproduced. For Líster's self-defence, see Líster, *Nuestra guerra*, 179.

[37] DR, L461, C9, cable from the Army of the Centre. The government was sympathetic but replied that the regulations did not allow such a promotion.

[38] Indalecio Prieto, *Convulsiones de España*, Mexico City [1942], 1968, 202ff.

[39] Mera, Beltrán and Durruti were promoted in the *Diari Oficial* of 29 April 1938. See Appendix 4.

[40] DR, L969, C14.

[41] *DO*, 13 August 1938 and 2 September 1938.

relaxing the regulation so that promotions could be granted by a mere ministerial Order approved by the Cabinet later. This may explain the bunching of posterior promotions.

If these 27 promotions of militia officers are compared with the 74 promotions of professional officers made in the Republican Army between April and September 1938, it becomes obvious that Prieto's departure from the Ministry of Defence in April 1938 did not give any real satisfaction to those who wanted the militia officers' role to be generously recognised. For example, no promotions were granted to the communists Ascanio and Vicente Pertegás, divisional commanders in the Army of the Centre, or to the communists who ran the Staff of the Army of the Ebro.

Militiamen could now be promoted up to the rank of lieutenant-colonel. Apart from the promotions published on 3 March 1939,[42] raising Modesto and Líster to the ranks of general and colonel, the only promotion above lieutenant-colonel was that of Juan Modesto, who was raised to colonel during the battle of the Ebro.[43]

Promotions of militia officers and their confirmation in their commands were negotiated through an organisation, announced by the *Diario Oficial* on 23 September 1937, called the *Comisión revisora de empleos de los oficiales de milicias* or Review Committee for Ranks of Militia Officers. Evidently this would be a slow bureaucratic process, which explains the large number of officers in command posts who were not on the professional active list but are not described as militia, either. For some time, this committee was chaired by Jesús Pérez Salas, after he left the command of the 30th Division following the battle of Belchite in August 1937 to join the Under-Secretariat of the Ministry of Defence, where he became Under-Secretary on 27 March 1938.[44] Pérez Salas, however, complains that the committee was actually run by a communist militia officer who favoured officers who held the membership card of the PCE, but whom he fails to name.[45] Given the particular circumstances of the Spanish Civil War, the appointment of Pérez Salas, a professional officer attacked by the anarchists[46] despite his strongly anti-communist stance, was an error, especially because he was preoccupied by the position of professional officers after the war,

42 *DO*, 3 and 4 March referred to in the *DO* of 15 March 1939.

43 *DO*, 26 August 1938, backdated to 25 July (opening of the Ebro offensive).

44 DR, L461, C8. The Minister, Prieto, announced the appointment of Pérez Salas in a circular with a lengthy justification which asked for all to cooperate with this officer, who may be assumed to have been unpopular.

45 Pérez Salas, *Guerra en España*, 162ff.

46 Peirats, *CNT*, III: 103, speaks of his 'well-known incapacity and lack of confidence' ('*conocida incapacidad y falta de confianza*').

an anxiety which may have hidden from him the seriousness of what was happening during the war.

By virtue of his post in the Ministry, Pérez Salas also sat on the committee which appointed commanders (the *Junta de Mandos*), together with Rojo, the previous Under-Secretary Fernández Bolaños and a co-opted member. This committee appointed brigade, division and army corps commanders, while the Personnel Section confirmed the other commanders and made promotion recommendations. Although he could not complain of the presence of communists, as he would frequently do in the book which he published in exile, Pérez Salas clashed with Rojo about the promotions of militia officers and the holding back, as he saw it, of the careers of professionals like himself, and that Rojo, as Chief of Staff, acted imperiously.[47] There is no proof of this and while Rojo certainly admired the military performance of the leading militia officers (see below) and was not very impressed by that of many career men, he would surely have done all he could to use every trained officer who was capable of leading units.

Some militia leaders

The figure of Juan Guilloto León, known as 'Modesto', is outstanding. He was not only the highest-ranking militia officer, a colonel from 25 July 1938 and a general from the beginning of the last month of the war, but is rarely if ever criticised in memoir literature. Rojo himself, the Chief of Staff, was greatly impressed by him. In February 1938, during the battle of Teruel, he wrote of Modesto to the Minister of Defence, 'he inspires great confidence in me' ('*me inspira gran confianza*').[48]

Three days later, 22 February, he was writing again about Modesto's qualities. He was

> truly admirable for his activity and the skill which he has shown in handling his units, since the collapse which we have seen here has been completely halted in his sector. Since he has taken over command, total order has been restored within the difficulties inherent in the tactical situation which he had to resolve.
>
> (*verdaderamente admirable por su actividad y por el acierto que ha tenido en el manejo de las unidades, ya que la descomposición que aquí había ha sido perfectamente contenida y en su frente, desde que vino al mando, los acontecimientos se han sucedido con el mayor orden dentro de las dificultades inherentes a la situación táctica que tenía que resolver.*)[49]

[47] Pérez Salas, *Guerra en España*, 186.
[48] DR, L461, C6. [49] *Ibid.*

Modesto had previously distinguished himself in the eyes of Rojo in an attack on the Cerro de los Angeles, a tactically important hill south of Madrid,[50] and, referring to the fighting retreat through Catalonia in 1939, Rojo writes that Modesto was both confident and calm.[51]

Modesto rose rapidly, as he had done in the PCE, which he joined in 1930 at the age of 24.[52] After three years in his native province of Cadiz he was summoned to Madrid and then selected to attend a course in Moscow on Marxist theory. Given that he had not even completed primary school, this is an indication of his perceived abilities. He was not obliged to leave Spain, as was Líster, for political reasons, or others who spent some time in the Soviet Union before the Spanish Civil War. When Modesto returned to Spain in 1936 he was made responsible for the MAOC, the Workers' and Peasants' Antifascist Militias. His military career in the war began on 27 July 1936 when he left for the sierra north of Madrid at the head of a group to repel General Mola's advance on the city from Pamplona, Burgos and other garrison cities of Old Castile.

He recalls that he was soon discussing military matters on equal terms with professionals. From then onwards he was the first militia officer to receive a promotion or command of a larger unit. He was made an unofficial major when commanding the battalion whose members had decided to name it after the German anti-Nazi Thaelman. Even so, there is no indication that his militia were any more successful than others. When Enrique Líster was given command of the 1st Mixed Brigade of the Republican Army, Modesto took over the *Quinto Regimiento.*

His next move up was to be named to command one of the divisions formed on the Madrid Front in the winter of 1936–7. In contrast to other militia commanders who in the memoirs tend to forget to mention their professional Chiefs of Staff, Modesto praises Major Federico de la Iglesia, his Chief of Staff in the 4th Division. At the battle of the Jarama River, in February 1937, he commanded a much augmented 4th Division. When the V Corps was formed as the nucleus of a mobile army in March 1937, Modesto was given command. To command an army corps which included divisions under other well-known

[50] Rojo, *Madrid*, 120.

[51] Rojo, *Alerta*, 169. JPA, an officer on Rojo's Staff, who knew all the principal commanders of the Army of the Ebro (which Modesto commanded), confirmed that Rojo thought highly of Modesto, underlining that Modesto's abilities were considered high not only for a militia officer but also in comparison with the professionals (conversation in Madrid, 9 November 1971).

[52] Personal details from Modesto's autobiography, *Soy del Quinto Regimiento.*

communist militia commanders gave the tone for the sort of command he would exercise. For example, in May 1937, Líster's 11th Division, part of Modesto's V Corps, was ordered to take the Cerro del Aguila, an artillery observation point overlooking Madrid. The attack was disastrous but while Líster recounts that he retired his troops and challenged General Miaja, who was in overall command, to dismiss him, Modesto recalls that he 'persuaded' Miaja to suspend the attack.[53] If these accounts are true, they show that Modesto was a leader capable of exercising influence on his superiors.

The next step in Modesto's military career was the battle of Brunete in July 1937, where he led a powerful force, the V Corps, consisting of the 11th, 35th (International) and 46th Divisions, as well as a cavalry regiment, 12 artillery batteries and 30 tanks.[54] This was a major part of the main thrust of the operation. The criticisms made by Matallana, Chief of Staff of the Army of the Centre, were limited here to suggesting that more attention should have been paid to the flanks, but in general the action was successful.[55] Modesto himself comments that the V Corps and the XVIII, which received most of the adverse criticism, had acted with insufficient coordination.[56] It was true that the leadership of Valentín Gonzalez ('El Campesino') and his 46th Division left much to be desired, since his tactics consisted of furious frontal attacks with great losses in an attempt to take the village of Quijorna.[57] The commander of the 35th Division (the Polish General 'Walter') also wrote a report on the deficiencies of the training of his own division, which the battle showed up. Líster, commander of the 11th, the other division in Modesto's V Corps, restricts himself to praising his men, which was appropriate, and, without criticising Modesto, blames the higher commanders for not taking advantage of the initial gains.[58] Leopoldo Menéndez reported to Azaña that 'El Campesino' and Líster hated each other, and completed his scornful description of the militia commanders by saying that, while Modesto at least could read a military map, 'El Campesino' not only could not read the map but saw no need to do so and used his as a tablecloth.[59] Modesto had given indications of a high level of military competence, while 'El Campesino' had not

53 Líster, *Nuestra guerra*, 122; Modesto, *Soy del Quinto Regimiento*, 95.
54 DR, L482, C1, cited in Martínez Bande, *Brunete*, document 4.
55 DR, L669, C3.
56 Modesto, *Soy del Quinto Regimiento*, 105.
57 See, for example, several reports quoted by Casas de la Vega, *Brunete*, Madrid, 1967, in his appendices. See also Montero, *Brunete*, on Brunete.
58 Líster, *Nuestra guerra*, 145.
59 Azaña, *Obras Completas*, IV: 712–13.

overcome the faith in crude attacks and military ignorance more typical of the earliest days of the militia. The disdain which the highly trained artillery officer Menéndez felt for the militia commanders was transmitted and appears in Azaña's diaries in a paternalist tone which more than anything else reflects the corporative attitude of Spanish officers, alarmed at the threat of militia officers reaching the top of the military tree, in the same way that they had resisted the concession of battlefield merit promotions over seniority.

Modesto's V Corps, reinforced with tanks, artillery, armoured cars and other arms so that it became a small army, took part in the battle of Belchite which began on 24 August 1937. The V Corps took the town of Belchite but there was a complete lack of follow-through. The lower-ranking officers were blamed for this, as Prieto told Azaña,[60] while, writing years later, Antonio Cordón, Chief of Staff to General Pozas, who had overall responsibility for the operation, blamed the failure on the absence of a supreme commander who would have been able to launch supporting offensives on other fronts.[61]

Modesto was briefly in command in the battle of Teruel, which was taken by Republican Army forces on 8 January 1938, although the 11th, his best division, was attached to another corps. His other division, 'El Campesino's' 46th, was implicated in the withdrawal from the city, which led to a major scandal. 'El Campesino' himself accused Modesto of abandoning his troops.[62] Modesto himself avers that 'El Campesino' was a coward who evacuated Teruel against his express orders and when the 46th Division was in no immediate danger.[63] However, the conflict between 'El Campesino' and the other senior communist militia commanders had deeper roots and was connected with the former's violent antipathy towards Líster. It would reach its peak during the battle of the Ebro, when Líster, now with a higher rank and commanding a corps, sacked 'El Campesino' for cowardice.[64] In the case of Teruel, however, a study of the documents suggests that the situation there was not completely understood even by the Chief of Staff, Rojo himself. The 46th Division suffered great losses. Enemy reports said it had fought valiantly.[65] Furthermore, on 14 April 1938, presumably after an exhaustive investigation, 'El Campesino' was decorated with the Medal of Valour of the Republic, despite the two accusations of cowardice. Prieto, the

60 *Ibid.*, 759. 61 Cordón, *Trayectoria*, 362ff.
62 Valentín González, *Comunista en España*, Mexico City, 1952, 24.
63 Modesto, *Soy del Quinto Regimiento*, 150–1.
64 Líster, *Nuestra guerra*, 224.
65 CGG, L285, C36.

Minister of National Defence, writing to the Chief of Staff, Vicente Rojo, declares that 'El Campesino' was a liar and that he had not had to fight his way out of Teruel at all, a statement clearly contradicted by an Insurgent report of 26 February 1938, which states, 'the encirclement completed by our troops caused this unit a bloodletting so serious that it practically disappeared for good' (*'el copo que nuestras fuerzas hicieron al entrar en Teruel ocasionó a esta unidad una sangría tal que a poco desaparece para siempre'*).[66] Nevertheless, 'El Campesino's' disgrace and imprisonment in the USSR after the war tends to discredit anything that Modesto wrote about him later.

On 16 April 1938, following a reorganisation impelled by the disastrous retreats of March, Modesto was given command of the Independent Ebro Group (*Agrupación Autónoma del Ebro*) which on 30 May 1938 became the Army of the Ebro. It included three corps, the V, XV and later the XII. It is significant that Modesto insists that he appointed his divisional commanders personally.[67] This independence is confirmed, in a hostile tone, by the anarchist Ricardo Sanz, commander of the 26th Division:

> The arrogance of this army had reached such a degree, that its leaders refused to accept orders from their immediate superiors in the military chain of command ... Commanders were dismissed and appointed dispensing completely with military rules and procedures.
>
> (*Había llegado a un estado tal el engreimiento de los componentes de este ejército, que sus principales jefes se negaban a recibir órdenes de sus inmediatos superiores dentro de la jerarquía militar ... prescendiendo en absoluto de los trámites y normas militares.*)[68]

There is no doubt that Modesto's leadership of the Army of the Ebro in the battle of that name, which lasted from late July until early November 1938, was highly competent. 'Modesto has conducted himself extraordinarily well and once more shown proof of his extraordinary qualities' (*'Modesto se ha portado extraordinariamente bien, dando una vez más pruebas de sus excelentes condiciones'*), wrote Rojo to his friend Manuel Matallana in Madrid.[69] The secrecy of the operation, the night crossing of the river, the rapid advance and the leadership of an army which at times during the battle included 11 divisions, on the part of a man of 32 helped by a Staff where only the chief was a professional officer

[66] Republican references in DR, L471, C6 and L482, C3; Insurgent references in CGG, L285, C36.
[67] Modesto, *Soy del Quinto Regimiento*, 170.
[68] Sanz, *Los que fuimos a Madrid*, 237.
[69] Letter from Rojo to Matallana, quoted by Martínez Reverte, *Batalla del Ebro*.

and whose heads of artillery and engineers were either low-ranking officers or promoted NCOs, demonstrate great administrative, organisational and inspirational ability. Modesto's own opinion was that despite the obvious problems caused by the lack of appropriate air cover for the essential pontoon bridges over the Ebro, the 'political and moral preparation', that is to say the psychological preparation of the troops, made up for the deficiencies of armaments.[70] The most serious mistakes were more of a strategic than a tactical nature. There should have been diversionary attacks and guerrilla activities that would have prevented the Insurgents bringing such an overwhelming force from other fronts. Modesto's final achievement was to bring back his army to the north bank of the Ebro without panic and without the loss of large quantities of war material.[71]

Modesto was at the head of his army during the battle of Catalonia, from 24 December 1938 until early February 1939, when he led it over the French frontier. Tagüeña, commander of the XV Corps, recalls that Modesto was the last to cross into France.[72]

Communist policy was to fight to the end to defend Madrid and the remainder of Republican territory. Modesto flew back to Republican Spain from France on 14 February. On 3 March an order in the *Diario Oficial* promoted him to the rank of general. Colonel Casado, the principal figure in Republican Spain from his uprising on March 5, claims to have seen Modesto's appointment to command the Army of the Centre (see below).[73]

Evidently the communist leaders did not think there was any point in attacking Casado, whose forces had defeated communist-led units of the Army of the Centre, in a minor but bloody civil war in the capital. They remained in Elda (Alicante), where Negrín was living.[74] The party decided that the successful Casado coup had done away with any possibility of continuing resistance to Franco. Thus the PCE leaders ought to use the time and means at their disposal to organise the departure from Spain of those who faced the greatest peril if captured.

70 Modesto, *Soy del Quinto Regimiento*, 245–6.

71 See the valuable study of L. M. Mezquida, *La batalla del Ebro*, 3 vols., Tarragona, 1963–70. The recovery of the material was confirmed in a report to a Cabinet meeting noted by Azaña in his diary, *Obras Completas*, IV: 893.

72 Personal communication from Tagüeña to the author, 28 November 1970.

73 The decree, assuming Negrín signed it, did not appear. See Salas Larrazábal, *Historia del Ejército Popular*, 2332–4, who discusses the complex issues of appointments and promotions made at this stage by Negrín. Casado's version is in his later book, *Así cayó Madrid*, Madrid, 1968.

74 For a rather cynical description of the PCE leaders in Elda see E. Castro Delgado, *Hombres 'Made in Moscú'*, Barcelona, 1965, 650–3.

Modesto went to the Soviet Union, where he was enrolled in the Frunze military academy with the rank of *kombrig* or brigade commander, higher than the other Spanish militia leaders. He took no active part in the Second World War. Towards the end of the war he was attached to the new Polish Army and, in 1945, left for France, where he headed the *Agrupación de Antiguos Oficiales Republicanos* (Association of Ex-officers of the Republic), but took no part in the guerrilla war launched against Franco Spain from France in 1946. He died in Prague in 1969.

The youngest of the militia leaders was Manuel Tagüeña Lacorte, born in 1913. He was 23 when the war began and 26 when it ended. In contrast to the working-class Líster and Modesto, he came from a middle-class background, though this seems not to have had any effect on his military career, except that he was able to select fellow university science students to head his Staff. When the war began, Tagüeña was preparing his doctorate in physics and teaching as an assistant professor at Madrid University.[75] His political activity had begun early. By 1930 he was active in the students' union, the *Federación Universitaria Española*. Two years later he was a member of the Communist Youth. After being implicated in the unsuccessful attempted coup in Madrid in October 1934 he thought he had avoided court martial by luck. Nevertheless, reports on his political activities prevented him acquiring the rank of *alférez de complemento* or reserve lieutenant to which his educational level entitled him. However, his period of military service was shortened because his mother was a *maestra nacional* and a widow and he was able to pay the fee required. His military knowledge was thus very poor, much less that that of Modesto, who had served with the *Regulares* in Morocco, and of Líster, who had received some training in Russia. In the year before war broke out he spent time organising the militia of the United Socialist and Communist Youth.

After taking part in the crushing of the military insurrection in the Carabanchel depot near Madrid and the earliest skirmishes in the sierra, he received his first appointment as adjutant to the Italian political exile Fernando de Rosa, who commanded the militia battalion *Octubre No. 3*. This battalion claimed pay for 260 men in July 1936, but by September it had recruited 2,827.[76] When de Rosa was killed in August 1936, Tagüeña took his place with the rank of major. The battalion continued to grow and at the beginning of 1937 had 16 companies. It was

[75] Information from Tagüeña's *Testimonio* and his letters to me before his premature death.

[76] DR, L1335.

then militarised as the 30th Mixed Brigade, which Manuel Tagüeña continued to lead for several months, aided by the Chief of Staff, lieutenant of *Carabineros* Alejandro Veramendi, who went on to be Head of Services on the Staff of the I Corps.

On 1 August 1937, Tagüeña took over command of the 3rd Division, relieving a career officer. This division remained in training as part of the I Corps of the Army of the Centre and did not take part in the battles of Brunete and Teruel. When the Insurgents broke through the Aragon Front in March 1938, Tagüeña was sent with his division to the Eastern Front, and in one of his letters he mentions a Russian source who praises his excellent logistics. At the suggestion of Modesto and with the approval of Rojo, Tagüeña was given command of the reconstituted XV Army Corps on 15 April 1938.[77]

The Chief of Staff of one of the divisions in the XV Corps recalls that the very young Tagüeña enjoyed growing prestige, as did his divisional commanders, who had considerable latitude.[78] The XV Corps played a vital part in the battle of the Ebro and the fighting retreat through Catalonia. There are indications that Tagüeña, perhaps trying to justify his command despite his youth, acted very harshly, ordering the execution of deserters when the Army of the Ebro was about to cross into France.[79] Order no. 44 of XV Corps contains threats of execution for officers who retreated.[80] Such orders were instituted in the Army of the Ebro. Tagüeña said in later correspondence that threats of execution for retreating without orders were frequently made but rarely carried out, though there were several cases during the Ebro battle itself.

One of the very rare instances of a report from a British officer comments that Tagüeña was 'a most courteous gentleman', though young for the responsibilities he bore as an army corps commander. Later, the same British officer, Brigadier Molesworth, member of the Control Commission for overseeing the departure of foreign volunteers in Spain, said that discipline was scant, salutes rare and that the uniforms and footwear of Republican troops were in bad condition.[81]

[77] Modesto, *Soy del Quinto Regimiento*, 167.

[78] Henríquez Caubín, *La batalla*, 109.

[79] Information from JPA, who was on the General Staff.

[80] Henríquez Caubín, *La batalla*, appendix.

[81] FO 371, W16462/84/81 of 14 December 1938. This and other comments from British officers are less informative than might be hoped from a senior officer who had facilities to undertake a more penetrating analysis of the Army Group East. But one does not find such reports in Great Britain, where more searching observations are found in reports by journalists, sometimes revised by a military expert. Articles in specialised military and regimental journals show no more than a patronising and superficial interest in the Spanish Civil War and none in the particular problems of the Republican Army.

Tagüeña's XV Corps was the last to cross the French frontier. Tagüeña, with Modesto, the political commissars and the Staff of the Army of the Ebro, left Spain on 9 February 1939. He returned to Spain by air with other leaders five days later, but he was given no command, though Colonel Casado assured his readers that Negrín intended to give him charge of the vital evacuation port of Alicante. Other communists were put in command of Alicante (Etelvino Vega) and Cartagena (Francisco Galán).

Finally, Tagüeña left Spain once more for France. He spent the Second World War in the USSR as a student and then instructor at the Frunze military academy, which indicates his capacity. In 1946 he was sent to Yugoslavia, where his sympathy for Tito in the latter's dispute with the Soviets led the PCE to send him to Czechoslovakia. There he was separated from fellow Spaniards and occupied himself with university studies. He was interrogated but writes, 'I shall never know in how much danger I really was.' The result was that he left the PCE. Reaching Mexico in 1955 he worked as a technical adviser for pharmaceutical companies and in research until his death in 1971.

The best-known anarchist commander was Cipriano Mera Sanz, who at 40 was already much older than most other militia leaders. A stonemason by trade, he led the building workers in Madrid and, when the war began he was in prison for his activities. He became the political officer for the del Rosal column. His anarchist-based antimilitarism, according to the anarchist sub-commissar-general Miguel González Inestal, once reduced the career officer del Rosal to impotent tears of rage. However, although Mera once told a senior general that he obeyed only the orders of the CNT, on 17 December 1936 he was telling the noted anarchist leader Buenaventura Durruti that self-discipline was not enough and that discipline had to be imposed *manu militari*.[82] Mera in a sense discovered his military capacity when taking part in the crushing of the Insurgent military of the garrisons of Alcalá de Henares and Guadalajara, and in a lightning if unsuccessful attack on Teruel.[83]

Mera's abilities were recognised by his appointment, proposed by the CNT and confirmed by General Miaja, to lead the CNT column in the Pozuelo sector during the battle of Madrid in November 1936.[84] Four months later he was commanding a division during the battle of Guadalajara in March 1937, where he reached all his objectives.[85] At Brunete, in July 1937, Juan Modesto's memoirs include a scene in which

[82] Mera, *Guerra*, 69, 89 and 116.
[83] Martínez Bande, *Aragón*, 71.
[84] Rojo, *Madrid*, 105, and Mera, *Guerra*, 112.
[85] J. M. Martínez Bande, *La lucha en torno a Madrid*, Madrid, 1968, document 7.

Mera admitted that he was not up to the job and asked to be relieved.[86] This may have coincided with the time when Mera was undergoing his *crise de conscience* about militarisation, which many people observed.[87] Modesto's account is difficult to accept because Mera's division reached its objective at Brunete. However, his change of attitude had indeed been remarkable, so much so that the CNT-appointed Sub-Commissar General Serafín González Inestal recalled many years later that he once approached Mera about some reports to be made to the CNT. Mera shouted that he gave information only to the headquarters of the Army of the Centre. González Inestal retorted that he had had great difficulties in making Mera accept militarisation and that now he seemed to have too much respect for it.[88]

His military superiors had great respect for Mera and backed his promotion after the Republican Army's defeat of the Italian fascist *Corpo di Truppe Volontarie* (CTV) at Guadalajara, for which Mera earned much credit. He was appointed to command the IV Army Corps and remained in that post until the end of the war. In spite of his high position, the editor of the Madrid daily paper *CNT* wrote the following about Mera:

> Under his lieutenant-colonel's uniform, Mera had not lost the frank and simple aspect he had previously. He was still a stonemason, a workingman, and the ease with which he moved in senior military circles reflected the grave air of a man who is determined to do his duty, just as in previous years he had gone from the Union to prison and from prison to the building site.
>
> *(Bajo su uniforme de teniente-coronel, Mera no había perdido la apariencia franca y simple de su vida anterior. Seguía siendo un albañil, un trabajador, y la soltura con que se movía en los altos círculos militares reflejaba el aire serio de un hombre que está cumpliendo con determinación su misión del mismo modo que en los años anteriores había pasado del sindicato a la cárcel y de la cárcel al tajo.)*[89]

Mera's role in the Casado coup of March 1939 has led communist authors to condemn him. Modesto, for, example, claims that Mera abandoned his lines while the former insists that the IV Corps troops he sent to aid the *casadistas* were in reserve and not front-line units.[90] In a more violent tone, Líster writes that Franco rewarded Mera by not condemning him to death.[91] It may be true that Mera's support for

86 Modesto, *Soy del Quinto Regimiento*, 118.
87 Bolloten, *Spanish Revolution*, 251, quoting the anarchist press.
88 Interviews with Serafín González Inestal, Madrid, 1971.
89 García Pradas, *Cómo terminó*, 70.
90 Modesto, *Soy del Quinto Regimiento*, 286; Mera, *Guerra*, 210n., confirmed by Salas Larrazábal, *Historia del Ejército Popular*, 2339.
91 Líster, *Nuestra guerra*, 260.

Casado counted in his favour at his court martial. Mera, of course, did not know the outcome of his actions but, if Casado is considered a traitor to the Republic, as the communists have always judged him to be, then those who, like Mera, aided him are tarred with the same brush. The fact is that, from the anarchist point of view, since the majority of units which had emerged from the CNT sphere were now interned in France, resistance in the central-south zone to the bitter end would have meant the end of the CNT. The possibility that Casado would be able to negotiate a conditional armistice must have seemed remote.[92] Mera himself got away to North Africa but was returned to Spain, sentenced to death, reprieved and imprisoned until on his conditional release in 1946 he left for France, where he lived until his death in 1975.

Another anarchist militia leader, Miguel García Vivancos, was a Barcelona activist who emigrated to South America during the repression of the 1920s.[93] Together with Durruti, the Ascaso cousins, Ricardo Sanz and other CNT leaders, he helped to crush the military insurrection in Barcelona on 19 July 1936, after which he left for the Front as second in command of the *Aguiluchos* column. During the siege of Huesca in September 1936 he began to advocate militarisation, a change which his own column strongly advocated, though he describes how he had to dismiss the leader of a group called *Los Puritanos*, which wanted to preserve the anarchist flame of resistance to all authority. There were disputes within the anarchist groups, because some saw militarisation of their militias as inevitable while others wanted to keep the undisciplined 'spontaneity' of the early militia days. García Vivancos planned the militarisation of his column with Gregorio Jover, later a corps commander, against the opposition of extremists such as Domingo Ascaso. Nevertheless, militarisation was not complete until February 1937.

Vivancos was appointed to command the 125th Mixed Brigade of the 28th Division (ex-*Ascaso*, *Aguiluchos* and *Rojo y Negro* columns). He recalls having to exhaust his energies in arguing with anarchist extremists and with a large group of Italian anarchist refugee volunteers. During the conflict in Barcelona in May 1937, between the Government, supported by the PCE and the PSUC on the one side, and the POUM and the CNT, on the other, he persuaded the POUM's

[92] Acracio Ruiz, political commissar of a brigade and briefly of the IV Corps, was convinced that neither the CNT nor Mera himself knew that Casado was planning to negotiate with the Insurgents (interview May 1973).

[93] Most of the following information comes from the unpublished memoirs of García Vivancos, kindly lent to me by Miguel González Inestal. See also W. Runacre, 'Portrait of an Anarchist General: Major-General Miguel García Vivancos', at http://flag.blackened.net/revolt/spain/general_vivancos.html.

29th Division not to abandon the Front to march on Barcelona, and he also had to pacify his own men, many of whom wanted to return to the city and fight it out with the hated communists. Men such as Vivancos, Jover and Sanz contributed importantly to keeping the Aragon Front stable at that time when, had they returned to Barcelona with their forces they might have been able to defend their interests and those of the persecuted communist dissident POUM. Later, Vivancos persuaded the POUM division to parade and verified that it had purged its ranks of some who were sabotaging the militarisation process. But when the order came to dissolve the POUM he realised that this was a political rather than a military necessity. Unless the 29th Division was dissolved the flow of Soviet arms would cease.

Vivancos was appointed to command the 25th Division in September 1937, which demonstrates that he was reliable and that it is unlikely that he would have defended the 29th POUM Division if that body had been a nest of concealed fascists, as the communists insisted as part of their determination to destroy dissidents in Spain who continued to take the revolutionary stance which was counter to the Popular Front policy.[94]

The 25th Division had been commanded previously by Antonio Ortiz, who, according to Vivancos, had not been cooperative during the battle of Belchite in August 1937. Yet, though Vivancos was appointed on the recommendation of General Pozas, commander of the Army of the East, he writes that he had to seek the approval of the CNT before accepting the post. He writes this without seeming to realise that this admission invalidates his other affirmation that most of even the CNT extremists had accepted militarisation, and demonstrates just how far politics predominated in purely military matters. In contrast, neither traditionalists nor Carlist militia leaders can be imagined insisting on a right to confirm appointments to divisional commands made by Franco. In this case, however, the CNT agreed that Ortiz should be relieved of his command.[95]

The 25th Division was coupled with the communist-led 11th, during the battle of Teruel. In an imaginary or perhaps reconstructed conversation with the 11th Division's commander, Líster, before the battle, Vivancos describes the two leaders swearing that they would not allow political differences to interfere with their mutual loyalty. In his book,

[94] The principal anti-POUM publication was the untrue 'Max Rieger' [Wenceslao Roces], *Espionnage en Espagne*, Paris, 1938.

[95] Cordón, *Trayectoria*, 349 (Cordón was Chief of Staff of the Army of the East at the time).

Líster does not mention this, though he praises Vivancos and other 'magnificent and disciplined' anarchists.[96]

However, when the time came, Líster did not cooperate fully. Vivancos says that he abandoned the 25th Division. He thinks that it was favouritism and Soviet influence which allowed Líster to remove his troops without orders. Ibarrola, the corps commander, could do nothing and Rojo avoided making a decision. Military documents on Teruel confirm that Vivancos's opinion was in general correct, though he avoids mentioning his own division. A quarrel blew up between the 25th Division and the 40th *Carabineros* Division about booty, and it became necessary to relieve the 25th.[97] One of its brigades, the 117th, was returned to the Front without sufficient rest and was destroyed from the air by the enemy. The brigade was reconstructed but in February, at the end of the battle of Teruel, even with 600 new recruits, it was still seriously undermanned, while the recruits knew only basic drill but not how to use a rifle or throw a grenade properly. In any case, rifles were insufficient and many were in bad condition. The combination of exhaustion, inexperience, shortage of weapons and lack of air cover led to a disorderly retreat.[98] Vivancos says nothing of this, though he describes at length the Siberian temperatures that Teruel suffered in the winter of 1937–8, comparing his men's suffering with the luxurious heated railway coach occupied by the high command.

The 25th Division suffered serious losses in the retreat of March and April 1938, remaining in the central zone, after the Republic had been split, as part of the XVII Army Corps. García Vivancos was relieved from command. He had been given an impossible task at Teruel, but he had contributed successfully to the militarisation of the CNT columns. After a career in France in later life as a *naïf* painter, he returned to Spain, dying in 1972.

Officers' and NCOs' training schools

The need for short training courses for officers was expressed in general terms during the first three weeks of the Spanish Civil War. They would be organised in three branches, continuing the traditional division between infantry, artillery and engineers.[99] However, nothing concrete emerged at that time. One month later, on 9 September 1936,

[96] Líster, *Nuestra guerra*, 161.
[97] CGG, L371, C8. This information would have been gleaned from prisoners.
[98] *Ibid.* See also the study of Teruel by R. Casas de la Vega, *Teruel*, Barcelona, 1973.
[99] *Gaceta*, 11 August 1936.

Largo Caballero published a decree according to which schools for infantry and cavalry officers would be opened at the Carabanchel depot near Madrid; artillery officers would be trained in the barracks of the Regiment of Horse-Drawn Artillery, with a section in the Cartagena naval base specialising in coastal artillery; signals would be the speciality at the Retamares depot near the city. There would be 14-day courses for new officers and for militia already commanding battalions and companies. Promoted NCOs would also attend. Courses would be intensive, lasting a minimum of eight hours daily. Emphasis would be laid on practical knowledge with only the indispensable minimum of theory. The instructors would be professionals.

Meanwhile the first operative officers' school had been set up in Barcelona in one of the religious buildings which, given the hasty departure, the arrest or the murder of clergy, were coming vacant. This was the Escolapian convent in the Barcelona district of Sarrià. The school was directed by the CNT activist Juan García Oliver, now in charge of militias. There are several descriptions of the way it was conducted, but it seems to have consisted of a common course for all branches of the Army, followed by exercises and practice within each Arm. Later, men living outside the city were required to live in, and strict hygiene was enforced. Subjects studied included tactics, weapons, signals, fortification, topography, musketry, explosives, horse-riding and book-keeping (*sic*).[100] The first new officers who graduated were reported to be of excellent quality, but the standard soon declined because of what would be a permanent problem in the Republican Army: a shortage of men with adequate basic education,[101] together with the unwillingness to participate of those who had had more years in school, who in any case tended to be politically distrusted. Besides this, the new officers were not well received by the militias, who looked on them as the classic *señoritos* of the idle upper classes. At first, some new officers went to the Front for the first time after their two weeks at the officers' school, while other young men entered the school on the urging of their fathers, who presaged a general mobilisation and thought that their sons would be better off to take this brief and free training to be officers.[102] This was not the only officers' school organised by the Catalan *Generalitat*. There was a school for NCOs which was soon boycotted because of the

[100] Details in J. M. Soler, *La guerra en el frente de Aragón: junto a la línea de fuego*, Barcelona, 1937, 168, and M. (Domingo) Benavides, *Guerra y Revolución en Cataluña*, Mexico City, 1946, 314–15.
[101] See Miralles Bravo, *Memorias*, ch. 17, who attended this school.
[102] A. Artís-Gener, *556 Brigada Mixta*, Mexico City, 1946, 100–2.

opposition of both García Oliver and Caballero.[103] In Valencia there was a school for armourers, valuable because indiscipline and ignorance had rendered many weapons useless, but only one cohort graduated from it. Lastly, the CNT organised an artillery school in Barcelona. According to the communist-controlled *International Press Correspondence* of 19 December 1936, the Minister of Agriculture (*sic*; the minister, Uribe, was a member of the PCE) had created a school which produced a hundred new officers every month who could command a company or a battery. The mere assumption that a battery commander could be trained in a month indicates to what extent the training of new officers for the Republican Army ran the risk of becoming another means for a political or ideological group to enhance its prestige. It also shows the great service that Largo Caballero and his military adviser Asensio rendered to the Republic by centralising military education.

After some time, the new schools which had been announced in the *Gaceta* were opened. At first there were five, for infantry, artillery, cavalry, engineers and signals, located mostly in small garrison towns in the Valencia Division's territory such as Paterna (Valencia), Chinchilla (Albacete), Godella (Valencia) and Almansa (Albacete). These schools ran courses which lasted for a sensible three months for infantry and cavalry officers and four months for new artillery officers.[104]

A later decree, of 9 December 1936, numbered the schools and named them *Escuelas Populares de Guerra* or People's War Schools. Entrance tests, even for the technical Arms, were not particularly demanding. There were large numbers of candidates. Three thousand applied to enter the artillery school or *Escuela Popular de Guerra No. 2* at Lorca (Murcia). The entrance test consisted of a brief psychotechnical examination, a long set of mental arithmetic problems, an elementary mathematics examination and one of verbal reasoning. In the entrance examination of 15 December 1936, some of the surviving papers show the very low level of some candidates. A primary school teacher was unable to solve a simple arithmetical problem and a secondary school mathematics teacher could not continue a simple number sequence. Even a university graduate could not do some of the tests.[105] These candidates were not, presumably, admitted, but the mere fact that they could think of applying and present a recommendation shows the low level of studies of potential officers and the poor outlook for the new Republican Army. Alternatively, the standard

[103] Voronov, in Malinovski *et al.*, *BLB*, 101.
[104] *DO*, 27 November 1936. [105] DR, L519, C3.

might indicate that the educational system did not enable the students to face a set of surprisingly modern exercises.

In contrast, in the Insurgent army, future junior artillery officers underwent a three-month course, but they had to start off with a good level of mathematics. As a point of reference, candidates for artillery officers' courses in the British Army in the Second World War had to have served in the ranks and have a basic practical knowledge of artillery before their six-month course.

The first course at Lorca was attended by 273 men. They were the cream of the recruitment and the average level soon declined.[106] Many primary school teachers applied, which is not surprising, for few other men with higher educational qualifications could have obtained a political guarantee from a political party or union, as was required.

Students who failed were allowed to resit once. Men were eager to don an officer's uniform and most studied hard.[107] Having passed out, the new officers were dispatched to the Permanent Artillery Centre (*Centro Permanente de Artillería* or *COPA*) at Almansa to follow a two-month practical course. One of the instructors was a Russian adviser, but his explanations were considered abstruse.[108]

In *Escuela Popular de Guerra No. 3* for infantry, cavalry and supply officers, 400 places were announced in the *Diario Oficial* on 29 December 1936. This huge number proves that the insurrection could not have been tackled with the loyal professionals who remained with the Republic. Entry was limited to Spanish citizens aged between 19 and 36, who were already in militia battalions, the regular army or police forces, and who could present a certificate guaranteeing their loyalty. The entrance examination consisted of a four-hour test of writing and grammar, three questions on elementary history and geography, optional translation from a foreign language and basic mathematics. Successful candidates would follow a common course for three weeks and then specialise in one Arm of the service.[109]

In the Army of the North, covering the Basque Country, Santander and Asturias, General Llano de la Encomienda was authorised to open an *Escuela Popular de Infantería* in Bilbao, and one for artillery officers in Trubia, centre of an armaments industry. There were also schools in Santander.

[106] According to EGF, an engineering student in 1936 and one of the first graduates of the Lorca school.
[107] According to Bazal, *¡Ay de los vencidos!*, 155, 159, who took the course.
[108] *Ibid.*, 162. [109] DR, L519, C2.

The Basque autonomous government opened its own officers' school, called the *Academia Militar de Euskadi*, for 250 infantry and 130 artillery and engineer officers. One hundred and eight had their commissions ratified by the Ministry of Defence. Writing to the Minister, the Basque President, Aguirre, announced that the second course was full and asked for the academy to be recognised by the Republican Government, but when Bilbao fell to the Insurgents on 19 June 1937 the academy ceased activity.[110]

Escuela Popular de Guerra No. 1 was the school for the instructors in Catalonia. Founded by Juan García Oliver, who was President of the War Sub-committee of the Militias Committee which virtually ran Catalonia in the early weeks of the war, and headed by Lieutenant-Colonel Juan Plaza Ortiz, one of the few loyal officers in the area, it had enjoyed prestige in Catalonia, preparing literally hundreds of officers for the militias and the *Exèrcit de Catalunya*. After the central government took back the military functions that the *Generalitat* had unconstitutionally arrogated, the *Diario* Oficial published a decree on 24 May 1937 requiring the school to adapt to ministerial requirements.

Schools 2, 3, 4 and 5 were, respectively, to train new officers of artillery, infantry, cavalry and supply and engineers and signals. No. 6 was the *Escuela Popular del Ejército del Norte*. The Staff College or *Escuela Popular de Estado Mayor*, listed by the *Diario Oficial* on 16 December 1936, announced a total of six entrance examinations. The final one was on 2 October 1938. Most of the Staff cohorts were small, consisting largely though not entirely of professional officers, some of whom were acting as untrained Staff officers already. Regulations required all new Chiefs of Staff of large units as well as section heads to be either career officers or provisional Staff officers. All men who were already occupying such Staff posts were required to attend a course. The *Diario Oficial* of 2 October 1938 announced that attendance at a course would soon be required for brigade Staff officers.

Among the new students in November 1938 were, for example, the Chief of Staff of the II Corps, the Head of the Services Section of the Army of the East and the Chiefs of Staff of several divisions.[111] Most of these men do not appear on the 1936 Army List. They were either retired officers, promoted NCOs or even militia officers, which illustrates the grave problem of shortage of competent, trained Staff officers in the Republican Army. When General Pozas was in command of

[110] Letter to Prieto from Aguirre of 10 June 1937, archived in DR, L54, C8, quoted by Martínez Bande, *Vizcaya*, document 9.

[111] Names listed in *Diario Oficial* of 22 November 1938.

the Army of the Centre he complained that Staff officers in Madrid, where the number was adequate, were being removed and posted to other armies.[112] Nevertheless, in the Army of Extremadura, even as late in the war as April 1938, the only qualified Staff officer was the Chief of Staff, Eduardo Sáez Aranaz, while the other Staff officers were a war-temporary lieutenant and a militia officer.[113]

The entrance test for the Staff College was of course more challenging than for others officers' schools. It seems to have been designed for men who were already acting as Staff officers. There was a two-hour essay, a two-and-a-half-hour topographical description of an area, one hour to interpret a military map and an exercise in composing battle orders. This was the first part, while the second was a test of tactical skill based on an imaginary mixed force of artillery and infantry, for which the candidates were required to write a set of operational orders. Only 50 places were available and hundreds of well-qualified men applied for them. This last course finished abruptly when the Insurgent armies crossed the River Segre and invaded Catalonia at the end of December 1938.

On 11 August 1938 the *Diario Oficial* announced a major reorganisation. Until then, according to the announcement, military education had been spasmodic. The schools had lacked unity and coordination. Furthermore they had attracted inappropriate students. What this last observation meant was not specified, but it may be supposed that the entrance tests favoured men who had had good education, while the character of the Republican Army tended to favour militia officers. Service at the Front, moral strength and political awareness were now to be considered more important than the ability to pass examinations. However, apart from the word 'unification', no change in the schools themselves seems to have taken place. The most important development in military instruction in general was the organisation of a training scheme in the fighting units themselves. All training was put on an official basis. Each battalion would organise courses for aspiring corporals and each mixed brigade would do likewise for sergeants. Divisions would organise compulsory short courses for officers up to company commanders if such officers had not already completed a course in one of the *Escuelas Populares de Guerra*. At army corps level, *Escuelas de Aplicación* would train officers for the specialised Arms. Finally, the Armies of the South, Centre and East would have courses for divisional and higher commands. All of this would be under the Training Section

[112] DR, L968, C2.
[113] DR, L575, C2, telegram to Matallana, Chief of Staff of the Central Army Group.

of the Ministry of National Defence. Just to have passed a course did not qualify an officer for promotion, but it would be a good mark on his record.

In 1937 it was already evident that the *Escuelas Populares de Guerra* were not training sufficient new officers to keep up with the expansion of the Republican Army. Rojo, the Chief of the General Staff, told President Azaña that they produced very little (*'rinden muy poco'*), so the Army had to train battlefield-appointed officers very fast.[114] Even a year later, the provisional Army List includes only 6,444 war-temporary officers (*oficiales en campaña*).[115] In the artillery, there were 907 new lieutenants and 19 who had risen to the rank of captain. There had been 793 casualties among these *oficiales en campaña*, while 2,225 graduated later,[116] but even this total of 9,458 would have included dismissals and desertions, while the later graduates would have passed through the schools hastily. Nine thousand to ten thousand war-temporary officers compares poorly with the Insurgent figure of 22,936 *alféreces provisionales*. The British military attaché commented that there was a shortage in the Republican zone of men with the required educational level. This was true, though perhaps it was less a question of men with the required studies than their unwillingness to apply for officers' school or to ask for the required political guarantee or *aval*. Conversations with better-educated men who did not want to wear the bars of an officer in the Republican Army lead one to believe that the revolutionary excesses of the early days of the war, the crushing of the POUM and the need to have communist support in some armies, added to the lack of confidence in the capacity of higher commanders and pessimism about the outcome of the conflict, led many to avoid coming forward. In the circumstances of a civil war which was so politicised that being an officer meant totally accepting Republican propaganda, such an attitude is understandable.

There was also a marked shortage of suitable instructors. These were often officers and NCOs who had not enjoyed a favourable report from the *Gabinete de Información y Control*, as well as people whose plans of study demonstrate a lamentable lack of imagination about the type of instruction that was appropriate in the circumstances. In *Escuela Popular de Guerra No. 1*, for example, a one-month course was held for sergeants aspiring to officer's rank. The course included: organisation, information, logistics, tactics, weapons (from rifles to cannon

[114] Azaña, *Obras Completas*, IV: 840.
[115] DR, L506 of 25 July 1938.
[116] José María Gárate, *Tenientes en campaña*, Madrid, 1976.

and anti-tank guns), telemetry, explosives, fortification (detailed in 11 tightly typed lines), signals and topography.[117] Most of this instruction would have been theoretical. The result could have been little more than a palimpsest of confused notions. A report on instruction given in the *Escuela Popular del Norte* between 14 January and 25 July 1937 gives a fuller idea of the method employed. The school was organised on traditional lines, with an orderly officer, barracks inspections and written reports. There was a great emphasis on cleanliness. The regulations were copied directly from older ones dating back apparently to the previous century, for the style was semi-archaic, using at times the future subjunctive mood![118] Such respect for tradition was surprising, for the School was commanded by an ex-militia commander, though he was probably a long-service NCO.

Altogether, 13 courses were held at this school. At the beginning only a few of the students were proposed for promotion. Not till the third course were some graduates proposed or promoted to sergeant. The fourth course began a specialisation in mortars and machine-guns, while the following were of irregular length because of the urgent demands from the Front. All graduates of the eleventh course became NCOs. The General Staff demanded expansion, so that in July 1937 the school could house 1,500 students and 27 instructors. Nevertheless, that one of the latter was an instructor in fencing reflects the permanence of outdated plans of study. The course was never full. The maximum number ever studying was 658. Naturally, the school lacked weapons for instruction purposes. Most of the rifles were Japanese, which were rarely to be found in use even in the Republican Army, which acquired weapons where it could, though some single-shot French weapons were used as well as 23 other types from different countries. In its six months of existence the training battalion of Noreña produced 2,971 corporals and 1,182 sergeants, 16 of whom went on to take courses for officers.

Some brigades and divisions published reports on their internal training schools. The 44th Mixed Brigade, for example, based at El Pardo, north of Madrid, organised courses for NCOs in the summer of 1937, publishing an attractive photograph of General Miaja and María Teresa León, the wife of the communist poet Rafael Alberti, who visited the camp and distributed prizes.[119] The course lasted from 14 May to 14 June 1937. The day began at 6 a.m. and finished at 9.30 p.m. It was

[117] DR, L519, C2.

[118] *Memoria del batallón de instrucción*, Ejército del Norte (Asturias), Noreña, 1937; *Obligaciones por las que han de regirse los oficiales y clases instructores afectos a esta escuela*, Noreña, 1937.

[119] 44th Mixed Brigade, *Escuela de cabos y sargentos*, Madrid, 1937.

typical of most courses which were held in brigades and divisions, with its physical training, emphasis on personal hygiene, classes on elementary military subjects and lectures on politics, moral education and so forth. Yet as so often, the formalism and conservatism suggest that the training itself and the ideas which were inculcated were narrowly conventional. Few courses seem to have tried to tell the future corporals and sergeants what to do in a given situation. Rather they tended to fill them with knowledge which might or might not be of future value. The innumerable remarks about the very low level of commanders, particular at lower level, which are widespread in the records of the Republican Army, show that the intentions were laudable but the results of training were disappointing.

Yet it was not impossible to organise such short courses in a suitable manner. Rojo himself approved such a course for militia officers when he was Chief of Staff in Madrid.[120] It was held at Barajas, today Madrid's airport, then a military aerodrome. The teaching staff were young career officers, an officer from the *Comandancia de Milicias* and an inspector of the Madrid army corps. Two battalions were always undergoing training, each one undergoing intensive work for three days, which would be repeated as often as possible when they were out of the front line. The entire battalion and its officers would be required to attend. Rojo underlined that only the minimum of theory should be taught, and one sign of this practical orientation is that the regulation required the demonstration of one mortar of every type actually in use. The courses dealt with the deployment of units, stripping and reassembly of all the types and calibres of rifles used, approach marches, mock attacks and map-reading. This was not a school for officers but officers and NCOs were required to attend. In contrast to many others, this course demonstrated a high order of imagination and planning.

The requirement that candidates for officer schools had to produce evidence of membership of a trade union or Republican political organisation unless they had been in the army in 1936 was constant throughout the war and for all schools, and had to be confirmed by the unit's political commissar. Three months' service at the Front was also a condition of entry. A primary selection of suitable candidates was made at divisional level. However, for most schools, the entrance test seems to have been little more than a formality, which as has been seen was the result of the changes made after the first few months of the war. Literacy, the ability to express oneself clearly, a little history and geography, and basic mathematics were all that was required. Slightly

[120] DR, L68, C3. Plan signed off by Rojo on 22 December 1936.

more was demanded for the more specialised courses. Engineers and signals officers were required to know the principles of electricity, but in that subject, and even in mathematics, the aspiring signals officer could begin the course with a mark of only 40 per cent. If he could not reach this he could attend a preliminary course, which he could resit if he failed.[121] The low level of candidates is evident, as is possibly the reality that a candidate approved by the political commissar could not be allowed to fail.

The insistence on affiliation to a union or political party had the effect of continuing the influence that such organisations wielded. This was reflected in the preparatory academies which were run by the socialist PSOE (*Academia preparatoria socialista para el ingreso en las Escuelas Populares de Guerra*) and the anarchist CNT. The regulations imposed in the latter included prohibitions on scribbling on the walls, committing *inmoralidades* (what could these be?) and, significantly, sending protest delegations.

Russian advisers were rarely used in the *Escuelas Populares de Guerra*, although there were some in the Artillery School at Lorca and the Archena (Murcia) tank depot.[122] The language problem was serious. Colonel Krivoshein and his fellow instructors, not supplied with interpreters, had to teach Spanish tank drivers with mime.[123] A similar problem arose in the specialist school for machine-gunners at Albacete, where the commissar requested interpreters and was told by the Ministry that in future it would be better to select Russians who could speak a more 'common' language.[124] Presumably French was meant.

On 12 October 1938 the *Diario Oficial* published another reorganisation which came too late to have a decisive effect. Its main contribution was to set up the *Inspección General de Instrucción Militar*, something which the Insurgents had done over a year before on 25 March 1937 under General Orgaz. The inspector-general was to be General Mariano Gámir Ulíbarri, who had been deposed by the Asturias politicians and had later been Spanish representative on the international commission dealing with the withdrawal of foreign nationals.[125] Beyond Gámir's appointment, however, lay a far-reaching and well-conceived plan. The *Escuelas Populares* were to become 'polytechnics' with academics rather than officers who would lecture on specialised topics. NCOs and temporary officers would be trained within their divisions and brigades.

[121] *DO*, 25 December 1937.
[122] See Voronov and Krivoshein, in Malinovski *et al.*, *BLB*, 99 and 321.
[123] *Ibid.*, 325. [124] DR, L474–1, C6.
[125] Gámir, *De mis memorias*, II: 297.

Specialised schools would train only divisional and higher commanders, Staff officers and specialists. In January 1939, practical application of this plan began with the *Escuela de Aplicación Táctica del Ejército*, which, in a four-month course, would train a pool of future commanders or *cuadro eventual* for divisions and army corps.

The changeover to training NCOs and junior officers within their units was an improvement, but it could not take place until the units themselves were in a proper state of efficiency. It is difficult to say that the *Escuelas Populares de Guerra* were wrongly conceived, except in so far as the courses were unimaginative and overloaded with theory. Given the level of development of the Republican Army there seemed to be no other way of doing it. The comparison sometimes made with the Red Army during the Russian Revolution is invalid, because the Soviets had a large number of war-experienced officers following the First World War. Even so, if the Republican Army had had the time and if the balance of arms supply had been more equitable, the Republic might have finally succeeded in producing as many good junior officers and NCOs as its enemies. There was no evident lack of ability to organise military training, but it took nearly until the collapse of the Republican Army to do so. Very likely the most important factor was the lack of trust in the professional officers. This, together with the antimilitarism of the CNT, lowered the status of training and discipline in general. Secondly, the insistence on political guarantees, allied with the social revolution and the violence which had taken place in the early weeks of the Spanish Civil War, discouraged young men of better education from applying for entrance to officers' schools. Thirdly, the shortage of suitable instructors forced the schools to rely on men of doubtful enthusiasm for what they were doing and on others who were merely hidebound, lazy or inefficient. Again, while the Insurgents relied for instructors on the efficient services of German NCOs, the Russians do not seem to have acted as such except in the specialist schools which trained men to use Soviet equipment, but here the language problem was a hindrance. In contrast, the German instructors were men who had trained South American armies in the years of the Weimar Republic, when the German army had been restricted in size, and who spoke Spanish.[126] The problem was aggravated by the higher responsibilities that Republican Army NCOs and officers bore because their superiors were often insufficiently competent.

[126] José Llordés gives a vivid description of the German instructors at the sergeants' academy he attended in San Roque (Cádiz) in his *Al dejar el fusil*, Barcelona, 1968, 185ff.

Uniforms and insignia

The professional officers had to accustom themselves to considerable changes in the army they knew. The decree abolishing the rank of *alférez* (second lieutenant), calling a major *mayor* rather than *comandante*, granting immediate promotion to loyal officers, promoting sergeants to lieutenant, the re-entry of retired officers, the investigation of all officers and the rejection and sometimes the arrest of many, all that must have had a bewildering effect on men who had lived monotonous garrison lives for 10, 20 or more years. They would now have to accustom themselves to changes in their uniforms and salutes, as a decree in the *Diario Oficial* of 31 October 1936 announced. Thin and thick gold-coloured bars replaced the traditional six- and eight-pointed stars to indicate officers' ranks. Lieutenants and captains would wear two or three thin bars sideways and above one another, while majors, lieutenant-colonels and colonels would display one, two or three thicker bars. Junior officers would wear the bars above the sleeve hem and senior officers below.[127] Thus the traditional distinction between juniors and field officers or *jefes* was retained. In summer, in shirtsleeve order, the insignia would be worn on a tab over the left side of the chest. Corporals were to wear a red chevron on the sleeves and sergeants one upright red bar. No reason was given for introducing bars for officers' insignia but since they were used to distinguish rank in the French Army they would probably have been the obvious alternative to the traditional Spanish silver and gold stars. What was revolutionary was the five-pointed red star worn by all ranks from sergeant up, and the clenched-fist salute given with the right arm, as prescribed by an order in the *Diario Oficial* on 7 October 1936. The red star was abolished by Colonel Casado's National Defence Council because of its communist associations but ostensibly 'since it has no hierarchical significance' ('*por no tener significación jerárquica*').[128]

At the outset, officers tended to wear the workingmen's overalls of the militia, if not more varied attire. Francisco Ciutat, for example, Chief of Staff of the Army of the North, appears to be wearing a track suit in a photograph of late 1936.[129] A British journalist noticed that even the dignified General Riquelme was wearing a boiler suit with general's insignia, and Major Rojo the same when they entered the Alcázar of Toledo to try to persuade the besieged *Guardias Civiles* to surrender.[130]

[127] Martínez Bande, *Brunete*, includes a photograph of the new insignia on p. 32.
[128] *DO*, 17 March 1939.
[129] Martínez Bande, *Norte*, opposite p. 152.
[130] H. Buckley, *Life and Death*, 226.

However, José Asensio Torrado, as commander of the Central Front and later Under-Secretary for War, insisted that officers wear correct uniforms, after which a Dutch volunteer recalled that even sergeants were ordered to go and be measured for theirs.[131]

Ranks did not necessarily correspond to the commands held, so the authorities later approved a set of distinguishing command insignia (*distintivos de mando*).[132] These were three-pointed black stars, later changed to gold, to be worn under the rank bars with a single angle upward, to indicate brigade, division, corps or army command. Chiefs of Staff wore similar stars in the traditional light-blue colour of the Spanish Staff.

Conclusions

The main impression is of the dominance of political attitudes affecting questions of officer training and promotions. It was not so much that one party, the PCE, imposed its will, but that the development of the Republican Army could not free itself from the political tensions of the civilian world, regardless of party or ideology.

At the same time, political pressures seem to have been the goad for any sort of progress within the Army, but where the military bureaucracy was supreme, traditionalism and backwardness persisted.

The promotions question continued to be as bitter as it had always been and was exacerbated by political tensions, in contrast to most countries at war, where promotion blockages dissolve.

It would be incorrect to say that purely military considerations did not determine many promotions and appointments, but here the most persistent impression is of improvisation. Time was clearly the element most lacking in the formation of the most appropriate criteria for creating a new officer corps and new cadres of command.

[131] J. Last, *The Spanish Tragedy*, Routledge, 1939, 161.
[132] *DO*, 19 and 26 July 1937.

7 The experience of individuals

Conscripts

Historiography has been influenced by both written and filmed journalism of the dramatic scenes in the cities of Republican Spain in the early days of the Civil War, where a major role was played by the militias. Nevertheless, the maximum number of militia volunteers at that time on all fronts on the Government side was probably not more than about 130,000. Unlike the Insurgents, who could count on the professional forces based in Spanish Morocco – once they were able to cross the Strait of Gibraltar – the Republican Army had at its disposal only some barely trained troops who were undergoing their compulsory military service. The rest were either volunteers and, within a short time and overwhelmingly, conscripts.

Although both sides resorted to conscription, the Republic summoned 27 classes of reservists – *quintas* or *reemplazos* – about twice as many as the Insurgents. Young men reaching their twenty-first birthday in 1934 and 1935 were serving their time in the Army when the war started. The Republican Government released them from their oaths of obedience to their Insurgent officers, but they were at once recalled and required to join the militia. The 1932 and 1933 cohorts were called up on 29 September 1936, and another six *reemplazos* were called before the end of 1937. By the end of the war, cohorts from 1915 (men of 45) and 1942 (boys of 17) had been summoned. The latter were jokingly known as the 'feeding-bottle class' (*la quinta del biberón*).[1]

The procedure for call-up was that the local *Caja de Recluta* or Recruitment Depot, which came under the CRIM, *Centros de Reclutamiento, Instrucción y Movilización* or Centres for Military

[1] See Michael Seidman, *Republic of Egos: A Social History of the Spanish Civil War*, Madison, WI, 2002, and James Matthews, 'Conscripts in the Republican Popular Army and the Nationalist Army in the Spanish Civil War (1936–1939). A Comparative Study of the Armies of the Central Region', unpublished doctoral thesis, University of Oxford, 2008.

Recruitment and Training, would instruct the local authority (*Ayuntamiento*), which had the relevant names and addresses, to publicise the call-up by poster and loudspeaker. The conscript was examined medically. The result might be *útil* (fit), *inútil* (unfit) or *apto para servicios auxiliares* (suitable for auxiliary services). Memoirs speak of friendly or pro-Insurgent doctors classifying men as physically unfit when they were not.[2] Training was brief in the extreme. In the CRIM, the recruit was given some rudimentary instruction for two or three weeks[3] and then dispatched to his brigade, in which he might continue his training in a depot company.

The Republican Army was disadvantaged compared with the Insurgents, who overran large areas of territory quickly, particularly in Andalusia and the north of Spain, and were able to 'recycle' tens of thousands of prisoners into auxiliary, rearguard and garrison troops, and were thus able to use their Legion, Moors, *Falange* and Navarrese Carlist *Requetés* as shock attack troops, which in turn freed their own conscripts from such dangerous roles. Republican Army conscripts spent long periods of time in front-line trenches and were used, even though poorly trained, as assault troops, which in some cases meant cannon-fodder.

The tools of persuasion

Given the absence of a harsh disciplinary framework within established military parameters, the Republican Army resorted, more than its opponents, to propaganda and a marked emphasis on what would be seen now as political correctness. Since the Communist Party was particularly adept at this, and since also communist policy was to stress the policy of the Popular Front and the defence of the bourgeois, parliamentary and liberal Republic, downplaying and discouraging the revolutionary aspects which had characterised the militia period, the political indoctrination of new recruits, contradictorily to what was intended, might well have been scorned, particularly by some of those older recruits who were not over-sympathetic to what they saw as the formal military ideals of the Republican Army. The clenched-fist salute and the five-point star (abolished in March 1939 by Colonel Casado's National Council of Defence) were obviously communist symbols.

[2] Lluis Puig Casas, *Personal Memories of the Days of the Spanish Civil War, in Catalan and English*, ed. and annotated Idoya Puig, Edwin Mellen Press, 1999, 237.

[3] See Miralles Bravo, *Memorias*, 165. The author was in charge of training at the CRIM at Tarragona in late 1938.

Men conscripted into the Republican Army were not necessarily all convinced that any regime which an Insurgent victory would bring would be markedly different from what they had experienced under Primo de Rivera in the 1920s or during the 1933–6 period of right-wing government. Men from an anarchist background might well have been discouraged by the repression in 1937 and 1938 of the left-wing communist POUM, the constant complaints from the CNT about communist domination and ultimately by the institutionalisation of what they saw as militarism on the Republican side, with its uniforms, rank badges and ceaseless propaganda.

The tools used for persuasion, that is the abundant military newspapers, the competitions between units and all types of activity directed by the political commissars directed towards making recruits think in a 'correct' way, may well, in some cases, have proved to have a negative value. The dynamic of relations between the ranks may well have made older recruits see the new army as a 'people's' one, but whether they had as much trust in the competence of their officers as did the Insurgent conscripts is doubtful.

Nevertheless, the principle that soldiers of the Republican Army were not fighting for colonial oppressors as had been the case of the Riff wars of the 1920s, but for their own families, together with the institution of the political commissars who stood between the officers and the men, as well as the emphasis on self-discipline rather than the discipline of hierarchy and punishment, were to a considerable extent efficient, and even perhaps the only way to mobilise the support of large numbers of conscripted men who may have been indifferent and possibly even hostile to the principles for which the commissars told them they were fighting.

Milicianos de la cultura

One visible result in the Republican Army of putting its principles into operation was the literacy drive, headed by the *milicianos de la cultura*, usually primary school teachers. In 1937, over 40,000 men were regularly attending classes. The aim was to put an end to illiteracy. The principal textbook used was the *Cartilla Escolar Antifascista*. Its name implied that literacy would itself inculcate appropriate thought. It was a successful campaign. For example, between January and March 1937 one battalion of the 31st Mixed Brigade reduced the number of men unable to sign for their pay from 34 to 16.[4]

[4] Matthews, 'Conscripts', 147. For a detailed study of the educational effort of the Republican Army, see Christopher Cobb, *Los milicianos de la cultura*, Bilbao, 1995. See

Literacy increased cultural awareness. In his memoirs, the militia officer Enrique Líster writes about how important he found poetry, which he describes as 'several hours of speeches summed up in a few moments'.[5] In the Spanish war many of the famous poets of the time, among them Rafael Alberti, Miguel Hernández, Juan Herrera Petere, Pedro Garfías and Emilio Prados, went into the trenches and inspired men with their poems.

Food and clothing

The majority of soldiers in the Spanish Civil War were conscripts, and most of them spent most of their time on inactive and thinly manned fronts. Some idea of this can be gleaned from the reports of the Army of Extremadura, where each battalion of the 109th Mixed Brigade covered 5 km. The British volunteer Tom Wintringham, who had served in the 1914–18 war, noted that '[by] the standards of the Great War they [Spanish troops] were as thinly dabbed on the ground as English mustard needs to be on British beef'.[6] Trenches were rudimentary, often only 60 cm in width and a maximum of only 1.20 m in depth, that is, less than a man's height.[7] Deep dug-outs for semi-permanent habitation, shelter and protection from bombardment were rare even though units occupied sections of the line for many months.

Consequently, matters such as food, clothing and supplies in general became more important than military action as such. Despite the propaganda on both sides, on quiet fronts there were frequent occurrences of fraternisation, exchange of newspapers, food and tobacco and even temporary truces. Republican Army soldiers were short of tobacco while the Insurgents had an ample supply from the Canaries, but were short of paper in which to roll it.[8] In many places, both sides wanted a quiet life.

However, almost all reports, usually from prisoners captured by the Insurgents, indicate that, in the Republican Army, the actual amounts of food and its variety and quality were substantially inferior to the official rations as well as to the abundance reported in the Insurgent army.

also C. Foquet i Boreu, 'Cultura y teatro en las trincheras: la 31a división del Ejército Republicano', *Teatro*, 13–14 (1998–2001), 137–72.

[5] Líster, *Nuestra guerra*, 65: 'varias horas de discursos resumidos en unos pocos minutos'.

[6] Tom Wintringham, *English Captain*, Penguin Books, 1941, 15.

[7] José Hinojosa Durán, *Tropas en un frente olvidado: el ejército republicano en Extremadura durante la guerra civil*, Mérida, 2009, 166.

[8] Seidman, *Republic of Egos*, 82, 111 and 207; Matthews, 'Conscripts', 240.

This would, of course, vary according to the season and the location of the unit in question, but almost every deserter or prisoner from the 109th Mixed Brigade in Extremadura, for example, complained about the monotonous diet of chickpeas, rice and lentils. The meat was either horseflesh or tinned meat from the Soviet Union. Bread was largely maize and thus coarse. Much of the food had to be brought long distances on mule-back. On the Catalan Front, Esteve Mas Alsina wrote to his wife in 1938 that his battalion of the 131st Brigade, in the 30th Division, had been served lentils and Russian tinned meat for three days running.[9] But at least he had food, which made him worry all the more about his pregnant wife, Paquita, writing from Terrassa, who wrote in every letter about her efforts to obtain food.[10]

In the militia period, men had looted items of uniform and kit from the sacked quartermasters' stores. The recently acquired 'coal-scuttle' steel helmet, which is associated with the German Army, looks strange in photographs of Spanish militiamen when worn with odd bits and pieces of webbing, straps and cartridge belts buckled on over civilian clothes. But when winter came, the lack of warm and waterproof clothing became a cause of complaint and of sickness. Especially in the trenches in the University City outside Madrid, and in the mountainous areas of Aragon, men wore whatever they could find to protect them against the harsh climate: balaclava helmets, heavy leather or cloth jackets and baggy trousers closing at the ankles. Esteve Mas Alsina, writing to his wife from the Catalan Front as winter neared in 1938 (letters came with remarkable regularity), wanted a heavy leather coat but tried to dissuade his wife from buying one costing the immense sum of 700 pesetas. This was over two months of his pay, which, as he complained in a letter of 25 August 1938, had not yet arrived for the previous month. Remarkably missing from uniforms of the Republican Army are the regulation puttees or leggings. Indeed, this is one way of being able to tell Insurgent troops in photographs from those of the Republican Army, whose officers, in particular, were often photographed with loosely flapping trousers and low boots, although some wear high boots (much desired by the Insurgents, whose zone lacked footwear factories) or even leather 'tubes' when they dress like pre-war officers. Nevertheless, in summer particularly, the typical Spanish *alpargata* or espadrille was widely worn.

[9] Hinojosa Durán, *Tropas*, 179.

[10] E. Mas Alsina and Paquita Anglada, *En aquesta carta hi ha tabac: epistolari d'un soldat de l'exércit republicá*, Valls, 2010, 19.

The tassel on forage caps was rarely worn by the Republican Army. Perhaps it was Juan Modesto's experience as a sergeant in the Legion which inclined him to choose to be photographed wearing a tasselled cap, characteristic of that regiment. The men in his Army of the Ebro were pictured wearing a variety of caps, often indicating some particular revolutionary tendency, which makes them look like Russian or German revolutionaries of an earlier epoch, while even officers wore caps where sometimes the stiffening frame was removed.[11] Nevertheless, in most units, the formal items, regulation tunics and caps, especially for officers, made their reappearance after the brief period of the workingman's boiler suit or *mono azul*.

Health and hygiene

One subject which was hardly ever absent from the unit newspapers was health and hygiene. This was a major item in commissars' responsibilities. With the exception of periods of intense fighting, such as the battles of Brunete (July 1937), Belchite (August 1937), Teruel (December 1937–February 1938), the Ebro (July 1938) and Catalonia (January–February 1939), far more casualties were caused in the Republican Army by illness than by wounds.[12] In September 1937, 71.1 per cent of Republican Army soldiers hospitalised in Madrid were sick rather than wounded.[13] At times, malaria, scabies, avitaminosis and rheumatism created havoc.

Poor personal hygiene, insufficient sanitary facilities and slackness in dealing with venereal disease were the principal problems. A bane of the medical authorities was scabies, frequently mentioned in commissars' reports. It was caused by a combination of poor washing facilities and unhygienic habits. Unit newssheets often contained advice on how to avoid or cure the disease. Mental health, on the other hand, does not seem to have caused problems, or perhaps was not well recognised. Only 1.5 per cent of the troops of the Republican Army were discharged because of war-induced neurosis, though there was some malingering.[14]

Venereal disease was a major problem, particularly in militia columns based in the big cities. Prostitution in Barcelona had been tackled by

[11] On uniform see C. Flores Pazos and R. Recio Cardona, *Uniformes y pertrechos: Ejército Popular Republicano 1936–1939*, Madrid, 1997.

[12] Seidman, *Republic of Egos*, 108–10.

[13] Matthews, 'Conscripts', 159.

[14] Emilio Mira, *Psychiatry in War*, New York, 1943, 72ff. (Mira was a leading psychiatrist in the Republican Army).

a reform campaign, yet venereal disease was the commonest cause of militia casualties despite a poster campaign warning the militiaman about the dangers and advising him that catching VD was as serious an offence as desertion.[15] Women from the notorious red-light districts of Barcelona spread disease widely in the early militia columns in Aragon, to such an extent that the Council of Defence of the Catalan Government, headed by Colonel Felipe Díaz Sandino, threatened to charge any diseased militiaman with desertion. The anarchist militia leader Buenaventura Durruti sent many women back from the Aragon Front to Barcelona in cattle trucks and when some returned to the Front he had them shot.[16] The first commander of the Madrid-based communist Fifth Regiment, Enrique Castro Delgado, reports 200 cases in one month.[17] Though he mentions this primarily to discredit the PCE and in particular the communist leader Dolores Ibárruri for insisting on women taking an equal role with men and occupying the front line, the stress on caution in sexual encounters was also frequent in the Fifth Regiment's own paper, *Milicia Popular*. Figures for infection became seriously high as the war progressed. A British representative reported that in the year between August 1936 and August 1937 one hospital treated 2,200 in-patients and 87,800 out-patients for VD. Between September 1937 and March 1938 the same hospital reported 94,000 cases and this did not include milder infections treated in the units themselves. After spring 1938 military regulations required all out-patients to be treated in the line because of the extent of deliberate infection. Cure was frustrated also because of the shortage of drugs. No Salvarsan was available and its substitute was found to be of little worth.[18]

Commissars and medical authorities cooperated in the mass circulation of handbooks on medical hygiene. Occasional the advice tended to be unreal in the circumstances. One booklet advised total abstention from sex, while another recommended marriage.[19] The commissars sometimes began morality drives, which included confiscating pornography. One battalion newspaper, preaching against the widespread reading of erotic matter, claimed that the resulting masturbation produced

[15] See Franz Jellinek, *The Civil War in Spain*, Gollancz, 1938.

[16] The possibly tendentious source for this is Miralles Bravo, *Memorias*, 54. Paz's biography, *Buenaventura Durruti 1896–1936*, does not mention the episode, even to deny that it happened.

[17] Castro Delgado, *Hombres*, 303.

[18] British acting consul in Madrid to London in FO 371, W11897/29/41 of 24 August 1938.

[19] Dr Astro, *Consejos a los milicianos*, Barcelona, n.d.; F. Martí-Ibáñez, *Mensaje eugénico a los trabajadores*, Madrid, 1937; F. Fuente-Hita, *Salud del combatiente*, Madrid, n.d.

tuberculosis.[20] Pornography and prostitution were seen as the concomitants of corrupt pre-war Spanish society. Commissars preached that neither should be necessary in the New Order.

The Army of the Ebro, under its energetic commissar Luis Delage, took serious measures to arrest the spread of venereal disease. On 5 July 1938, it issued an order through the army command requiring all medical officers to see that sufficient prophylactic measures were available, to inspect brothels in towns behind the lines, to examine the men every two weeks and to report all new cases. These would be punished with one month's arrest, while reincidence would incur military prison. A further infection would be deemed self-wounding, which, in a highly disciplined force like the Army of the Ebro, might well incur the death sentence.[21]

The question of venereal disease and other self-inflicted illnesses not only illustrates the role of the commissar as a persuader. It demonstrates a characteristic of an army which intended to be conservative in some senses but revolutionary in others. It saw clearly that the absence of discipline was self-destructive. On reading the worthy and kindly advice, repeated in almost every issue of unit newspapers, to wash regularly, brush one's teeth, crop the hair and take care with women, it becomes obvious that the absence of an instituted discipline was an error. This was a contradiction within the Republican Army. Because it represented a revolution, in attitude if not in fact, it was felt that men could not be ordered to do anything outside the strictly military; they had to be persuaded. But prostitution was rife; the moral restraints of Church and family were absent. The latter point may have been more relevant than the absence of straightforward discipline. Conversations with officers in Franco's army and hospital personnel suggest that venereal disease was less of a serious problem for the Insurgents, and that scabies was infrequent. To some extent, this can be put down to better rotation of units, for some Republican Army units spent weeks in the line.[22] Furthermore, the Insurgents had field brothels. An Argentinian doctor serving with them reports that his 800-strong battalion was inspected monthly for parasites and VD, and received a weekly change of clothing.[23] Account must also be taken of the religious idealism of many of the Insurgent troops, who had volunteered precisely because they were hostile to what

[20] 1a batallón, 29a Brigada Mixta, *Combate*, 15 May 1937, no place mentioned.
[21] DR, L795, C1, *Orden general del Ejército del Ebro.*
[22] According to the commissar of the Army of Extremadura, the 63rd Mixed Brigade had been in the line for 18 months (DR, L473, C4).
[23] Héctor Colmegna, *Diario de un médico argentino en la guerra civil española*, Buenos Aires, 1941, 54 (cited Seidman, *Republic of Egos*, 122).

they considered the lax morality and sexual permissiveness of Republican Spain. However, it is also possible that the relative absence of venereal disease was due to the lack of big cities in the immediate rear of most of the Insurgent lines, whereas the largest body of Republican Army troops was stationed around Madrid and went there – and others to Barcelona or Valencia – when on leave. Another important reason was the high pay of the Republican soldier, which attracted prostitutes to him, especially since he had relatively little on which to spend it. There is yet another consideration: the publicity given to venereal disease by the Republican Army may itself contribute to the belief that it was more widespread than among their opponents. All the same, a later Spanish diplomat who was conscripted into the Republican Army recalled that as late as summer 1937 there was a prostitute serving as a militiawoman in the signals section of the XXI Corps. Hers may not have been an isolated case. A total ban on women at the headquarters of the Army of the Centre was not imposed until 27 November 1936.[24]

Women at war

The Civil War led to a temporary sea-change in traditional Spanish attitudes towards women. They were now to play an important part in the struggle to create the new society that a Republican victory, it was hoped, would bring. The Austrian social researcher Franz Borkenau noted that women in Barcelona were acting

> with a self-assurance unusual for Spanish women when they appear in public (and it would have been unthinkable for a Spanish girl to appear in trousers, as the militia girls invariably do) but with decency.[25]

He noticed that girls collected money in the elegant Madrid cafés, though they never walked alone. They talked to foreigners and sat down at their ease in cafés to chat to militiamen.[26] Consequently, women might have been expected to take a major part in the military defence of the Republic. Yes despite the progress which had been made in the years since 1931 and the significant parts played by women such as Dolores Ibárruri, Federica Montseny and Margarita Nelken, Spain remained an intensely patriarchal society.

The Spanish Civil War may have been the last European war in which women continued to play the parts they had always done in

[24] Seidman, *Republic of Egos*, 55.
[25] Franz Borkenau, *The Spanish Cockpit*, Faber and Faber, 1937, 72.
[26] *Ibid.*, 126–7.

armies. Some were straightforward whores, attracted by men without women and with cash to spend, as Mika Etchebéhère discovered when she joined the POUM militia in Madrid.[27] Others were the wives and *compañeras* of militiamen, who accompanied them to do their washing and sewing, and to cook for them. Yet others were adventurous and rebellious young women who saw themselves as equal to men although they were restricted to nursing, cooking and laundry. There were a number of female combatants, although the popular and newsworthy photographs of young women in militia uniforms being shown how to load and unload rifles may well have overshadowed those few women who did indeed fire their rifles at the enemy. María Luz Mejías Correa was one of the few to leave memoirs. She belonged to the JSU in Extremadura. Women often accompanied their husbands, fiancés, brothers or men whom they knew from the political or trade union bodies to which they belonged.

María Luz Mejías Correa accompanied her husband in the Pedro Rubio column. Local women called her a 'little whore' (*putilla*) but the militiamen treated her with respect: She later recalled:

> They accused the militiawomen of being prostitutes or women who went to bed with anyone and who spread venereal disease. There were some of these, I have to say. But that was a calumny against the majority of militiawomen who fought valiantly at the front. I went with the militia out of conviction, but especially because I had to follow my father, my brother and my husband. Like many other women, I did not want to stay on my own. And if there was an epidemic of venereal disease, I think that the men were just as much to blame, especially those in the rearguard and who were on leave, for they were the ones who went to the brothels.[28]

Some women did actually fight in combat roles, standing guard, taking charge of prisoners, making bombs and firing at the enemy. One or two outstanding examples were Lina Odena of the JSU, who organised militias in Almería, fought at Guadix and was killed on 13 September 1936. There was a women's company in the POUM militia, led by the Argentine communist Mika Etchebéhère. Among female bomb- and grenade-makers was the well-known Rosario Sánchez de la Mora, known as 'Rosario la dinamitera', who blew off her hand in an accident.[29]

[27] Mika Etchebéhère, *Ma guerre d'Espagne à moi*, Paris, 1976, 12.

[28] María de la Luz Mejías Correa, *Así fue pasando el tiempo: memorias de una miliciana extremeña*, Seville, 2006.

[29] Lisa Lines, 'Female Combatants in the Spanish Civil War: *Milicianas* on the Front Lines and in the Rearguard', *Journal of International Women's Studies*, 10, 4 (May 2009), 168–87. See also Mary Nash, *Rojas, las mujeres republicanas en la guerra civil*, Madrid, 1999, 159ff.

However, neither side in the Spanish Civil War recruited a uniformed and hierarchicised women's auxiliary service. Although Spanish women played important roles in the war effort of the Republic, working in munitions factories, making uniforms, in social work and in nursing, they were not militarised in formal, non-combatant, women's corps, as they had been in the USA and Britain in the First World War and would be much more extensively in the war of 1939–45.

The wounded

The Republican Army soldier had the advantage that some of the most experienced traumatic surgeons, and many foreign doctors and surgeons, often unable to practise in their own countries (several doctors in the Polish international battalion had been subject to the boycott of Jewish doctors in Poland), were serving in the Republican Army.

Two major advances in the treatment of war wounds were made on the Republican side in Spain. Many wounded men had died from loss of blood before they could reach a base hospital. Dr Norman Bethune, a Canadian thoracic surgeon, developed the mobile blood transfusion unit, which saved many lives.[30] Bringing the hospital to the wounded man (the predecessor of the famous Mobile Army Surgical Hospital as depicted in the television series *MASH*) was another novelty in Spain. Dr Moisés Broggi recalls that in the La Granja attack in June 1937 a field hospital close to the Front led to a remarkable fall in deaths from abdominal, thoracic and other wounds which required immediate surgery.[31] The most dramatic change in traumatic surgery was, however, introduced by Dr Josep Trueta, head of surgery at a leading Barcelona hospital. It had been found that wounds from bullets or shrapnel tended to be very deeply infected and, if sewn up, produced fatal gas gangrene His technique was to excise all dead and contaminated tissue, exposing the wound but not suturing it. The wound had to be thoroughly cleaned, packed with dry, sterile gauze and allowed to drain. The limb was immobilised in a plaster cast. Trueta's work would change orthopaedic practice completely and save thousands of lives in the Second World War. After the war he became Professor of Orthopaedic Surgery at Oxford until he went back to Barcelona in 1967.[32]

[30] See T. Allan and S. Gordon, *The Scalpel, the Sword: The Story of Dr. Norman Bethune*, Boston, 1952, 133ff.

[31] M. Broggi, *Memòries de un cirurgià 1908–1945*, Barcelona, 2001, 205–6.

[32] See his *Treatment of War Wounds and Fractures with Special Reference to the Closed Method as Used in the War in Spain, etc.*, Hamish Hamilton, 1939. For a general study of medicine and war in Spain see Nicholas Coni, *Medicine and War in Spain 1936–1939*, Routledge, 2008.

Desertion

By the time of the Ebro battle, the last great effort of the Republican Army, which began on the night of 25/26 July 1938, all able men between the ages of 18 and 36 had been conscripted. The commissars were having to combat a considerable amount of desertion, mostly among older men with families, some of whose opinions and circumstances probably made them uneasy in the Republican Army, even after formal militarisation had taken place. In earlier days, when revolutionary chaos was still uncontrolled, *Guardias Civiles* often passed over to the enemy because of the suspicions, jibes and threats of the militia and because they were uncomfortable at the looting and the killings that were taking place. But militiamen also went over. Ninety-seven men from the *Columna de Hierro*, who had perhaps joined the militia for that purpose, deserted to the enemy on 22 December 1936.[33] There were similar occurrences in Málaga before its fall and in Guadalajara.[34] During the battle of Brunete in July 1937 a group of men from the 3rd Battalion of the 21st Mixed Brigade murdered their officer and went over to the enemy, an event which the divisional commander, the Polish General 'Walter' (Swierczevski) attributed to a low level of political consciousness and preparation.[35] These were exactly the deficiencies which the commissars strove to remedy but not always with success. The Northern Front, where the Basques did not entirely share the aspirations of the rest of the Republic, also saw much desertion. General Mariano Gámir Ulíbarri, commander for some time of the Army of the North, comments that the small number of deserters from Asturias contrasted with the higher number from the predominantly conservative province of Santander.[36] So serious did the situation in Santander become that towards the end of the campaign in August 1937 deserters were sometimes fired upon.[37] Among the troops during the final defence of the north, desertion reached such proportions that an autonomous government, headed by the miners' leader Belarmino Tomás, assumed power on 28 August 'owing to desertions from the Army' ('*debido deserciones ejército*').[38] The last commander in the north, Colonel Prada, felt it necessary to shoot three brigade and six battalion commanders.[39] If this

33 *Nosotros*, Valencia, 2 January 1937, quoted in Bolloten, *Spanish Revolution*, 261n.

34 Martínez Bande, *Andalucía*, 157, and *La lucha en torno a Madrid*, 173.

35 DR, L669, C3.

36 Gámir, *De mis memorias*, II: 37.

37 *Ibid.*, 77.

38 Cable from Tomás quoted in Zugazagoitia, *Guerra y vicisitudes*, II: 30–1.

39 Azaña, *Obras Completas*, IV: 847; For desertion from the International Brigades see J. Hopkins, *Into the Heart of the Fire: The British in the Spanish Civil War*, Stanford,

was the situation among the leaders, desertion among the rank-and-file was not surprising. Desertions later in the war tended, to the extent that credible reasons were discovered, to be on account of poor conditions and because of low morale among conscripts. Desire to pass over to the Insurgents was common among better-educated conscripts serving in technical branches, as JDP, an engineering student posted to the signals section of a corps headquarters, and who went over to the Insurgents, recounted. The battle of Teruel, which took place over the winter of 1937–8 in freezing conditions, gave rise to a great many desertions and consequent executions. A report signed by Rojo on 31 December 1937 and carefully stored in Franco's headquarters, perhaps for later propaganda purposes, refers to the shooting of six 'agitators' after a panic retreat, and summons unit commanders to execute such men 'at once, as an example' (*'de manera fulminante, para que sirva de ejemplo'*).[40] In the 84th Mixed Brigade, formed from the original Torres-Benedito column, two battalions mutinied and refused to return to the line. Forty-six men were executed on 20 January 1938; 60 were still to be court-martialled.[41] Such information was carefully noted by the enemy, one of whose documents, of 15 February 1938, estimates that as many as a hundred men from the 84th Brigade were shot.[42] The routs of March and April 1938 posed very serious problems of desertion, especially as in many cases the men were not far from their homes in the Levante and Catalonia, where they might hope to find shelter. A decree of the Defence Ministry went as far as accusing civilians of harbouring deserters, and set up special regrouping centres (*Centros de recuperación de personal*). In an attempt to tighten up the situation, local authorities were required to account for men of military age who were not in the armed services, and a comb-out of men in reserved occupations or *embuscados* was begun. Regular officers and NCOs who were still not being used and were in *disponibilidad* were instructed in the *Diario Oficial* of 11 April 1938 to report to the Personnel Section of the Under-Secretary for Defence. The problem was men who were known as *embuscados*, often those who, by volunteering and not waiting to be conscripted, had got 'cushy jobs'. Signals (*Transmisiones*), or supply (*Intendencia*) with its abundant food, were thought to be safe postings. Sometimes the *embuscados* were or claimed to be skilled workers who were 'mobilised in their place of work'. Men might be *enchufados* ('plugged in'), a term meaning having influence in

CA, 1998, 266–8; and R. Baxell, *British Volunteers in the Spanish Civil War: The British Battalion in the International Brigades, 1936–1939*, Warren and Pell, 2007, 140–3; R. Skoutelsky, *Novedad en el frente: las brigadas internacionales en la guerra civil española*, Madrid, 2006, 352–9.

[40] CGG, L285, C29. [41] DR, L781, C2. [42] CGG, L285, C29.

high places. Until Prieto tightened matters up, the higher ranks of the Political Commissariat were thought to be a good *enchufe*, while political parties and trade unions retained the right to issue exemptions from military service until 1938.[43]

It was difficult to keep check of evaders of military service, so, in August 1938, the Defence Ministry again issued an amnesty for conscripts who had not registered for service when they should have, and deserters if they returned to their units. To encourage further such men, on 19 August 1938 the *Diario Oficial* announced that all cases, even of men serving sentences in disciplinary battalions, were to be revised.[44] Several death sentences were commuted. Angel Gil Roldán, the sub-commissar-general of the Eastern Army Group and a CNT nominee, made an attempt to analyse the problem of desertions in a report addressed to the commissar-general.[45] He pointed out that the question was complex. Some deserters returned to their units; other deserters had been early volunteers and proven antifascists. The political work of the commissars (reading between the lines, this seems to mean the insistent propaganda by the communists) was insufficient in the case of bad material conditions. Gil Roldán underlined the real causes of desertion. These were 'A SENSE THAT THEY HAVE BEEN ABANDONED. IT IS HERE PRECISELY THAT IN MY JUDGEMENT THE KEY CAN BE FOUND TO MOST OF THE DESERTION.' (*'EL ABANDONO EN QUE SE ENCUENTRAN Y ES PRECISAMENTE EN ESTO DONDE A MI JUICIO RESIDE LA CLAVE DEL ORIGEN DE LA MAYOR PARTE DE LA DESERCION.'*)[46] Rations, he added were insufficient, many men lacked sufficient clothing and footwear, pay was irregular and the political organisations were causing bitterness because of favouritism in the distribution of food parcels. The troops, he ended, were worried about conditions for their families. This report mirrors the resentment of non-communist units which complained that the communists were treated as the élite and always provided with the best available equipment, clothing and food.[47] Nevertheless, communist units also had their share of deserters, because they were, as much as others, filled with new conscripts and unwilling men who had been rounded up, as Julián Henríquez Caubín, Chief of Staff of the 35th Division of the Army of the Ebro, admits.[48] However, specific figures

[43] Matthews, 'Conscripts', 323, and P. Corral, *Desertores*, Madrid, 2006, 532. Also Seidman, *Republic of Egos*, 56–7, and Miralles Bravo, *Memorias*, 121.

[44] See Miralles Bravo, *Memorias*, ch. 20. The author commanded a disciplinary battalion whose task was to build fortifications.

[45] DR, L786, C3 of 25 August 1938.

[46] In capitals in the original. [47] Peirats, *CNT*, III: 219ff.

[48] Henríquez Caubín, *La batalla*, 344.

for the Army of the Ebro are hard to find. Neither the commander, Modesto, nor Líster, who headed the V Corps, is forthcoming, because to admit substantial numbers of deserters would be to deny the value of their and the commissars' leadership, which is a major aim of their accounts. Henríquez Caubín, however, claims that desertion had reached a serious level.[49] Insurgent sources also comment on the phenomenon.[50] The Army of the Ebro set up a very tight disciplinary system, including a correctional company in each corps and by publicising in the military newspapers that military law imposed death for desertion,[51] but the extent of executions appears to have been concealed. This is likely to have been the case with the application of the decree of 19 June 1937, which allowed the summary execution of those who retreated in the face of the enemy. There were instances of machine-guns being set up to kill retreating soldiers.[52] Self-wounding was also known.[53]

Morale became ever lower. Many men felt that they were neglected.[54] They worried about their families, to whom they sent part of their pay, whose apparent generosity was affected by inflation. This was a serious problem in the Republican rear, while in contrast prices in the Insurgent zone were strictly controlled. Insurgent pay was low but soldiers' families were subsidised. Food shortages in the Republican zone were serious. In the 1990 film *¡Ay Carmela!* the shortage of food is emphasised, and contrasts with the heaped platefuls of spaghetti from an Italian field kitchen that the two main characters enjoy when they are captured by the Insurgents.

Many Republican Army men simply did not identify with their cause. Nor was there much trust in the competence of their leaders. After the Insurgents had broken through in Catalonia at the end of 1938 desertion increased. According to General Rojo, town mayors encouraged and concealed fugitives.[55] Given the generally middle-class social structure of Catalonia, which had provided a comparatively small militia force in 1936, and the fact that thousands of young men had made their way to Insurgent Spain, even forming a Catalan regiment, the *Tercio de Montserrat*, it is not surprising that conscription into the Republican Army in full retreat was not popular among young Catalans.[56] Líster makes a point of defending the Catalans, which tends

[49] *Ibid.*, 13
[50] Manuel Aznar, *Historia militar de la guerra de España*, Madrid, 1958–63, III: 263.
[51] DR, L795, C1 (Ejército del Ebro, *Orden general No. 8* and *No. 11*).
[52] See Corral, *Desertores*, 294–5.
[53] Seidman, *Republic of Egos*, 84–5.
[54] Matthews, 'Conscripts', 203. [55] Rojo, *Alerta*, 39, 128, 169.
[56] J. M. Fontana, *Los catalanes en la guerra de España*, Madrid, 1956, 262–3.

to reinforce the view that their attitude during the war was not considered favourable.[57]

Military justice

On 15 September 1936, the People's Courts (*Tribunales Populares*), which had been set up on 26 August to try people who might otherwise be murdered by the mob or by self-appointed courts, were given jurisdiction over military offences. This was what the anarchist Minister of Justice, Juan García Oliver, wanted, but he clashed with the socialist Prime Minister, Francisco Largo Caballero, who wanted to restore the power of the State. On 16 February 1937, therefore, a *Gaceta* decree established Special People's Military Courts (*Tribunales Populares Especiales de Guerra*) to judge offences committed by soldiers. When Indalecio Prieto became Minister of Defence under the Negrín administration of May 1937, he abolished these courts, reintroducing standard military courts or *Tribunales Permanentes de Guerra*. This followed the State take-over of military justice with the creation of the *Servicio de Investigación Militar* on 9 August 1937.[58] Under Prieto's control, the Ministry of Defence issued further regulations about courts martial. These, published in the *Diario Oficial* on 18 June 1937, replaced the commissar by a senior officer as president of the court. Sentence would have to be confirmed first by an army commander and only then by the relevant commissar. One final adjustment, published in the *Diario Oficial* on 11 August 1937 over Prime Minister Negrín's signature, was to forbid the commissar to make a speech before the unfortunate man was shot. For those sentenced to imprisonment, life in disciplinary camps and units was hard, but available evidence does not suggest that it was cruel. Pay was reduced to 1 peseta per day, but the other 9 pesetas of the daily wage were sent to the prisoner's dependants. Food, equipment and post-war pensions were to be the same as for all troops.[59]

While in the early months of the Civil War it was felt inappropriate to punish desertion in the way it would be dealt with in a classic army, the extent of evasion and desertion among the conscripts of the Republican Army, and, surprisingly, among early volunteers as well,

[57] Líster, *Nuestra guerra*, 242–7.

[58] See Antonio González Quintana, 'Justicia militar en la España republicana durante la guerra civil española (1936–1939)', in *Justicia en Guerra*, Archivo Histórico Nacional, Sección de la Guerra Civil, Salamanca, November, 1987, Madrid, 1990, 171–89.

[59] *DO* of 4 December 1937. For a description of a disciplinary camp see E. Torres, *La batalla de l'Ebre*, Barcelona, 1971. A more hair-raising description is provided by Luis Romero in reply to a question from a reader in *Historia y Vida*, 78 (September 1974), 4–5.

led to the construction of a rigorous system of military justice, although the severe penalties quoted by historians were imposed for acts of indiscipline and desertion which would have been treated in any army, and certainly the Insurgent one, just as severely. For example, a sentry was found stretched out dozing on the parapet of his trench. He refused his officer's order to get up. He was sentenced to 30 years' imprisonment and sent to a disciplinary unit. Most courts martial would have handed down a death sentence for the joint offences of dereliction of duty and refusing an order. However, one of the particular characteristics of the military justice of the Republican Army was that the commissar of the unit to which the accused belonged had to agree with the sentence, and in case of disagreement the case went to the Supreme Court. In some cases the commissar was able to ensure a lower sentence because of the man's record. However, during the crisis of spring 1938, when the Insurgents split the Republican zone in two, the Central War Commissariat, with the approval of the Chief of Staff, issued an order permitting commissars to execute without trial 'those commanders who are not on our side and are declared enemies of the regime' ('*aquellos mandos que no estuvieran de nuestra parte y fueran enemigos declarados del régimen*').[60] This raises a problem. How could a 'declared enemy' become a commanding officer anywhere in the Republican Army? Be that as it may, in July 1938 shooting without trial was prohibited.

All these were problems that affected an army which was fighting mostly against its own compatriots. Indeed, a good deal of the mobilising propaganda was directed towards the 'foreignness' of the Insurgents, with their Moorish and Italian infantry. One scholar of the Spanish Civil War comments that both sides faced similar problems, but the Insurgents overcame them better.[61] Yet one might argue that the difficulties of feeding the Republican zone and the politically based reluctance to give complete control to the army by declaring a State of War were inherent disadvantages that the Republic faced, leaving aside the insoluble shortages of war material. These disadvantages led to a growing lack of confidence in the leadership of the Republican Army, which had its inevitable effect on individual soldiers.

[60] Salas Larrazábal, *Historia del Ejército Popular*, 1586, although the author mentions no names.

[61] Matthews, 'Conscripts', 338.

8 The political commissars

The officer with whom the conscripts in the Republican Army would perhaps have most contact was the political commissar. A political leader was to some considerable extent essential in an army so closely related to politics and ideology and where the rank-and-file, as a matter almost of principle, distrusted officers. The role of commissars in the Soviet army was well known and the Chief of Staff of the Republican Army claimed later, presumably as a justification for their existence, that there had been men with similar responsibilities in the armies of the French and American revolutions.[1] The communist *International Press Correspondence* reported on 10 October 1936 that the PCE was appointing commissars on the model of those of the Red Army in the Russian Revolution.

The role and the men, if not the term 'commissar' itself, existed from the beginning of the Spanish Civil War. The militia columns had a '*responsable*' or 'political delegate' who accompanied the column, explaining and often justifying the orders of the military command and seeing to questions such as the evacuation of wounded, the provision of supplies, communications and other matters which, at the time, were seen possibly as secondary to the main purpose of the fighting and for which there were rarely specialised professionals available.[2]

However, to some extent, the role of these leaders was limited to matters which would later come under military Staff responsibility and it was the communists who first realised the value of the commissars themselves as having an individual part to play in the conflict. In the pages of *Milicia Popular*, the newspaper of the Fifth Regiment, can be found many references to the militia committees, which were, in theory at least, representative of all Popular Front organisations, whose tasks included:

[1] Rojo, *Madrid*, 139.

[2] These matters are discussed *passim* in the account of the work of the militia command published by the Comandancia de Milicias, *Un esfuerzo en 1936*, Madrid, 1937.

1 order and organisation in captured towns
2 political and military security
3 guidance of political and social activities
4 visits to militiamen's families
5 discipline and order within the column.

These committees had no command functions but were to cooperate closely with the military leaders.[3]

Through the newspaper *Milicia Popular*, the Fifth Regiment established committees in each of the diverse and scattered units that it had engendered. The method of organisation was as follows, according to *Milicia Popular* of 23 September 1936. The correspondent of *Milicia Popular* in the unit would organise discussions on problems mentioned in the paper. He would edit a newssheet himself, while another committee member would arrange talks on political, social, military and medical (*sic*) questions. One member was to be elected political commissar. This is the first mention of the term and was printed in capitals, as was the following description of his function:

THE POLITICAL COMMISSAR IS THE DIRECTOR OF THE COMMITTEE. HE IS IN CLOSE CONTACT WITH THE MILITARY COMMAND (*EL COMISARIO POLITICO ES EL DIRIGENTE DEL COMITE; ESTA EN LIGAZON ESTRECHO CON EL MANDO MILITAR*).

The company commissars formed the battalion committee. The latter appointed a sector commissar who would receive his orders from the Fifth Regiment.

That some kind of intermediary was required between the military leadership and the militia emerges clearly from the reports of the officers who commanded the columns. It was confirmed by a note from the Ministry of War published in the press heralding the official recognition of commissars.[4] It was clear that the militia were unwilling to obey unconditionally the orders of the professional officers and that they mistrusted them. Furthermore, the absence of a realistic attitude towards the danger of the situation expressed itself not only in frequent refusal to obey orders but also in an unwillingness to accept that discipline was as important as courage and indeed often created courage, that pillage was unjustified and that revolution did not mean licence. One of the most vivid examples of these problems became evident in the abortive landing on Majorca (16 August to 3 September 1936) where the commander, Captain Alberto Bayo, had insuperable difficulties with the Catalan and

[3] *Milicia Popular*, 28 August 1936. [4] *El Sol*, Madrid, 16 September 1936.

Valencian militia who formed the bulk of his force, and who ignored his orders and looted. Bayo had to go as far as executing some men.[5]

Six weeks after he became Prime Minister and Minister of War, in decrees published in the *Gaceta* of 16 and 17 October 1936, Francisco Largo Caballero instituted the War Commissariat (*Comisariado de Guerra*). The decree instituting the Commissars was preceded by a prologue explaining their purpose:

The political and social nature of the armed forces which are fighting over the whole of the territory of the legitimate government of the Republic, together with the very origin of the Civil War, makes it necessary both to endow the army combating the rebellion with the greatest possible efficiency, and to exercise constant influence over the mass of combatants so that they should at no moment fail to be aware of the spirit which should animate each and every one of the men fighting in the cause of liberty. In no case is this necessity in conflict with the absolute need to maintain the prestige of the military commanders. On the contrary, this measure, as well as what has already been described, is intended to establish a spiritual and social current between senior officers, officers and NCOs of the loyal Army, and the soldiers and militiamen who make up its mass, in such a way that the noble urge to fight which unites us all in the present circumstances is multiplied one hundredfold and, translated into fact, each action taken by the loyal Army should be a firm and definite step towards total victory.

(*La naturaleza político-social de las fuerzas armadas que actúan en todo el territorio sometido al gobierno legítimo de la República y el motivo mismo de la guerra civil hace necesario, a la par que imprimir la máxima eficacia militar al ejército en armas contra la rebelión, ejercer en la masa de combatientes constante influencia, a fin de que en ningún caso esta necesidad esté en pugna con la absoluta conveniencia de prestigiar la autoridad de los mandos. Antes al contrario tiende, además de a lo que consignado queda, a establecer una corriente espiritual y social entre los jefes, oficiales y clases del ejército leal y los soldados y milicianos que componen el volumen total de éste, de tal suerte que el noble afán combativo que a todos nos agrupa en los momentos actuales se centuplique, y al ser traducido en hechos, tengan éstos la virtud de que cada acción del ejército leal al régimen sea paso firme y definitivo en orden al logro de la victoria total.*)

Evidently, Caballero visualised the possibility that the combatants might lose the fighting spirit which ought to animate them. The quoted document, taken at face value, could suggest merely that too many militiamen were undisciplined, but, in view of the later history of the Republican Army, in particular the large amount of desertion, the phrase takes on a more profound meaning. Though it might not have been in the minds of those who framed the decree establishing the

[5] Bayo, *Mi desembarco*, 92–3, 95, 99, 103–4; see also DN, L8, C1, quoted by Martínez Bande, *Aragón*, document 4.

Commissariat or *Comisariado de Guerra*,[6] they nevertheless expressed the reality of the later situation. One of the primary tasks of the commissars during the conflict would be to remind the new conscripts in particular of the reason for and origins of the war.

The decree placed great stress on the commissars not undermining the authority of the officers. This may be seen both as a warning to those who had pressed for the commissars to be institutionalised and as a reassurance to loyal officers.

By the Government decree that set it up, the *Comisariado General de Guerra* was required to 'exercise control of a political and social nature over the soldiers, militia and other loyal forces' and 'to achieve coordination between the military command and the combatants'.[7] The Minister of War reserved the right to appoint the commissar-general, the four sub-commissar-generals and the *comisarios delegados* provided for in the decree. The wording makes it clear that the Minister retained his power over the commissars. Although an unlimited number of junior commissars might be appointed, each would have to be approved by the Minister.

A further decree of 18 October 1936 made the appointments. Julio Alvarez del Vayo was named as commissar-general, though he retained his portfolio of Foreign Affairs. Felipe Pretel of the PCE became secretary-general, and appointed as sub-commissar-generals were Antonio Mije of the PCE, Crescenciano Bilbao, a union leader belonging to Indalecio Prieto's moderate wing of the PSOE, Angel Pestaña, a CNT leader in Barcelona in the 1920s and founder of the Syndicalist Party, which had been established to counter the extremism of the anarchist FAI, and Angel Gil Roldán, that probably rare figure of a professional man (he was a dentist) in the CNT.

One might wonder why the important post of commissar-general was entrusted to Alvarez del Vayo while he remained in charge of Foreign Affairs. At the time, given the international situation as it affected the Spanish Civil War, negotiations with other countries were of vital importance. It is unlikely that del Vayo did more than sign documents. Nor were the other senior commissars outstanding figures. Pestaña's party, for instance, had won only two seats in the general elections of February 1936. Strikingly absent are the leaders of the various Republican parties, representing the middle classes, though two sub-commissar-generals

[6] *Comisariado* is translated as 'Commissariat'; 'Corps of Commissars' might be an alternative.

[7] '*Ejercer un control de índole políticosocial sobre los soldados, milicianos y demás fuerzas armadas al servicio de la República*' and '*lograr una coordinación entre los mandos militares y las masas combatientes*', *Gaceta*, 16 October 1936.

from such parties were later appointed. In fact, the decree and its subsequent amplifications do not seem to demonstrate any clear idea or purpose in the establishment of the Corps of Commissars. It conveys the impression that it was conceded by Caballero when he did not really grasp the significance that the commissars would come to have. Some credence is lent to this theory by a statement by Gregorio Gallego, a Madrid CNT militant, that Pestaña himself proposed the decree.[8]

If this was so it negates the view that the commissars were imposed by the PCE and the Soviet advisers.[9] Nor do later communist authors claim that the PCE suggested the decree, though they insist, and correctly, that commissars were first appointed in communist-led militia.[10] On 17 October 1936 the *Gaceta* published two Circular Orders extending and clarifying the mission of the commissars, who would: 'At no time act in a manner detrimental to the prestige and authority of the military command.' ('*No irá en momento alguno en menoscabo del prestigio y autoridad del mando militar.*') The commissar's most important duty was to ensure confidence between officers and men. They were not to interfere in military planning, but were obliged to facilitate carrying out the plans of the commanders. The latter would sign orders relative to weapons, ammunition and other supplies, but these would be countersigned by the commissars in order to ensure 'greater speed in requests and the satisfaction of the mass of combatants' ('*la mayor rapidez de las peticiones y la satisfacción de las masas de combatientes*'). Once more, the vagueness of the expression shows that those who drew up the document were not clear about what they wanted it to achieve. If the commissars were only there to ensure trust between officers and men, why did they have, for example, to countersign an indent for ammunition? Why would a commissar's signature guarantee greater promptness in fulfilling the order? These questions imply that different pressures were at work and that the role of the commissars might change into what they themselves wanted it to be. What would happen, for instance, if a commissar failed to countersign a request of a commander or if, even more seriously, he refused to confirm an order from a senior to a junior officer, as was also required by the Circular Order of 17 October 1936?

The second of the Circular Orders attempted to spell out the commissars' duties. They were to exercise 'decisive moral influence' ('*una influencia moral decisiva*'). This would be done through their personal

[8] Gregorio Gallego, in *Historia y Vida*, 55 (October 1972). The author confirmed his view by personal letter.

[9] James Cleugh's view that the decree resulted from a conversation between Caballero and the Soviet ambassador lacks evidence. See his *Spanish Fury*, Harrap, 1962, 80.

[10] For example by Malinovski, in Malinovski *et al.*, *BLB*, 19.

public and private conduct. They were to remind the men continually of the political and social nature of the Popular Front. The order went on to explain briefly the consequences of a fascist victory, citing as examples the massacres which Francoist troops had carried out in occupied parts of Spain, news of which had been brought by the substantial number of refugees. The commissars were to tell the militiamen that once the war was won a New Order would be introduced. The order underlined that the men had to obey the officers, and that the latter had the confidence of the Republican authorities, while the commissars had to persuade the professional officers that they had nothing to fear from the new institution. Commissars were to settle quarrels arising from political disputes, keeping impartial and seeing that requests went through correct channels only.

These Circular Orders were both instructions to the commissars who were already functioning unofficially, and more importantly they were guidelines for the conduct of the delegated commissars, both to them and the parties and other organisations which proposed them. The vagueness of the ideas is still striking. The orders themselves are ill-conceived, confusing general recommendations with the exact ideas that the commissars were meant to convey. They suggest not only that the militias were ill-disciplined, amply demonstrated by reports from their commanders and many memoirs, but also that the significance of the war was imperfectly understood.

The decree of 16 October 1936 had mentioned only one commissar-general and four sub-commissar-generals, but had allowed the Minister of War to appoint lower-level commissars as required. Six weeks later, as the new mixed brigades of the Republican Army were being formed, the *Gaceta* of 25 November published another decree which laid down that there would be commissars at company, battalion and brigade level. Later, in the *Gaceta* of 12 February 1937, divisional commissars and commissar-inspectors at army level were appointed. To take as an example the communist-led 11th Division, by 1938 it enjoyed the services of a divisional commissar, three brigade commissars, 13 at battalion level and 92 *delegados políticos* who acted as commissars in the companies.

The communists and the commissars

The PCE was the first organisation in the Spanish Civil War to recognise the importance of commissars. Consequently, PCE and JSU members provided most of the commissars in the first few months of their existence. According to Mikhail Koltsov, the *Pravda* correspondent in

Spain, the PCE had sent out commissars to the fronts in September 1936 and had already about 200 in post by the time the formal order establishing the Corps of Commissars was circulated.[11] On the Central Front, 80 per cent of the commissars were reported to be communists by the *International Press Correspondence* of 24 December 1936. This preponderance was reflected in casualties. According to Francisco Antón, Inspector-General of the Corps of Commissars on the Central Front, 52 communist commissars had been killed or wounded on that Front between October 1936 and March 1937, compared with 27 belonging to other political organisations, 18 of whom were in any case members of the United Socialist and Communist Youth or JSU.[12] Soviet archives report that 125 of the 186 battalion commissars on the Central Front by April 1937 were communists.[13]

The reason for this preponderance is not hard to fathom. The commissar-general, Alvarez del Vayo, explains it succinctly. Communists were preponderant in the Corps of Commissars because they took their function seriously and sent their best men to be commissars.[14] In contrast, the anarchist CNT, despite the immense mass of its members in the militias, did not believe that the institution had any great importance and consequently delayed in making appointments. Their sub-commissar-general, Angel Roldán, was proposed because the CNT thought that the commissars were insufficiently important to give the post to somebody who ought to leading at the front or organising in the rear.[15] Thus he did not effectively defend the interests of the CNT in the appointment of unit commissars, which led to his replacement by Miguel González Inestal.[16] The manifest purpose and drive of the communists in organising the recruitment and appointment of commissars contrasts with anarchist and other indifference. As González Inestal recalled in conversation, when he protested to the CNT about his appointment, he said that he knew nothing of military matters, only to be told that however little he knew others were even more ignorant.

In the spring of 1937, Caballero reacted very strongly to the growing power of the PCE in the Corps of Commissars. He launched an attack on appointments which had not been submitted to him for

[11] Koltsov, *Diario*, 112, 142.

[12] F. Antón, *Madrid, orgullo de la España antifascista*, Valencia, 1937, quoted in Payne, *Spanish Revolution*, 332.

[13] Maidanik, *Ispanskii proletariat*, 310.

[14] Alvarez del Vayo, *Freedom's Battle*, 125.

[15] This was the view of Miguel and Serafín González Inestal, CNT militants, in conversations in 1971. Alvarez del Vayo, *Freedom's Battle*, 124–5, confirms that only the PCE understood the real value of the Corps of Commissars.

[16] *Gaceta*, 6 October 1937.

confirmation.[17] It was a fierce reminder that only the Minister of War could appoint commissars, that all existing holders of the office had to have their appointments confirmed and that new applicants would need to show that they had been members of a Popular Front organisation before the war (when the PCE was very small). From then onward, the *Comisariado General de Guerra* confirmed and appointed new commissars over Caballero's signature almost daily until his Government fell on 17 May 1937.

His successor in the War Ministry, now called Ministry of National Defence to include the war at sea and in the air, was Indalecio Prieto, who continued striving to bring the commissars under Ministry control. As an emergency measure, he confirmed most of the battalion and brigade commissars in their post, but he dismissed the communist sub-commissar-general Antonio Mije.[18] Later that year, after the summer battles of Brunete and Belchite and with the formation of three new armies, of Andalusia, Extremadura and the Levante, and the increase in the size of the Republican Army with the extension of the call-up to younger and older men, an order in the *Diario Oficial* of 8 October 1937 demanded a full list of commissars with their ages. This was followed closely by an order that men within the age groups affected by conscription could serve as commissars only up to brigade level. This affected Francisco Antón, the 27-year-old commissar-inspector in the central zone, who suffered demotion by being sent to be commissar of a brigade. According to the Minister, Antón ignored the order, the brigade was badly mauled and Prieto dismissed Antón from the Corps of Commissars, to the anger of the communists and particularly of Dolores Ibárruri, whose lover he was reputed to be.[19]

A further order of Prieto in the *Diario Oficial* of 18 November 1937 stopped the commissars engaging in propaganda activities directed at the Insurgents, a task now reserved for a section of the army command.

Both Caballero and Prieto attacked proselytisation in favour of the PCE, as carried out by the commissars.[20] Prieto's insistence that commissars of call-up age should go to front-line units or leave the Corps of Commissars and his refusal to confirm many appointments led to a virulent attack on him by 'La Pasionaria' at a plenary session of the Central Committee of the PCE in Valencia on 13 November

[17] In the *Gaceta* of 16 April 1937 and repeated for three successive days in the *Boletín Circular del Comisariado General de Guerra* (archived in DR, L480, C6).

[18] *DO* of 22, 25 and 26 May 1937.

[19] Prieto, *Cómo y por qué*, 35. On 'La Pasionaria' and Antón, see Castro Delgado, *Hombres*, 234.

[20] Largo Caballero, *Mis memorias*, 211–13, and *DO* of 10 October 1937.

1937.[21] She had noticed a growing lack of energy among the commissars, which she put down to the bureaucratisation of the senior office-holders. This can be construed as an accusation against Prieto's replacements. She also spoke of the 'incomprehensible attitude' of the Minister, who had refused to confirm the appointments of 'hundreds of commissars with admirable records'. In some cases, continued 'La Pasionaria', 'these unofficial commissars had been killed and their families were receiving no support'.

Prieto's intention apparently had been to try to effect a balance of commissars according to the ideological forces supporting the Republic. He concluded, after being forced out of office, that he had not succeeded because he had not received the support of the National War Council.[22]

Nevertheless, in some way Prieto did manage to counter communist influence by some judicious appointments, among them the socialist leader Alfredo Nistal as secretary of Commissar-General Alvarez del Vayo. Since the latter was taken up entirely by his duties as Foreign Minister, Nistal's post became very important, because he was the counterweight to Enrique Castro Delgado, who replaced Pretel as secretary-general.[23] Similarly, during a brief absence of Alvarez del Vayo in January 1938, the UGT representative, Crescenciano Bilbao, took his place.

Prieto was under pressure not only from the communists but also from the CNT anarchists, who put a set of suggestions to him on 23 October 1937. These were that five sub-commissar-generals, one socialist, one anarchist, one communist, one syndicalist and one from the Republican parties, should be appointed and that the entire corps of political commissars should be replaced on a basis proportional to the influence and support that the different factions represented in the country. According to this suggestion, socialists and anarchists would have 33 per cent between them of commissars, and communists a bare 14 per cent.[24]

Such a major reorganisation, which appears to be based on the overwhelming size of the membership of the PSOE, UGT and CNT, would be undesirable and indeed impossible because it would dismiss many men who had joined the PCE or the JSU and were doing excellent work, replacing them with unprepared newcomers. All Prieto could see

[21] Quoted in part in Ibárruri, *En la lucha*, 214.
[22] Prieto, *Cómo y por qué*, 31.
[23] This explanation was provided by Miguel González Inestal personally.
[24] DR, L481, C3.

himself doing was to restrict the entry to the Corps of Commissars of PCE and JSU members, which might in turn make the PCE and JSU less attractive.

The nub of the matter was that the Corps of Commissars was political by its very nature and could not be depoliticised. Commissars guided the men differently according to their political beliefs and also because, in the circumstances, only the political parties and the CNT possessed the resources from which the commissars could be drawn.

Prieto, in his role of Minister of National Defence, had the right and indeed did transfer many commissars, 131 according to one report.[25] Not all of these were communists, for Prieto was also wary of the power of the CNT. He told President Azaña that, though he had no great enthusiasm for the institution of the Corps of Commissars, he hoped he could correct its imbalances – this at a time when perhaps close on one half of the commissars were members of the PCE or JSU – but only when vacancies occurred. He had, he told the President, vetoed the appointment of only one brigade commissar.[26] Evidently, Prieto saw a clear difference between vetoing communist nominations and refusing to confirm appointments already made, which he did frequently.

Continuing with his policy of reducing the sphere of action of the commissars and bringing them more closely under control, Prieto instructed the sub-commissar-generals to restrict themselves to inspecting the work of their subordinates. They should cease all other activities. All office and advisory staff were dismissed. The commissar-general was told to re-interview only candidates for essential positions.[27] In the *Diario Oficial* of 15 December 1937, Prieto appointed 65 new brigade commissars, but the *Diario Oficial* did not state their political affiliations. Commissars who had held office in the Army of the North, a fraction of which had returned through France to Republican territory after the Insurgents had overrun Asturias, were told that their appointments were unconfirmed. The *Diario Oficial* of 17 January 1938 told them that no salary would be paid after October 1937, when Gijón, the last redoubt, had fallen. Prieto's last action was to abolish the rank of the political delegate, who represented the commissar at platoon and squad level. Henceforward, that post would be occupied by an NCO. The holder would receive a pay supplement to compensate for the extra work required. He would have to be over 21, have served at the Front

[25] F. Antón, *El comisariado en el Ejército Popular*, Madrid, n.d. This communist source was confirmed personally by the CNT commissar Miguel González Inestal.

[26] Azaña, *Obras Completas*, IV: 786.

[27] *DO*, 26 November 1937.

for over 6 months with good conduct and have belonged to a Popular Front organisation before the war.[28]

It might have been considered that Prieto's fall, engineered by the communists, and his replacement at the Ministry of National Defence by his fellow socialist Juan Negrín, would have reinforced the role of the commissars. In fact, there was surprisingly little legislation and no definite evidence of such a change. Negrín restored the rank and the importance of the post of commissar-general, which had been neglected after the resignation of Alvarez del Vayo in November 1937. The new occupant of the post was Bibiano Fernández Ossorio y Tafall, at the time Under-Secretary for the Interior (*Gobernación*) and a member of the Left Republican Party (*Izquierda Republicana*).[29] Ossorio was provided with a secretary, possibly to act as a counterweight to Castro Delgado, the secretary-general.[30] And on 19 August 1938, the *Diario Oficial* published an order underlining that the Corps of Commissars were subordinate to the Minister of Defence – Negrín himself – that the sub-commissar-generals were restricted, as Prieto had decreed, to the role of inspectors, and that propaganda outside the Republican Army was a matter for the General Staff. These were restatements of Caballero's and Prieto's orders. They signified not that Prieto wished to limit the role of the commissars, but that previous orders had been disobeyed. The phrase, in the same order, '[t]he commissar will complement the functions of the commanding officer, but without interference with them ... his authority must stem from his educational work and his behaviour' (*'[e]l Comisario completará las funciones del Mando militar sin interferencia en el mismo ... Su autoridad debe ser ganada por su trabajo educativo y su comportamiento'*) clearly indicates that Negrín was not going to allow any 'political creep' in the activity of the commissars.

The political balance was, however, upset when in the *Diario Oficial* of 30 April 1938 Negrín appointed the communist Jesús Hernández to be commissar of the Central Group of Armies or GERC. Hernández's appointment might be seen as indicating that Negrín was already suspicious of some of the army commanders and Staff in the GERC, most of whom would support the Casado coup in the following year. On 19 September 1938 Angel Gil Roldán of the CNT was appointed commissar of the Eastern Army Group in Catalonia (GERO). The GERO had two armies, one of which, Modesto's Army of the Ebro, was almost

[28] Order of 12 April 1938, quoted in I Army Corps Commissariat, *Recopilaciones de las disposiciones más importantes sobre el Comisariado General de Guerra*, Madrid, 1938.
[29] *DO*, 2 May 1938.
[30] According to Miguel González Inestal, who had frequent dealings with all these officials.

entirely under communist command. Gil Roldán, who was seen as a lightweight, was unlikely to have much influence outside the other army in the GERO, the Army of the East, whose commander, Juan Perea, was friendly with the CNT.

Negrín stated later, in his correspondence with Prieto after the war, that he had attempted to maintain a political balance among the commissars.[31] However, examining who held senior commissars' posts does not bear out Negrín's statement to Prieto. It is true that there was a balance between the two army groups in the sense that the senior commissar in one was a communist and in the other an anarchist. However, the latter was not officially appointed until 19 September 1938 when the communist-led Army of the Ebro had already established its identity. The intensity of its political work (see below) was not likely to allow a CNT commissar like Gil Roldán to be very effective. In the same issue of the *Diario Oficial*, Negrín appointed the communist Enrique Castro Delgado to be Secretary-General of the Corps of Commissars. According to Castro's account, the PCE asked him for his opinion of the sub-commissar-generals. He reported that Crescenciano Bilbao and Miguel González Inestal would not help the communists, but that Felipe Pretel of the UGT could be suborned and that the new commissar-general, Ossorio y Tafall, would be a useful ally.[32] In addition, four of the army commissars, Ortega of the Army of the Levante, Piñuela of the Army of the Centre, Luis Delage in the Army of the Ebro and Ignacio Mantecón of the Army of the East, were PCE members. The commissar-inspector of the Army of Extremadura was Serafín González Inestal of the CNT. It would seem, thus, that most senior commissars were members of the PCE although at other levels there was a steady increase in CNT, UGT and PSOE representation during 1938.[33] There was no hurry to confirm communist commissars in their posts or to promote them. Santiago Alvarez, for example, who had been commissar of the 11th Division since March 1937 and of the V Corps since April 1938, was fulsomely praised and confirmed in his post only in the *Diario Oficial* of 11 December 1938. Similar decrees of 12 and 14 December 1938 promoted Fusimaña of the XV Corps, Mantecón, who as Government delegate had suppressed the semi-autonomous anarchist

[31] I. Prieto, 'Epistolario Prieto–Negrín', *Indice*, 263/4 (February 1970).

[32] Castro Delgado, *Hombres*, 585. The author turned against the PCE. His book was published in Franco's Spain and should be judged appropriately.

[33] According to Miguel González Inestal in a letter of 25 February 1973. However, Santiago Alvarez, *Memorias II. La guerra civil de 1936–1939. Los comisarios políticos en el Ejército Popular de la República*, La Coruña, 1986, 186, denies that Mantecón and Piñuela were PCE members. Mantecón joined the PCE in 1948.

Table 8.1 *Pay of commissars*

Rank	Military equivalent	Annual salary
Commissar-general	General of division	22,000 pesetas
Sub-commissar-general	General of brigade	17,000 pesetas
Inspector of division	Colonel	13,000 pesetas
Brigade commissar	Lieutenant-colonel	11,000 pesetas
Battalion commissar	Major	9,000 pesetas
Company commissar	Captain	7,500 pesetas

Council of Aragon in 1937 and was now commissar of the Army of the East, and Sevil of the 45th Division. Most of these men were communists in the Army of the Ebro who had served with the militia leaders Modesto and Líster since the birth of the Republican Army.

The role of the commissars

The Spanish term *comisario* did not bear the Soviet connotation that 'commissar' does. It may mean police inspector or a person charged with any particular responsibility, as for instance the *comisario* of an exhibition. It was also a rank held by officers in the *Cuerpo de Intervención*, which dealt with internal military accounting and finance. There was no reason to believe that the Soviet model was being imitated merely because the same name was adopted. Nevertheless, the choice of term was hardly coincidental.

Commissars were to be paid from their units' payroll, thus attempting to obviate any suggestion of financial irregularity or that they were paid by the political bodies which they usually represented. Table 8.1 lists their pay.[34]

On 15 December 1938, the *Diario Oficial* announced a pay increase for commissars. Company commissars, for instance, were to receive a combat bonus of 15 pesetas daily, added to their salary of 625 pesetas per month.

It did not follow that commissars holding posts necessarily had the equivalent rank. In view of the slowness in confirming appointments it would in fact be rare for this to happen. There is some evidence that commissars were not promoted to a higher rank than the commanding officers of the relevant unit. For example, the commissar of the 35th

[34] DR, L480, C1 of 30 December 1936.

Division was promoted to lieutenant-colonel some time after its commander was upgraded to that rank.[35]

On 6 and 7 January 1937, the *Diario Oficial* issued details of uniforms for commissars, with illustrations.[36] Commissars would wear a peaked cap, a dark-brown uniform with a gilt 'C' on the collar and their rank on the sleeve in gilt for senior commissars and red silk for brigade and lower-level commissars. The large 'C' was to be worn in the middle of their caps.

Many handbooks were issued for the guidance of the commissars.[37] Their duties were manifold and expanded to exceed by far those which Largo Caballero had envisaged in his decrees of 16 and 17 October 1936. They were required, for example, to examine the condition of weapons, to check signals and to oversee supplies and medical services. Most officers were inexperienced and not the professionals whom the decrees of October 1936 had envisaged leading the troops. Their level of capability was low and the commissars had to press for them to attend special courses. The commissars' handbooks recommended joint meetings with the officers to analyse the results of operations. The commissars were enjoined not to engage in party politics but to stimulate discussion in the 'fighting-man's corner' (the '*rincón del combatiente*'), a discussion room, library and lecture room similar to the Soldiers' Home (*Hogar del Soldado*) in larger units. Every brigade had to have its newspaper, with contributions from the men rather than from the commissar himself and free from sectarian bias. Commissars had to see to the men's physical welfare, their facilities for delousing, to ensure that laundered clothes were available and to support the campaign against venereal disease. On the intellectual and spiritual side, they were to organise reading groups and political meetings and see that the civilian press was regularly received and discussed. They were to attend to the strengthening of political consciousness and awareness of the causes of the war, and to prevent the fraternisation that not infrequently took place with the enemy on quiet fronts.

[35] *DO*, 26 December 1938. The divisional commander, Pedro Mateo Merino, had been promoted previously during the battle of the Ebro.

[36] These are reproduced in the *Revista de Historia Militar* (Madrid), 17 (1964), opposite p. 73.

[37] Among them were, published by the *Comisariado de Guerra*, *ABC del Comisario*, Madrid, n.d.; *Comisariado 48a División*, *Guiones del trabajo del comisario*, n.p., n.d.; the PCE published *Instrucciones a los comisarios políticos, mandos militares y milicianos en general*, Bilbao, 1937; *Comisariado de la Zona Central*, *Instrucciones a los Delegados de Compañía respecto a su misión en período de combate*, Valencia, 1938. The number of such publications was large and many others have survived.

Commissars were to engage in constant activity. They appointed activists in the smallest units and ensured that what they achieved was publicised in the wall newssheets that battalions and even smaller units published. Regular talks, lectures, discussions and film shows were held. The commissar, aided by the *milicianos de la cultura*, supervised the teaching of illiterate soldiers.[38] He was to explain the purpose of attacks and ensure that officers were treated with respect and obeyed.

Commissars sent up reports to their superiors which were in turn summarised into a circular by army commissar headquarters. Some of these reports show that commissars were very much concerned with the military aspects of operations. A typical report from the commissar of the Army of the Levante, covering mid December 1937 to mid January 1938, during the battle of Teruel, summarises the reports of his subordinate commissars.[39] Each theme is neatly dealt with, from a description of the political work carried out to a criticism of the propaganda directed at the enemy, which had been weak because the commissars had been ordered (see above) not to involve themselves in it but to leave it to the Information Section of the Staff, who, in the opinion of the commissar of the Army of the Levante, were incompetent at the task. Officers were freely criticised, but the report was probably not publicised among the rank-and-file. The Chief of Staff, Sáez Aranaz, for instance, had not visited the Front in a long time, leaving this essential task to his deputy. The commander of the XVIII Corps, Fernández Heredia, was inefficient. These accusations are mostly confirmed from other sources.[40] Commissars' reports criticise Staff organisation and point out errors in the location of command posts, in the allocation of units to divisions and corps and in the constant replacement of officers. In fact the commissars reported on almost everything: transport, medical facilities, supplies, signals, artillery, fortifications, cavalry, armament and general discipline.

This document was a major report on a battle situation, but the commissars wrote day-to-day reports also from units on quiet fronts. For example, the commissar of the 41st Division of the XIX Corps, stationed in a quiet sector of the Army of the Levante, reported on 23 April 1938 that the Front was quiet, without apparent change in the enemy's force. A battalion had been relieved, trenches had been dug.

[38] See Cobb's enlightening *Los milicianos de la Cultura*.

[39] DR, L481, C4.

[40] For Sáez Aranaz see DR, L575, C2. The *Gabinete de Información y Control* had not been happy about him. For Fernández Heredia, see Modesto, *Soy del Quinto*, 156, and Malinovski, in Malinovski *et al.*, *BLB*, 51, though these communist sorces may be expressing their own political bias.

The report also gave a list of the arms held by the division. None of this information was relevant to the commissar's brief according to earlier decrees and might easily have led to a serious leak of information to the enemy. Certainly the commissar also reported on the political work he was doing, referring mainly to explaining the policy of the new Negrín Government, the *Gobierno de la Victoria*, as it was optimistically called. The 69th Brigade, he commented, had made an extensive study of the press, concentrating on the International Conference of Trade Unions.[41]

It was circumstances which had, to some extent, required the commissars to report on purely military matters. While he was Chief of Staff in Madrid, Rojo had ordered the commissars to go out to the columns defending the city, check and report fully yet precisely on all their services, in particular the supply of ammunition, food, transport and medical equipment.[42] Therefore it might well have been the case that the commissars were used precisely to compensate for the unreliability, overwork and inexperience of the professional and militia officers who would normally have undertaken these tasks. The commissar-general, Alvarez del Vayo, was asked by the Ministry of War itself to request the commissars at divisional level to report at length on clothing, food and the prompt arrival of pay, and to report irregularities.[43]

When new conscripts came to the brigades, the commissar was ordered to arrange a reception and to give them talks about why the Insurgents had risen and what the benefits of a Republican victory would be for the agricultural labourers and peasantry. This would be done against the background of anarchist collectivisations in Aragon and the communist policy of protecting the small farmer, a policy which was wise when so many young men from peasant families in Catalonia and the wealthy *huertas* of Valencia, Alicante and Murcia were being conscripted. Such protection was included in the advice given to Caballero by the Russian leaders in their letter of 21 December 1936 and agreed to by Caballero, who admitted that there had been excesses in compulsorily collectivising farmland.[44] The commissars were also to explain to the conscripts how the army was organised and the need for discipline. They were to be on their guard against enemy sympathisers who might desert, and to list the illiterates.[45]

41 DR, L481, C4.
42 DR, L968, C14, 6 December 1936.
43 DR, L474, C6, 9 February 1937.
44 See text in Ibárruri *et al.*, *Guerra y Revolución*, II: 101–3.
45 DR, L481, C1

The full range of commissars' activities was discussed at a conference held in Albacete in April 1937.[46] The functioning of all services was seen clearly as part of the commissars' responsibility, as was the maintaining of discipline and support in general for the officers. The main task was the political and psychological preparation of the troops for military operations. While out of the line, commissars' tasks were to attend to their units' press and the literacy campaign, and to maintain morale.

The military press

A major channel of the commissars' influence were the generally well-produced daily or weekly unit newspapers, whose superabundance is one of the peculiar characteristics of the Republican Army. They can be classified in three major types:

1 the newssheets containing items culled from the international press;
2 the unit sheet, which reflected the activities and aspirations of the brigade or division;
3 the propaganda publication, consisting largely of exhortations.

By June 1937 there were over 130 papers being published in brigades and divisions.[47] The sub-commissar-general in charge of press and propaganda, while recognising the enormous importance of the medium for the Republican Army, nevertheless reported several faults which needed correction, including the unintentional betrayal of information to the enemy, party sectarianism and 'lack of seriousness'. The Insurgents certainly did glean information from the Republican Army's press.[48] Later in 1937 the Commissariat created a press inspectorate which laid down guidelines.[49] Writers were to concentrate on the character of the war, the literacy campaign and internal issues of the unit concerned. Faults noted by the inspectors included over-intellectualisation of the issues and pedantic military education. The former was certainly a defect of many commissars. One senior commissar told Azaña that in the Army of the East lectures had been given to the troops on subjects so removed from the immediate situation (one was on 'Ulysses

[46] Reported in *International Press Correspondence* of 8 May 1937 and circulated in the *Boletín del Comisariado General de Guerra*.
[47] DR, L480, C7.
[48] See J. Bertrán y Musitú, *Experiencias de los servicios de información del nordeste de España (SIFNE) durante la guerra*, Madrid, 1940, 38.
[49] DR, L480, C4.

and War') that the troops had laughed at them and protested at being required to attend.[50]

Many newspapers were exceedingly well produced. Even a sheet which appeared very early in the war in the Ortiz column in Aragon had well-set type and no misprints.[51] A major characteristic of newspapers published by the commissars of primarily communist-led units was concentration on internal matters, with photographs of men who had distinguished themselves. This is especially noticeable in a comparison between the 25th, 26th and 27th Divisions; the latter, which was composed of ex-PSUC militias, produced a journal of far higher quality than the primarily CNT others.[52]

For a really interesting publication one must turn to *Acero*, the organ of Líster's V Corps, edited by Santiago Alvarez, the able commissar. This was more of a magazine and appeared monthly. It was printed on high-quality paper, with attractive typography and clear photographs. Its choice of material was varied. For instance, its February 1938 issue included an article commenting on the reversal of the decree which had restricted the promotion of militia officers – a change which had affected the corps commander, Líster, himself – an exhortation on the spirit of the V Corps, a piece on what life was like under the Insurgents in the city of Teruel, which the latter had recently retaken, a well-written piece on the factor of morale by the Chief of Staff of the V Corps, pages on the International Brigades and on the part the corps had played in the battle of Teruel, and articles about and photographs of the machine-gun battalion of the V Corps. The paper succeeds because of its concreteness and relevance to the men who would read it as well as because of its technical quality. The soldier could identify with it, which meant that the propaganda, which otherwise might be scorned, would have an audience. The intellectual demands of some articles were high, as was appropriate for a corps journal, but they were not rarefied. Within the V Corps, the 11th Division published an excellent paper which was free of propaganda and all about the division, with photographs of individual soldiers, officers and commissars, pieces in Catalan for new recruits from Catalan-speaking areas, humorous pieces and a commentary on the general news.[53]

In contrast, some publications were extraordinarily dull. One of the worst examples, especially given that it was an army newspaper and

[50] Azaña, *Obras Competas*, IV: 897.

[51] 2a Columna FAI, *El Combate*, alternate days, Caspe and later Híjar.

[52] 25a División, *Veinticinco División*, weekly, Híjar; 26th Division, *La Trinchera*, variable periodicity, n.p.

[53] 11a División, *Pasaremos*, weekly, Caspe.

could draw on more resources than unit sheets, was the one published by the Army of Extremadura.[54] This was *El Frente*, a poorly printed sheet with only snippets of news from the daily press and an editorial.

Education

Another major preoccupation of the commissars was the education of the men. Here again, the Fifth Regiment was first in the field. Its newspaper requested columns to advise headquarters whether they possessed libraries and how they were used, in order to systematise the distribution of books.[55] Soon afterwards, literacy classes were reported to be functioning.[56]

Literacy was the prime aim of the educational campaign. In the central zone, by October 1937, there were stated to be 42,493 men receiving instruction.[57] So important was literacy that the Ministry of Education (*Instrucción Pública*) was empowered to recruit a body of teachers, called *milicianos de la cultura* ('*cultura*' with the meaning of education in general), who might be mobilised for this purpose. They would continue to receive their salaries but would come under military regulation.[58] The *milicianos de la cultura* reported a total of 95,000 illiterates, who had been reduced to 52,750 by October 1937.[59] The total number of men who were taught to read has been given as 70,000.[60]

General education was also encouraged. Though in the early days of the war this was indistinguishable from war propaganda and consisted mainly of the screening of films about the Russian Revolution, it soon progressed. The library service (*Servicio de bibliotecas del frente*) was very active.[61] The commissar of the 45th Division reported on 20 May 1938, after the disastrous routs of that spring, that '[t]he battalion libraries have been restocked with cultural and historical works'.[62]

Some of the educational work was highly positive. Strip cartoons in the military press repeatedly illustrated the problems encountered by soldiers who did not follow the wise advice so freely given. One which

[54] Army of Extremadura, *El Frente*, daily, n.p.
[55] *Milicia Popular*, 11 September 1936.
[56] *Ibid.*, 18 September 1936.
[57] Antón, *El comisariado*, 31. [58] *DO*, 3 February 1937.
[59] United Editorial, *Spain at War* [later *The Voice of Spain*], London, 1938–9, No. 11 (May 1938).
[60] Hernández, *La grande trahison*, 114. He was Minister of Education in the early part of the war.
[61] United Editorial, *Spain at War*, May 1938, and *Bibliotecas del frente y de la retaguardia en la España republicana*, Barcelona, 1938.
[62] Quoted by Mezquida, *Batalla del Ebro*, III: 59.

became very popular and was syndicated in various newspapers dealt with the amusing misadventures of Canuto, whose name usefully rhymed with the word '*bruto*', meaning 'stupid'.[63] This was a well-drawn cartoon story with rhyming couplets describing Canuto's drunkenness, lack of hygiene, cowardice, venereal disease and other faults. While Canuto never suffered the worst consequences of his bad habits, the point was very well made.

Another telling argument frequently put to illiterate soldiers was that if they learned to read and write they could write home to their mothers and girlfriends, and read the latter's' letters without the embarrassment of an intermediary. Photographs of soldiers writing to and receiving answers from their mothers and girlfriends were often published.

The *Hogar del Soldado* recreational centre, which had existed in the pre-war army, spread until there was one as a matter of course in all rest depots, while there was a *rincón de cultura* for reading and studying in the lines wherever possible. Another obligation of the *milicianos de la cultura* was to collect works of art, manuscripts and books in occupied areas and send them to the Ministry of Education for safekeeping.[64] Communists considered that the sacking of Church property in particular by militias in the early days was an understandable but mistaken habit, particularly of anarchists.

At times, the efforts of the *milicianos de la cultura* and the commissars under whose authority they came were somewhat misplaced. In one manual, the troops were urged to cultivate their personalities in order to be able to combat injustice and as a 'spiritual refuge'.[65] The aim was worthy but the manual in which it appeared was a dismal failure, with chapters replete with quotations on abstract subjects from a variety of authors such as Emerson, Carlyle, Marcus Aurelius, Gladstone and Napoleon, together with the anarchist Minister of Justice, Juan García Oliver. Another chapter in the manual deals with questions of hygiene in alphabetical order of subjects. The style is turgid and the practical value nil. Any militiaman who was capable of understanding the manual would have had no need of it. An officer who was properly trained and had perhaps undergone a course dedicated to the particular circumstances of a civil war, aided by an education officer for specific questions and NCOs who enforced hygiene regulations, would have been much more useful.

[63] *Hay que evitar ser tan bruto como el soldado Canuto*, published by *La voz del combatiente*, Madrid, 1937.

[64] Líster, *Nuestra guerra*, 73.

[65] *Manual del miliciano*, Barcelona, 1937.

Competitions were another activity encouraged by commissars. These served the double purpose of maintaining morale and improving performance. One typical *curso de emulación*, as competitions were known, took place in autumn 1938 in the 17th Division.[66] The examiners consisted of the commanding officer, the divisional commissar, the senior *miliciano de la cultura* and an ordinary soldier. There was a prize for speedily built and efficient fortifications and another for the battalion in which the largest number of illiterate men had been taught to read and write in a given period. A corporal who wrote the best essay on a technical subject won a fountain-pen. Enthusiasm in teaching and achievement in learning were rewarded appropriately with books. The prize-giving took place at Brihuega, near Guadalajara, where the Republican Army had roundly defeated Franco's Italian allies in March the previous year. Each winner made a speech, followed by discourses by the commissar and the commanding officer, referring mostly to the bravery of the Army of the Ebro, which was making heroic efforts at the time to maintain its bridgehead south of that river, as well as to Dr Negrín's directives for winning the war.

Although this educational effort was highly laudable and civilised, it seems out of place when compared with the poor level of training described in the unimaginative manuals issued for instruction in the field.[67] The commissars do not seem to have concerned themselves with training procedures, despite the fact that the manuals used were based on the conservative *Reglamento táctico de infantería*, whose 1914 edition was reissued by the Ministry of War in 1937 and laid stress on traditional doctrines with no thought of taking advantage of the particular circumstances of the Spanish war. For once Spanish soldiers were not fighting an irregular enemy as in Morocco, yet the opportunities for irregular warfare were very great, because of the length of the fronts and the highly accidented nature of much of the terrain.

The commissars of the Army of the Ebro

Not until the records of the Commissariat of the Army of the Ebro and in particular of its V Corps – whose newspaper *Acero* has already been

[66] 17a División, *Firmeza*, irregular, Guadalajara, October 1938.

[67] See, among others, Comisariado de Guerra, *Datos sobre la utilización de la infantería en el combate*, Guadalajara, 1937; Comité Militar PSUC-UGT, *Como luchar para vencer*, Barcelona, 1937; XXI Cuerpo de Ejército, *Programa de instrucción de batallón*, Valencia, 1937.

described – are examined can the real possibilities of the institution be seen and appreciated.[68]

The Army of the Ebro was composed of Enrique Líster's V Corps, Manuel Tagüeña's XV Corps, and Etelvino Vega's XII Corps. Commanded by Juan Modesto and with Luis Delage, who had earlier been responsible for propaganda in the Madrid committee of the PCE, as commissar, the Army of the Ebro was the spiritual descendant of the Fifth Regiment. Consequently, the work of the commissars in the preparation of this army for its great strike across the Ebro and into Francoist territory was considered of paramount importance. As the commander, Modesto, writes:

> [P]olitical and moral preparation, a weapon which made up for other shortages, was the work of the Commissariat, from company commissar to the commissar of the Army, through those at battalion, brigade division and corps level.
>
> (*[L]a preparación politica y moral, arma que suplía las insuficiencias, era la obra del Comisariado, desde el comisario de compañía hasta el del Ejército, pasando por el de batallón, brigada, división y cuerpo.*)[69]

Líster, who commanded the V Corps, writes:

> In the operation across the Ebro and later in our resistance to counterattacks, the political and moral preparation of our men played a great part. The labour of the commissars under Delage, of the *milicianos de la cultura* and the group of writers and soldier-artists was tremendous ... It was the result of intense political work.
>
> (*En la realización de la operación del paso del río, y luego en toda la resistencia, desempeñó un gran papel la preparación política y moral de los hombres. El trabajo de los comisarios, dirigidos por el del Ejército del Ebro, Luis Delage, de los milicianos de la cultura y del grupo de escritores y dibujantes-combatientes fue enorme ... Ello era obra de un gran trabajo político.*)[70]

The problems had been outlined in a set of notes summarising a report on the Insurgent victories of March and April 1938, which had constituted a rout and led to the division of Republican territory into two. These notes were circulated with the general orders of the newly formed Army of the Ebro.[71] According to them, the factors which had caused the disaster were manifold, but they included some which it would be the task of the commissars to overcome, such as political dissension,

[68] The records of the commissar of the V Corps are found in DR, L795, C13. See also Mezquida, *Batalla del Ebro*, *passim*, and Santiago Alvarez, *Memorias II*, *passim*.

[69] Modesto, *Soy del Quinto Regimiento*, 182.

[70] Líster, *Nuestra guerra*, 202. [71] DR, L795, C1.

apathy, fatalism and defeatism, as well as a tendency to cast blame on subordinates.

Circular No. 4 of the Commissariat of the V Corps, signed on 2 April 1938, by Luis Delage just before he became commissar of the embryonic Army of the Ebro, describes how the corps was reorganised after the defeat and then the tasks of the commissars.[72] He criticises the commissars for their passivity or at least for restricting themselves to responding to situations rather than attending proactively to matters of morale. He warned them to watch out for enemy sympathisers among newly drafted men and to see that every soldier was personally spoken to about the importance of holding the line. Each commissar of division was given a specific mission. The entire message was to be discussed within the brigade in the presence of the divisional commissar.

Every one of Delage's circulars repeats and emphasises the duty of the commissars. They are written in clear, elevated yet concise style, expressing abstract ideas clearly so that the junior commissars in their turn could hammer home the message to their men. By means of the company delegate, the activists and the *milicianos de la cultura*, each soldier could literally be lectured personally.

Almost every circular includes instructions to the commissar of services such as the medical, signals and supply units, who were encouraged to become aware of how important their tasks were. As Líster would write later:

> There was a general tendency to reserve posts in the services for men who were not considered good enough for front-line duty. I always selected the men who had done best in combat and I put the most tested commanders at the head of the services.
>
> (*Existía una tendencia general a colocar en los Servicios a hombres que se consideraba no servían para misiones más combativas, de primera línea. Yo seleccioné siempre para los Servicios a hombres escogidos entre los mejores en el combate y puse a su cabeza a mandos de los más probados.*)[73]

While it is undeniable that the second-echelon services should be well manned and run, the fact is that in any army of the size of the Army of the Ebro with its 9 divisions (a total of perhaps 90,000 men), there will be men who have to be used even though they are indeed not suitable for front-line service. One must always take Líster's and other communist accounts with a grain of salt. Despite the real achievements and

[72] The documents of the Commissariat of the Army of the Ebro can be found in the appendix to vol. II of Mezquida, *Batalla del Ebro*, and quoted *passim*.

[73] Líster, *Nuestra guerra*, 283.

admirable performance of the Army of the Ebro, it still suffered from the faults of the Republican Army in general.

An illustration of daily work in the lengthy preparation of the army for the assault across the River Ebro on the night of 25–26 July 1938, and its months of resistance until Franco finally forced it back across the river in November, will show just how much effort was involved. On 11 May 1938, the Commissariat of the V Corps reported that new NCOs were being trained in the 45th Division, where discussions were being held about recent Chinese victories against the Japanese. Special groups were being formed for anti-aircraft and anti-tank units. For all this a great political campaign was under way in which soldiers were contributing to discussion about maintaining equipment in good order and about the importance of discipline in general. The 45th Division was running its classes for illiterates. A delegation had given bread and cheese to the factory it had adopted, while a friendship ceremony had been held with civilians in a rest depot. Establishing good relations with the civil population had been one of the basic points in the policy of the 11th Division, the one which Líster had originally led and which was still a part of the Army of the Ebro. The matter was important because discipline, at least while out of the line, was slack in the Republican Army. Looting, indeed, was not a rare occurrence. Therefore Líster made great attempts to cultivate good relations with the local civilians, especially in Aragon, where communist propaganda made a lot of the depredations of the anarchist columns in the summer of 1936.[74] The letter sent by the Russian leaders to Caballero in December 1936 had advised him not to confiscate or collectivise the property of landowning peasants.

All the battalions, the report continues, had wall newspapers. New recruits were being welcomed. On 9 May 1938, the Prime Minister, Juan Negrín, accompanied by Vicente Rojo, the Chief of Staff, had visited the 1st Brigade.

Shortly before the crossing of the Ebro, Santiago Alvarez, commissar of the V Corps after Delage's elevation to be army commissar, issued instructions to his subordinate commissars.[75] Well written and inspiring, they explained the purpose of the attack. The Ebro was to be crossed in order to relieve the pressure on the defenders of Valencia. Politically, the assault was intended to

> [s]how the pusillanimous and the cowardly in our own camp that we have a strong army, that our people do not want a compromise, that our brave soldiers

[74] *Ibid.*, 123; for pillage, see in particular CGG, L371, C1 for Teruel.

[75] *Instrucciones a los comisarios para el paso del río*, in Mezquida, *Batalla del Ebro*.

will fight until they expel the invader from our country ... and that the unity of our people in support of the government ... is real.

(*[d]emostrar a los pusilánimes y cobardes hasta expulsar los invasores de nuestra patria en nuestro propio campo que nosotros tenemos un fuerte ejército, que nuestro pueblo no quiere compromisos, que nuestros bravos soldados quieren luchar ... La unidad de nuestro pueblo alrededor al gobierno de Unión Nacional es un hecho real que cada vez adquiere más fortaleza.*)

This was the message; the method was to fight to the finish, which required renewed efforts by the commissars, implicit trust in the command, surprise, audacity, discipline and careful attention to detail and to preparing every single man. The pressure was continuous. The commissar of the 139th Mixed Brigade of the 45th Division received a message on 10 October 1938 pointing out that his unit had not been justified in abandoning two hills the previous day. Furthermore, officers and commissars were not to stay behind the front line on the pretext of rounding up stragglers. It was at such times that the men in the line were leaderless and provocateurs took advantage.[76] Apart from the regular misuse of the word 'provocateurs', by which the commissars really meant soldiers with low morale, the point seems valid.

The British assistant military attaché, Major Mahoney, wrote, late in 1938:

The Republican soldier is carefully tended by the Political Commissar. The Nationalist, if better fed physically, is not so well-nourished mentally. He is told, once a week on Sundays, that he is fighting for his Christ; the Republican is told, seven days a week, that he is fighting for his rights. The differences in the methods and in the force of the appeals to primitive and insensitive minds, do not need emphasis.[77]

Omitting the reference to 'primitive and insensitive minds', which says much about the vision of Spain possessed by Major Mahoney, the observation seems broadly accurate. Yet it is insufficient. It might have been more useful for him to examine the role of the commissar and whether he had a part to play, however modified, in any army. The British Army had relied on strict discipline and regulations, but even in the 1914–18 war, there had been sufficient old-style officers and NCOs to form the framework of a new and massive host. This was largely true also of the Francoist army. In a really professional force such as the Spanish Legion, or a fanatical body of volunteers such as the Traditionalists, the equivalent of the commissars were the traditions themselves and

[76] *Ibid.*, II: 163.
[77] FO 371, W14897/29/41, 14 November 1938.

the accompanying chaplains. In a civil war, with few professionals left, without chaplains, the commissar was the only solution possible for the problem of how to receive often unwilling conscripts, ignorant of what the war was about, whose ancestors had handed down anti-militarist sympathies, and forge a reasonably efficient army without reliance on external and traditional disciplinary methods.

Even though anarchist writers and anti-communists criticise the methods of the communist commissars, and Prieto made great attempts to reduce their grip, at least in the central zone, they do not attack the institution itself. Nor does General Rojo, who writes that faults on both sides led to friction between officers and commissars but that this was soon stopped.[78] Even the markedly anti-communist Colonel Casado thought that many commissars did excellent work, but that they 'impeded, undermined and annulled the Military High Command'.[79] This view was not rare among the career officers, but it is not easy to find definite evidence to prove his accusations.

What is likely to be true and unsurprising is that, once the Republican Army had been formed, the commissar became an irritation to men who had been in the militias and were politically aware, as many ex-soldiers have reported.

There is little evidence either, outside anarchist accusations, that the commissars engaged in a reign of terror, though that they did so at times seems true.[80] One document suggests that the commissar could '[d]owngrade and physically remove [*suprimir físicamente*] those officers who are not on our side [*de nuestra parte*] and declared enemies of the regime'.[81] This would seem to refer not to political opponents but to Insurgent sympathisers. In any case, it was probably only a recommendation. The date of the document is 28 March 1938, during the disastrous collapse of those weeks. It could refer to a specific situation or a particular officer. The letter is from a brigade commissar to the battalion commissar. It is not marked 'secret' and would seem to refer to the position in that unit alone.

The work of the political commissars, as it would be ideally, is perhaps best summed up by quoting part of a report by Luis Delage, commissar of the Army of the Ebro, on the activity of the commissars of that army from the beginning of the Ebro battle on 25 July 1938 until 10 September:

78 Rojo, *Madrid*, 139–40.
79 Casado, *Last Days of Madrid*, 58.
80 See evidence in Peirats, *CNT*, III: 254ff.
81 DR, L474/1, C1.

The commissars held meetings down to company level, some of them between commanders and commissars in which the first phase of the battle was analysed and conclusions for further action were reached. Close relationships with the troops were established. Thousands of leaflets were printed on the significance of the attack over the Ebro and the defence against Nationalist counter-attacks. Cases of heroism or distinguished conduct were quoted in order to stimulate all troops. We worked hard to establish unquestioning confidence in the command in order that difficult situations might not be created if orders were not obeyed to the letter and so that not a yard of captured territory would be lost. Propaganda was directed to the enemy using the few means that we had. Within the units competitions were held in order to speed up the building of fortifications with special mention being made daily of those men who had accomplished most ... Commissars were on duty every evening, talking to the troops in order to stimulate profound hatred of treacherous deserters. We commented on the notes sent by the War Commissariat about deserters and used to the full the details we had about the treatment meted out to Republican deserters by the enemy.

But fundamentally the most important aspect of our task was to explain the political and military significance of the offensive and therefore the need to RESIST, even under the most difficult conditions.

(Se celebraron reuniones de Comisarios hasta las compañías, algunas entre mandos y comisarios, en las cuales se hizo un análisis de la primera fase y se sacaron conclusiones para el futuro; se estableció una estrecha convivencia con la tropa; se tiraron millares de octavillas y manifiestos sobre el significado de la ofensiva y defensiva; se destacaron, con un sentido político justo, los casos de heroísmo y buen comportamiento para despertar el estímulo de todos; se encaminó un trabajo a crear una confianza ilimitada en los mandos, en el sentido de que no se podían crear situaciones difíciles si se cumplían a rajatabla las órdenes y no ceder un palmo de terreno reconquistado. Se hizo propaganda al enemigo, utilizando los pocos medios de que se disponía ... Se estableció un trabajo de emulación dentro de las mismas unidades para intensificar la fortificación, destacando diariamente a los que más cumplían ... Cada noche se establecían turnos de vigilancia con los comisarios a la cabeza y entre la tropa se orientó el trabajo a crear el odio profundo hacia los traidores que desertaban, comentando las notas enviadas por este Comisariado sobre penas impuestas a evadidos y desertores, y explotando datos conocidos sobre el trato dado por el enemigo a algunos que se pasaron a sus filas.

Pero fundamentalmente el más fuerte trabajo fue orientado a explicar la importancia política y militar de la ofensiva y la necesidad, por tanto, de RESISTIR aun en las condiciones más difíciles.)[82]

Conclusions

The institution of the Commissariat does not seem to have been a clearly thought-out decision. If the communists did not suggest it, they

[82] DR, L796, C3.

were quick to seize the opportunities it gave them. In view of the duties involved, the communists were, in general, the best commissars, though it is arguable that their self-publicity may have been greater than their actual achievements. It was never intended that the commissars should supplant and much less hamper the officers, but as the Republican Army expanded the commissars took a growing part in purely military matters. Commissars were essential for new recruits in view of the special circumstances of the Spanish Civil War. The masses of new recruits had to be convinced that, despite the major splits within the Popular Front and in the working-class and trade union movements, the Republic offered a better future for all, even those who were fighting on Franco's side, than the rhetoric of the Insurgents. Furthermore, great emphasis was laid on the war being in one sense international, in that it could be portrayed as a struggle against the German and Italian 'invaders' whom Franco's so-called 'Nationalists' had invited to Spain to fight against the Spanish people. These were the ideological positions of the Spanish communists. Yet the problem or almost contradiction lay in that for many the communist vision seemed to dominate, despite the undoubted value of the concept of national unity.

How successful the commissars were is a matter of debate, in view of the eventual defeat of the Republican Army. Yet it would be hard to blame the commissars for the defeat, because the Commissariat itself arose from the conditions which themselves contributed towards the defeat. It may be that, in the battle of the Ebro itself, arguably the greatest and most decisive struggle of the war, intensive labour on the part of the commissars contributed to prolonging the war. If, counterfactually, the war had indeed lasted until the general European war began in September 1939, it could perhaps be argued and indeed has always been the view of many, that the result of the Spanish Civil War would have been different.

This is mere speculation, but there remains the valid question of how far the infighting between the communists on the one hand and those who opposed them on the other was prolonged in the Republican Army by the commissars, and this will be examined in the next chapter. Finally, there seems little doubt that the most lasting contribution made was the spread of literacy and education in general. That a great deal of it was to have the result of making the new literates more available to written propaganda is also true, but, in its cultural aspirations, the Army of the Spanish Republic was exemplary.

9 The communists, the anarchists and the Republican Army

Communist policy and the army

The intense political activity of Republican Spain, together with the disappearance of many of the outward forms of the traditional Spanish army, inevitably led to political and ideological attitudes occupying a dominating position in the Republican Army.

The chaos of the first weeks of the Civil War brought about the emergence of the PCE as the organisation with which many of the career officers could identify their own aims, on the one hand because of its emphasis on order and discipline, and on the other because the policy of the Popular Front had made the PCE take on the role of the party which sought to defend the bourgeois, liberal and parliamentary Second Republic, which had come into power only in 1931, against those who thought that the military uprising of 18 July 1936 sanctioned the destruction of the State in those areas where the insurrection had been defeated, and permitted revolution, with its accompanying aspects of confiscation of property, indiscriminate murder and, in respect of the army, abolition of traditional structures and of accepted military forms. That the PCE was opposed to all this was evident from the beginning of the war. The Fifth Regiment, the writings of its commissar 'Carlos Contreras' in its daily paper *Milicia Popular* and speeches by leading communists praising those professional officers who had not risen in rebellion, left no doubt about the PCE's views on the army. As early as 24 July 1936, the Comintern sent a message to José Díaz, Secretary of the PCE, insisting that the army should not be replaced by militias and that professional officers should be encouraged, even with an amnesty if need be, to volunteer to defend the Republic.[1]

[1] Radosh *et al.*, *Spain Betrayed*, 13–14. See also A. Elorza and M. Bizcarredondo, *Queridos amigos, la Internacional Comunista y España 1919–1939*, Barcelona, 1999, 298.

At the same time as the PCE was concerned to support and not antagonise career officers, even the most traditional among them, it was concerned with 'fascists' within the army, by which was rarely meant true fascists, that is members of José Antonio Primo de Rivera's *Falange*, but rather officers who, whatever their views, put their loyalty to their fellow officers before their oath to what they now considered a regime which could not be allowed to continue in power. Even so, the necessary purging of the Army would have to be postponed, in the PCE view, until the insurrection had been crushed, stated Antonio Mije in September 1936, still confident of a rapid end to the conflict.[2]

Very soon after Francisco Largo Caballero became Prime Minister on 4 September 1936, the Central Committee of the PCE sent a delegation to him, emphasising the absolute necessity for central direction of the war, not only in its military aspects, to which Caballero had already attended by the appointment of Asensio to command in the Central Front and by the appointment of a new General Staff, by also by the creation of an all-powerful War Committee. Its proposed members were Caballero as President, Prieto as Minister of Defence, thus giving him control of the Army, whose responsibility had been assumed by Caballero, Antonio Mije of the PCE in charge of War Industries, Julio Just of Republican Left to run Transport, and a member of the anarchist CNT for Supplies. The PCE also proposed the building of a large reserve army in the south-west of the country.[3] This was at a time when the decision to form only six mixed brigades was being taken. The communist proposals demonstrated a high degree of realism, not appreciated by Caballero, who rejected them. Nor did Caballero, Prime Minister and Minister for War (in reality only the Army, since the Navy and the Air Force came under a different ministry and there was no joint Staff), accept the proposals of the CNT, which held a Plenary Session of its Regional Federations in the same month. Its conclusions recommended the establishment of militia-controlled Workers' and Soldiers' Committees, with equal representation of the CNT and the socialist UGT. Professional officers should be retained in the subordinate and advisory positions of *técnicos* which they held in anarchist columns. Supreme direction of operations should be by a National Defence Council under the Prime Minister, with equal representation of the CNT, UGT and Republican parties. Local administrations should be replaced by Defence Councils and public order assured by a People's

[2] In *International Press Correspondence*, 16, 43 (19 September 1936), cited by D. Cattell, *Communism and the Spanish Civil War*, Berkeley, CA, 1965, 57.

[3] Ibárruri *et al.*, *Guerra y Revolución*, II: 57.

Militia. Unity of command was demanded, which in view of the cumbersome plans of the CNT would seem rather difficult to attain.[4]

One or two communist civilians of importance appeared in the new General Staff. On the list of 20 October 1936, Alejandro García Val, the communist Secretary of the Clothing Workers' Union and one of the organisers of the Fifth Regiment, and later Director of Transport services, was appointed aide to Lieutenant-Colonel Estrada, the Chief of Staff, while Vittorio Vidali, the Trieste communist, who used the pseudonym 'Carlos Contreras', was appointed to head the Organisation Section of the Staff. However, the role of these men was that of *civilian* representative. It is unlikely that Vidali could spare the time from his duties with the Fifth Regiment to attend Staff discussions, and the idea that García Val could have any serious 'communist' influence on Estrada, the austere and dedicated Major Rojo and the other professional officers is untenable.[5] Emile Kléber also appeared on 20 October in the Operations Staff, when he was about to take over command of the first of the International Brigades (11th Brigade of the Republican Army). That certain names appeared on a list in the *Diario Oficial del Ministerio de la Guerra* ought not to be construed as meaning that they played significant roles on the Staff, as the CNT representative on the Staff and later sub-commissar-general Serafín González Inestal confirmed many years later.[6]

The PCE frequently called for mass conscription and the creation of powerful reserves. While on the one hand the existing militias, in the process of being militarised in the mixed brigades, might, if better armed, led and armed, and if the Republic's strategy had impeded Franco from bringing his professional Legion and Moroccan *Regulares* over the Strait of Gibraltar (both very big 'ifs'), have held the Insurgents, and while in the meantime a proper army might have been recruited and trained in the Levante, on the other hand the long-standing opposition to conscription and militarism in general, characteristic of the Spanish working class, but also the lack of weapons and officers to train a massive army, made the PCE demands seem unreasonable.

Though the demand for mass conscription may have been unreasonable, the Eight Conditions for Victory, published by the PCE's Central

[4] See *De julio a julio* (special issue of the anarchist newspaper *Fragua Social*), Valencia, 19 July 1937, and *The Times*, 1 December 1936, quoting speeches by the anarchist ministers Peiró and Federica Montseny. See also Maidanik, *Ispanskii proletariat*, 252, for a Russian opinion quoting *Izvestia* and Antonov-Ovseyenko, Soviet Consul-General in Barcelona.

[5] For the opposite view see Martínez Bande, *La marcha sobre Madrid*, 98n.

[6] Conversation, October 1971.

Committee on 18 December 1936, did demonstrate awareness of the situation. The conditions were:

1 a People's Army
2 traditional military structure
3 a single General Staff
4 an end to the militias
5 iron discipline
6 abolition of autonomous war zones and an all-embracing plan of operations
7 obligatory military service
8 respect for loyal professional officers.[7]

The Eight Conditions do not mention the commissars. This might be because the communists were satisfied with their achievements in this respect. They may have been right, for opponents saw the commissars as vehicles for ensuring that advancement would be granted to officers only if they joined the party. Luis Araquistáin, ambassador of the Republic to France in 1936 and 1937 and a close associate of Caballero, claimed that the commissars aimed to force men to take the PCE card by rewarding them if they joined and persecuting them if they did not. From the first, he wrote later, 'the Communists were the privileged, the aristocracy of the Republican Army'.[8]

Reaction of Largo Caballero and Prieto

Caballero turned fiercely against the communists. He once fiercely dismissed the Soviet ambassador from his office. He was aware of communist methods, according to one of his ministers, the Basque Manuel de Irujo, having received 'a bitter lesson which produced salutary effects' when the communists had taken over the Socialist Youth.[9] Caballero's reaction now consisted principally of ignoring communist demands for the replacement of General Asensio as Under-Secretary for War and for creating a large mass conscript army. He also reacted by refusing to sanction the large number of irregularly made appointments of commissars. In his memoirs, Caballero complained of communist

> favouritism in the matter of promotions, influence in hospitals to ensure that party members received better care, excessive praise of communist units by the

[7] Ibárruri *et al.*, *Guerra y Revolución*, II: 208–16, give the full text.
[8] Luis Araquistáin, 'The Communists and the Spanish Civil War', at www.whatnext-journal.co.uk/Pages/history/Araquist.html.
[9] Letter from Irujo, 23 September 1972.

communist press and the consequent entry into the PCE of men who would normally never have done so.[10]

In fact, Caballero's main reaction seems to have been one of anger and defiance, rather than using his power and prestige to prevent the more undesirable aspects of an apparent communist take-over. That the importance of the political commissars was fully understood only by the PCE is an example of this. Caballero would have done better to urge the UGT and the PSOE to suggest large numbers of men as commissars and defend his actions by pointing out that the UGT and PSOE together were immensely powerful in comparison with the PCE and JSU. He could have signed the appointments himself rather than complain later that del Vayo, the commissar-general, had done so over his head and packed the Commissariat with communists. Similarly, it might have been advisable not to have a scene with the Soviet ambassador but simply to threaten to request his immediate recall, which would have brought the latter up short. Yet Caballero's reply to Stalin's letter of 21 December 1936 referred to the ambassador in very approving terms.[11]

A great deal of the proselytisation complained of occurred because the politically conscious militias were already in units whose ideological complexion was established. This left the PCE to work on the conscripts of 1937 and 1938, a task for which its well-drilled and able commissars and activists were peculiarly suited.[12]

Communist statistics for PCE members serving, and in consequence the increase in membership, are impressive. In 1936 the PCE had claimed 35,000 members, a figure which had risen to close on 250,000 by March 1937.[13] Fifty-three per cent of the total membership was under arms by that month,[14] which indicates that the new membership was largely in the army. By March 1938, about one-third of the army were stated to be members of the JSU[15] and by May of that year a captured communist document spoke of almost 35,000 'militants' in the Army of the Centre alone and a recruitment of 500 every week. This document

[10] Largo Caballero, *Mis memorias*, 211–13. *Ibid.*, 293, for the scene with the Soviet ambassador, for which see also Bolloten, *Spanish Revolution*, 272 and 273n.

[11] Ibárruri *et al.*, *Guerra y Revolución*, II: 102.

[12] A good explanation of this is found in G. Hermet, *Les communistes en Espagne*, Paris, 1971, 47–8.

[13] Cattell, *Communism and the Spanish Civil War*, 21, quoting Jesús Hernández; Payne, *Spanish Revolution*, 331, quoting José Díaz.

[14] Hermet, *Les communistes*, 47–8.

[15] Payne, *Spanish Revolution*, 331, quoting JSU source.

was for internal party use and also quite critical of some other parts of party work, so its figures may be taken to be more or less genuine.[16]

The battles fought by Caballero and later Prieto to reduce communist influence in the War Commissariat have been examined in the previous chapter. In an attempt to depoliticise the Republican Army entirely, Prieto forbade officers to take part in acts of a political nature. The *Diario Oficial* of 5 October 1937 required ceremonial parades, often used as opportunities for political propaganda, to have to apply for authorisation. It is an interesting comment on the Spanish army that Diego Hidalgo, Minister for War in 1934, had issued similar orders in July of that year. Furthermore, in his preamble Hidalgo recalled that 13 other such decrees had been issued in the previous century. In this respect, it was the Insurgent army, where politics were strictly repressed in favour of military efficiency, that was the innovator, while the new Republican Army kept to the tradition.[17]

The communist counter-reaction

The PCE's reaction to Prieto's onslaught came in Dolores Ibárruri's report to the meeting of the Central Committee of the Communist Party on 13 November 1937. Her report consisted of a detailed analysis of the party's opinions on the way the war was being fought.

After criticising Largo Caballero for using unreliable professional officers and 'sabotaging' the Fifth Regiment, she went on to stress the greater importance of political work now that the Republican Army was to a great extent composed of conscripts rather than the enthusiastic volunteers who had formed the early militias. The decree forbidding proselytisation was no excuse for impeding political explanations that the Popular Front was a union of all parties to defend the parliamentary, bourgeois and liberal Republic against the threat of Fascism. Indeed, she said, the Popular Front had led to important collaboration between the PCE and the CNT. She made several detailed criticisms about the lack of discipline, proper fortifications, serious Staff work and concern for the welfare of troops. If those who ought to busy themselves with these matters did not do so, 'our military commanders', and by 'our' she meant communist ones, should take over these responsibilities.

The latter part of 'La Pasionaria's' speech contained suggestions about how the PCE should work within the Republican Army. The

16 Captured document in CGG, L284, C14.

17 Diego Hidalgo, *Cómo y por qué fui lanzado del ministerio de la Guerra*, Madrid, 1934. The title appears to have suggested itself to Prieto for his famous speech of 1938.

party had been correct in establishing cells at every level from company upwards and in organising politico-military committees at provincial level. Close liaison between militants at the Front and PCE headquarters had provided useful data and, in return, the PCE had given invaluable help to the Commissariat. Party militants had shown a good example to those of other political complexions and party work had lifted the morale of civilians.

Nevertheless, went on Ibárruri, there had been an excess of zeal in promoting the PCE in certain quarters and members must stop hindering the work of those who held different opinions. But Prieto's restrictions had led to political schisms within the army. While she conceded that communists were heavily represented in the Commissariat, this was because they were experienced and able to do the job.

At the same conference, the Party Secretary, José Díaz, after blaming Caballero for the loss of Málaga in February of 1937, complained that anti-communist prejudice had been responsible for the entry into the Commissariat of too many '*señoritos*', by which he meant men of higher education who were ignorant of the tasks they had to perform.[18]

Intense political work was still needed. It was approved by the party hierarchs even at the risk of being accused of sectarianism. By 1938 the PCE had liaison committees in army corps and in all lower units as far down as battalions and companies. There were party instructors at all levels. Whatever the fears of other groups, the PCE felt that the socialists in particular were strongly opposed to their committees and that even in units where both military commander and political commissar were PCE men, the activists were still not properly trained.[19]

A further anonymous report to the party with the title 'Some Experiences of the Ebro Offensive', dating from the latter part of 1938, praised the execution of the attack and underlined the respect which the professional officers had for the militia commanders. By now, according to the writer, 'The party committees were functioning well, but some weaknesses were still evident.' ('*Los comités del partido funcionaron bien, pero se notaron algunas debilidades.*')[20]

These speeches and documents indicate the extent of PCE influence in the Republican Army. They also betray an awareness of the danger of alienating other shades of opinion but point out that in the current situation the PCE's conclusions were correct. Yet, if Prieto's comments truly reflected the facts, he was also undeniably correct in trying to

[18] See extract of speech in *Labour Monthly*, London, February 1938.
[19] Quoted from a captured document in CGG, L284, C14.
[20] DR, L796, C3.

stamp out proselytism. His first decree, as Minister of National Defence, on 28 June 1937, on the question began in ringing tones: 'Political proselytism is invading military areas.' (*'Afanes de proselitismo político vienen invadiendo zonas militares.'*) He proceeded to forbid members of the armed forces to undertake propaganda intended to persuade anybody, whatever his rank, to join any political party. Even a mere suggestion from a superior to a soldier that he should change his political allegiance would be considered a military offence and entail loss of rank. His later decree, in the *Diario Oficial* of 5 October 1937, forbade officers to participate in public political acts, talk to the press or on the radio or hold parades without permission. It was preceded by an explanation that the peculiarly multicoloured political composition of the Republican Army made it essential that nobody should oblige any member of it to abandon his own ideas. The Army had to be seen as apolitical. 'The Army ... is the People itself.' (*'El ejército ... es el pueblo mismo.'*) As the communists realised, in some ways these statements contradicted each other. How was an army which was so strongly politicised suddenly to become depoliticised? The implementation of these decrees, together with the closer control that Prieto wanted to exert over the commissars, made it impossible for the PCE to see eye-to-eye with the Minister, and so in April 1938 they engineered his fall.

Verdict

The burden of the communist case is that, though it was true that their militants occupied a disproportionate number of posts of responsibility, Prieto's insistence on proportional representation made a mockery of the successful prosecution of the war. In the opinion of Antonio Cordón, later Under-Secretary for War, the appointment of Prieto's associate Julían Zugazagoitia as Secretary-General of the Defence Ministry was a pointless exercise in balancing the political see-saw.[21] Cordón had reason to be bitter because Prieto had twice removed him from posts, once from being Chief of Staff of the Army of the East and later as head of the Operations Section of the General Staff. Cordón attempts to demonstrate that, although as Under-Secretary under Juan Negrín as Minister of National Defence from April 1938 onwards he made all appointments to commands up to battalion level, senior commands were filled by a committee that he chaired but which had a wide representation of members of the General Staff, the inspector-general of the Arm concerned and the head of personnel in the Under-Secretariat.

[21] Cordón, *Trayectoria*, 393–4.

However, he was in the chair, the General Staff tried to avoid factional tension, Rojo himself, its chief, was indecisive on such questions and the inspector-general was an ageing officer who was not considered fit for active command.[22] It is probable that without Prieto in the Ministry, and with Negrín preoccupied with questions of state, appointments fell almost entirely under Cordón's control. One small reference hints at his procedure. À propos of a journey to the central-south zone he writes, 'I also gave a detailed account of my journey to the party leadership, of course.' ('*También di cuenta detallada de mi viaje a la dirección del partido, claro está.*')[23] He seems unaware of the gravity of his statement. A colonel who occupies the vital post of Under-Secretary for the Army reports to civilians on matters of great import and extreme security.

After the war it was the preponderance of communists in high commands which formed the basis of Prieto's correspondence with Negrín. He wrote that communists held the Under-Secretaryship of the Army (Cordón), of the Air (Núñez Maza), and command of the Air Force (Hidalgo de Cisneros). Pedro Prados was Chief of Staff of the Navy, Jesús Hernández was commissar of the central-south zone, Cuevas was in charge of police and Marcial Fernández was Director-General of *Carabineros.*[24] But were these men appointed because they were members of the PCE and, once appointed, did their membership affect their judgement and conduct so that they made decisions which were not in the best interests of the Republic? The case of Cordón has been considered. As for Jesús Hernández, he received his appointment as part of a political share-out between the two zones into which the Republic had been split. In the *Carabineros* and police, an internal PCE document analysing recruitment into these forces noted that the party had had little success among men who had been in them before the war and was not too successful with new officers, either. In the very important *Servicio de Investigación Militar,* the redoubtable SIM, the document commented that the few communists there had had their lives made difficult by socialist sympathisers.[25] In Madrid, the commander of 9 of the 14 *Seguridad* groups held party cards, which is not an excessive figure given the strength of the PCE in Madrid, its leadership in the war

22 For example, the Inspector-General of Infantry was General Llano de la Encomienda, whom the Basque President Aguirre had described as 'the personification of military incompetence' (DR, L54, C6).

23 Cordón, *Trayectoria*, 422.

24 Prieto, '*Carta a Negrín*' of 3 July 1939, in *Convulsiones de España*, 74–5. Cuevas later claimed to have broken with the PCE and not to be under its influence. See E. Cuevas, *Recuerdos de la guerra de España*, Montauban, 1940.

25 DR, L558, C1. This appears to be draft of a report on PCE work in the paramilitary forces in May 1938.

effort and the lead it had taken in advocating the reestablishment of proper police methods rather than the vigilante bands which had rampaged through the city in the early weeks of the war. There were few PCE members in the elite *Carabineros*, a force which was a socialist fief. This observation by a communist confirms the comments of Dr Rafael Méndez, who was told, when he was in charge of the force, by Negrín that the *Carabineros* had to be 'impenetrable to communist influence' (*'impenetrable a la influencia comunista'*).[26]

Negrín answered Prieto's letter with a lengthy defence of his own appointments policy,[27] claiming that his choices were made strictly on apolitical grounds and pointing out that he made no appointments of communists when he had previously been Finance Minister nor in the Prime Minister's own office. As for the military, he wrote that they already had a large complement of communists in command posts when he arrived at the Ministry of National Defence in April 1938, and it was Caballero and Prieto who had appointed them. As for the powerful Cordón, Negrín know that he was widely disliked, but he was nevertheless quite extraordinarily competent in reconstructing the remains of the army which had been routed so disastrously in the spring of 1938. As for Nuñez Maza, he had replaced Antonio Camacho, another communist about whom no complaints had been made. He had appointed non-communists to the Under-Secretaryship for the Navy (Játiva) and the office of Head of Supplies (Trifón Gómez). He had left the socialist Alejandro Otero in charge of arms procurement. As commissar-general he had appointed Ossorio y Tafall, a member of the Republican Left Party and the socialists Belarmino Tomás and Bruno Alonso as commissars of the Air Force and the Navy respectively. Among the sub-commissar-generals, Negrín claimed to have established proportional representation but with a marked predominance of socialists. Hernández had been balanced by the CNT nominee Gil Roldán in the Army Group of the East (GERO). Manuel Ulíbarri, a socialist, was put in charge of the SIM, where he carried out a purge of communists. As for Pedro Prados, Navy Chief of Staff, Negrín said he had dismissed him for his partiality. Regarding the military commanders, Negrín listed his appointments as army group and army commanders: Hernández Saravia, Jurado, Perea, Casado, Moriones and Escobar, none of whom were communists. Modesto had become an army commander fortuitously. Negrín continued to claim similarly in respect of less senior posts. But, finally, he pointed out that the communists were

[26] *Indice*, 303 (March 1972).
[27] *Ibid.*, 263/4 (February 1970).

not the enemy. They were the Republic's 'brothers in arms' ('*hermanos de lucha*') and deserved respect as such. In the end, protested Negrín, they could not have been so dominant as Prieto alleged when one considers the success of Casado's coup in March 1939.

Inevitably, there is some special pleading here. When Negrín refers to socialists, he may easily refer to some who were within the communist orbit, such as Ossorio y Tafall, who was not in fact a PSOE member. He says nothing about the virtual communist control of the Air Force when, as will be seen later, the General Staff seems to have had little authority over it and it was probably controlled by Russian advisers. To claim that Modesto was appointed 'fortuitously' to lead the Army of the Ebro is unacceptable. Modesto was given command of the *Agrupación Autónoma del Ebro*, composed of the V and XV Corps. What Negrín should have said was that when the decision to give the Group the status of an army, the command should have been given to somebody else. But Modesto was the man most fitted to command the army which he had formed and trained specifically for the Ebro operation.

No reply from Prieto has been forthcoming. Negrín's defence of his own appointments and the particular appointments that Prieto criticises seems more or less convincing, with the possible exception of Cordón, who was not the only competent officer available and who virtually controlled all but the highest appointments, and of the Political Commissariat, where the communists clearly predominated. Argument at this level is difficult. One sentence quoted from Cordón's memoirs does not prove that he always took and obeyed his orders from the Communist Party. In the final analysis it is impossible to establish whether it mattered that some posts were held by communists, especially in view of the fact that so many men became communists during the war because they thought that the communists had the right ideas and attitude about conducting the conflict. What seems more worrying and depressing is that so many arguments revolve around the particular political membership of men in important posts, when this should not have been significant. In contrast, none of this ideological quarrelling was significant among the Insurgents, where, though large numbers of the new troops belonged to the *Falange*, or the Carlists, or the youth section of the Catholic conservative CEDA, the military was supreme. In April 1937 Franco simply ordered the *Falange* and the Carlists to merge under his leadership. He selected his own Cabinet, under the guidance of his brother-in-law, Ramón Serrano Súñer, some of whom had no specific political allegiance, while the others were expected to lay aside any loyalties they might have to the old monarchy or the new *Falange*.

Grievances of the anarchist CNT

The CNT in particular laboured under a heavy sense of grievance, among other reasons because the PCE had probably attracted many CNT sympathisers to its ranks given what they considered the more realistic communist attitude towards the Civil War. The CNT had many members who were not convinced of anarchist doctrines but who did not feel at home with the gradualist UGT. It was quite natural for such men to accept a PCE card when the communists were at the height of their dynamism and prestige because of the aid provided by the USSR.

The CNT had seen the PCE's doctrines about how to construct an army, so totally opposed to its own, adopted by Largo Caballero and instituted by the process of militarising the militias. The CNT had had to dissolve its own columns of militia, had seen its members conscripted, had seen communists become officers and commissars because anarchist ideology objected to officers who gave orders and had to be saluted. Then its power was sharply reduced after the Barcelona troubles of May 1937. That summer, its agricultural collectives in Aragon were destroyed by communist military forces on the orders of the Government. Many CNT members wondered what sort of Spain they were they fighting for.

Reports went regularly to the FAI and the Defence Committee of the CNT, complaining of communist influence and the ill-treatment of CNT members. According to them, men with first-class records had deserted from communist-commanded units and returned to CNT formations because they refused to be preached to by the commissars. If they were attached to communist units they felt that they were treated as cannon-fodder. As an example, the 116th, 117th and 118th Brigades of García Vivancos's 25th Division (ex-Ortiz column) had been divided amongst newly formed corps with the express purpose of dissolving an anarchist division which had been together since the outbreak of war. Much sought-after postings in special units, such as tank drivers, were denied to CNT members for specious reasons, and they found it hard to obtain entry to the *Escuelas Populares de Guerra* and thus to become new officers.[28]

A frequent complaint was that PCE members were favoured for promotion. A FAI circular of September 1938 said that communists had been granted 5,500 promotions out of the 7,000 made between May and

[28] For a summary of these reports see Peirats, *CNT*, III: 219ff.

September that year.[29] In fact, about 20,000 promotions had been made. The FAI report probably refers to promotions to the ranks of lieutenant and captain, which did amount roughly to 7,500.[30] Without being able to collate a list of names with lists of CNT members, it would be impossible to verify the FAI's complaint. Moreover, it seems unlikely that the FAI could have substantiated it. However, there is no doubt that there was a very large number of promotions in the 27th Division, which had been formed from the column organised in Barcelona by the PSUC – the united socialists and communists of Catalonia – at the same time as the anarchist columns (later the 24th, 25th, 26th and 28th Divisions) and the POUM militia (later 29th Division). In the 27th Division, on 9 May 1938, the *Diario Oficial* announced 46 new captains, 157 lieutenants and 395 sergeants. Was there a military reason for such discrimination? There are no similarly long lists for the 25th Division at any time. In its newspaper, *La Trinchera*, on 17 April 1938 the 27th Division gloried in its promotions and in the large number of medals awarded.

This is not to say that undeserved promotions were granted because of communist pressure. However, promotions to officer rank should be to recognise abilities which must have been more or less equally present in all these divisions. From the CNT's point of view, the distribution of new NCOs and officers among other units was, it feared, part of the plan to spread communist influence in the Republican Army.

It cannot be said that all the promotions in the 27th Division went to communists, or that their being communists increased their suitability for promotion. Ironically, the commander of the division, José del Barrio, would break with the PCE in 1948 and, probably for that reason, was criticised by Modesto in his memoirs for his wartime shortcomings.[31] There were frequently other reports about discrimination against the CNT by the all-powerful communists. At high levels, Rojo was accused by the CNT of having followed communist instructions. The heads of the Staff Sections of Information (Estrada) and of Personnel (Díaz-Tendero) were said to be party members. Cordón, the Under-Secretary, often came under CNT fire. He was accused of protecting communist officers who murdered CNT men and for being behind the policy of splitting up long-existing CNT units.

The CNT complained that it had no influence at all in the *Servicio de Investigación Militar* and the Air Force. Even within the Republican Army itself it complained that it was poorly represented at command

[29] *Ibid.*, 225.
[30] *Nueva España*, newspaper of the 49th Division, 31 December 1938.
[31] Modesto, *Soy del Quinto Regimiento*, 173.

Table 9.1 *Senior commands in CNT hands, September 1936*

	Total	Commanded by CNT or friendly
Army groups	2	0
Armies	6	2 (Perea and Casado)
Corps	21	2 (Jover and Mera, but commanders of the XIII (Romero), XVI (Palacios), VI (Gallego) and VIII (Joaquín Pérez Salas) were anti-communist and hence friendly to the CNT)
Divisions	70	9

level, in spite of its huge contribution to the war effort. In the GERO or Eastern Army Group, the commander, Juan Hernández Saravia, was said to be a tool of the communists, though his last-minute dismissal and replacement by the artillery general Jurado was probably due to his inability to work smoothly with Modesto.[32] The only friend of the CNT in the GERO was Perea, commander of the Army of the East, in which the X Corps (Gregorio Jover) and the 26th Division (Sanz) were headed by anarchists. In the other army in the GERO, the Army of the Ebro, under Modesto and corps commanders Líster, Tagüeña and Vega, there was no CNT influence. In the Central Army Group or GERC, the CNT described Miaja as 'a characterless nonentity' ('*elemento sin carácter*'), Menéndez of the Army of the Levante as 'a communist who should be shot' ('*comunista y elemento fusilable*') and Prada of the Army of Extremadura as 'a socialist fellow-traveller of the communists' ('*socialista comunizante*'). There were a few corps and divisions whose commanders sympathised with the CNT (Mera's IV Corps was one of these), but brigades which had been recruited largely among CNT members had been widely distributed in order to keep them apart. Table 9.1 shows the CNT's position in September 1938, as reported by the military secretariat of the CNT.

The report went on to analyse the CNT content of commands in recruiting depots, transport battalions and rearguard battalions. As far as the commissars were concerned, only Gil Roldán of the GERO, González Inestal of the Army of Andalusia and a few corps commissars belonged to the CNT.[33]

[32] Rojo, *Alerta*, 83, and Azaña, *Obras Competas*, III: 536 and 538.

[33] Report to the military secretariat of the National Committee of the FAI, 30 September 1938, quoted by Peirats, *CNT*, III: 228.

Other points frequently made in reports to CNT and FAI committees were that the PCE maintained cells in all units, as the latter admitted, and the serious accusation that communists plotted to murder uncooperative officers and commissars, a matter which affected in particular the 43rd Division during the time it was trapped in the Pyrenees in 1938. The socialist commissar of this division, Máximo de Gracia, had reported that he had had to watch carefully over the safety of the commander and the Chief of Staff of the 102nd Mixed Brigade.[34]

How should these reports be judged? Were they merely examples of paranoia on the part of the CNT, which was facing a challenge from a political party that was efficient and resolute and played a militant game? Was the PCE really so determined to run the army that no trick was too low to stoop to in order to seize power? The difficulty with judging such reports is that no objective enquiry into the complaints seems to have taken place. As for the commanders of the armies, corps and divisions, the complaint that the CNT was poorly represented is factually correct, but it is not surprising. Few professional officers could be expected to have much sympathy for libertarians who had taken indiscipline as a principal and a threat to traditional values in a way that the socialist UGT had not done. The only officers that the CNT described as 'friendly' were either strongly anti-communist, such as Casado, or had come to know CNT leaders well during the Primo de Rivera dictatorship, such as Perea. While the reports were correct in their judgement of Cordón, in so far as he was a communist, it would nevertheless be difficult to substantiate the accusation that his being so was itself responsible for the treatment which the CNT saw as unfair. To describe Menéndez as a communist who should be shot was hysterical. Nevertheless, what seems important is not so much to judge how far the CNT was accurate in its complaints, but rather to take note of its attitude and the fact that political bitterness of this kind grew steadily greater in the Republican Army, when the whole point of the militarisation of the militias had been, among other things, to merge political differences. Furthermore, merely because the CNT was a large organisation and its numbers were as heavily, if not more, represented in the armed forces as those of the socialist PSOE and UGT, or the communist PCE and JSU, did not mean that it should enjoy a proportionate number of high commands. Communists accepted military discipline; professional officers were familiar with it. Rightly or wrongly, the Government had decided that a standard (*regular* was the

34 *Ibid.*, 246.

adjective used) form of army rather than irregulars, run in a classic way, was needed. Communists believed this also, but anarchists had accepted that structure against their will. The CNT produced military leaders, but not so many as the communists, even though it might be claimed that some of the latter were successful only because of the skill of their professional Chiefs of Staff. In contrast, the anarchist columns in Aragon in 1936 and 1937 had accepted militarisation unwillingly. There had been bitter infighting within the CNT and among its units about militarisation and the acceptance of professional officers in the columns.[35]

By 1938 the CNT was more aware of the situation it faced than it had been earlier. It had not been on its guard, which had permitted much of its power in Barcelona to be taken away in May 1937. When it had witnessed the hunting-down of the revolutionary communist and anti-Stalinist POUM, the imprisonment of its leaders and the murder by the NKVD or Soviet secret police in Spain, headed by Alexandr Orlov, of the POUM leader, Andrés Nin, and later the destruction of the anarchist-run Council of Aragon, it became more aware of the peril. 'We could have wiped them [the communists] out in 1937; we did not do so in order not to be accused of imperilling the Front, but even now I wish we had', said Miguel González Inestal 34 years later in Madrid.

In March 1938 the CNT invited the reservists of the 1926, 1927 and 1928 classes, who were about to be called up, to join volunteer CNT battalions.[36] The anarchist newspaper *Solidaridad Obrera* of 13 March 1938 proclaimed to these older men that they needed no discipline beyond 'the imperative of their antifascist awareness' ('*el imperativo de su conciencia antifascista*'). The idea was to protect anarchist sympathisers from going through the recruiting depots and being sent against their will to brigades where they would perhaps be ill-treated unless they accepted all the brainwashing to which the CNT feared they would be subjected from the commissars. Secondly, it would be a way of ensuring that new recruits with anarchist attitudes would strengthen the anarchist units. Indeed, all those who volunteered were directly enrolled in the 26th Division, which was based on the ex-Durruti column.[37] While volunteering to get into a particular regiment without waiting to be conscripted and sent somewhere else was not unknown elsewhere, in Spain it demonstrated the degree to which political and ideological fears and considerations predominated.

[35] As is evident in García Vivancos's unpublished memoirs.
[36] Peirats, *CNT*, III: 91. [37] *Ibid.*, 90.

Conclusions

Inevitably, the PCE increased enormously in influence and members because of the evident opportuneness of its views on how to fight the war, the better discipline of its militias and its opposition to the revolutionary attitudes and deeds of the CNT. Hence the attempts of the socialists Francisco Largo Caballero and Indalecio Prieto to limit communist influence. Republican Spain included people of all classes, who might not be supporters of the military coup but were not enthusiastic about a revolution, either. The letter from the Russian leaders to Caballero in December 1936 had advised him to look after the interests of that class. The efforts of the socialist Largo Caballero and Prieto to block the overwhelming communist influence, at least in the central zone of Republican territory, in the end brought about the fall of both politicians and the rise of another socialist, Juan Negrín, who was probably a better manipulator of the situation.[38]

With the communist Antonio Cordón, the Under-Secretary for Defence, in day-to-day control of the Republican Army, it might have seemed that the army was a communist one, yet the PCE, as can be seen from Soviet documents, was never happy with the situation. They had abolished the collectivisations of independent farmers' lands in Aragon, and had reduced much of the power of the CNT in Catalonia. The revolutionary and anti-Stalinist Marxists of the POUM had been arrested and their leader, Andrés Nin, murdered, but this had increased anti-communist resentment in much of Republican Spain, so that the Casado coup was able to overcome communist-led opposition and present itself as an uprising to remove Soviet influence from Republican Spain. Communist influence may have been exaggerated, perhaps because Prieto's allegations have been taken at face value and Juan Negrín left only his brief answers to Prieto in their post-war correspondence. Yet Negrín's insistence on keeping the communists out of the elite *Carabineros* and the SIM suggests that he was quite aware of the danger. The final round of appointments of communist militia leaders to important posts occurred because Negrín's hand was forced by the strong pressure to surrender of the professional army commanders. However, despite Casado's allegations (see below), Negrín did not appoint Líster, Modesto and others to the army commands.

[38] On this question see Helen Graham's magisterial study, *The Spanish Republic at War 1936–1939*, Cambridge University Press, 2002.

10 International aspects

The International Brigades

There were six brigades of foreign volunteers who came to defend the Spanish Republic against the insurrection. These were numbered the 11th, 12th, 13th, 14th and 15th Mixed Brigades. While they formed only a very small numerical part of the Republican Army, and from late 1937 they were increasingly filled with Spanish recruits, the International Brigades took a major part in almost all the great battles of the Spanish Civil War. Moreover, they represented in a concrete form the reaction of the foreign militant working-class and left-wing parties towards the Civil War. Discussion here, however, will be limited to their military role within the Republican Army.

The Communist International or Comintern gave the French Communist Party (PCF) the task of mobilising volunteers to fight for the Spanish Republic. One of the first decisions of the PCF was to send Vital Gayman, a Parisian local councillor, and André Marty, who had led a mutiny in the French fleet in the Black Sea in 1919, and was a leading French communist and a member of the directorate of the Comintern, to Spain. The exiled German Communist Party (KPD) appealed to those of its adherents who had military experience to volunteer to fight Fascism. The Italian Left leaders, Luigi Longo, Randolfo Pacciardi and Pietro Nenni, left for Spain. These efforts, however, were uncoordinated until the Praesidium of the Comintern met and decided, on 20 September 1936, two months after the Spanish conflict had begun, to recruit, among workingmen from all countries, volunteers with military experience with a view to sending them to Spain. Later, in a speech before commanders and commissars of the 11th Brigade, Gayman said that the idea was to contribute the special military skills that the 1914–18 war on the one hand and compulsory military service on the other had enabled thousands of antifascist workers and peasants to obtain in France, Belgium, Italy, Germany, Central Europe and the Balkans.[1]

[1] Skoutelsky, *Novedad en el frente*, 75–6.

Almost all the narratives and accounts of the International Brigades show that the reality was very different from the illusion. Given the logical requirement that the volunteers ought to have had some military experience, it might have been thought that men not possessing genuine and useful capacities would not have been sent to Spain. Yet Marty and his commissar, Mario Nicoletti, wrote to Paris as early as 27 October 1936, when the first brigade was still being organised, complaining that in a group of 515 recently arrived volunteers close on 42 per cent had not even done their military service.[2] There were even men who were physically unfit. Moreover, this group was worse than the preceding one. There was a lack of officers, so companies were put under NCOs and battalions under low-ranking reserve officers. Every volunteer who had a minimum of military experience was given some command responsibility. As Skoutelsky comments: 'How far away was this from the shock infantry of international communism organised in a disciplined army directed from Moscow!'[3]

The 1st Battalion of the first International Brigade (the 11th Mixed Brigade of the Republican Army) marched through the Gran Vía, the main avenue of Madrid, on 8 November 1936.[4] The good military order and firm marching step of the men, who were mostly German anti-Nazi refugees, made some spectators believe they were Russians, whose arrival to save Spanish democracy was expected from one day to the next.[5] If the observers had known that the marching men were Germans, with their military reputation, they might have been even more impressed, yet nevertheless mistaken. The ages of these German volunteers made it unlikely that they had served in the army even in the last months of 1918. To have acquired some useful military experience in the 1914–18 war a man would have been almost 40 in late 1936. The average age of the German volunteers is not known, but it cannot have been markedly different from that of other International Brigaders, who were mostly between 18 and 36 years old. Furthermore, the Versailles Treaty had prohibited compulsory military service in Germany. It was not reintroduced until 1935, by which time the volunteers, affiliated to the German socialist and communist movements, powerful yet so quickly broken up by the Nazis, had probably already fled their country.

[2] *Ibid.*, 120–1. [3] *Ibid.*, 87.

[4] This date has been disputed. However, 8 November was the date given by *The Times*, which reported on Monday 9 November 1936 that 720 International Brigaders had marched through the Spanish capital the day before.

[5] According to *News Chronicle* journalist Geoffrey Cox, in his *Defence of Madrid*, Gollancz, 1937, 37–67.

As for the French volunteers, their average age was between 26 and 34.[6] In France, however, there was military service. One of the results was that the French volunteers included reserve officers and so, exceptionally, the proportion of French volunteers with military experience was significant, despite the complaints sent by PCF leaders from Spain to Paris.

In the case of the approximately 2,200 British volunteers, 74 per cent were between 21 and 35 years old. It is true that some of the best-known British volunteers had played an active role in the Great War. This was why Major Nathan and Captain Wintringham, and MacCartney, Fry and Bert Overton, plus a few more, reached high rank in the British battalion. But Britain, like the United States, did not have compulsory military service. Though a tiny minority of the British had been army cadets in private schools, the immense majority of the volunteers were working-class in origin, had left school at the latest at the age of 14 and were inherently men of rebellious natures, uncompliant and hostile to discipline. Many were of scant military value, as Will Paynter of the Miners' Union complained to Harry Pollitt, Secretary-General of the Communist Party of Great Britain. About 250 or 19.6 per cent of the British were over 36 years old and might have been in the armed services in 1918, but only 6 declared that they had been professional soldiers.[7]

Among the Americans, Robert Merriman, first commander of the Abraham Lincoln battalion, had been in the Reserve Officers Training Corps (ROTC) of the University of Nevada, while another commander, Oliver Law, had been in the US Army for six years. It was precisely for these reasons that they became commanders, though the famous *El Lobo*, a nickname translated from the surname of Milton Wolff, a later commander of the Lincolns, had no military experience.

The figure of 34 per cent of Americans with military experience, quoted by Skoutelsky, seems doubtfully high.[8] Given that the volunteers wanted to go and fight Fascism in Spain and that military experience was required, their statements that they possessed such experience

[6] R. Skoutelsky, *L'espoir guidait leurs pas: les volontaires français dans les Brigades Internationales 1936–1939*, Paris, 1998, 142.

[7] See Baxell, *British Volunteers*, 14, 17 and 21, although this author opines in general that many of the British did have military experience. On Will Paynter's view, see Hopkins, *Into the Heart of Fire*, 157. See also Michael Alpert '"Una trompeta lejana". Las Brigadas Internacionales en la guerra de España: una reconsideración sesenta años después', *Espacio, Tiempo y Forma*, series 5, *Historia Contemporánea*, 12 (1999), 225–38.

[8] Skoutelsky, *Novedad en el frente*, 180.

should not be taken at face value. In any case, Spaniards were no more ignorant of military matters than foreigners. Spain did have military service; many militiamen would have served in the Moroccan campaigns of the 1920s, while others had been in the Legion. It is difficult to accept the view that the foreign volunteers, even if they had been in the World War for a few months in 1918, could contribute more than the undoubtedly very important sense of solidarity and awareness that the Republic had not been totally abandoned to its fate.

The idea that the Internationals were the equivalent of the Spanish Legion, a well-trained, fiercely disciplined and savage force, was seriously mistaken. Nevertheless, in the first year of the Civil War, the Internationals were treated as if they really possessed the weapons and the abilities of the Legion. The decree, published on 27 September 1937, which gave the Internationals a precise status read: 'As a substitute for the Foreign Legion, the International Brigades will be created within the units of the Army of the Republic.' ('*En sustitución del Tercio de Extranjeros … se crearán las Brigadas Internacionales como unidades del Ejército de la República.*')[9]

The appalling consequences of this mistaken comparison were enormous losses among the Internationals. Entire brigades had to be reconstructed. On 4 March 1937, Vital Gayman, the Parisian municipal councillor stationed in the Internationals' base at Albacete, wrote a report protesting that 'taking advantage of the particularly high morale of the international units, armed only with their valour … without sufficient artillery support or tanks, against the machine-guns … of the enemy, should be forbidden'.[10] On 21 August 1937, Colonel Simonov, one of the Russian advisers, sent Marshal Voroshilov, People's Commissar for Defence, who in turn passed it to Stalin, a report from André Marty, in which the latter complained of great weariness in the political morale of the Internationals, their lack of trust, shown by constant and reiterated demands for leave to go home, friction between the different nationalities and what the paranoid Marty called the activities of 'provocateurs'.[11]

The International Brigades suffered such heavy casualties that they were steadily reinforced with Spanish conscripts. In December 1937, the International command in Albacete announced that, of a total of 48,814 men, 27,725 or 57 per cent were Spanish.[12] That summer, the battles of Brunete and Belchite had destroyed the International Brigades.

[9] *Ibid.*, 319. [10] *Ibid*, 159.
[11] Radosh *et al.*, *Spain Betrayed*, 249–50.
[12] Skoutelsky, *Novedad en el frente*, 225.

Officers were refusing to obey orders; whole battalions fell to pieces; the XII International Brigade had to be dissolved.[13] Colonel 'Gómez' (the German Wilhelm Zaisser) reported to Moscow in July 1938 that the collapse of morale among the Internationals, added to the undermining which he blamed on Fifth Columnists, had filled the Internationals' base at Albacete with demoralised soldiers, whom he had had to concentrate in a special 're-education' camp through which 4,000 had already passed.[14] Another report, signed on 14 January 1938 by Sverchevsky (known as 'Walter' in Spain), the Pole who commanded a division of three International Brigades, criticised the military qualities of the international units after the bloodlettings of Brunete and Belchite in summer 1937, followed that winter by Teruel. The distinguished communist military leader writes that the Internationals fought worse at Brunete than inexperienced Spanish brigades, and refers to panics and flights. Sverchevsky does not spare his harsh comments. He blames the fall in military competence of the Internationals on their idea that they had come to save Spain, which made them take a superior attitude. Moreover, discipline in the International Brigades was poor, they neglected to clean their weapons, their Staffs were grossly overfull, training was not as good as it should be and, finally, the Internationals were obsessed with politics and ignored instruction and training.[15] Again, Grigory Shtern, the principal Soviet military adviser, wrote to Moscow on 23 June 1937:

> I have begun to worry a great deal about the state of the International Brigades ... the attitude towards them of the Spaniards and of them towards the Spaniards; the questions about morale; the chauvinism of the nationalities (especially the French, Poles and Italians); the desire for repatriation; the presence of enemies in the ranks of the Internationals.[16]

General Kléber, who had led the XI International Brigade until the Spanish Chief of Staff of the defence of Madrid, Vicente Rojo, had complained about his behaviour and discipline, repeated similar views in a report of 14 December 1937.[17]

There were five International Brigades. Later another, the 129th, was created, but most of its troops were Spanish. The Internationals helped to raise Spanish morale, giving an example of solidarity, altruism and heroism, particularly as, contrary to what had been hoped, they were

[13] *Ibid.*, 315.
[14] Radosh *et al.*, *Spain Betrayed*, 431ff.
[15] *Ibid.*, 436–60. Although the documents selected by the editors of *Spain Betrayed* may not have been absolutely representative, such comments by a commander of Sverchevsky's status cannot be ignored.
[16] Radosh *et al.*, *Spain Betrayed*, 240.
[17] *Ibid*, 345.

not gladiators with extensive war experience, nor well equipped, nor led by generals who were masters of the art of war. Though they took part in most of the great battles of the Spanish Civil War and suffered huge losses, they cannot be said to have given an example of discipline or military ability to the Spanish troops, nor was their achievement greater than that of the Republican Army or at least its best fighting units.

How many international volunteers went to Spain? According to the most trustworthy figures discovered since the Comintern archives were made available to scholars, calculations refer to 32,256 men having reached the Albacete base by August 1938.[18] By this stage in the war no more volunteers were arriving. Possibly this figure may be an overestimate. The same man may have been counted twice if, for instance, he returned to Albacete after a period of hospitalisation.

Not all the Internationals were in Spain at the same time. Furthermore, many non-Spaniards fought in the Republican Army but were not enrolled in the International Brigades (George Orwell, who was in a POUM militia, is an example). However, the figure of 32,256 mentioned above does not include the auxiliary personnel, especially the British and US medical teams, nor the foreign airmen such as the squadron organised by André Malraux. Lastly, the Soviet advisers, airmen, tank-drivers and interpreters have to be counted separately.

The Russians

The precise dates of the arrival of Russian military advisers are hard to identify, but some of them are known to have accompanied the first shipments of Soviet weapons, while many more came to Republican Spain during October, November and December 1936.[19] In his account, Colonel Casado, who from his position on the Staff must have been well informed, writes that they arrived in the second half of September 1936.[20] The letter which Stalin, Marshal Voroshilov and Molotov, the Soviet Foreign Minister, sent to Largo Caballero dated 21 December 1936 refers to the advisers as already present in Spain and to the insistent requests for specialists made through Marcel Rosenberg, the Soviet ambassador,[21] and underlines that the Russians could be no more than

[18] Skoutelsky, *Novedad en el frente*, 169.

[19] On the Soviet decision to aid Spain see Michael Alpert, *A New International History of the Spanish Civil War*, rev. edn, Palgrave Macmillan, 2004. For details of shipping see Alpert, *La guerra civil española en el mar.*

[20] Casado, *Last Days of Madrid*, 51.

[21] Ibárruri, in Ibárruri *et al.*, *Guerra y revolución*, II: 101, writes that the letter from the Soviet leaders was in response to one from Caballero, which she does not cite.

advisers. The Soviet leaders asked the Spanish Premier to indicate to what extent he valued their contribution. Caballero answered on 12 January 1937 praising the Soviet officers:

> The comrades who, *summoned by us*, have come to help us, are giving excellent service. Their great experience is very useful and is contributing efficiently ... I can assure you that they are fulfilling their task with real enthusiasm and extraordinary valour.[22] (Italics added)

The exact number of Russians who came to Spain cannot be established, but there are various statements which can be compared. President Azaña had been told by Caballero, presumably towards February 1937, when most of the advisers had arrived, that the total figure was 781.[23] The President noted in August 1937 that most of them had left. He adds in his memoirs, probably repeating the views of his military aide and other loyal professional officers who came to visit him, that 'The Russian masses, who have never amounted to more than a thousand, distributed in different parts of the armed services, are dwindling to nil ... It is no great pity ['*No es para lamentarlo*].')[24]

Walter Krivitsky, a Soviet secret agent who fled to the USA and who would not have reason to underestimate the figures, said that there were never more than 2,000 Russians in Spain. Only the pilots and tank-drivers took part in active conflict while the rest were Staff advisers, instructors, engineers, war industry and chemical warfare experts, aircraft mechanics, radio operators and artillery experts.[25]

International Solidarity with the Spanish Republic, published in Moscow, appeared in English in 1975. It gave the following figures of Russian personnel in Spain: 772 pilots, 351 tank drivers, 222 military advisers and instructors, 77 in the Navy, 100 artillerymen, 52 other military experts, 130 engineers and others in aeronautical industries, 156 specialists in radio and communications and 204 interpreters. The total was 2,064, of whom no more than between 600 and 800 were in Spain at any one time.[26] The same figures were provided by Vittorio

[22] *Ibid.*, 102–3. The original text, in French, reads: '*Les camarades, qui, appelés par nous, sont venus nous aider, nous rendent de grands services. Leur grande expérience nous est très utile et contribue d'une manière efficace ... je puis vous dire qu'eux* [sic] *accomplissent leur charge avec un véritable enthousiasme et un courage extraordinaire.*'

[23] Azaña, *Obras Completas*, III: 477.

[24] *Ibid.*, IV: 768.

[25] W. Krivitsky, *I was Stalin's Agent*, Hamish Hamilton, 1939, 114.

[26] Academy of Sciences of the USSR, Soviet War Veterans' Committee, *International Solidarity with the Spanish Republic*, Moscow, 1975, 328–9 (copyright for the translation into English is dated 1974, but the first printing was in 1975).

Vidali.[27] Investigations in Soviet archives have recently produced a slightly different total of 2,082.[28]

The Spanish archives have preserved some paysheets for 'foreigners' attached to the Ministry of National Defence for October, November and December 1937 and for January, February, March and July 1938.[29] The total figures range from 258 in September 1937 to 426 in December of that year. The paysheets are drawn up in rank order of the recipients, from general of division to lieutenant. For every month they include close on 150 interpreters, of the 204 who served in Spain.[30] The future Marshal Rodion Malinovski signs for his monthly pay in this set of sheets, as well as other generals: Perpich, Kreming, Leonidov, Maximov, Duvrovich, Alexander, Bikov and Schilov.

The most important Russian in Spain was Jan Berzin (Pavel Ivanovich Kiuzis Peteris), whose other *noms de guerre* were 'Donizetti' and 'Grishin'. When Malinovski arrived he presented himself to Berzin at once.[31] Known among the Russians as 'the old man', he appears to have been a popular figure. He had founded and run the Soviet Military Intelligence service.[32]

Vladimir Efimovich Goriev, known as 'Sancho', was the military attaché. The writer Arturo Barea, who probably met him when Barea was working in the censor's department in the tall Telefónica building in the Gran Vía, used as an artillery observation point, describes him as 'tall, good-looking, with prominent cheekbones ... speaking good Spanish, excellent English, and with an unlimited capacity for hard work'.[33] During the battles for Madrid over the autumn and winter of 1936–7 he collaborated closely with Vicente Rojo, the Chief of Staff in the city. Rojo's impression was that Goriev was intelligent, courteous and never tried to impose his opinions.[34] While one would expect a Spanish officer to say that he had never permitted himself to be lectured by a foreigner, Rojo would probably have complained if necessary about Goriev, as he did about Kléber, who commanded the XI

[27] Quoted by Ricardo de la Cierva in answer to a reader's letter in *Historia y Vida*, 48 (March 1972), 10.

[28] Kowalsky, *La Unión Soviética*, 208, table 5.3.

[29] DR, L511, C4.

[30] P. and A. Abramson, *Mosaico Roto*, 277, who were interpreters in Spain, refer to 204 Russian interpeters.

[31] Malinovski, in Malinovski *et al.*, *BLB*, 14.

[32] Y. Rybalkin, *Stalin y España: la ayuda militar soviética a la República*, Madrid, 2007 (originally published Moscow, 2000).

[33] Barea, *La llama*, 231.

[34] Rojo, *Madrid*, 215. See also J. A. Rojo, *Vicente Rojo, retrato de un general republicano*, Barcelona, 2006, 108.

International Brigade and who was dismissed for his public boastfulness and for not working harmoniously with the Spaniards.[35] For some time at the end of 1936, Goriev was in Bilbao (*The Times* correspondent on 28 October reported that the presence of a Russian general was rumoured). The journalist concerned, probably the famous George L. Steer, who published the news of the German bombing of Guernica on 26 April 1937, thought that Goriev was pleasant enough. He had organised the first tank counter-attack on the Madrid Front but he was 'inexperienced in war', and the Basques rejected his advice.[36] This was probably a mistake. In contrast with central Spain, where the Russian advisers seem to have worked in close contact with the Spaniards, Goriev advised Basque President Aguirre to dismiss his professional officers and take over supreme command himself, which he did on 5 May 1937. Considering the scanty achievements and later desertions and even treason of the career officers in the Basque Country, the Russian advice seems to have been good.[37] From Goriev's point of view, it was probably a matter of carrying out a disagreeable task as well as possible, for Aguirre, who headed a government of the Catholic and conservative Basque Nationalist Party (PNV), did not appreciate communists, had resisted the introduction of the commissar system and had probably been referring to his communist Chief of Staff, Captain Francisco Ciutat, when complaining about 'pernicious and politically mistaken elements' ('*elementos perniciosos y políticamente equivocados*') in his letters to Prieto.[38] Goriev seems, according to the account of Steer, who was present at high-level discussions before Bilbao fell, to have given his views with a certain diffidence.[39] After Bilbao fell on 19 June 1937, Goriev and 26 of his Russian colleagues remained in the North as advisers to the forces of Colonel Adolfo Prada. When Gijón, the final redoubt, fell they were evacuated by air.

The tank expert sent by Moscow to Spain was Colonel Semion Krivoshein. In his report, he does not hesitate to say that he maintained close relations with local committees of the PCE, which provided him with a car and driver. He headed a small group of Russian tank specialists and organised the first training depot for Spanish tank-drivers at Archena (Murcia). He gives an interesting résumé of the first tank battle in the Spanish Civil War, which took place at Seseña (Toledo), some

35 Rojo, *Vicente Rojo*, 107.
36 Steer, *The Tree of Gernika*, 99.
37 Martínez Bande, *Vizcaya*, 128.
38 See letter from Aguirre to Prieto of 24 May 1937 in DR, L54, C6, quoted by Martínez Bande, *Vizcaya*, 128nn. 193 and 194.
39 Steer, *The Tree of Gernika*, 323–4.

miles south of Madrid, on 29 October 1936. In Krivoshein's view the T.26 Russian tanks, which had arrived in Spain only two weeks earlier, did well (even though there was no common language and the Soviet advisers taught the Spanish drivers using hand signals), but there was a lack of efficient follow-up by the insufficiently trained Spanish infantry.[40] Poor preparation led to tank-drivers not knowing where they were, and lack of fuel forced them to return to their starting points.[41] While it took a year to train a Soviet tank-driver, in Spain Madrid taxi-drivers were pressed into service and expected to master the art in a month. Krivoshein provides a revealing comment on Soviet frustration in the face of Spanish dilatory bureaucracy. In charge of a programme to convert civilian vehicles into armoured cars he complained that the Ministry of War took a month to authorise oil and petrol. 'All this for want of a piece of paper', he sneers.[42] This document, which Voroshilov, the People's Commissar for Defence, sent to Stalin on 10 March 1937 with a note to say that Stalin would find it interesting (perhaps because the delays of the Soviet bureaucracy were also frustrating), contains many more complaints about how difficult it was to work with the Spaniards.[43]

Krivoshein's successor was Dimitri Pavlov, alias 'Pablo', who formed a brigade of Russian T.26 tanks at Archena in December 1936, which he commanded in the battle of Guadalajara in March 1937. Though a successful tank commander (he would become Director-General of Armoured Forces in the Soviet Army),[44] he was relieved that summer, according to the Soviet authorities' habit of repatriating even highly competent officers after a relatively short period in Spain.[45]

Despite their successes in Spain, the disasters in the first few months of the German onslaught against the Soviet Union in 1941, which were due to the Russians not having absorbed the new tank tactics and having divided their armoured forces up instead of using them as their spearpoint against the enemy, led to Pavlov's execution. Such was the fate of many of the Russian advisers. Berzin disappeared in 1937, replaced by Shtern, and Goriev and Kulic ('Kupper') were also purged.[46]

[40] Krivoshein, in Malinovski *et al.*, *BLB*, 319–41. See Rybalkin, *Stalin y España*, 105, who also provides a detailed description by Captain Pavel Arman of the training procedure in the two weeks spent at Archena before the battle, 91–2.

[41] Kowalsky, *La Unión Soviética*, 309.

[42] Quoted *ibid.*, 270.

[43] Radosh *et al.*, *Spain Betrayed*, 146–8.

[44] Rybalkin, *Stalin y España*, 127.

[45] Kowalsky, *La Unión Soviética*, 329.

[46] Rybalkin, *Stalin y España*, 117–28, and Kowalsky, *La Unión Soviética*, 335–8.

The most difficult aspect to interpret and assess in the role of the Soviet advisers is what their precise contribution was. They claim to have had a decisive influence, so Nikolai Voronov (alias 'Voltaire') writes that, although José Luis Fuentes, commander of the Republican Army's artillery, was somewhat distant in manner, Voronov's instructions about how to place guns and other technical matters were printed and used by the Spanish gunners. He had to teach new techniques, organise cooperation with the infantry, draw topographical maps and write manuals and tables.[47] Similarly Malinovski ('Malino' in Spain) claims a vital role in the battle of the Jarama, in advising Líster, on the Staff of the Army of the Centre and as adviser to General Leopoldo Menéndez.[48]

One of the fullest and most self-aggrandising accounts is by Kiril Afanovich Meretskov (alias 'Petrovich'). According to him, though Berzin was the chief adviser, Meretskov would approach the Spanish Staff directly. He claims to have had the ear of Largo Caballero and to have proposed a new Staff to him. It may be that Caballero's Staff appointments of 20 October 1936, consisting of a number of civilians in advisory roles but still mostly of career officers, could have been based on Russian advice. Yet if this was so, there was a radical change soon after, for the General Staff announced on 30 November 1936 was much changed, with the Chief and the Section Heads all replaced. Meretskov's most excessive claim is to have persuaded Caballero to leave Madrid for Valencia when the city seemed about to be occupied by Franco's forces in early November 1936, a claim which he makes soon after grumbling about how difficult it was to reach the Prime Minister. According to Meretskov, the Russians directed Staff conferences and suggested the formation of the mixed brigades. They even exerted authority over the anarchist CNT, which began to turn to the Soviets for help, going so far as to request advice in planning an attack on Teruel in the winter of 1936.

Meretskov's judgements of Miaja and Rojo are more balanced. Miaja, he writes, was difficult to work with, as he knew nothing of the interests of the working class and hindered the organisation and direction of military operations. Nevertheless, he was a competent general (this is probably the only expression of Miaja's competence to be found in the whole of Spanish Civil War literature). Rojo was businesslike and significantly further to the left than Miaja, which may be interpreted as meaning that he was more compliant. As has been seen, Rojo was

[47] Malinovski *et al.*, *BLB*, 99.
[48] *Ibid.*, 25, 28, 37, 44.

distant and tried to avoid conflict. He cannot be said to have been politically to the left, but description of this sort applied to Spanish career officers is largely irrelevant. Meretskov persevered with Miaja, who gradually began to accept his advice. In the mornings Miaja would outline his plans as agreed with Meretskov the previous evening. Rojo would support them and disputes arose only on matters of detail.[49]

On the basis of available evidence, it is not possible to reach a decision on how far the advisers persuaded or imposed their views on Spanish officers. Understandably no Spanish officer, not even the communist militia commander Líster, admits that they did. The latter, for instance, avoids saying anything direct except that, where he disagreed with the Russians, he said so plainly.[50] Casado's opinion was that the Russian proposals were usually rejected by the General Staff but that their advice often prevailed in the end.[51] But Casado's memoir is self-justifying on the grounds that his March 1939 coup was aimed at ousting the communists and Soviet officers who, in his view, were in charge of the Republican Army.

Certainly, many documents bear the words 'Russian comrade' in their distribution lists. The apparent absence of documents signed by Russians in the archives of the Republican Army leads to the conclusion that such documents were removed or destroyed or that most advice was oral and informal. The reports of the advisers emphasise their hard work in composing plans of action for the Spanish Staffs. This, in addition to being self-justifying, is probably true, but the plans would have had to be translated into Spanish before being handed to the Spanish officers, and whether the latter actually read them, leave alone inwardly digested them and put them into operation, cannot be known.

Major planning, however, shows scant evidence of Russian advice. Even in a work as tendentious as the *Historia de la Cruzada española*, published in the early post-war years, admits that, despite rumours, foreign experts do not seem to have had anything to do with the Ebro operation of July 1938. This is confirmed by a strange episode recounted by General Rojo. Five days before the date set for the operation, Colonel Maximov, the Russian adviser to the Spanish Staff, came to advise Rojo against the planned operation. The latter wrote at once to Negrín saying that the Russian had known and approved of the Ebro crossing from the beginning but that *he knew how influential Maximov was* (my italics:

[49] K. A. Meretskov in *Voprosi Historii*, Moscow, December 1967, 109–21.
[50] Líster, *Nuestra guerra*, 105.
[51] Casado, *Last Days of Madrid*, 52.

MA).[52] The operation went ahead but from Rojo's words it seems that while this senior Russian adviser was kept informed of plans, his views about them were probably not solicited. He may not have been as influential as Rojo thought.

One major example, however, of the possible imposition on the Spanish Staff of the Soviet advisers' views was the offensive planned in Extremadura in the spring of 1937. This plan was worked out by Casado, at the time Head of the Operations Section of the Staff.[53] It consisted of a two-pronged drive towards Mérida and along the Tagus River towards Oropesa, thus striking the enemy at a weak point and cutting the Insurgent zone in two. When everything was ready, it was discovered that the required brigades were not being detached as ordered from Miaja's Central Front, where there was a plan to use them in the Brunete attack. When Miaja finally agreed to move the troops, the Russians refused to allow the Air Force to provide the necessary air cover.[54] All the evidence points to the conclusion that the Russians imposed their view, but Miaja's characteristic opposition to having units removed from his command should not be overlooked and it is irrelevant perhaps that his attitude was Russian-inspired. Nevertheless, there is probably more to the question than an argument about strategy, where the opponents of the daring Extremadura plan may have been right.[55] Azaña was told that the communists in the Cabinet did not want to give Caballero a chance to ask for their resignation, so when the Premier criticised Miaja for disobeying his orders, they did not object even though Miaja's refusal concurred with the Soviet advisers' views. Hernández and Uribe, the two ministers in question, merely asked for documentary proof of Miaja's indiscipline which would justify his dismissal. By then Miaja had probably issued the necessary orders to detach the brigades.

The conclusion to the question about the precise contribution of the Soviet advisers must be non-committal. Half a dozen senior Russian generals is a large number to be in Spain at one time, even though the prevailing Russian view was that there were nowhere near enough advisers given

52 Rojo, *Vicente Rojo*, 222–3, publishes a photograph of Rojo, General Jurado and a smiling Maximov relaxing in an observation point overlooking the Ebro.

53 Casado, *Last Days of Madrid*, 69.

54 *Ibid.*, 69–73. This episode is not mentioned by the commander of the Air Force, Ignacio Hidalgo de Cisneros. See his *Cambio de Rumbo: Memorias*, vol. II, Bucharest, 1964.

55 Colonel Martínez Bande, author of an excellent series on the military history of the Spanish Civil War, and who was not likely to have underestimated Russian influence, believed that the Brunete plan was very likely more sound that the Extremadura project (conversation Madrid, October 1971).

the amateur nature of the Republican Army. The advisers must have given their opinions, nearly always through interpreters. Their views may quite often have coincided with those of the Spanish professional officers. When they did not it is impossible to say whether the Russian view predominated. Certainly it cannot be said that the predominance of either a Russian or a Spanish opinion had a decisive effect.

The opening of Soviet sources[56] to scholars has allowed them to read comments by the advisers on the Spaniards and their own Russian colleagues, made objectively and not with propagandistic aims or written with extreme caution like the accounts in *Bajo la bandera de la España republicana*. Among them, one of the first letters of Goriev, the military attaché, to Voroshilov, People's Commissar for Defence, describes the lack of an adequate system of command in the Republican forces, the absence of proper control, the lack of officers and NCOs, the unsatisfactory distribution of material and food and the general attitude of neglect.[57] He confirms the attraction that the PCE had for the career officers. A month later Goriev describes the lack of coordination between the Chief of Staff, Major Estrada, and the recently promoted General Asensio, to whom Caballero had handed command in the central theatre of operations. Here can be seen the start of the criticisms to which Asensio would be subjected by the communists in the coming weeks. Goriev explains that Asensio had not yet understood that the militia commanders were not well enough trained to understand his laconic instructions and then writes some interesting sentences: 'You remember how orders were written during our civil war. It wasn't orders that were received, but rather instructions explaining what to do and how to do it.'[58] These observations help to understand the marked wordiness of the instructions which would later emerge from the Operations Sections of the Staffs of the Republican Army. They also explain that, while Goriev believed that Asensio was loyal, he thought that, however tactically brilliant this ex-*africanista* officer might be, he was of little use for the military situation at that precise moment.

Berzin, in charge of the military advisers, writing to Voroshilov on 12 January 1937, makes much less tactful criticisms than Goriev.[59] He uses the word 'sabotage', which should not be taken literally but in the Soviet context in which it was used to mean any sort of incompetence, and here to castigate the Spanish bureaucracy. Berzin rages at the Spaniards:

[56] The results of the opening of Soviet military archives are to be seen in Rybalkin, *Stalin y España*, Radosh *et al.*, *Spain Betrayed* and Kowalsky, *La Unión Soviética*.
[57] Radosh *et al.*, *Spain Betrayed*, document 16, 25 September 1936.
[58] *Ibid.*, document 17, 16 October 1936, 64–5.
[59] *Ibid.*, document 31, 12 January 1937.

> Sometimes my hands itch to take some of these bastards out of their offices and put them up against a wall. Such unpunished, unbridled sabotage of necessary measures, such sloppiness and irresponsibility as reign here in the General Staff and in the bureaucracy … I could never have imagined … People simply do not carry out the orders of the War Ministry, or they do the opposite and calmly continue to stay where they are.[60]

Berzin returns to the attack on 19 March 1937, after Caballero, much against his will, had in the end dismissed Asensio. 'Every measure is delayed and sabotaged by the General Staff', wrote Berzin to Voroshilov.[61] His words echo how idleness and irresponsibility had characterised Russian officers in Czarist times. It had been a very difficult task to impose order and discipline even on Russian revolutionary forces – the Red Army itself.

Finally the Russian advisers got their way. Asensio, Martínez Cabrera and Martínez Monje, and Colonels Hernández Arteaga and Villalba were arrested, accused of responsibility in the loss of Málaga. But Villalba was acquitted, while the cases against the others were suspended.

Despite the critical Soviet view of the Spanish bureaucracy and the professional officers, their own actions cannot be said to have been brilliantly planned and carried out. Apart from the shortage of advisers and the problems caused by the lack of interpreters, Goriev complains about restrictions imposed on his colleagues:

> Every trip to the Front must include a number of precautions. To go to a unit, to view training, to give instructions on the spot, to help, are not permitted, so as not to break the rules. It's dangerous to be with various [Spanish] military men too often, in case people talk about it too much.[62]

It was a difficult problem. The advisers were obliged to advise, but at the same time they were not to force their ideas on the Spanish officers nor draw too much attention to their presence. Grigory Shtern, the principal adviser after Berzin, summarised the issue briefly: before leaving the USSR, Voroshilov had told him, 'In no case give an order but … do everything necessary for victory.'[63]

The advisers had few illusions about their own ability. Colonel Sverchevsky ('Walter' in Spain) wrote, in mid 1938, that, as the commanding officer of a division of the Republican Army, he had come to know far more Spaniards than most of the other Soviet advisers.

[60] *Ibid.*, 127. [61] *Ibid.*, document 37, 149.
[62] *Ibid.*, document 19, 16 October 1936.
[63] Kowalsky, *La Unión Soviética*, 260.

What is more, he could speak Spanish, which made it easier for him to understand how Spaniards considered the Russians. Certainly, insisted Sverchevsky, the Republican Army owed a great deal to the advisers. Pavlov in tanks, Shmuskievich in the Air Force, Shtern, Malinovski and many others achieved a great deal in the building of the Republican Army. However, it was not only a question of material but also of moral aid. Some advisers had failed. Many operational errors had been committed in the battles of Brunete, Belchite and Teruel. A large proportion of the advisers overestimated their own abilities, thinking that a brief visit to a few army units gave them the right to express their opinions about the Republican Army. Spain needed much deeper study. Sverchevsky criticised individual tank officers and pilots. Furthermore, if some advisers made unwelcome comments, it reinforced the objection of other Spaniards to their very presence.[64]

What was worse, added Sverchevsky, were the arrogant attitudes and tone of too many of the Russians in their dealings with the Spanish officers, whom they treated as if they were amateurs with little experience and as if the Republican Army were still in its infancy. Tactlessness, bad manners and lack of respect were only too evident, especially when the Soviet advisers tried to give lessons to the Spanish professional officers. (Sverchevsky mentions the distinguished artillery officer Juan Hernández Saravia, as an example, who was made, in the presence of his subordinates, to listen to unnecessary advice in an incompetent translation.) Getting down to details, he criticises the untidiness of some Russian officers, who appeared in public unshaven, wearing unkempt civilian clothes, and who contrasted with their elegant Spanish hosts. Lastly, Sverchevsky slates the ignorance of Spanish among the advisers, even if they had spent many months in Spain. Even graver were the charges sent on 22 September 1937 to Moscow by a party organiser, who informed his superiors that some advisers were drunkards, spent their time seducing Spanish women and even misused the funds provided.[65]

Advisers, most of whom were self-effacing and of some value if not as much as might have been thought, were in fact a minority of the Russians in Spain. The largest individual group were the pilots who flew the new and up-to-date machines that the Soviet Union sent. In all, 772 pilots crewed aircraft until sufficient Spanish pilots were trained to fly machines which were, however, not replaced and updated as Germany and Italy replaced theirs.

[64] Radosh *et al.*, *Spain Betrayed*, document 77.
[65] *Ibid.*, document 58.

The Republic had retained the larger part of the mostly obsolete military aircraft in Spain.[66] However, lists of dismissed officers in the *Gaceta* show that 333 Air Force officers were dismissed the service in February 1937, many of whom were in Franco's forces. A scrutiny of various Republican sources shows a total of 65 pre-war officers who served in the Republican Air Force. Even if not all have been discovered and this total is doubled it remains smaller than the number that the Insurgents had at their disposal. As an example, although Andrés García Lacalle, who commanded the fighter aircraft of the Republic, had held a pilot's licence since 1929, he had no command experience and had only just been promoted to the most junior officer's rank.[67] On the other hand, pre-war records of Insurgent squadron and wing-commanders, leave alone individual pilots, demonstrate how much experience of flying and command they had. Out of 27 fighter squadron leaders, 21 had been pre-war Air Force officers, while this was so of only 15 out of 43 equivalents in the Republican Air Force.[68] The Insurgent flying ace Joaquín García Morato had been an instructor for six years,[69] and, if Adolf Galland, a later ace in the Battle of Britain, was typical of the German pilots of the Condor Legion which rotated about a hundred aircraft regularly to the Insurgents, they were the result of rigorous selection and meticulous training.[70]

Russian pilots began to fly their newly arrived high-speed 'Katiuska' SB bombers from 28 October 1936.[71] These forces were, as far as can be seen, controlled by Yakov Shmushkievich, the air attaché to the Soviet embassy. November saw the first actions of two fighter groups of ten squadrons, each of ten I-15 and I-16 fighters, followed by three squadrons of R-Z 'Natashas'. By the end of November 1936 there were close on 300 Soviet pilots flying in the skies of Spain and protecting Madrid from bombing by enemy aircraft. Over the winter and early spring of 1936–7 Soviet aircraft dominated the sky in central Spain.

66 On aircraft see Gerald Howson, *Aircraft of the Spanish Civil War*, New York, 1990, and the same author's *Arms for Spain: The Untold Story of the Spanish Civil War*, John Murray, 1998.

67 A. García Lacalle, *Mitos y verdades: la aviación de caza en la guerra civil española*, Mexico City, 1973. See his entry in the *Anuario Militar* for 1936.

68 General Jesús Salas Larrazábal, *La guerra desde el aire*, Barcelona, 1966, appendix 13.

69 J. García Morato, *Guerra en el aire*, Madrid, 1950, 25.

70 For an analysis of air force personnel and tactics see Michael Alpert, 'The Clash of Spanish Armies: Contrasting Ways of War in Spain 1936–1939', *War in History*, 6, 3 (1999), 331–51.

71 Kowalsky, *La Unión Soviética*, 292.

Their greatest triumph was the rout of Italian forces at Guadalajara in March 1937.

However, detailed studies show that the Soviet Union did not maintain its rate of supply and so failed to replace lost aircraft and catch up with the ever increasing supply of new and ever more advanced models by Germany and constant and large arrivals of Italian Fiat fighters. Moreover, how many of the 250 Russian machines assembled in Spanish factories were really finished for service, given that there was always a lack of motors or armament?[72]

One of the results of the shortage of aircraft and the failure to rotate pilots was their overwork and exhaustion. This in turn led to extraordinary figures of machines lost through accidents (147 during 1936–8, almost as many as lost to enemy action).[73] The majority of the accidents were due to pilot error, and a large part of these to landing errors, which suggests insufficient training, overwork or perhaps poor maintenance of airfields. In addition, 99 Soviet pilots lost their lives in Spain.[74]

The number of Soviet pilots diminished rapidly, from over 300 in 1936 to 276 in 1937 and 183 in 1938, as they were replaced by Spaniards trained in the USSR. Of these, 413 were trained in time to return to Spain and take over flying duties, while the last cohort of 185 who were still in the Soviet Union when the war ended either went to Mexico or stayed in the Soviet Union. In all, the Russians trained nearly 700 Spanish pilots.[75] However, the insufficiency of the five months' training continued the trend of accidents and fatalities.

In contrast with the Republican Army, there are indications that the Air Force was not controlled by the Spaniards. Frequently, aircraft were required for operations but not provided. For example, on 19 February 1938, Rojo commented on the incessant attacks from the air that his forces were enduring and the absence of the Republican Air Force. The next day the Minister of National Defence, Prieto, asked Rojo if he had a senior Air Force officer posted to his Staff. Rojo answered that … he did not know! He had a link with an Air Force commander in the rear, but there was no official connection.[76] This is an extraordinary admission. The memoirs of Ignacio Hidalgo de Cisneros, commander of the Republican Air Force, are singularly uninformative about who actually controlled the aircraft of the Republic. However, from autumn 1936

[72] *Ibid.*, 297 and ch. 13. J. Salas Larrazábal, *La intervención extranjera en la guerra de España*, Madrid, 1974, 427.

[73] Kowalsky, *La Unión Soviética*, 299, table 5:4.

[74] *Ibid.*, 305. [75] *Ibid.*, 303.

[76] DR, L482, C3–1, cables exchanged between Rojo, Hernández Sarabia and Prieto during the battle of Teruel.

the Fighter Group was commanded by the Russian Colonel Pumpur.[77] Eighty per cent of the pilots at the time of the battle of Brunete in July 1937 were Russian.[78] Nevertheless, it is difficult to discover who made the strategic decisions about their use.[79] The Russians supplied the aircraft and for the first two years most of the pilots, so there was little the Republican Army General Staff or even Prieto, Minister for the Air Force and the Navy, could do.[80]

Russian war material

The question of how much war material the Soviet Union sent to Republican Spain is fundamental, because the quantity of all armaments existing in Spain, or which Spanish factories were capable of producing, was relatively small and, had foreign material not reached both sides of the conflict in large quantities, the Spanish Civil War would not have reached the scale of intensity that it did. The hope of France and Britain, the major sponsors of the so called non-intervention policy, was indeed that both sides in Spain would run so short of arms that the war could not be continued.[81]

For the Republican Army, the problem of war material was grave. In the early weeks of the conflict, the loss of the cartridge factories in Seville and Granada, the lack of trust in the expert engineers and artillery officers, together with trade union leaders' preoccupation with forming militias rather than producing weapons, gave rise to severe shortages of even basic arms. Such shortages continued throughout the war. Another problem was the enormous variety of calibres and models of rifles and artillery which were accumulated. In Madrid, the arms depots of the 1st Division had been looted by the militias, which then abandoned vast quantities in their disastrous retreats in the summer and autumn of 1936. A report for November 1936 lists 24,192 rifles available for 38,000 men in the forces defending the city.[82] These rifles were of 16 different types, of 6.5, 7, 7.5 and 7.7 mm calibre,

77 Rybalkin, *Stalin y España*, 98.

78 *Ibid.*, 100. 79 Rybalkin has little to say about this.

80 In Rybalkin's well-researched work there are only two references to the Head of the Air Force, Hidalgo de Cisneros, neither of which refers to strategic or tactical matters.

81 See Alpert, *New International History*, for an account of the decisions taken by Germany, Italy and, somewhat later, the USSR to supply arms to Spain. The major and highly detailed work on this has been done by Gerald Howson, in his *Arms for Spain*. For Soviet arms shipments to supply the Republican Army, Air Force and Navy, see Kowalsky, *La Unión Soviética*.

82 Rojo, *Madrid*, 25. Also DR, L953, C9.

made in Germany, Czechoslovakia, Russia and Spain. There had also been 2,000 Mexican rifles urgently sent in September by President Cárdenas.[83] Unfortunately, the latter had almost all been lost in retreats that month. There had originally been 65,000 rifles kept in Madrid, though most of the bolts were kept separately in the Montaña barracks, which were looted by the mob. Thus it may be reasonably assumed that the lost rifle-bolts were never properly accounted for.[84]

References in Republican Army sources to other weapons, such as machine-guns, mortars, cannon, anti-tank guns, heavy artillery and so on, invariably underline the great variety in their type and calibre, as well as their capacities. Azaña summed it up well: 'The supply of arms is always slow, problematic and never sufficient.' ('*La entrega de armas es siempre lenta, problemática y nunca suficiente.*')[85]

Social disruption and the unreliability of specialists hampered arms production in the industrialised region of Catalonia. Demand for arms in the central zone, with the largest army, meant that a large part of the increase in production in the Barcelona industrial belt was taken by Madrid.[86]

To some extent, the arms question is one where there is evidence both of shortage and of abundance. In the Basque region, for instance, the Basque minister Irujo himself had to go to Bilbao and bring back 6 mortars and 20 rifles in his own car,[87] but other evidence points to large amounts of material arriving in the north.[88] It is very hard to make a reasonable assessment of any given situation without taking into account a large number of unknown factors such as the suitability and condition of the weapons when they arrived from the view of both their quality and their relevance to the particular military situation, the availability of spare parts and the supply of ammunition of the appropriate calibres. A Republican Army document produced during the Santander campaign of August 1937, for example, refers to 261 pieces of artillery, but they were of 25 differing manufactures and of 37, 47, 70, 75, 76.2, 77, 80, 105, 115, 127, 150, 152.4 and 210 mm calibre. Not surprisingly, the document complains of a constant shortage of ammunition.[89] The dearth of men with the appropriate skills to use to the best advantage whatever arms there were has also to be borne in mind.

83 *The Times*, 3 September 1936, quoting a speech of Cárdenas.
84 Martín Blázquez, *I Helped to Build*, 105.
85 Azaña, *Obras Completas*, III: 477.
86 Memorandum of Colonel Guarner, Chief of Staff of Militias in Catalonia and Aragon.
87 A. de Lizarra (pseud. of Manuel de Irujo), *Los vascos y la República Española*, Buenos Aires, 1944, 66–7.
88 Martínez Bande, *Vizcaya*, 54n.
89 DR, L853, C16.

Figures tend to lack meaning unless they can be related to requirements. By the end of the Spanish Civil War, the Insurgent Nationalists under General Franco possessed:

1,090,000 rifles and other personal weapons
35,000 automatic weapons
7,600 mortars
651 tanks.[90]

In contrast, in the autumn of 1938 the Spanish Premier and Minister of National Defence, Juan Negrín, told a British diplomat that, in order to be able to hold Catalonia and the Central-Southern Front, the Republican Army needed a further:

500,000 rifles
12,000 machine-guns
1,500 cannon
200 tanks
400 aircraft.[91]

General Matallana, Chief of Staff of the Central Army Group, reported in February 1939, that only 800 cannon, 80 tanks and 350,000 rifles were available for use.[92]

Earlier, in the Republic's last major offensive after crossing the River Ebro on 25–26 July 1938, the Nationalists had 76 artillery batteries on that battlefield, including 22 of the very large 149 mm calibre.[93] At the 3 guns per battery which was standard at this stage of the war, the Insurgents had 228 guns. Total figures of artillery for the Republican Army of the Ebro have not been found, but just before the offensive, when the attacking forces would have accumulated all their strength, the V Corps (one of three) had only 48 functioning pieces.[94] And by January 1939, even though the Army of the Ebro had brought its still usable material back over the river in November 1938, the losses of the Eastern Army Group (Armies of the Ebro and the East) in those weeks as they retreated through Catalonia to the French frontier must have been sizeable. Internal reports listed only 173 usable pieces in the entire army group.[95]

[90] Analysis by the *Servicio Histórico Militar*, quoted by R. de la Cierva in *Historia Ilustrada de la guerra civil española*, Madrid, 1970, II: 421.
[91] FO 371, W14601/29/41 of 31 October 1938.
[92] Somoza, *El general Miaja*, 260.
[93] Ignacio Moyano, 'La batalla del Ebro: la acción de la artillería', *Ejército*, 23 (December 1941), 18–27.
[94] *Ejército del Ebro, Comandancia General de Artillería*, 23 July 1938, quoted by Mezquida, *Batalla del Ebro*, II: 68.
[95] DR, L766, C4 of 30 January 1939.

Even when the artillery was there, the shells often were not. Rojo recalls that the 105 mm howitzers always ran out of shells and then used up one day's supply in a single barrage.[96] Modesto speaks of a ration of 80 shells per day.[97] Shells were frequently dud. In two weeks in summer 1938, in 8 different factories, 5,035 75 mm and 105 mm shells were seen to be defective on inspection.[98] Much of this may have been due to inefficiency and indiscipline but it may also be recalled that the Insurgent secret agent in Madrid, Colonel Centaños, who revealed his role to Colonel Casado, was in charge of an artillery armourers' workshop.[99] The large number of officers who received unfavourable but not condemnatory reports from the *Gabinete de Información y Control* must be considered as being at least potential saboteurs in the rear.

General Rojo summed up the problem in a teletype to Prieto towards the end of the battle of Teruel in February 1938:

> Our problem, as I am tired of repeating, is tragically simple: material, material, material, everything comes down to this. If we had only a half or one third of what the enemy has, our victory would soon be assured.
>
> (*Nuestro problema es, como me he cansado de repetir, de una trágica sencillez: material, material, material. Con que tuviéramos la mitad o la tercera parte del material del que dispone el enemigo, nuestra victoria estaría prontamente asegurada.*)[100]

Rojo's possible exaggeration here, together with his failure to discuss whether the Republican Army used its material appropriately, should not hide the truth of the matter. Neither side in the Spanish Civil War was manufacturing more than a small part of what it was consuming.[101] The non-intervention agreement forced the Republic to seek out arms in the murkier parts of the private dealers' market, while the Insurgents were well supplied, when necessary, with German and Italian material which was suitable, available when it was needed and, compared with the Soviet aid, constantly updated and supplied until the end of the war.

The Soviet Union agreed to non-intervention in Spain on 5 August 1936, hoping that doing so would free it from any obligation to send war material to Spain. If the USSR did send arms to Spain, it would create distrust in Britain and France at a time when the USSR's major aim was to present itself as no longer interested in revolution in the West but in achieving alliances which would protect it against Nazi

96 Rojo, *Alerta*, 50. 97 Modesto, *Soy del Quinto Regimiento*, 213.
98 DR, L535, C1. 99 Casado, *Last Days of Madrid*, 207.
100 DR, L461, C5.
101 This was the Foreign Office view (FO 371, W10814/1/41 of 3 May 1937).

Germany.[102] However, the Soviet ambassador in London, Ivan Maiskii, who represented his country at the meetings of the Non-Intervention Committee, consisting of the major countries which had agreed not to send arms to Spain, stated that the USSR would consider itself released from its word if Germany and Italy, who had also accepted non-intervention believing that not to do so would harm them diplomatically but that they could safely ignore the agreement, did not cease the stream of war material which they had begun to dispatch to Franco during the first week of the war. On 23 October 1936, Maiskii said that the USSR would begin to send war material to the Republic.[103]

What armaments had the Republic been able to buy before this date? On 25 July, one week after the military insurrection, José Giral, who had taken over Government in Madrid after Santiago Casares Quiroga had resigned and Diego Martínez Barrio's short-lived Cabinet had been unable to persuade the Insurgents to return their forces to barracks, doubtful whether the French Premier, Léon Blum, would be able to overcome the opposition within his own coalition towards supplying arms to the Spanish Republic, had sent this message to the Soviet ambassador in Paris (as yet there was no Soviet diplomatic representation in Madrid):

> The Government of the Spanish Republic needs to supply its army with a large amount of small arms to fight the war which has begun ... knowing the possibilities and availability of armaments of the USSR, I have decided to ask you to inform your government of our wish and our need to look to your country to supply us with a large quantity of arms and all kinds of military equipment.[104]

Giral as yet was not asking for advisory and much less combat personnel. Five days later, the USSR stated: 'The Spanish government has never asked for help. We are sure that it will find sufficient resources in its own country to crush this mutiny of Fascist generals who are following other countries' orders.'[105]

On 23 August the Commissar for Foreign Affairs, Maxim Litvinov, rejected Giral's plea officially. He listed his reasons: the cost would be too high, Spain was too far distant, the shipments would run the risk

[102] See Alpert, *New International History*, and Enrique Moradiellos, *El reñidero de Europa: las dimensiones internacionales de la guerra civil española*, Barcelona, 2001, for the diplomatic background behind arms supply to Spain as well as the dates and sources for the events described.

[103] Maiskii's own account is in his *Spanish Notebooks*, Hutchinson, 1966.

[104] Kowalsky, *La Unión Soviética*, 25.

[105] FO 371, W7236/62/41, from British ambassador in Moscow to London, 29 July 1936.

of interception and the USSR had agreed to non-intervention.[106] Soviet Military Intelligence and the Comintern were of course aware of the Republic's plight. At the beginning of September, Marcel Rosenberg, the newly arrived Soviet ambassador, Koltsov, the very influential *Pravda* correspondent and personal informant of Stalin in Spain, and Dr Marcelino Pascua, the Spanish ambassador in Moscow, underlined the gravity of the situation to the Russian political and military leadership. The People's Commissar for Defence, Voroshilov, proposed to Stalin that massive dispatch of war material should start, and the Soviet leader agreed. On 29 September 1936, the Political Bureau of the Central Committee of the Communist Party decided to carry out the plan for military aid to the Spanish Republic. It was to be known as Operation X and to be executed by Section Y – parallel with Germany's Sonderstab W and Italy's Ufficio Spagna, which directed armaments towards Franco's forces. All were kept at a distance from official structures. Though the intervention of Italy, Germany and the Soviet Union was soon well known, even to the public, the agencies which organised it had to remain secret and in theory non-existent. Operation X was to be headed by Semyon Uritsky, director of the Red Army's Intelligence service,[107] and Slutsky, head of the NKVD (Soviet secret police) overseas department.

All decisions as to the volume and dates of supplies of arms to Spain were personally taken by Stalin in telephone conversations with Voroshilov from the Black Sea resort of Sochi, where the Soviet leader was vacationing. The messages reveal that Stalin reduced by half whatever amounts of armament were proposed.[108] However, it may well be that the amounts suggested by Voroshilov on the suggestion of the Spanish Republic (and perhaps by Koltsov and Rosenberg) were swollen in anticipation that Stalin would reduce them.

Movement of the armaments by train from the depots to Odessa or another embarkation port on the Black Sea was closely supervised by security forces. The wagons were marked 'Vladivostok' though whether experienced observers were misled is unknown.

The number of sailings to Spain, known as 'Y's' (*igreks*) totalled 48.[109] The first ship was the Spanish merchant *Campeche*, which docked at Cartagena on 4 October 1936 with six 115 mm British howitzers

[106] For the initial Soviet rejection of the Republic's appeal see Rybalkin, *Stalin y España*, 50.
[107] See text of decision in Rybalkin, *Stalin y España*, 51.
[108] Rybalkin, *Stalin y España*, 53.
[109] Howson, *Aircraft of the Spanish Civil War*, 278–303.

(corresponding to the wish of Kulik, the Director-General of Soviet Artillery, to get rid of 280 British, French and Japanese pieces,[110] which probably dated from the beginning of the century), 240 German grenade-launchers with 100,000 grenades, 20,350 rifles with 16.5 million cartridges, and 350 machine-guns.[111] The second *igrek* was the *Komsomol*, which docked on 12 October 1936 with Colonel Krivoshein's 50 T.26 tanks, with spares, shells and fuel. The shipment does not seem to have been expected, according to Krivoshein's account in *Bajo la bandera de la España republicana*.[112] He had to make his own way to Archena (Murcia), a distance of 60 km along a main road from Cartagena to Murcia, through Murcia itself and along a side road to Archena. It was unlikely that tank-transporters were available, so how the tanks themselves travelled is a mystery. Krivoshein's surprise, already aroused by the harbour pilot directing the *Komsomol* to dock between several foreign warships, must have increased when his tanks probably had to drive to Archena under their own steam using vast amounts of fuel, chewing up the road surfaces and drawing everyone's attention. Krivoshein had no interpreter with him, so the local PCE supplied him with one who spoke French, as well as a car and driver. The absence of a formal Spanish reception must have come about because the Republican Army Staff had hardly been formed. Either nobody had been told that Russian tanks were arriving or nobody had communicated with Krivoshein at sea, possibly because the *Komsomol* was observing radio silence. Nevertheless, the absence of a high-ranking Spanish officer to receive the Russian colonel in Cartagena is striking.

The contrast between the quality of the tanks which arrived in the *Komsomol* and the material which was landed from the *Campeche* was startling. The latter brought the rifles which engendered the frequently made statements that the USSR had sent ancient and useless weapons. Indeed, the weapons were of six different calibres, including a totally obsolescent Japanese 11 mm model. Of the 58,183 rifles sent by the USSR in 1936, about 26,000 were old models with few cartridges, while another well-used 6,000 came with half the cartridges which they would normally have.[113] The case was similar with the American Colt machine-guns, whose ammunition belts were so perished that they could not feed the guns efficiently. They were thought to have been

[110] Note from Voroshilov to Stalin of 2 November 1937, quoted by Rybalkin, *Stalin y España*, 52–3.
[111] Details of the first 25 cargos in Rybalkin, *Stalin y España*, 209–13.
[112] Malinovski *et al.*, *BLB*, 319–41.
[113] Howson, *Aircraft of the Spanish Civil War*, 139; Kowalsky, *La Unión Soviética*, 212.

sold to the White Russians during the Russian Civil War. In contrast, the Maxim machine-guns were rugged and reliable, with a carriage and a trail.[114] The French St. Etienne and Chauchat machine-guns had been retired from the Front in the First World War because of their tendency to jam. However, much of the foreign material, such as the 280 British artillery pieces that Voroshilov told Stalin he was going to send to Spain, was not necessarily old or in bad condition. Table 10.1 provides estimates for the material sent to Spain, 1936–9.

Debate is still continuing about the total volume of artillery sent by the Soviet Union. Nevertheless, the constancy of supply of aircraft and heavy artillery from Italy and Germany, together with the regular upgrading of the German aircraft at least, is evident.

Tanks and aircraft

In 1936, tanks were the most modern of battlefield arms. If properly used, they could give an army the best chance of victory. The Russian tanks which arrived on the *Komsomol*, and later deliveries, were the best available. The T.26 was the most powerful weapon used in the Spanish Civil War. Nevertheless, T.26 tanks had their problems, proved by the Insurgents' success in capturing and reusing between 30 and 50 of them during the war.[115] The T.26 weighed 9 tons, and was heavier by far than the Panzer Mark Ones and the small Fiat-Ansaldo 'tankettes' that Franco's suppliers sent him. However, the T.26 did not possess the thickness of armour sufficient to resist the impact of the German 37 mm anti-tank guns which accompanied the Condor Legion. Furthermore, because the machine-guns of the T.26 revolved in the same turret as its cannon, they could not be depressed sufficiently to allow them to target an individual soldier who had learnt the technique of getting very close. The T.26 was difficult to manoeuvre. It was hard to direct fire from its interior, so the tank-drivers drove it with the turret open. A resolute enemy could destroy the T.26 by throwing a bottle of petrol with a lighted wick inside the turret, a device later known as the 'Molotov Cocktail'.

The Spanish army of 1936 was equipped with about 20 1919 vintage Renault FT-17 tanks, one regiment of which was stationed in Madrid and theoretically available, but not used. Consequently, Colonel Krivoshein's tanks, based at the winter spa at Archena, had to be brought

[114] For the Colts and Maxims see Jason Gurney's closely observed account of the early days in the International Brigades, *Crusade in Spain*, Faber, 1974, 78–9.

[115] Kowalsky, *La Unión Soviética*, 219.

Table 10.1 *Estimated amounts of war material sent to Spain 1936–9*[a]

	Republican Army	Insurgents	
Type of material	USSR	Germany	Italy
Aircraft	648	632–732	689–99
Tanks and armoured vehicles	407	122	149–55
Cannon	1,186	838	1,801
Mortars[b]	340	?	1,426
Machine-guns	20,486	5,000	3,436
Rifles	497,813	157,306	223,784
Cartridges	862 million	257 million	320 million
Shells	3.4 million	1.1 million	7.7 million[c]

Notes: [a] The figures for Russian material are from Rybalkin, *Stalin y España*, table 2, p. 69. The German and Italian aircraft figures are according to Howson, *Aircraft of the Spanish Civil War*, 305, and for other Arms from calculation by the historian Angel Viñas in personal communication to Rybalkin.

[b] There may be a difference of nomenclature here. The Soviet figures seem to refer to grenade-launchers.

[c] Italy also sent a number of old destroyers and some modern submarines to reinforce Franco's naval strength. The USSR sent four torpedo launches. See Alpert, *La guerra civil española en el mar*.

up to defend the approaches to Madrid before their Spanish drivers had been sufficiently trained. A company of 15 tanks with the Soviet instructors as crew and Spanish soldiers as loaders and gunners commanded by Captain Paul Arman, who later became a Hero of the Soviet Union, went into action on 29 October 1936 at Seseña, 15 km south of Madrid. The action had been announced vaingloriously by Caballero the previous day, but it still seems to have caught the enemy by surprise. The tanks managed to disperse enemy troops, destroying a number of vehicles, and advanced about 6.5 km westwards as far as Esquivias, but since the Russians reported that the untrained Spanish militia did not keep up with the tanks, it is evident that the machines were being used as accompaniments to the infantry and at what was hoped to be their pace, though other reports state that the tanks raced ahead. If in fact this was so, the infantry could not fairly be blamed for not keeping up with tanks travelling at 25 or 30 miles per hour. Yet at the same time, if tanks were to be used as military thinkers such as Captain Basil Liddell Hart, General Heinz Guderian and Colonel Charles de Gaulle were advising, that is fast and in mass, and as the Germans demonstrated so effectively in 1939 and 1940, their drivers needed far more training and there had to be far better communication between them. They also needed accompanying fuel tankers. The Spanish drivers and their commander had not previously studied the terrain. Captain Arman's tanks ran low on fuel and had to return to base.[116] The complaint that the infantry did not keep up with the tanks would arise many times, but it displays a lack of up-to-date tactical thought. Consequently, not much could be learnt from the Spanish Civil War about the use of tanks.

Another 56 T.26 tanks arrived during November 1936. With these the 1st Armoured Brigade (*Primera Brigada Blindada*) was formed. Successes were claimed, but losses were heavy. Altogether 52 machines, over half of those sent, were lost in the first month of combat. Shortages of spares, insufficient training, poor repair facilities, even difficulties in finding and siting fuel dumps adequately, indicated the amateur nature of the operation.

By early September 1937, the USSR had sent 306 tanks to Spain, of which 80 had been destroyed and 17 needed major repairs.[117]

The Russian BT.5 tank, 50 of which arrived on 14 August 1937, weighed 20 tons, travelled at 40 km per hour, was equipped with a 45 mm gun and protected by 60 mm of armour. It had been designed for the independent use of tanks in mass. These machines suffered a major reverse on 13 October 1937 at Fuentes del Ebro, about 30 km south-east of Zaragoza. The tactical use of tanks was still dependent on the infantry occupying the ground which the machines had conquered. The problem of how the infantry were to keep up with fast-moving tanks was, it was thought, solved by mounting the men on the tanks themselves. Mounting troops on tanks, however, needed thought and careful preparation. The 14th (International) Brigade, which was to carry out the operation, had not been carefully rehearsed. Nineteen of the 45 tanks which went into action were lost. Terrain was uneven and some machines were stuck in deep ditches or bogged down in fields flooded when the enemy opened dykes, while infantry losses were heavy. Those BT.5 tanks which did manage to reach Fuentes del Ebro could not manoeuvre in the narrow streets and became easy prey for the enemy and their antitank guns.[118]

116 There are many accounts of this action, among them Rybalkin, *Stalin y España*, 105, and Kowalsky, *La Unión Soviética*, 308–9. Setting aside the hostile tone, one of the best is Martínez Bande, *La marcha sobre Madrid*, 106 and n. 97.

117 Kowalsky, *La Unión Soviética*, 315.

118 There is a useful analysis of the battle in U. Kelsey, 'Fuentes del Ebro', *Military Modelling* (December 1994), 45–7 and 58–60.

The BT.5 was the best Soviet tank of the time. If handled by adequately trained crews in a well-prepared operation, over suitable terrain, with air cover and radio communication, it would have been a formidable weapon. As it was, in Spain there were insufficient Russian tank experts, while the crews were under-trained and inexperienced. It would not have been practical for interpreters to have ridden in the tanks and interpreted between Russians, Spaniards and the occasional International Brigaders who also crewed the tanks, so the language problem created difficulties. The Staffs and the commanders had not made a thorough study of the ground. Thus the BT.5s suffered accidents and breakdowns which exposed them to enemy fire. They were vulnerable to the magnificent German 88 mm anti-tank guns. In other words, it is not the theoretical and potential power of a war machine that counts but its use in particular circumstances and by troops who are well trained to use it. This should have been obvious in the first tank action at Seseña on 29 October 1936, where the T.26s advanced swiftly, but left the infantry behind and without air support, of which there was none made available. True enough, they did a lot of damage to the enemy, but the absence of preparation and of radio meant that the crews ended up not knowing where they were and short of fuel, not having appeared to have considered the distance they had to cover.

It was these errors that led to the loss of so many of these precious and expensive tanks. By the time of the battle of Brunete in July 1937, 68 Soviet tanks had been destroyed and 116 required repairs.[119]

That the Soviet tanks were more powerful than the German and Italian machines supplied to Franco's army turned out to be irrelevant. At any given moment, despite the 347 tanks which were sent to equip the Republican Army, rarely could a hundred be assembled at the same time. Normally operations were conducted with a few companies totalling 40 or 50 machines, which was more or less what the Insurgents did. Further, the level of competence of the crews was low. When the British tank expert Colonel Martel had watched annual Soviet tank manoeuvres in 1936, he had remarked that the commanding officers could not control or coordinate the movements of the tanks through lack of adequate tactical training.[120] Furthermore, the tank drivers were mostly Spaniards who suffered from the improvisation which was so characteristic of the Republican Army. Sometimes foreign volunteers were used, with the consequent linguistic chaos. They were given few

[119] Kowalsky, *La Unión Soviética*, 312, table 5.8.

[120] See A. and J. Seaton, *The Soviet Army, 1918 to the Present*, The Bodley Head, 1986, 92ff.

ideas of tank theory or doctrine. Given the almost complete absence of tanks in the pre-war Spanish Army, and the scant enthusiasm shown by Spanish military attachés in the 1930s when reporting on manoeuvres with tanks which they witnessed abroad, the officers of the Republican Army had very little if any idea about how to use tanks in combat despite the translations of the British General Fuller's works on mechanised warfare which Rojo had published in the *Colección Bibliográfica Milita*.[121] Lastly, the Russian tanks needed technical maintenance for which only rudimentary facilities were available.[122] Thus few valid conclusions could be extracted from Spain about the use of tanks. The Staffs realised this. Rojo criticised the lack of coordination with the infantry, while Matallana, Chief of Staff of the Army of the Centre, complained that before Brunete there had been no plan for coordination between the tanks and the infantry. Without such coordination, wrote Matallana, tanks were bound to fail. There was no advantage in using them. The origin of the problem, he continued, lay in the complete independence (*gran autonomía*) of the tank command. As a result, the Staff of the Army of the Centre did not know how many tanks had been allocated to each corps or how many were kept in reserve, where they were and how many had been lost.[123] This and other statements by senior officers of the Republican Army support Colonel's Casado's assertion that 'Neither the Air Force nor the tank corps was controlled by the Ministry of National Defence, nor in consequence by the Central General Staff.'[124]

If the tank was a new weapon in Spain, the aeroplane was not. Spanish pilots had been flying pioneers. In most countries in the 1930s, the function of the air Arm was seen primarily as a tactical aid to ground forces. Strategic use of aircraft was limited to the bombing of civilians, such as had been done by colonial powers almost from the beginning of the introduction of aircraft to the armed services. In the Spanish Civil War, Madrid and Barcelona had been bombed by German and Italian airplanes, and there had been occasional bombing of cities in the Insurgent zone by the Republican Air Force. These events did not, however, have an important effect on the progress of the war even though they led to loss of human life. However, the destruction of the Basque town of Guernica, where the use of incendiary bombs by the German

[121] See Alpert, *La reforma militar*, 72–4.

[122] There is a very useful discussion in Steven J. Zaloga, 'Soviet Tank Operations in the Spanish Civil War', at http://bobrowen.com/nymas/soviet_tank_operations_in_the_sp.htm.

[123] DR, L669, C3, quoted by Martínez Bande, *Brunete*, document 9.

[124] Casado, *Last Days of Madrid*, 54.

aircraft of the Condor Legion was an experiment in how to spread terror in the civilian population, also had the tactical motive of cutting of the retreat of troops towards Bilbao.

The Soviet Union sent, as has been seen, 648 aircraft, while small numbers of machines were acquired by the Republic at different times from other sources. The figures for German and Italian supplies are as yet not definitely established, but they would see to be at least double the numbers from the USSR. Soviet aircraft were also assembled in Spain, but the machines lacked either motors or cannon or both. Soviet reports criticised the slowness of production and blamed Spanish bureaucracy.[125]

As for the tactical use of aircraft, the technique of concentrated bombing of enemy trenches and strong points by the Insurgent Nationalists contrasts strongly with the absence of such a practice by the Republicans. The Insurgent technique goes some way towards explaining the frequent occupation by their troops of well-fortified enemy positions, even in mountainous areas, such as in the Asturias campaign of 1937. In spring 1938, the Republican Army's lines in Aragon were destroyed using the technique of air to ground intensive bombing by large concentrations of aircraft. Joaquín García Morato, one of the Insurgent aces, developed the 'chain' (*en cadena*) attack which succeeded in destroying the bridges over the Ebro which linked the Army of the Ebro with its rearguard on the left bank of that river during the hard-fought battles of July to November 1938. In his memoirs, the chief of the Republican fighter Arm emphasises that there was less air–ground cooperation on the Government side than on the Nationalist one.[126] Furthermore, both qualitatively and quantitatively, German anti-aircraft fire was more abundant and productive in terms of results than that of the Republican Army, especially as the war was coming to its end. At the end of 1938, aircraft of the Condor Legion were attacking enemy airfields undefended by anti-aircraft fire.[127] At the same time, the sheer lack of aircraft in the Republican Army forces reached such limits that Insurgent infantry and artillery rarely bothered to camouflage themselves.

The Russian I-15 and I-16 fighters, known respectively as the 'Chato' ('Snubnose') and the 'Mosca' ('Fly'), were supreme in late 1936, dominating the skies over central Spain and Madrid so long as there were sufficient of them and enough Russian pilots who knew how to get the best performance from these machines, the most advanced of their

[125] Kowalsky, *La Unión Soviética*, 290, 297.
[126] A. García Lacalle, *Mitos y verdades*, 408, 431.
[127] Adolf Galland, *The First and the Last*, Collins, 1955, 34. The author was a *Luftwaffe* ace pilot who served in Spain.

time. Altogether 771 Russian pilots flew in Spain, and the maximum figure at any one time was 298 at the end of 1936. In comparison with Germany, which sent the pilots of the Luftwaffe to Spain to acquire combat experience, the Soviets withdrew their airmen as soon as possible, either to ensure that they lost few, or so that their presence should not be noted by foreign observers. For this reason, the USSR trained cohorts of Spanish pilots in the 20th Military Flying Academy at Kirovabad (Azerbaijan), at the expense of the Spanish Republic, which had sent the Spanish gold reserve to the USSR in October to pay for Soviet and other material which they bought in the international arms market. On 1 February 1937, 193 Spaniards left for the Soviet Union to undergo an intensive 5-month course. Altogether, several hundred Spanish pilots were trained, including 185 who completed the course in May 1939 after the Spanish Civil War had ended, and another 200 who did not get as far as flying in Spain.[128] The new Spanish pilots, despite the intensity of their teaching, lacked flying hours in comparison with their enemies. In addition, they were insufficiently qualified to fly advanced aircraft.

In contrast, Germany, which used the Spanish war as a testing ground for their constantly developing and expanding military aviation, improved its Messerschmitt Bf109 so that by 1939 this fighter could fly for two hours without refuelling, at a maximum speed of 516 km or 323 miles per hour, and was equipped with efficient radio communication. When fitted with additional fuel tanks, it could fly long enough to escort bombers. No Republican fighter could do this, with the result that the Republican Air Force could not take advantage of all the potential superiority of its SB 'Katiuska' bombers, whose insufficiently protected fuel tanks made them vulnerable to fighter fire.[129]

The Russian R-5 'Rasante' ('low-flying') reconnaissance and bombing biplanes, 31 of which arrived in Spain in November 1936, were used for low-flying bombing missions. Nevertheless, their heavy losses displayed their vulnerable slowness. They could not operate safely without a fighter escort. The history of this squadron does, however, suggest that the Republican Air Force could have developed a tactical technique of constant harrying of the enemy infantry if the USSR had continued to send squadrons of R-5s. The same thing could be said about the R-Z 'Natasha', a more modern form of the R-5, 31 of which arrived in Spain in January 1937. The Russian flying instructor stationed at El Carmolí airfield (Cartagena province) trained Spanish

[128] Kowalsky, *La Unión Soviética*, 300 and 303.
[129] Howson, *Aircraft of the Spanish Civil War*, 277.

pilots particularly for low flying and defence against fighters. In the battle of Guadalajara in March 1937, the 'Natashas' did brilliantly, strafing the Italian divisions from low levels. The USSR sent a total of 155 R-5s and 'Natashas'. But, given the inevitable losses and the large number of accidents, the Republican Army suffered the consequence of the Soviet unwillingness to provide more planes, despite the requests even of the Russian advisers themselves in Spain.[130] Furthermore, had the Russians developed more advanced types of their justly famed fighters and sent them to Spain in similar numbers to the Condor Legion, and with pilots who were better trained than the Spaniards who completed intensive courses in the USSR, the course of the Spanish Civil War might have differed. Once some of the I-16 'Mosca' fighters received Wright-Cyclone motors, which allowed them to operate effectively at heights where the most modern German Messerschmitts functioned well, they gave better results, but by then it was too late.[131]

Germany and Italy sent their aid to Insurgent Spain on credit, but the Soviet Union already had the 700 million dollars' worth of gold belonging to the Bank of Spain.[132] Commentators hostile to the USSR often make critical remarks about the relative value and price of Soviet war material. It may be interesting to look at an anonymous document in the military archives,[133] summarising and discussing the prices in the Soviet invoices. Each T.26 tank, for instance, had been charged at 247,845 pesetas, which the author of the document considered reasonable. The rifles had cost an average of 153.75 pesetas, which the author considered too much since the weapons were not new. The machine-guns and automatic rifles varied in price between 1,200 pesetas for an automatic rifle and 7,380 pesetas for a new Maxim. Since each Spanish-made Maxim cost 5,000 pesetas, the author thought that the Russian price was high, as he did that of pistols, at 180 pesetas, though he thought that prices for the artillery were reasonable, provided the pieces were not old. Given the circumstances, the author of this paper thought that the prices were not too high. Up till that moment, 28 January 1937, 440 million pesetas had been spent.

Some recent investigations, however, suggest that the USSR manipulated the exchange rates applicable to the costs of the material it sent to

[130] Kowalsky, *La Unión Soviética*, 296–7.
[131] Howson, *Aircraft of the Spanish Civil War*, 200.
[132] For an account of the financing of the Spanish Civil War see Angel Viñas, *El oro de Moscú: alfa y omega de un mito franquista*, Barcelona, 1979.
[133] DR, L71, C7.

Spain, all chargeable to the product of the gold reserve, very much in favour of its own interests.[134]

Ever since the Spanish Civil War there have been reports of the poor quality and old age of some of the equipment provided by the Soviets, particularly of rifles and machine-guns (see above). Elsewhere, some artillery was supplied without recoil-damping mechanism. These guns, thought to date from the Russo-Japanese war of 1904, reared back, endangering the gunners themselves.[135] Presumably, these were from the old stock of foreign material which the Russians decided to get rid of (see above). The communist defence of this poor-quality armament can be summed up in a few lines by the militia commander Líster, who insists that some Spanish Government purchasing agents were deceived by arms dealer into buying it.[136] The tanks and the aircraft were the very best that the Soviet Union had to offer. It is also true that some material bought by the Republic from elsewhere was deficient. In one case the Insurgents captured a ship carrying war material, which the armourers had to repair before it could be used.[137] Krivitsky recalls arms purchasers buying material in Germany in bad condition.[138] The other side of these arms purchases is revealed by the German Admiral Canaris, head of the German secret service, the Abwehr, who organised the purchase of old material, which was then deliberately rendered unserviceable in Germany by filing down firing-pins, extracting some of the charge from grenades and so on. The material was sold back to the dealer, who then sold it to the Spanish Government.[139]

The relative values of the supply of war material to the Spanish Government and to the Insurgent Nationalists can also be described in financial terms. Both sides in Spain had to face the problem of how to make international payments. Since the gold reserve of the Bank of Spain was in Madrid, the Republic was able, by Cabinet decree, to get over certain legal restrictions, and use it to buy arms abroad. At the beginning, hoping to acquire the war material it needed in France, it sold gold to that country to a value of US$195 million. When the international non-intervention agreement prevented European dealers and arms industries selling war material legally to Spain, and the Soviet Union announced in October 1936 that it could not bind itself

[134] Howson, *Arms for Spain*, 146–51.

[135] Bazal, *¡Ay de los vencidos!*, 163. EGF, an artillery lieutenant in the Army of Andalusia, told me the same personally in 1971 (MA).

[136] Líster, *Nuestra guerra*, 75–6.

[137] CGG, L292, C1, 25 May 1937.

[138] Krivitsky, *Stalin's Agent*, 105.

[139] Ian Colvin, *Camaris, Chief of Intelligence*, rev. edn, Pan Books, 1957, 36–7.

to non-intervention any further than Germany and Italy, who were sending arms to Franco despite being parties to non-intervention, the Caballero Government decided to deposit the rest of its huge gold reserve in Moscow. In all, the Republic spent US$518 million through Soviet banks, as well as selling US$20 million worth of silver. Adding other small quantities, the total treasure spent on the defence of the Republic is calculated to have amounted to US$744 million, without including credits and transactions in kind.

The Insurgents financed their effort in various ways but above all by credit. Since calculations after the war were made in different ways, the total foreign support received by Franco's Insurgents totalled between US$694 million and US$716 million.[140] To this should be added the value and importance of the credit for fuel extended to Franco by Texaco,[141] together with the commercial and mining influence gained by Germany, as well as the not inconsiderable amounts donated by individual people of wealth (the multi-millionaire Juan March paid for the British airplane chartered to bring Franco from the Canary Islands to Morocco to take command of the professional Spanish forces in the Spanish Protectorate).

The joint German and Italian contribution to the Insurgents' armaments was much greater in aircraft and artillery, while the Soviet contribution was greater in tanks and small arms. However, the day-to-day history of the Republican Army, as followed through its documents, shows that it ran short of essential material at critical moments. The Republican Army, for example, was never able to assemble the huge quantities of artillery needed for massive shelling before its major offensives, as in the battle of the Ebro. The revolutionary circumstances of the earlier weeks of the war caused great losses of material from arsenals, many of which had fallen immediately into the hands of the more disciplined and efficient Insurgents. Yet inability to use what it had was a constant of the behaviour of the Republican Army. An Insurgent message of 4 April 1938, admittedly during the routs which the Republican Army suffered at the time, refers to the capture of the Army of the East's artillery depot, and lists a vast number of pieces of artillery, armoured vehicles and other material, commenting that the 'large quantity of weapons thrown anywhere [*tiradas por doquier*] is so enormous that it cannot be calculated'.[142]

[140] Angel Viñas, *El oro español en la guerra civil*, Madrid, 1976, his *El oro de Moscú* and his article 'The Financing of the Spanish Civil War', in Paul Preston (ed.), *Revolution and War in Spain*, Methuen, 1984.

[141] See the article on the Texaco–Franco negotiations by M. Aznar in *La Vanguardia Española* (Barcelona) of 8 July 1973.

[142] L. Mezquida, *La batalla del Segre*, Tarragona, 1972, 61. On relative efficiency of this sort see also Alpert 'The Clash of Spanish Armies'.

The SIM

In complete contrast to the Insurgents, where, despite the existence of large political forces, the army was all-powerful, in a situation such as the one in which the Spanish Republic found itself in the Civil War, the limits of authority were vague. The military insurrection had allowed all sorts of groups to assume the power to act independently and autonomously. Policing and investigatory organisations proliferated, including officers of the War Ministry and of the General Staff's Information Section, the internal security systems in the Republican Army itself, and particularly in the International Brigades, into which it must be assumed that different countries' security organisations infiltrated their own agents, the Special Investigation Department of State (DEIDIDE), and organisations run by the Basques and the Catalans.[143]

The arrival of many foreigners, among them high-ranking Soviet secret agents such as Alexander Orlov, increased the variety of Intelligence agencies. There was much to investigate, for there were many people in the Republican zone who could be described as sympathetic to the Insurgents, or as defeatists, even if large numbers were in prison. Speculators and hoarders had to be checked, as well as the '*incontrolables*' who had been responsible for the assassinations and robberies of the early weeks, people who had taken advantage of the chaos to slake their criminal thirst, as well as agents of the enemy.

In an attempt to bring some order, Prieto set up the *Servicio de Investigación Militar* or SIM, announced in the *Diario Oficial* on 9 August 1937. Article Five of the establishing decree stated that SIM officials would be entitled to arrest military officers, which was an indication of the extent of the suspicion of unreliability among the officers, despite the labours of the Office of Information and Control. Prieto later explained that he was careful to make the SIM politically representative and to exclude Soviet influence. One person whom he appointed in the Army of the Centre was Gustavo Durán, a communist who, according to Prieto, attempted to recruit fellow PCE members as sub-agents, and was dismissed by Prieto. The Minister then appointed Manuel Uribarri, and, in his speech to the PSOE after he had left the Ministry of Defence, Prieto admitted that this had been a mistake.[144] Uribarri, a *Guardia Civil* officer in Valencia, had led a militia column, quarrelled with Captain Bayo over who should command the attempt, in the end

[143] M. Uribarri, *El SIM de la República*, Havana, 1943, quoted in M. García Venero, *Historia de los internacionales en España*, Madrid, 1957, III: 334–5.

[144] Prieto, *Cómo y por qué*, 57–8.

abandoned, to recapture Majorca from the Insurgents and had then led the *Columna Fantasma* (see above). One may wonder what qualifications he had to lead the SIM, except that Uribarri was one of a trusted group of career officers who had conspired against the Primo de Rivera dictatorship, was known to socialist politicians and considered above all suspicion. Yet he later confessed to Prieto that he had been forced to report to Soviet agents.[145] What pressure could have been exerted on him is unknown, but he left Spain with a sum in gold and jewels, probably fleeing from the communists over a matter which remains a mystery.[146] One may merely speculate that the SIM accepted bribes and that Uribarri became involved and was subjected to threats or blackmail.

In 1938 Negrín appointed a socialist, Paulino García, to make good the '*atrocidades*', which probably means financial irregularities introduced by Uribarri, and to purge the SIM of communists.[147] However, communist sources indicate that their participation in the SIM was very limited. In April 1938, according to a Soviet source, in the central-south zone, 248 SIM agents were members of the PSOE or UGT, while only 2 held PCE cards.[148]

Post-war, the main publication in Franco Spain detailing the murders and other outrages committed accuses the SIM of acts of torture.[149] The proofs suggest that the accusations are well founded. They are even echoed by the CNT.[150] Like other such bodies, it may be that the SIM attracted sadists, but after 1938 it was not, if ever it had been, a communist-dominated organisation into which the Soviets had an input. Colonel Casado, in fact, had sufficient confidence in the SIM and its head in Madrid, Angel Pedrero, to give him instructions in preparation for the coup of 5 March 1939.[151] Nevertheless, the short-lived National Defence Council abolished the SIM only a few days before Madrid was occupied by the enemy.[152]

Conclusions

Soviet aid to the Republican Army consisted of advisers, who do not seem to have exceeded that function, except perhaps in some highly

[145] *Ibid.*
[146] Both Bayo, *Mi desembarco*, 322, and Peirats, *CNT*, III: 289, mention his desertion from different political standpoints.
[147] Negrín to Prieto, 23 June 1939 ('Epistolario Prieto–Negrín').
[148] J. García, *Ispania Narodnova Fronta*, Moscow, 1957, 166.
[149] *The Red Domination in Spain*, translation of *La causa general*, 4th edn, Madrid, 1961.
[150] Peirats, *CNT*, III: 281ff.
[151] Casado, *Last Days of Madrid*, 131.
[152] *DO*, 26 March 1939.

specialised areas such as the command of the few and unreliable Republican submarines. Most of them had left by the end of 1937. Their most important influence on the Republican Army was their control of the tanks and, more importantly, the Air Force, which prevented the development of an integrated air–land strategy, but they are unlikely to have exerted any influence on strategic decisions in general. When Russian armaments were available they constituted vital aid for the Republic, but problems of transport through the Mediterranean or through France meant that they were of less value to the Republican Army than German and Italian material was to the Nationalists. The prestige of the PCE increased thanks to the support shown for the Republic by the Soviet Union and the presence of the Russians, but it is doubtful that the USSR ever wielded pressure in favour of the PCE itself.

The Soviet command in Spain obeyed the orders it had received and avoided as best it could any involvement in internal Spanish divisions about the role of the PCE, leaving such matters to the representatives of the Comintern. The secretary-general of that organisation, Dimitrov, wrote on 31 July 1937 to Voroshilov, People's Commissar for Defence, in which he complained that Prieto, Minister of National Defence, was doing everything he could to obscure the valour, capacity and deeds of the communist commanders Líster, Modesto, Campesino and others.[153] Dimitrov makes a significant comment:

> Prieto is afraid that the People's Army, headed by commanders who have come from among the people, hardened in battle, represents a enormous revolutionary force and, as a result of this, will play a decisive role in determining the social and economic life, the political system of a future Spain. This is why he would like it if the People's Army were antifascist in an indeterminate way, and far from political activity, especially from communist activity, and in this the professional military, including Rojo, supports him. He at least wants the command staff not to consist of active revolutionaries.

Actually, Dimitrov is moderate in describing what Prieto would have wanted. But the Minister's views were *fears*, not facts. Everything leads one to believe that at that moment neither the Communist International nor the Soviet Union envisaged creating a sort of 'People's Democracy', such as Stalin would do in Eastern Europe after 1945 in very different circumstances.[154]

[153] Radosh *et al.*, *Spain Betrayed*, document 46.

[154] Commenting on Dimitrov's letter to Voroshilov, on page 211 the editors of *Spain Betrayed* omitted the words with which he began his sentence ('He is afraid that'), which can be interpreted in the sense that Prieto's fear was unjustified.

Both views, the communist and the anti-communist, have some justification, but the importance for the Republican Army is that there was so much mutual fear and hatred among its members. That circumstance, despite the undeniable cooperation between all parties and ideologies in creating the army, together with the excess of politicisation, reduced the confidence and the readiness of the *Ejército Popular de la República*.

11 Reorganisation

Reorganisation

By July 1937, the Republican Army was rapidly evolving from the chrysalis stage of the spring. The Army of the Centre, formed during the battles around Madrid, was well established with its five Corps (I, II, III, IV and VI). The Army of the South was about to be divided into the Army of Extremadura and the Army of Andalusia, and was composed of the VII, VIII, and IX Corps. The militia columns of Aragon and the short-lived *Exèrcit de Catalunya* had been militarised into the Army of the East, with the X, XI, XII and XIII Corps. The Army of the North, now falling back on Santander, was composed of the XV, XVI and XVII Corps, and striving to reorganise the remains of the Basque Corps (XIV). A new Corps, the XVIII, would be launched into battle at Brunete on 6 July 1937, and the V Corps would be coupled with it to form the nucleus of an Army of Operations (*Ejército de Maniobras*). Around the cities of Cuenca and Teruel were the remains of earlier militia columns called *agrupaciones* and soon to be formed into the Army of the Levante, that is, eastern Spain south of Catalonia. An Insurgent estimate at the time was that, in all, the Republican Army could boast of 16 fully organised army corps composed of 157 of the new mixed brigades. The report estimated an average of 2,700 men for each brigade (well under the theoretical establishment), and thus a round total of 424,000 men of whom 374,000 were at the fronts.[1]

Continuing the rapid organisation of the new Army of the Republic, the *Diario Oficial* issued a decree on 16 July 1937 which ordered the dissolution of the pre-war structure. The eight *divisiones orgánicas* or territorial administrative divisions, three of which (Madrid, Barcelona and Valencia) had remained under the control of the Republic, together with the Cavalry Division and the different brigade system of the pre-war Army, as well as the Albacete Division which had been set up

[1] CGG, L292, C1.

in August 1936 to organise the volunteer battalions, were to be wound up. Henceforward, for administrative purposes, Republican Spain's military structure would be on a provincial basis. Recruitment, which by now was almost completely by conscription, would be channelled through the Recruitment, Training and Mobilisation Centres (*Centros de Reclutamiento, Instrucción y Movilización*), known by the acronym CRIM, which would take over the installations of the old recruitment depots (*cajas de reclutas*). The CRIM would also deal with demobilisations, dependants of dead and wounded, regrouping of scattered personnel and recovery of equipment. The decree also established rearguard battalions (*batallones de retaguardia*) in each area, to act as military police and to which older men who had spent a long time at the Front would be posted.

Despite this forward-looking decree, it was becoming evident to many that the mixed brigades, known as the small 'big units' (*grandes unidades*, translated from the French concept of *grandes unités*, normally divisions and corps), were in practice unsatisfactory. Formed at speed in the process of militarising the militia, there were too many of them to be maintained at the regulation strength of about 4,000 men. The shortage of suitable officers and of equipment of all sorts meant that the Republican Army was not using its limited resources and its considerable strength in manpower to the best effect.

In view of the inherent problems of the mixed brigade it is interesting to examine an anonymous plan for reorganisation preserved in the records of the Republican Ministry of National Defence.[2] In view of the shortage of officers and weapons, it suggested that the Republican Army should be reorganised on the following lines.

There should be only four armies, of the Centre, South, East and Operations. The Army of the Levante and the Army of the East should be merged. No more army corps should be formed, leaving the number at 17. This dates the (undated) document to about November 1937, by which time the corps numbered XIV, XV, XVI and XVII, of the Army of the North, had ceased to exist. The XVIII, XIX, XX and XXII Corps had been formed by October 1937. Added to the existing 13, the total was 17. The document went on to suggest that each army corps should consist of two rather than three divisions, a sound suggestion which would ease the task of the relatively low-ranking and inexperienced corps commanders. The main battle unit or *gran unidad*

[2] DR, L474-1, C3. The undated paper is described as by a Staff colonel. Perhaps the author was Segismundo Casado, in view of his criticisms of the brigade system. See Casado, *Last Days of Madrid*, 60.

should be the division rather than the mixed brigades. Thus the brigades would lose their Staffs, which could not be efficiently manned for lack of trained Staff officers. Furthermore, the brigades should be reconstituted with three, rather than four, battalions with a depot battalion as a supply and training base, which the brigades had lacked, and which would 'feed' men to the serving battalions. To economise on officers, the report continued, each battalion should have 930 men rather than the 786 of the late 1937 revised establishment, and with 21 rather than 24 officers. Similar reforms were suggested at company, platoon, section and squad level, all with the aim of saving officers and increasing firepower.

The author calculated that his plan would save the commanding officers of one army, 60 brigades, 302 battalions and 1,510 companies. Given the dire shortage of trained officers, such a major change would certainly have meant that many more units would have been commanded by career soldiers. Distrust of the militia officers may have well have been one of the considerations of the author.

However, there is no record of an answer to these suggestions and, although establishments of units, big and small, were frequently changed, no alteration was made in the classic system of army = three corps; corps = three divisions; division = three brigades; brigade = four battalions; battalion = five companies. The weight of tradition and bureaucracy was too great, for even the Minister himself, Indalecio Prieto, suggested a reduction in the number of units in order to make better use of the competent commanders available, but nothing changed.[3]

The inexorable demand for conscription continued regardless of widespread shortages of almost every item of equipment. Current estimates would agree broadly with Rojo's statement to Azaña that conscription of men born in a given year would produce, given exemptions and failures to report for service, about 50,000 new recruits.[4] The classes of 1934 and 1935 had been called up on 7 October 1936. By May 1937, those of 1931 to 1937 had received their summons. By the end of the Spanish Civil War the Republic had mobilised 27 classes, ranging from men who had done their service in 1915 to boys from what was jokingly known as the *quinta del biberón*, the 'feeding-bottle class', of 1942. However, not till 14 January 1939 was the mass conscription demanded by the communists, of all men aged between 17 and 55, ordered. In comparison, the Insurgents called only the 15 classes between 1927 and 1941, aged 18 to 33. However, the latter were reinforced by over 80,000

[3] DR, L471, C6, 23 February 1938.
[4] Azaña, *Obras Completas*, IV: 840.

Moroccan volunteers and over 70,000 Italian infantry, and they used large numbers of their prisoners, especially after the collapse of the Northern Front, for labour, thus freeing men for front-line service.[5]

In late 1937 eight new divisions were formed, numbered 63 to 70 (numbers 48–62 had been destroyed in the north. Only some of these numbers were reallocated in 1938.). Five new army corps were created, numbered from XIX to XXIII, under the professional officers Joaquín Vidal Munárriz, Leopoldo Menéndez, Juan Perea, Ricardo Burillo and José María Galán. A new army, the Army of the Levante, was established on 19 August 1937, by which time the Armies of Andalusia (IX and XXIII Corps) and of Extremadura (VII and VIII Corps) had been created out of the original Army of the South. In due course, Insurgent Intelligence recognised the speed of the Republican Army's organisation and that its training methods were improving.[6]

Completing the new structure of the Republican Army, Vicente Rojo, its Chief of Staff, issued a General Order on 11 December 1937 intended to avoid confusion in nomenclature and to determine which commands should have a Staff.[7] Such a concern with formality and prestige was noticeably absent in the Insurgent army, which had maintained its traditional regimental system, creating brigades and divisions where needed for tactical purposes. Organising the Republican Army in a formal way, however, was part of the project of recovering Republican legality after the chaos of the early weeks of the war.

Below the Ministry and the Under-Secretariat of Defence, continued the General Order, each Arm had its inspector-general. Services such as transport, railways, signals, etc. had director-generals. As units, only armies, army corps, divisions and brigades were officially recognised. As tactical units, only the infantry battalion, the cavalry squadron and the artillery battery had status. No recognition would be given to any militia-style body. However, there is no evidence that militias were still functioning, so these statements of Rojo may be taken as a reflection of the actual state of affairs. The Republican Army was in being, in the classic form of any other army.

Training was to be recognised only in the numbered *Escuelas Populares de Guerra* and some special institutions for the *Carabineros* and other para-military bodies. Having abolished the *divisiones orgánicas*, territorial demarcations now consisted of *comandancias militares*

[5] See Pedro Corral, *Desertores: la guerra civil que nadie quiere contar*, Barcelona, 2006, 95–6 and 529–32, for statistical calculations of manpower in the Popular and Insurgent armies.
[6] CGG, L292, C1 of 14 December 1937.
[7] DR, L474-1, C3.

which controlled the rearguard battalions, all of which were numbered. Recruitment could take place only through the CRIMs. Armour, artillery and engineers had their bases and permanent centres (*Bases de Carros de Combate*, *Centros Permanentes de Artillería* (COPA) and *Centros Permanentes de Ingenieros* (COPI)).

Brigades were not deprived of their Staffs despite the shortage of qualified officers even at higher levels. Where available, one Staff-trained officer would be allocated to a division, three or four to a corps, and seven or eight to an army. In the meantime, units were to appoint Staffs according to the official establishment. Rojo would later claim that by 1939 the Republican Army had Staffs in all armies, corps, divisions and a large number of brigades.[8] Their quality, however, was deficient. In the Army of Extremadura, for example, a year after it had been formed, the Chief of Staff, Javier Linares, a professional officer, was described in a major investigation as a 'bon viveur'. The heads of the Operations, Information and Services Sections were all untrained for their posts. The Services Section in particular had in it militia officers who 'certainly did not know the regulations' ('*desde luego no conocían los reglamentos*'). Colonel Burillo, the army commander, was not cooperating with his Chief of Staff. This SIM report condemned the Staff for idleness, using the phrase 'complete paralysis' ('*parálisis completa*'). All the Staff were junior officers or militiamen. Blame for a recent disaster was attached primarily to the Chief of Staff and the heads of sections who, it was suggested, should be demoted to battalion commands.[9]

Poor-quality professional officers were, of course, worse than committed and energetic militia officers, even in the context of Staff work. The Army of the Ebro, for instance, had only one career officer on its Staff, who had accompanied Modesto, the army commander, since 1937. This was the engineers officer Captain José Sánchez Rodríguez, who was in possession of the Staff diploma. But the rest of the Staff were all militia officers, and they had been carefully chosen by Modesto himself. As he writes:

When you have a Staff which you have created, choosing the best, caring for them, observing their qualities, encouraging their initiative and learning from

[8] Rojo, *Alerta*, 114.

[9] DR, L473, C4. This is 'Investigation of the Army of Extremadura after loss of a line between Castuera and Don Benito in July 1938'. The investigation was the first public function undertaken by General José Asensio Torrado after the charges against him in connection with the loss of Málaga had been dropped. Reading between the lines, it seems that his condemnation of the Army of Extremadura command and Staff could have been justifiably harsher.

their example, you can rely on them and be confident that the missions which are required of you will be carried out.[10]

This shows that in a war such as the Spanish one, fought with indifferent commanders on the whole on the Republican side, the role of the Staff was vital. Yet the structure of the Republican Army was such as to require more Staff officers than could be provided.

By the end of 1937 the Army of the North had disappeared but the Armies of the Levante, Andalusia and Extremadura had been formed. Rojo's concept of an Army of Operations was a reality. It came under his control and included the V Corps, the newly numbered XIV Corps, which was a guerrilla force, and three other army corps, the XX, XXI and XXIII, which were partly of recent creation. The Army of Operations included well-experienced units with strong *esprit de corps*: the 27th (PSUC) Division, the 25th and 28th (CNT) Divisions, and the 45th (International) Division and the 11th Division. Under the Army of Operations came the tank and armoured car brigades and about 65 artillery batteries, as well as cavalry and most of the aircraft. However, very few of such non-infantry forces were attached to other armies.

However, the description of the Republican Army published on 18 December 1937 is to be taken as only an outline.[11] Many of the units shown were non-existent, as a final note remarks. Discounting those brigades which were in the process of reconstruction, there were in reality only 148 brigades out of the 225 numbers allocated. Only 49 divisions were at readiness. To some considerable extent this was a paper army.

A few months later, in April 1938, the Armies of Operations, the East and the Levante were reeling from the rapid Francoist advance in Aragon. The Ministry of National Defence was listing entire army corps as 'in reorganisation'. Divisions were being cobbled together from straggling groups of men who were being picked up by *Centros de recuperación de personal* as far north as Gerona and even close to the French frontier at Figueras. The XVIII Corps had been dissolved and its divisions and brigades redistributed, as had the XX, XXI and XXII Corps. It had been necessary to transfer units from the five corps of the Army of the Centre from around Madrid to the east in order to bolster Republican defences. In fact, considering the extent of the Insurgent breakthrough, which reached the Mediterranean on 15 April 1938, it was thought best to transfer nine divisions. Rojo, probably correctly, decided that to

10 Modesto, *Soy del Quinto Regimiento*, 176. 11 DR, L462.

transfer more was taking too great a risk.[12] The Insurgents might attack Madrid. This, nevertheless, seems unlikely. A city which has had time to fortify its defences and has high morale is an enormously challenging obstacle. It ought to have been possible to hold Madrid with the minimum of forces, while maintaining a large mobile force which could be transferred rapidly to threatened fronts. However, this requires a high degree of logistic efficiency, an area in which the Insurgents showed marked superiority. As Rojo wrote during the battle of Teruel:

I have a very bad impression of the personnel attached to transport. None of the faults so characteristic of these garage people has been corrected. On the contrary, there has been great laxity in the running of transport, which has magnified the defects. Cities and their comforts are too attractive for drivers.

(*Tengo muy mala idea, cada día peor, del personal afecto a los servicios de transportes por carretera, pues no se ha corregido ninguno de los defectos de esta gente de garaje. Sino por el contrario una gran flojedad en la dirección ha servido para acentuarlos y las poblaciones con sus comodidades suponen grandes atractivos para chóferes y demás elementos garagistas.*)[13]

Rojo's criticisms of shortcomings in the Republican Army in general became more frequent. On 30 March 1938 he was writing about the disastrous retreats taking place. The following month, after seeing the alarmingly large figures for arms abandoned in flight he insisted that a better sense of discipline had to be inculcated. The Republican Army did not use the discipline of fear, wrote the Ministry of Defence official who summarised Rojo's reports, so political and moral education must be intensified in order to instil a better sense of responsibility. This opinion probably led to a strengthening of the Political Commissariat in the spring of 1938. The report went on to claim that discipline had reached a high level of effectiveness in 1937, but had fallen off by 1938. This was not surprising, for the volunteers and militia who had formed the new Republican Army in early 1937 had fought mostly around Madrid, in the defence of the city and the battles of the Jarama, Guadalajara and Brunete which had finally caused Franco to desist in his attempt to take Madrid. Around the capital, furthermore, there had been a greater presence of professional military men. The influence of the PCE had also been very strong. By 1938, however, the Republican Army was fighting mainly in Aragon and the Levante, and it was composed much more of probably unwilling conscripts, among whom there may well have been a large number of men who were politically neutral or even sympathetic to Franco's Insurgents. The illusion of a militia

[12] DR, L507, C1. [13] DR, L461, C5.

army had disappeared with the militarisation. Many men must have looked on the Republican Army as a force in which they would receive plenty of political indoctrination, but poor food and insufficient footwear and clothing, together with indifferent leadership. A Ministry report commented: 'All the commanders are criticised.'[14] Any stick was good enough to beat them, so, went on the anonymous official, once one had been appointed, it was vital that he be accepted by his men. If he turned out to be a poor leader, then he should be publicly sanctioned. Next came a statement which epitomised the whole problem of the Republican Army:

> We have gone too rapidly along the road, in view of our resources, for we have created an army in name, with all the nomenclature and command system of a standard army, because that was essential if we were to be able to maintain and handle all the services. But we forget that we climbed only the first steps to reach the summit in this feat of organisation which we have undertaken.
>
> (*Hemos caminado también demasiado más deprisa de lo que nuestras disponibilidades consienten, pues hemos creado un Ejército con el nombre de tal, con toda la nomenclatura y sistema de mandos de un Ejército regular, porque así era obligado para poder mantener y articular todos los servicios, pero olvidamos que en esta organización emprendida sólo hemos subido los primeros peldaños para alcanzar la cumbre.*)[15]

Guerrillas

One potentially important advance had been made in October 1937 when 'Special Services' or guerrillas had been formally set up as the *Servicio de Información de Acción Militar* or SIAM. Its purpose was to provide information for the Information Section of the General Staff, and to carry out sabotage behind enemy lines.[16] The first actions of the new structure were planned to impede the arrival of enemy reinforcements at Teruel, which was to be attacked in December 1937. In early 1938 the guerrilla groups were given the title of XIV Corps, under Domingo Ungría González as inspector-general. Ungría had been an anti-Primo de Rivera career officer who had had to leave Spain. He formed militias in Valencia at the time of the insurrection but otherwise he remains a shadowy figure.

The XIV Corps had a total of 3,480 men, grouped into 6 divisions numbered 48, 49, 50, 51, 75 and 76, each with 4 brigades of 145 men each. The brigade bases were well in the rear, at Figueras, Gerona and

[14] DR, L507, C1. [15] *Ibid.*

[16] See Rodríguez Velasco, 'Las guerrillas'.

Manresa in Catalonia, and at Carcagente in Valencia. As for commanders, only two had been appointed. These were Luis Bárzana and Manuel Cristóbal Errandonea. The former had been a MAOC leader in the northern city of Gijón. His brother, who was a schoolmaster like him and had been killed, was a member of the Madrid committee of the PCE. Cristóbal was also a PCE member. A Basque, he had taken a prominent part in the battles for Irún and San Sebastián.

A large amount of minor guerrilla activity was seen in 1938 in Andalusia, where the lightly held Front and accidented terrain permitted the lines to be crossed and recrossed easily. Some of the activity was conducted by local inhabitants who had fled in 1936 and had been organised in the Republican zone.[17] A major coup was the freeing of 300 prisoners from Carchuna Fort, near Motril (Granada), directed by two American International Brigaders posted to the XIV Corps. This was a spontaneous action, without orders, consultation or even a report made to the head of the Information Section of the GERC. Perhaps this was one of the reasons for its success.

Although the actual damage done by these guerrilla bands was minimal, the Insurgents were worried by the frequency and the impunity of their exploits. Between January and April 1938 there were over 60 attacks, many of them frustrated by the warnings of civilians. Indeed, although Insurgent reports may be biased and lean in the direction of telling superiors what they wanted to hear, they do seem to point to the absence of support for the guerrillas from the civilian population and there were even denunciations. Expeditions failed in several places because they ran short of food. A point emerging from information collected from interrogated prisoners was that military hierarchy was maintained in guerrilla units. Prisoners said that the objects of raids were not explained to them.[18] There is nothing strange in this. The less a man knew the less he could betray, but on the other hand not engaging all the men in a plan does not allow each one to know what his precise task is and how it fits into the whole.

By 11 August 1938, the guerrillas were causing sufficient trouble for Franco personally to order his Military Intelligence service, the *Servicio de Información Periférica Militar* (SIPM), and other relevant authorities to stamp them out. Manpower was insufficient to prevent guerrillas crossing the lines. An order was issued to use shepherds for information

[17] References in Modesto, *Soy del Quinto Regimiento*, 25; Ibárruri *et al.*, *Guerra y Revolución*, II: 92; Castro Delgado, *Hombres*, 468; Koltsov, *Diario*, 397; and E. Comín Colomer, *La República en el exilio*, Barcelona, 1959, 365.

[18] Unless otherwise stated, all Insurgent information on guerrillas is taken from CGG, L281.

purposes and to move all civilians out of zones where they might aid the guerrillas. The SIPM proposed collective punishments if civilians did not report the presence of enemy guerrillas but Franco, more realistically, ordered rewards to be paid for denunciations.

Specifically the Republican Army used special units in the months before the battle of the Ebro began on 25–26 July 1938 to spy out the dispositions of Insurgent forces.[19] This probably contributed to the success of the initial assault.

Early 1939 saw a great increase in guerrilla activity in Extremadura. On 4 February, a 48-hour delay was caused by blowing up a railway line. How much more effective such a demolition would have been in the two or three days following the crossing of the River Ebro, when the Franco army was hastily transferring forces from the south and west of Spain! By now there was somewhat more information available on the guerrillas. Their headquarters had been set up at Alcalá de Henares, a few miles west of Madrid. The XIV Corps was composed of six divisions, two of which were numbered 200th and 300th. Each division had 4 brigades, each of 150 men. (The reason for the nomenclature is unknown: 150 men was no more than a large company. The 'division' of 600 equalled a battalion.) The 'corps' had 3,600 men. Guerrillas received extra pay. Unfortunately, Insurgent information was based on disjointed prisoner accounts and was often contradictory. One of the final reports speaks of guerrilla activity in the Avila region north-west of Madrid. The Insurgent officers who reported it seemed quite worried. With typical respect for anything non-Spanish, this report spoke of 'Russian dynamiters'. This probably referred to Americans from the International Brigades, or the Russians, who had a special centre for training guerrillas instructors, many of whom were Eastern Europeans detached from the International Brigades at Pins de Valls, about 20 km north of Barcelona.

In view of what appears to be the beginning of some success for guerrillas in the last two months of the war, together with the alarmed reports from the Insurgents, who were apparently disturbed by this unconventional way of waging war, widespread guerrilla activity, had it existed and had it been properly organised by the Republican Army, might have done considerable damage to the enemy, at least during battles where the latter's logistics were under pressure and susceptible to disruption. Even though evidence suggests that the civilian populations

[19] Modesto, *Soy del Quinto Regimiento*, 176; M. Pérez López, *A Guerrilla Diary of the Spanish Civil War*, André Deutsch, 1972; Tom Wintringham, *New Ways of War*, Penguin Books, 1940, 26.

gave little support to guerrillas, the latter might still have contributed much to the campaigns. That they did not do so is an example of an opportunity lost.

The principle of guerrilla war is that the guerrilla fighters are not under the authority of the formal army organisation, whether this is the division in whose territory they are operating or the Information Section of the General Staff. In the latter case they are more like the British Long-Range Desert group in North Africa during the Second World War than the Special Operations Executive or the advisers to French Resistance groups. The guerrillas of the Republican Army seem to have fallen between several stools. Were they established to engage in sabotage or to gather information? These are different aims. Information usually is gathered by undercover agents, whose skills are different from those of saboteurs. If the purpose was, as was sometimes stated, to raise the local populations in rebellion against the Insurgent occupiers, one may perhaps be thankful that they never managed to do so, because the savagery of the inevitable repression would have been hideous. The reality is that the purpose of the guerrillas was never agreed by politicians and Staffs, who wanted to keep control over them.

The anarchist leadership of the FAI proposed an increase in guerrilla war in a long report of 20 August 1938.[20] Later, however, when machine-gun battalions, the successors to the guerrillas, aligned in groups of five, each with three machine-gun companies and one of automatic rifles intended to provide intense fire-power, were formed,[21] the CNT, which was invited to participate, refused to send men without guarantees as to the commanders, fearing communist control.[22] In fact, one conclusion of Insurgent Intelligence, drawn from interrogating a man who had come over to their lines in Catalonia, was that the Republican Army had decided to abolish guerrillas as part of a plan to re-establish the old-style army. Even the old insignia and salute were to be restored. Since this is what indeed happened during the Casado period in the last three weeks of the Spanish Civil War it has the ring of genuineness about it and indicates that rumours of the sort were flying about as the Eastern Army Group or GERO fought a retreat towards the French frontier in January 1939. It also explains how the guerrillas were now to be used as special escorts. The Insurgent report added that José María Galán, commander of the XI Corps, had such an escort.[23]

[20] Quoted in Abad de Santillán, *Por qué perdimos*, 216ff.
[21] Rojo, *Alerta*, 129–30.
[22] Abad de Santillán, *Por qué perdimos*, 287.
[23] CGG, L281, C9.

Later, guerrillas under communist control were used to guard aircraft at Monóvar (Alicante) which were ready to take the PCE leaders into exile.[24] Here again, the idea of special commando-like forces was conceived but never came to fruition.

The Republic split in two

The great Insurgent push into eastern Spain of the spring of 1938 was finally halted north of Valencia. Franco's forces had reached the coast, thus dividing the Republic in two: Catalonia north of the Ebro River, and the central-south zone, a triangle with its apex in Madrid and its other two angles in Valencia and some distance south-west of Almería. Between 8 March and 15 April 1938, roughly 100,000 men of the Republican Army, casualties or prisoners, had been lost, together with large quantities of equipment. Considerable numbers of the Army of the East, of the Levante and of Operations had been left north of the River Ebro, so that by 1 May 1938, after recovery of scattered forces and a further call-up, there were 197,678 men in the armies in Catalonia. There were also 491,511 in the other zone (Levante, New Castile, La Mancha and those parts of Extremadura and Andalusia not occupied by the enemy).

The division of Republican territory had important political consequences, one of them being the forcing out of office of Indalecio Prieto, the Minister of National Defence, and his replacement by Juan Negrín, when the latter formed a new Government on 7 April 1938. Several important appointments were made, of which the most significant for the Republican Army was that of Antonio Cordón as Under-Secretary for the Army. A retired artillery captain in 1936, Cordón now proceeded to undertake an immediate and far-reaching reorganisation of the commands. He was soon working hard to set up the two new army groups which would compose the Republican Army until the fall of Catalonia in 1939. Miaja received command of the *Grupo de Ejércitos de la Región Central* (GERC), to include the Army of the Centre (Casado), the Army of the Levante (Menéndez), the Army of Extremadura (Burillo, then Prada) and the Army of Andalusia (Moriones). Hernández Saravia was appointed to head the *Grupo de Ejércitos de la Región Oriental* (GERO) to include Modesto in command of the new Army of the Ebro, and Perea heading the Army of the East. The GERO had six corps, Modesto's V, XII and XV, and Perea's X, XVIII and XX, together with the XXIV as a general reserve. The GERC included 16 corps as well as 3 brigades

[24] Líster, *Nuestra guerra*, 256, and Castro Delgado, *Hombres*, 651.

of cavalry, coastal defences, tanks and some other forces.[25] A whole series of director-generals were appointed or confirmed: Jurado to anti-aircraft, Azcárate to engineers, Bernal to transport, the socialist civilian Trifón Gómez to supplies, Dr José Puche to medical services and Ignacio Hidalgo de Cisneros to the Air Force. In some cases appointments were made which Prieto would later attack as being a result of communist pressure.

A swift and great effort was needed to provide these two army groups with the necessary personnel, equipment and supplies. The drafts of 1926, 1927, 1928 and 1941 were called up. According to Cordón, Negrín postponed an agreed plan for general mobilisation prepared in the Under-Secretariat because of the opposition of the CNT and the PSOE.[26]

Léon Blum's second Government reopened the French frontier for a few weeks in June 1938, allowing the entry of substantial amounts of armament.[27] Among the tasks which Cordón and his staff had to accomplish and did so sufficiently well so as be able to launch the battle of the Ebro on 25–26 July 1938, as well as hold the other fronts, were the reorganisation of supply and artillery depots and the regrouping of unnecessarily disseminated forces. For example, in all corps *Guardias de Asalto* were posted as military police. A round-up of all weapons held in the rearguard ensured that many more small arms were made available. Artillery and engineer units were to be restricted in the number of small arms they might keep. All horses were withdrawn from unit headquarters where they had been used for the entertainment of officers and were sent to bring the cavalry brigades up to strength.[28]

Considering the mangled condition of the Republican forces in Catalonia in April 1938, the reorganisation, which allowed the Front to be stabilised north of Valencia and the launching of the Ebro assault, which in its turn delayed the Insurgent attack on Catalonia until the end of 1938, goes far to justify Negrín's defence of his appointments policy.[29]

Further reorganisations

In September and October 1938 the battle of the Ebro was pinning down large numbers of Insurgent troops and succeeding in holding

[25] Cordón, *Trayectoria*, 412–13.
[26] *Ibid.*, 392–3.
[27] On this, see Alpert, *New International History*, 155, and Howson, *Arms for Spain*, 240.
[28] Cordón, *Trayectoria*, 412–13.
[29] See Michael Alpert, 'Negrín y el Ejército', in *Juan Negrín, médico y jefe del Gobierno, 1892–1956*, Madrid, 2006, 181–8.

off Franco's push towards Valencia. Germany's demands in Europe were appeased for a short time in October 1938 by the Munich agreement, but Spanish Republicans hoped, in vain, that the Western powers would seek to counterbalance Hitler's support for Franco by abandoning non-intervention and allowing the Republic to buy arms freely. The other Spanish fronts, central and southern, were holding steady. It seemed that there was no immediate danger.

At this moment, on 1 October 1938, Negrín issued yet another description and regulatory account of the Republican Army. This, in the form of a circular (*Orden Circular*) was communicated to all units and thus many copies were preserved in the archives. Was it designed to impress not only the enemy but also foreign countries?

The circular order, issued so that in its own words the army might achieve 'a stable structure and continuous improvement' ('*una estructura estable y continuas mejoras*') begins with a reference to the creation of new units in 1938 and affirms the belief in the efficiency of the standard army organisation imposed in 1937. The army, continued the order, consisted of 2 army groups and 6 armies of variable composition, 23 army corps, consisting of either 2 or 3 divisions, 70 divisions and 200 mixed brigades. There were two coastal defence groups, two armoured divisions, four anti-aircraft brigades and four brigades and two regiments of cavalry as well as the various specialised groups within each army group or army.

All details of establishment were to be respected; no units were to be formed without authority. Only the High Command could abolish units. At this late date it does not seem likely that these ringing commands were intended as an attack on the CNT or other group which did not like the formal army. Perhaps they were intended to warn General Miaja that his semi-autonomy in Madrid did not make him completely independent of the control of the Ministry of National Defence and the General Staff in Barcelona.

Units which had been temporarily attached were to be returned to their 'home' brigades or divisions. Reserves were to be held at the disposal of the army group command rather than of any lower-level authority. The commander of any unit was to be in command of all subordinates in his sphere of operations. In particular, the inspector-general of any Arm was to have no authority over it within a war zone. That is to say that the artillery, engineers and other service units were to come unquestionably under the orders of the brigade, division, corps, army or army group commander in whose zone they were stationed.

Brigade organisation was to be respected '*rigurosamente*'. Light artillery which had been stripped from the brigades to be assembled as a mass was to be returned and all the various sections of a brigade were to be properly established. Where possible, a depot company would be formed to assist in training. All brigades would have a nucleus of heavy arms which would not be dispersed. A similar levelling-out of men and weapons would be effected at division and corps level. This was a return to the original concept of the mixed brigade as an independent force. In view of the supply of war material required to provide each of the 200 brigades with its complement of accompanying artillery, for instance, it looks as though Negrín, ever the optimist, was hoping for a renewed flow of armaments. The order did realise that in certain cases it might be necessary to assemble all the artillery or engineers in a division or corps for a particular operation, but it was stressed that they could be separated only temporarily from their parent brigades.

The service echelons – sappers, signals, medical corps, supplies, motor pools and so forth – were regulated in depots coming directly under the orders of the Under-Secretariat for National Defence, which was fixed as the obligatory channel through which all material purchased or manufactured had to pass.

Much of the emphasis in this circular order was, understandably, on the full use in fighting units of all men available and the reduction of second-echelon troops to the minimum possible. From then on, rearguard units and service echelons might use only war invalids and others exempt from active duty. Nobody would be permitted to remain for more than three months in any of the main artillery or engineer depots. This seems to echo Vicente Rojo's frequent complaints in his *¡Alerta los pueblos!* about '*emboscados*' in comfortable rearguard posts during the last desperate stages of the fighting retreat of the Republican Army through Catalonia.

Finally, from Article 23 of the order, it seems as if no imminent end to the war was expected, for it required all brigades to have a History, which should be 'clear, concise and true' ('*claro, conciso y veraz*'). (See an example in Appendix 2.)

To this order were added detailed establishments for armies, corps, divisions and brigades.[30] Clearly it was felt that regulations at all levels were necessary. The detail of the order is reflected in the list of units to be attached to an army (that is, any one of the six in the Republican Army):

one battalion of HQ troops
one battalion 'special' corps (probably guerrillas)

[30] DR, L474–2, C5, C6, C7, C8.

one cavalry brigade*
one heavy artillery group
one sound-location group
one battalion of sappers
anti-aircraft units
two companies of road-builders
one disciplinary battalion
one signals battalion
one cycle and motor-cycle battalion
one remount depot*
one artillery depot
two fortifications battalions*
one supply group*
medical services
anti-gas unit
one motor transport group*
one horse transport battalion*.

If this establishment is compared with the return of the Army of the Ebro at the end of May 1938,[31] the artificiality and ideal character of the list becomes clear. The Army of the Ebro had attached to it only the units asterisked in the above list. Furthermore, its transport units were companies rather than battalions. However, it possessed a special machine-gun battalion and three tank battalions as well as companies of armoured cars. It had a battalion of bridgebuilders, essential in view of the planned crossing of the Ebro. The tank units were removed from army commands by the order of 1 October 1938. Thus an Insurgent report on the Armies of Extremadura and Andalusia in February 1939 wrote that the 27 tanks in the entire zone covered by the 2 armies depended not on the army commanders but on the commander of tanks, whose headquarters was far away in Cuart de Poblet (Valencia).[32] This seems to confirm Casado's insistence that tanks, supplied by the Soviet Union, were not under the control of the Spanish General Staff (and, by implication, they were directed by Russian advisers).[33]

These establishments and figures, like those issued many times for the mixed brigades, were to a large extent prescriptive rather than descriptive of the actual situation. They must have been seen as indications for a professional-style army, which by now had the backbone of organisation which might have been able to put Cordón's recommendations

[31] DR, L795, C1. [32] CGG, L292, C3.
[33] Casado, *Last Days of Madrid*, 54.

into practice had time and an abundant supply of war material been available.

If these schemes had been imposed in 1937 many difficulties would have been avoided, but it was not until after the disasters of April 1938 that Antonio Cordón became Under-Secretary of Defence. The circular order of 1 October 1938 was obviously his, with the powerful backing of Negrín, because for all practical purposes he ran the Ministry. Cordón believed in the ability of the Republican Army to fight on, or so he writes in his memoirs.[34] Despite the possibility that, writing many years later, he was embroidering the truth, his expression of confidence in the Republican Army does not seem to be a communist stratagem to provide the PCE with a heroic history nor a stance planned to cast even greater discredit on Colonel Casado's coup of 1939, one of the justifications for which was precisely the inability of the Republican Army to continue the war. Nevertheless, in Catalonia, Cordón was mistaken in his confidence. When Franco's offensive came just before Christmas 1938, the two armies of the GERO were defeated in six weeks. Even so, the possibility of resistance in the south-central zone still remains unknown. It was the diverse and mutually contradictory opinions on this question which led to the Casado coup and long post-war recriminations.

Negrín was clearly confident of the arrival of a steady stream of arms. As the GERO desperately fought back in its retreat towards the French frontier, abandoning Barcelona on 26 January 1939, Negrín and Rojo requested Ignacio Hidalgo de Cisneros, head of the Air Force and a prominent communist, to take their request for war material to the Soviet leaders. The numbers required seemed disproportionate to the Spanish airman, for the list included 250 aircraft, 250 tanks, 4,000 machine-guns and 650 pieces of artillery.[35] He arrived in Moscow at the end of November. Stalin, to Hidalgo's astonishment, did not demur but agreed to send everything which had been requested and to extend the necessary credit, given that the gold sent to Moscow had now been used up.

The Soviets shipped some of what had been requested, 168 aircraft, 40 tanks, 539 pieces of artillery and 2,770 machine-guns. By the time they arrived, however, there was no way of assembling the aircraft and little time to distribute the rifles and machine-guns which did get across the frontier, because the two armies, of the East and of the Ebro, had abandoned Spain by 9 February 1939.[36]

[34] Cordón, *Trayectoria*, 413.
[35] Hidalgo de Cisneros, *Memorias*, II: 242.
[36] Howson, *Arms for Spain*, 242–3.

12 The Casado uprising

Behind the surrender of the Republican Army at the end of March 1939 lay the conflict between the professional officers, who feared a communist take-over and a fight to the bitter end, and the Negrín Government, whose validity had been seriously impaired by the resignation of the President of the Republic, Manuel Azaña, and the refusal of Vicente Rojo, the Chief of Staff, to return to what remained of Republican territory after the two armies in Catalonia had sought asylum in France. The central figure in the surrender in the south-central zone, garrisoned by the Armies of the Centre, of the Levante, of Extremadura and of Andalusia, was Colonel Segismundo Casado López, commander of the Army of the Centre.

With the defeat of the Republican armies in Catalonia and their internment in France in early February 1939, the question was whether the remaining territory of the Republic, a triangle with its apex in Madrid and its other two angles in Valencia and some distance south-west of Almería, could continue the war. The leaders of Republican Spain, President Manuel Azaña, Diego Martínez Barrio, President of the *Cortes* – the Parliament – and General Vicente Rojo, Chief of the General Staff, were, it seemed, determined not to encourage what they saw as a useless policy of resistance. Having crossed into France, they did not return to the Republican zone of Spain.

The case of Rojo has been investigated in recent years. His grandson, José Andrés Rojo, quotes a bitter letter that Rojo sent in February to Juan Negrín, Prime Minister and Minister of National Defence, about the sufferings of soldiers of the Republican Army now interned in the winter in primitive shelters on wind-swept and sand-whipped French beaches. In a telegram sent on 18 February 1939, Rojo refused to accept the promotion to lieutenant-general which Negrín had awarded him on 12 February 1939, saying that he did not have the right to order other officers to return to Spain while they did not know how their families would survive in France. Yet Rojo said he would go back to Spain if Negrín, constitutionally his hierarchical superior, or Generals Miaja and Matallana, senior commanders in the south-central zone, ordered him to.[1] No such order appears to have been given. On 28 February 1939, General Jurado, the last commander of the Eastern Army Group, told Ralph Stevenson, who had been British consul-general in Barcelona but was now in France, that Negrín had 'asked' Jurado and Rojo to return with him to Spain (the service from Toulouse to Alicante was still operating), but they had refused.[2] On 3 March, Negrín, through Martínez Barrio, President of the *Cortes*, again asked Rojo to go back to Spain. Rojo replied that he would go when the journey was possible.[3] Soon after, Martínez Barrio told Rojo that the journey had been postponed (*suspendido*).[4] The Chief of Staff's return to Spain may have been postponed because Negrín suspected that he was involved in Casado's planned coup. This may have been a grave error, because the Chief of Staff's prestige and personal knowledge of high-ranking officers might have been able to put a brake on the conspiracy. However, this is a moot point. Is it likely that Rojo had the level of personal influence that would have empowered him to put paid to a movement which had such deep roots among so many professional and high-ranking officers?

Negrín, some of the Cabinet, and the leaders of the PCE, insisted on resistance. They were convinced that a general European conflagration, which they considered imminent, would save the Republic. However, this could be no more than a possibility, for while a European war would probably have made the Germans withdraw their forces from Spain, there is no reason to think that Britain and France would have done anything to stop Franco launching all his armies against Madrid.

Despite the peaceful surrender to Franco's forces of the Balearic island of Minorca on 8 February 1939, facilitated by Britain through Lieutenant-Commander Alan Hillgarth, consul at Palma de Mallorca, and accompanied by the evacuation in a British warship of people in most danger of reprisals,[5] nothing similar seemed possible in the central-south zone of the Spanish mainland. Hopes for a peace based on allowing evacuation following the example of Minorca were an illusion. Minorca was an island of relatively little significance to the Spanish Republic but important for Britain because the surrender was negotiated on the understanding that Italian forces would not be

1 Rojo, *Vicente Rojo*, 276–7.
2 FO 371, W3762 in volume 24153, quoted by A. Bahamonde and J. Cervera, *Así terminó la guerra de España*, Madrid, 2000, 12.
3 Rojo, *Vicente Rojo*, 293.
4 *Ibid.*, 310.
5 See Alpert, *La guerra civil española en el mar*, 348–51, and the same author's 'Los enigmas de la rendición de Casado', *Historia 16*, 16, No. 185 (September 1991), 8–16.

allowed to land there. An Italian military, air and naval presence in the Balearics, with all it might threaten for British hegemony in the western Mediterranean, was a major concern to London. It was quite a different matter to demand that Franco should accept the surrender of Republican Spain and allow his enemies to be evacuated (even if this were possible) merely because the British Government asked him to. Franco had closed his eyes to the departure of a few hundred people from Minorca because a British warship had agreed to take his emissary and had indeed had talked the Republican commander into surrender. To allow a massive evacuation from Mediterranean ports went against Franco's insistence on due punishment for those he considered guilty. The only alternatives for the Republican Army were resistance or the organisation of some sort of staggered retreat to the coast so as to protect an orderly evacuation of those in most danger. It was this tension between, on the one hand, seeking terms from the enemy and, on the other, resisting in order to protect an evacuation, which provoked feelings of hate and distrust towards Negrín, and allowed his enemies to support the *coup d'état* of Colonel Casado.

Since 23 January 1939, when the State of War had at last been declared in the remaining territory of the Republic, General Miaja had enjoyed absolute power in the south-central zone. If Negrín hoped that Miaja was resolved to fight on he would have had an unpleasant surprise when, on 9 February, he met Antonio López Fernández, Miaja's private secretary, whom the general had entrusted with a confidential mission. López spoke to Rojo, who was in Le Perthus, and then offered Negrín a full account of the situation in what remained of the Republic. There was no possibility, said López, repeating Miaja's views, of resistance.[6] The Prime Minister, nevertheless, ignoring this, flew back to Spain.

The solution of fighting in order to protect a staggered retreat towards the naval base of Cartagena, evacuating the most compromised people, whose departure would be protected by the Republican Fleet en masse, assumed that there would be sufficient ships to allow large numbers of people to be evacuated and that the safety of the base was itself fully guaranteed against naval blockade or bombardment. No plan seems to have been made for such an evacuation. Although the Republican Fleet was in being, consisting of three cruisers and several destroyers and other ships, it was seriously defeatist and several of its commanders were to some considerable extent sympathetic to the enemy.[7]

[6] López Fernández, *General Miaja*, 265–8.

[7] Alpert, *La guerra civil española en el mar*, 348–51.

Once President Azaña had resigned on 27 February 1939, refusing to return to Spain, from the constitutional aspect the remaining Republican territory had no governing authority. Many thought that Negrín Government was no longer legitimate, and this was the legal basis for the Casado coup of 5 March. Nevertheless, Negrín considered himself still the Prime Minister of the Republic and its Minister of National Defence, so when he arrived in Valencia on 10 February he proclaimed his determination to continue the war and promoted Miaja to the rank of lieutenant-general, perhaps to win him over to his cause and to establish his hierarchical superiority over the other generals of the Republic who were in the central-south zone.

Casado led the Army of the Centre, which was the largest and most important army given that it was based around Madrid. Negrín thus went out of his way to convince him of his point of view. He talked to Casado on 12 February, but Casado merely repeated to Negrín what Miaja had already indicated through López Fernández a few days earlier, that is, that the situation was hopeless. It was following this disappointing meeting with Casado that the decisive meeting of all the senior commanders and Negrín took place, on 16 February, at the airfield of Los Llanos near Albacete.[8] At this meeting, the commanders of the armies, and of the navy and the Air Force, agreed that further resistance was pointless. In particular, Admiral Buiza threatened to order the Fleet to sail away from Cartagena if peace negotiations were not begun at once.

Who was Segismundo Casado, the central figure in the surrender of the Republican Army to Franco in March 1939 and thus the end of the Spanish Civil War?

He was born in 1893, son of a man who had done his military service but, according to Casado, was now a farm worker.[9] He entered the

[8] Most historians give the date of this meeting as 26 and 27 February, but contemporary documents, albeit from Franco's headquarters, give February 17 (CGG, L277, C10 and C11). Casado, whose account of the entire episode of his rebellion has significant variations between the first version as published in London in 1939 and the later version he published when he returned to Spain as *Así cayó Madrid*, Madrid, 1968, gives 16 February as the date (p. 119) but the 1939 London edition gives 25 February (p. 115). In 1939 Casado, whose memory of such a recent event should have been accurate may have given the later date in order to show that he did not decide to mount his coup until he was sure that he had the support of all the army commanders, but nearly 30 years later he gave the earlier date. Since it is most unlikely that Casado had any access to archives in 1968, his change of date was intentional. Either he remembered it more clearly, or it was no longer necessary to give a false date.

[9] Casado's two books seem to be economical with the truth. Casado's father, for instance, was an army captain. See 'Casado', in García Fernández, *25 militares*.

cavalry academy at the age of 14. A man of obvious ability, he studied in the Higher War School and taught in the academy for NCOs. During the Primo de Rivera dictatorship of 1923–30 he defended some anti-Primo de Rivera conspirators. It was from this time that his friendship with some CNT leaders dated. On 31 January 1935, during the Republic, his loyalty and capacity in teaching in the Higher War School was recognised by his appointment as commander of the Presidential Guard. He also became, significantly, a Freemason (in Spain this generally meant a person of liberal and anticlerical views), though he later claimed he had been a mason for a very short time.[10]

An intellectual, his main interest was military organisation. In 1931, he gave a lecture at the Army Cultural Centre on the French Army, considered to be at the acme of military skill after the victory of 1918. In his lecture, Casado criticised Spanish military organisation, which caused some protest.[11] This interest in organisation re-emerged in the discussion in his books on the faults of the mixed brigade system, which he blamed on the pressure from the Russian advisers, although he himself did not express doubts while involved in the creation of the brigades.[12] Possibly some of the proposals discussed above for reorganising the Republican Army may have come from Casado. After a spell at Albacete organising the mixed brigades, an order in the *Diario Oficial* of 30 November 1936 sent him to the wartime capital Valencia as head of the Operations of the General Staff.

Casado's wartime career was a distinguished one. He remained as Head of Operations until May 1937, when he was given the back-room posts of Inspector of Cavalry and Director of the Staff College. This move may have been a result of the rejection of his plan for an offensive in Extremadura, a rejection which he blamed on Russian advice. However, when Colonel Jurado, commander of the XVIII Corps, which, together with Modesto's V Corps, had taken an important part in the battle of Brunete, fell ill in July 1937, Casado was ordered to take command. He thought he had been given the command to discredit him, because the XVIII Corps was badly prepared. In reality, the command was merely temporary and the fact that Casado left the command after the battle does not indicate that he was being discredited, although Casado's complaints about the impossible nature of his task are confirmed not only by his own reports but also those of Jurado.[13] Casado's

10 M. de Paz Sánchez, *Militares masones de España. Diccionario biográfico del siglo XX*, Valencia, 2004, under 'Casado'.

11 Miguel Alonso Báquer, *El Ejército en la sociedad española*, Madrid, 1971, 297.

12 Casado, *Last Days of Madrid*, 59–61. See Chapter 4 for a discussion of this issue.

13 *Ibid.*, 75. The reports are in Martínez Bande, *Brunete*, documents 10 and 11.

next combat command was the XXI Corps, formed in August 1937. He does not mention that he had disagreements with Líster, commander of the 11th Division, at the time part of Casado's corps. According to Líster, the argument took place because the inhabitants of Alcañiz (Teruel) refused to billet his troops and Casado supported them over Líster's head. The 11th Division had recently taken an important part in destroying the collectives of Aragón, and it may well be that this was the origin of the villagers' refusal to accommodate it. Antonio Cordón, who was Chief of Staff of the Army of the East, recounts the episode and claims that Casado was dismissed,[14] but it is likely that Cordón brought the matter up only because of Casado's crushing of the communists after his coup in 1939. It does not seem an important episode except to show how pettiness and political and ideological squabbles affected the conduct of the Republican Army. The important point is that the statement of Castro Delgado, which reflects the communist view of Casado's motives, according to whom Casado was 'full of rancour against everybody because he felt he had been held back' ('*cargado de rencor contra todos por creerse postergado*')[15] is unjustifiable in view of Casado's later promotions and posts. In March 1938, he was given command of the Army of Andalusia and two months later, even with the influential communist Cordón as Under-Secretary of Defence and effectively in control of the Republican Army, Casado, now a colonel, was given charge of the largest and most important force, the Army of the Centre.

To trace the chronology of Casado's coup and his negotiations with the Insurgents, his first and second version of the events and the relevant Insurgent documents can be interestingly collated (see Table 12.1). There are other discrepancies also. The Insurgent account relates that in the last week of February 1939 Francoist agents met Republican Army officers openly. Casado does not mention this in either of his versions. In his *Last Days of Madrid* (1939) he claims to have refused the promotion to general that Negrín had decreed on 24 February, but says nothing about it in *Así cayó Madrid* (1968).[16] On 5 March he met the commander of the Air Force, Hidalgo de Cisneros, a communist. In the earlier version of his account Casado writes that Hidalgo assured him of his loyalty, but in the second book he says that the air chief prevaricated.[17] At the meeting at Los Llanos, according to Casado's 1939

[14] Cordón, *Trayectoria*, 310.
[15] Castro Delgado, *Hombres*, 566.
[16] Casado, *Last Days of Madrid*, 149.
[17] *Ibid.*, 170; Casado, *Así cayó Madrid*, 169. Hidalgo de Cisneros himself writes that he told Casado that the idea of surrender was absurd (*Memorias*, II: 253–4).

Table 12.1 *The Casado coup: contrasting chronologies*

	Last Days	*Así cayó*	Insurgents[a]
Republican commanders meet at Los Llanos	26 February[b]	16 February[c]	16 February
Casado meets Colonel Centaño	12 March[d]	5 February[e]	20 February

Notes: [a] CGG, L277, C8, 'Memorias de un agente del SIPM'.
[b] Casado, *Last Days*, 11.
[c] Casado, *Así cayó Madrid*, 121.
[d] Casado, *Last Days*, 207.
[e] Casado, *Así cayó Madrid*, 205.

account, Admiral Buiza 'produced a most unhappy impression' while in the second book 'he impressed us all by his frankness and courage' ('*nos impresionó a todos por su franqueza y su gallardía*').[18]

There are other points of difference between the two versions, accounted for by the passage of time and reconsideration in greater tranquillity. The first book was written so soon after the events which it describes took place that it ought to be absolutely true in detail, but there are many inaccuracies. Writing in England (the book was never published in Spain) Casado had to justify his actions to a British audience and thus trying to show that he had no thought of revolt until Negrín appointed communist militia officers to major military commands on 3 and 4 March 1939. When he wrote the second book he was back in Spain and trying to establish his right to a military pension.

Taking the two versions into account, the true sequence of events can be reconstructed with the help of the Insurgent record.

The underground *Falange* in Madrid was involved. Its leaders thought that Casado was ready for surrender even before the armies of the GERO crossed into France, that is before 6–8 February 1939. However, Casado wanted Franco to grant conditions. If pressed, reported the Insurgent agents in the capital, the Army of the Centre, which Casado commanded, would resist to the end. This agrees with Casado's statement that at the Los Llanos meeting he said that stopping the war was in the best interests of all and that they should try to obtain the best terms possible and to resist if the enemy refused to grant them.[19] However, this paragraph is not in *Así cayó Madrid*. In the 1939 book, Casado dates this meeting ten days later than it took place,

18 Casado, *Last Days of Madrid*, 123; Casado, *Así cayó Madrid*, 126.
19 Casado, *Last Days of Madrid*, 122–3.

presumably to persuade his readers that he resisted as long as possible. The accurate date in his later version may have been given because interested readers would know or be able to discover the true date. Nor was Casado eager in 1968, when he was trying to get a pension, to emphasise that he wanted to prolong resistance.

According to the Insurgent account, Colonel Prada, Casado's successor at the head of the Army of the Centre, together with other professional officers, wanted to surrender and were in contact with the Madrid *Falange*. It might be thought that this account, not being written for publication, was reliable, but it has to be taken guardedly because it was basically a plea from the *Falange* that it should be recognised as an effective shadow administration in the capital. In view of later events, however, it does seem that the professionals of the Republican Army were prepared to surrender honourably. What the significance of their contacts with the *Falange* was cannot be judged.

Reports coming from the SIPM (*Servicio de Información y de Policía Militar*), the Insurgent Intelligence service, on 11 and 17 February 1939 suggested that General Matallana, commander of the Central Army Group (GERC) and two senior Staff officers, Colonels Muedra and Garijo, were ready to surrender. This rumour must have been circulated and is the basis of the accusation that the two latter were traitors to the Republic. Yet it was Matallana who handed over a plan of the defences of the city, while Lieutenant-Colonel Bernal Segura was reported to have agreed to collapse the XXIII Corps Front in Andalusia.[20] Matallana was court-martialled after the surrender like the other officers, but, despite a prison sentence of 30 years, he served a relatively short sentence, almost certainly because of his collaboration with Casado. On 20 February 1939, Casado took the formal step of meeting Colonel Centaño, a SIPM agent in command of an armourer's workshop in Madrid. Casado dates this meeting to 5 February in *Así cayó Madrid*, showing that he was in contact with Nationalist agents very early, but on 12 March in *Last Days*, that is after his coup and when he was fighting the communists. Casado did not want his British readers to know that he was meeting an agent of the Insurgents. The weight of evidence, nevertheless, inclines to the earlier date. In fact, Insurgent records indicate that it was through his army doctor, Captain Diego Medina, that the SIPM approached Casado, who suffered severely

[20] CGG, L277. The map bears a note saying that it was conveyed by Matallana. See J. M. Campanario, C. Díez Hernando and J. Cervera Gil, 'El enigma del general republicano Manuel Mantallana Gómez', at www2.uah.es/jmc/matallanacongresogce.pdf for a detailed study of Matallana's self-defence at his trial.

from stomach problems, as early as 1 February. The general suspicion was that Casado was playing for time, to try to force more concessions out of Franco, but that the communist 'take-over' of high commands forced his hand. Another source claims that the SIPM had been trying to recruit him for a long time.[21]

It is clear that Casado's attitude to continuing the war was negative and that he was in contact with the enemy.[22] If the latter made the first move, it must have been because, perhaps through his doctor, the SIPM thought it would be knocking at an open door. His motives, however, require further examination.

The report on his interview with Colonel Centaño may be taken as the extreme expression of Casado's views coloured by his concern for the future of himself and other professional officers. He claimed to loathe Azaña, the *bête noire* of the Insurgents ever since his reform of the Spanish Army in 1931–3, to have resigned from Freemasonry, the second bogeyman, because of its 'Jewish' associations (Judaism being another enemy despite the almost complete absence of Jews from Spain except in Spanish Morocco, where, paradoxically, the military got on with them quite well), and to be violently anti-communist. Thus he made the enemies of the Insurgents his own. He stressed his love for Spain and said he would kill himself if Moors or Italians took part in a Nationalist victory parade. He intended to leave Spain in any case but requested good treatment for his Staff, finishing by saying that his surrender would be 'an example for History'. The tone of this summary of his interview, admittedly written at second or third hand, raises suspicion about Casado's mental state. The acute strain of the war may well have impaired his finer judgement. His references to Azaña and Freemasons were, however, clearly attempts at pandering to Insurgent prejudices and obsessions.

It has been widely stated that Casado was unduly influenced by a British 'agent', Denys Cowan.[23] The rumour may have grown because of the role of Muirhead-Gould, captain of HMS *Devonshire*, the British warship which had enabled the peaceful surrender of Minorca (see above). Santiago Garcés, head of the SIM, said or wrote, 'It was then

[21] A. Bouthelier and J. López-Mora, *Ocho días: la revuelta comunista*, Madrid, 1940, 146.

[22] Rojo, *Alerta*, 295, notes that Casado's negative attitude was well known. If this is so and not merely a question of being wise after the event, why was Casado entrusted with the largest of the armies of the Republican Army?

[23] See Hugh Thomas, *The Spanish Civil War*, 3rd edn, Penguin Books, 1977, 887–8 and note.

[after the surrender of Minorca] that he [Casado] decided to negotiate a peace.'[24]

Casado states that his relations with Cowan and other diplomats were limited to interviews after his 5 March 1939 coup, and later negotiations about being allowed to come to the United Kingdom.[25] However, there is some evidence that he had had previous contacts with the British chargé d'affaires, who had brought offers of British intervention to avoid reprisals if Casado surrendered his Army of the Centre.[26] This was a journalist's report and must be treated with care. In general, Foreign Office discussions on how Britain should act at this juncture insisted that British representatives should interfere as little as possible although the end of the war was much desired in London because Spain was a hindrance in the Chamberlain Government's desire to come to an agreement with fascist Italy. Britain was happy to cooperate in the evacuation from Spain of Italian soldiers held as prisoners of war. But on 16 February, Denys Cowan, a Spanish-speaking ex-consul in Havana and a member of the International Committee for Prisoner Exchanges in Spain, visited Julián Besteiro, the socialist university professor who would back Casado's coup, and on 20 February he saw Casado. Both men told Cowan that they were trying to find a way of concluding a peace. This was before Casado's coup. Casado said that he was loyal to Negrín but hoped that Azaña, now in Paris, would dismiss him from office.[27] As for negotiations about evacuating those people in most danger of Francoist reprisals, the British consul in Valencia, Goodden, reported that members of Casado's future National Defence Council approached him before the 5 March coup.[28] However, nothing indicates that Casado was a British 'agent' or in receipt of British funds. The fact that he was taken off from the port of Gandía by a British warship may well reflect a certain understanding, but not as a sort of reward for bringing the war to an end, which Casado certainly wanted to do. Nevertheless, his efforts to safeguard prisoners, both Spanish civilians and Italian military, impressed the consul, Cowan and the British naval officers and, through them, the Foreign Office. The captain of the light cruiser HMS *Galatea* sent a signal from Gandía to the senior British officer in the area to say that Casado and his Staff had been in danger

[24] D. Pastor Petit, *Los dossiers secretos de la guerra civil*, Barcelona, 1978, 465. For the surrender of Minorca see Alpert, *La guerra civil española en el mar*, 348–51.

[25] Casado, *Last Days of Madrid*, 273.

[26] K. Scott-Watson, in F. Hanighen (ed.), *Nothing but Danger: Thrilling Adventures of Ten Newspaper Correspondents in the Spanish War*, Harrap, 1940.

[27] This is what Cowan communicated to London. See FO 371, W5827/2082/41.

[28] FO 371, W6704/8/41.

in Valencia but had stayed on to keep order: 'He and his party seem fit persons for embarkation in one of HM ships.'[29] In fact, Casado was invited to leave on board a French warship but declined because he felt too ill to move and wanted to stay with his party.[30]

Yet, doubts persist. Cowan may have suggested something to Casado in the meetings he had with him over the matter of evacuating prisoners. But what could it be? It seems absurd to suggest that Cowan told Casado the outright lie that London had received guarantees from Franco that professional officers' careers would be protected, even though Casado certainly believed this and continued to do so even in exile, by which time it was a fantasy.

Furthermore, Casado and others may well have discussed the possibility of evacuation in a British warship. If his coup and the surrender are seen as a triumph for the Foreign Office or some sort of British secret service operation, the foot-dragging unwillingness of London to authorise Casado and his party to embark on the *Galatea* until the very last moment needs an explanation. The *Galatea* visited the British-owned harbour installation at Gandía at 16.50 hours on 29 March 1939, which may suggest that it was known that Casado would be waiting there. Nevertheless, British ships, including naval vessels, habitually used Gandía to evacuate non-Spanish citizens, prisoners being repatriated to Italy and occasional Spanish citizens.[31]

Casado and the CNT

Casado's main support came from the anarchist CNT, which had been driven to the limit by communist and Government pressure, the export of treasure by Negrín and the unfair manner in which the CNT judged that passports were being issued. The CNT believed – naively perhaps – that the elimination of communist influence would favour diplomatic negotiations for surrender with the aid of Britain and France.[32] The CNT hoped that it would thus be possible to avoid large-scale decimation of the *Confederación* when Franco took over. Nevertheless, Casado did not willingly call in anarchist units to help him fight communist ones when the latter attacked the National Council of Defence after

[29] FO 371, W5263/2082/41. [30] FO 371, W5943/2082/41.

[31] See the interesting account by E. Mainar, J. M. Santacreu and R. Llopis, *Gandia i el seu port, marc 1939*, Gandía, 2010, 95. For a more detailed account see The National Archives, ADM 1/10221. For further interpretation see Alpert, *La guerra civil española en el mar*, 352.

[32] According to the CNT historian José Peirats in a personal communication to the author (5 September 1975).

the coup of 5 March 1939. Yet it was Cipriano Mera's IV Corps, based on the original CNT *Milicias confederales del Centro*, which assured Casado's success. The communist-led three other army Corps were also moving into Madrid from their positions around the capital.[33] The new Ministries, at that time on the outskirts, and other strategic areas, had been occupied by communist-officered troops.[34] Nevertheless, the I, II and III Army Corps led by Bueno, Ortega and Barceló, apparently unaware of Casado's plans, had reacted slowly to his coup.[35]

The CNT saw further resistance to Franco as useless. They hoped that shaking off the communist incubus would assure an honourable peace. Perhaps most realistically, they needed to find a way to save the lives of the most compromised militants of the movement.[36] Communist policy was to fight on, knowing that the party could expect no clemency from the victors and in the hope that Hitler's real intentions would at last dawn on Britain and France, who would abandon non-intervention and allow the large quantities of Soviet arms that had been sent following Hidalgo de Cisneros's mission to Moscow, and which may have been still in France, to be shipped to Alicante or Cartagena and rearm the armies of the Republic in the central-south zone. It had been to some extent a realistic view. On 12 September 1938, a German diplomat, worried about the Czech crisis, had certainly thought so: 'In the event of war, Red Spain could expect extensive military support from France, Russia and probably England', the German chargé d'affaires in San Sebastián had written to Berlin.[37]

It was now, however, March 1939. Two Republican armies were interned in France and Catalonia was lost. It is impossible to say what Britain and France would have done about Republican Spain if, counterfactually, the two democracies had declared war on Nazi Germany when Hitler occupied Czechoslovakia on 16 March 1939.

The main lines of Casado's policy, once he had defeated the opposition to his take-over, can be followed in the *Diario Oficial del Consejo Nacional de Defensa* (hereafter DOCND), published in Madrid from 15 to 28 March 1939. However, once it is understood that Casado had been in contact with the enemy for some considerable time before his rising,

[33] J. M. Martinez Baude, *Los cien últimos dias de la República*, Barcelona, 1973, 184 and ff. described these movements.

[34] Casado, *Last Days of Madrid*, 172.

[35] See A. Viñas and F. Hernández Sánchez, *El desplome de la República*, Barcelona, 2010, 349–50, 363.

[36] Peirats, personal communication, 5 September 1975.

[37] *Documents on German Foreign Policy 1918–1945*, series D, vol. III, *The Spanish Civil War*, HMSO, 1951, No. 658.

and that his major concern was to protect the careers of the professional officers, his decrees acquire a particular significance. It becomes clear that they were published to a considerable extent to impress the Insurgents.

Casado annulled the decrees of 3 and 4 March published in the *Diario Oficial del Ministerio de Defensa Nacional.* The Central-South Army Group (GERC) had been dissolved and the four armies (of the Centre, Levante, Andalusia and Extremadura) were to come directly under the orders of Negrín and not of Miaja. In the issue of 3 March Modesto had been promoted to General and Líster to Colonel. Well-known communists had been appointed to take charge of points of evacuation: Lieutenant-Colonel of Militias Etelvino Vega in Alicante, Air Force Lieutenant-Colonel Leocadio Mendiola in Murcia and Air Force Major Inocencio Curto in Albacete. However, for many years afterwards it was not possible to locate a copy of the *Diario* for 4 March 1939. This issue, according to Casado's confused memory, had given Antonio Cordón supreme military command, while the communist militia officers Modesto, Líster, Valentín González ('El Campesino') and Tagüeña had been made respectively commanders of the Armies of the Centre, Levante, Extremadura and Andalusia. The fact that Casado alleges the appointment of 'El Campesino' reflects how doubtful his statements about these appointments are, for the other communist militia leaders despised 'El Campesino', even accusing him of cowardice.[38] Neither Negrín nor Cordón would have entrusted him with an army, when his largest command had been a division. If Casado had owned a copy of the issue of the *Diario Oficial* of 4 March, the normal thing would have been to carry it with him and publish it in the two versions of his book as proof of his allegation that communists had taken over the crowning heights of the Republican Army. Evidently he did not keep a copy of that issue, because the *Diario Oficial del Ministerio de Defensa Nacional* of that date does not contain anything to indicate Casado's accusations, though it confirms Miaja's removal from command and his appointment as inspector-general.[39]

Casado could not have seen the alleged appointments of the communist militia commanders as supreme military leaders in the *Diario*

[38] Modesto, *Soy del Quinto Regimiento*, 229; Líster, *Nuestra guerra*, 224–5.

[39] The issue is among Negrín's papers in the Ministry of Foreign Affairs (RE 149, C6). Further appointments were made in a number of the *Diario Oficial* which appeared on 5 March, but none which would justify Casado's statements that the communist leaders were to take over the major commands (Juan Miguel Campanario, 'Los ascensos y nombramientos de militares comunistas en marzo de 1939', at www2.uah.es/jmc/an40.pdf).

Oficial because they were not made. However, considering what the army and navy commanders told Negrín at the meeting, held probably on 16 February at Los Llanos, the airfield four miles south of Albacete, it would not be surprising if the Prime Minister had thought of entrusting Líster, Modesto and Tagüeña, the most capable and determined militia leaders, with the supreme commands of the remaining forces of the Republican Army. These three men would certainly have obeyed Negrín's orders and done their best to take over command. So why did Negrín not appoint them? Perhaps he feared that their appointment would precipitate the coup. In their detailed study of the Casado episode, Angel Bahamonde and Javier Cervera suggest:

> It was one thing for Negrín to intend to carry out a reconstruction of the army commands. Probably, he had the communist militia leaders in mind, but we do not know how far he would go and how he would make the changes.
>
> (*Otra cosa … es que Negrín tuviera … la intención de llevar a cabo una remodelación en el seno del ejército y, probablemente, contaba para ello con militares comunistas, pero no sabemos cuál sería su volumen, ni la forma en que se hubiera efectuado.*)[40]

In the naval base of Cartagena, Colonel Francisco Galán, appointed to take control, defeated a pro-Casado movement in the garrison on 4 March, though he left with the Fleet when on 5 March it raised anchor and sailed to Bizerta, where it was interned.[41] Even if sufficient shipping had been available to take off the thousands of desperate people awaiting evacuation on the quays of Alicante, there would now no longer have been warships to protect them against Franco's navy.

Casado annulled the decrees calling up the reserve classes of 1915 and 1916, together with Rojo's promotion to lieutenant-general and his own to general. Casado considered these promotions to have been granted by a government which he wanted the Insurgents to see that he considered illegal. Many new appointments were made. Casado himself became Councillor for Defence. He replaced himself at the head of the Army of the Centre by Colonel Prada. Colonel Moriones, who had warned Matallana, the commander of the GERC, that Casado was thinking of rising and whom the Insurgents thought was determined to continue resistance, was dismissed from command of the Army of Andalusia and replaced by Menoyo, one of his corps commanders.[42] Escobar, head of the Army of Extremadura, promised support and crushed resistance

40 Bahamonde and Cervera, *Así terminó*, 365.

41 The departure of the Republican Fleet is described in full in Alpert, *La guerra civil española en el mar*, 353–60.

42 Casado, *Last Days of Madrid*, 129. For the Insurgent view of Moriones, see CGG, L277, C10.

to the coup, while the Army of the Levante under Menéndez offered no resistance to Casado. General Toribio Martínez Cabrera, who had been military governor of Madrid since December 1938, replacing the retired General Cardenal, was made Under-Secretary under Casado. Martínez Cabrera had been a general before the war, when Casado was a mere major. Of the corps commanders, Barceló was shot for his responsibility in the execution, indeed murder, of three members of Casado's Staff: Arnaldo Fernández Urbano, José Pérez Gazzolo and Joaquín Otero Ferrer, during the struggle between Casadist forces and communist-officered troops.[43] Bueno of the II Corps and Ortega, the ex-*Carabineros* sergeant who headed the III Corps, were replaced. General Bernal became military governor of Madrid and Colonel Ardid, Inspector-General of Engineers. Several changes among the political commissars were made, but the institution itself was retained. Significantly the red star on military uniforms was abolished[44] and the SIM was dissolved. Presumably, if time had allowed, many other commanders throughout the zone would have been replaced.

Peace negotiations

One of the main concerns of those who supported Casado's coup and the subsequent brief rule of the National Defence Council over the territory within the Madrid–Valencia–Cartagena triangle which composed nearly one-third of Spain was the personal safety of supporters of the Republic who remained in Spain, together with the wish to obtain safe conduct for those who wanted to leave. How would the victors act? Their behaviour earlier in the war left little room for optimism. While the murders, robberies and other outrages committed by the mob, semi-criminal gangs, vengeful peasants, church-burners, priest-killers, rebellious sailors and, in a few cases, people at a certain level of power had in their turn been taken by the Insurgents as justification for their mass killings of anybody they judged to be a threat, an enemy or to have taken up arms – that is to be rebels against the declaration of the State of War which was what had constituted the military uprisings of 1936 – by early 1939 the situation was different. The Insurgents were no longer fighting desperately, which had been the excuse for Franco's Army of Africa to murder everyone whom they dared not leave alive as they hastened towards Madrid in the summer and autumn of 1936 and well into 1937. Militiamen captured in the early weeks of the war were executed

[43] Casado, *Last Days of Madrid*, 175–80.
[44] *Diario Oficil del Consejo Nacional de Defensa*, 18 March 1939.

as a matter of course, as was the case with the bullring massacre at Badajoz and the killings in Málaga. Professional officers suffered the same fate after drumhead court martial.[45] But in 1939 their stated judicial procedures must be considered from the angle from which Casado and even the anarchist CNT weighed the chances of a just peace.[46]

In 1937, Franco's Supreme Command published regulations about the classification and treatment of prisoners of war.[47] Classifying committees were to be set up, on each of which there would be a legally trained officer. Prisoners would be rapidly classed, so that those against whom there was no charge could be incorporated into the Franco forces or into labour battalions. After Bilbao fell in June 1937 it was feared that many sympathisers of the Insurgents were in the labour battalions, so in September *Falange* representatives began sitting on the classifying committees in order to identify any of their supporters among the hordes of prisoners taken when the Republican Army of the North surrendered.

The committees would ask for information on the prisoners from their local town or village, from the *Guardia Civil*, the mayor, the parish priest or other important local people. This had to be done in three days, after which the final classification had to be made. It was informal and no written report was to be made. The classifications were:

A: men who had been conscripted into the Republican Army. These were to be freed at the end of the war. They would have to report regularly to the police without prejudice to further denunciations of their conduct.

B: volunteers in the Republican Army but against whom there were no other social, political or criminal accusations. 'Social accusations' might mean union activities or anticlerical attitudes. 'Political' referred to any role, however minor,

[45] On Badajoz see the account of the Portuguese journalist Mario Neves, *La matanza de Badajoz*, Mérida, 2007. Excavations at the San Rafael cemetery in Málaga point to 4,000 violent deaths. For officers executed in the north see Gobierno Autónomo de Euzkadi, *Report on the Administration of Justice in the Basque Country during the Civil War*, Paris, 1938.

[46] The question of deaths, apart from battlefield ones, in the Spanish Civil War is at the time of writing a major issue, as remains of people executed by the Insurgents and buried in open country or in common graves in cemeteries are being disinterred and identified. The major difference, apart from the relative numbers, is that the Republican authorities were horrified at murders committed but, bereft of forces of order, were unable to control them, while killings in the Insurgent zone were controlled by the army, even if sometimes carried out by *Falange* and other militia. See on this Santos Julià (ed.), *Víctimas de la guerra civil*, Madrid, 1999, and Paul Preston, *The Spanish Holocaust*, Christie Books, 2011.

[47] CGG, L55, C1.

in Republican parties. Their place of residence was laid down and their backgrounds investigated by the *Guardia Civil*, local *Falange* and parish priest.

The first two classifications did not free prisoners from future consequences. They merely allowed the Insurgent army to free itself from the heavy burden of maintaining prisoners of war, requiring the local authorities, when the place concerned came under Francoist authority, to undertake the task of investigating the background of every prisoner.

C: professional military men, political or social leaders, people whose acts could be legally interpreted as treasonous, rebellious or 'crimes of a social and political nature', committed after or before 18 July 1936. This was a catch-all, for the government of the Popular Front itself had been declared illegal by the Insurgents. Thus any pre-war political, union or intellectual activity could be declared illegal.

D: people clearly guilty of common-law crime before or after 18 July 1936.

Those who belonged to categories C and D. were to be subject to court martial.

In 1937 a new category was introduced of people who had families in the Insurgent zone and had changed their views. Naturally, errors were made, which led to correspondence between the Staffs of the Insurgent armies about the relative reliability of ex-prisoners enlisted in consequence of a favourable report. This in turn led to the publication of orders that the categories had to be strictly defined, especially regarding the identity, political reliability and truth of the written guarantees sent in by people who knew the prisoner or could be persuaded to vouch for him.

Strictly speaking, every soldier of the Republican Army was guilty, in the eyes of the Insurgents, of 'military rebellion' because by definition they had not respected the declaration of the State of War by the insurrectionist garrisons on 18–19 July 1936. However, a difference was made between *adhesión* and *auxilio* to rebellion. Those guilty of *adhesión* had identified with its aims (that is they had refused to accept the military uprising), while those whose offence was *auxilio* were less culpable because they had merely aided the former. The definition of their guilt conditioned the sentence: death in the first case, life imprisonment in the second. Death was recommended in cases of 'social danger' or 'as an example'. Yet another crime was *inducción*, which was further broken down into *inducción* whether followed or not by effects. Special regulations were published about how to treat the large number of Republican Army soldiers who had deserted to the Nationalist ranks. They were not to be accused of military rebellion unless they had been volunteers, in which case the length of time which had passed before they came over, their rank and their pre-war activities would be taken into account. Every decision taken was subject to revision if further 'responsibilities' were later discovered.

Furthermore, in February 1939, Franco had signed the *Ley de Responsabilidades Políticas*.[48] Not all those accused of a political offence would also face the charge of military rebellion, but the (British) Foreign Office commented that everybody whom a court martial convicted of military rebellion was *ipso facto* guilty of a political crime, which brought with it a possible 15-year prison term and a huge fine. Mr. Jerram, British consul in the wartime Insurgent capital of Burgos, noted that while having served in the Republican Army or merely having belonged to now prohibited organisations that had opposed the military insurrection did not imply *criminal* responsibility, 'there is no guarantee that they would not be punished as political offenders'.[49]

Against these stated Insurgent intentions and their record may be set Casado's declared intention to demand as a principal and essential condition for surrender, as dated 11 March 1939:

> The security that all civilians and soldiers who have taken part honourably and cleanly ... in this hard and lengthy struggle, shall be treated with the greatest respect, both as persons and in the question of their interests.
>
> Respect for the lives and liberty of soldiers in the Army and of Political Commissars who are not guilty of any criminal offence.
>
> Respect for the life, liberty and employment [that is, rank] of professional officers who have not been guilty of crime.[50]

The immediate impression of these terms is their extreme naivety. As the Insurgent Intelligence service commented scornfully, Casado thought he could make a gentleman's agreement between brother-officers, many of whom had known each other, belonged to the same academy graduation class and, tragically, were sometimes closely related. Casado had delayed his coup until he was forced to carry it out for fear of communists taking over the top commands, but this last-minute change of heart by

[48] *Boletín Oficial del Estado*, 13 February 1939. English translation and commentary in FO 371, W44129/8/41.
[49] FO 371, W423/8/41, March 29 1939.
[50] Casado, *Last Days of Madrid*, 201–2.

professional officers would not save them, especially since Casado was giving the really guilty people time to make their getaways.[51]

Before negotiations began, Franco's representatives sent Casado a list of concessions. These were in response to the conditions for surrender of the National Council of Defence. In regard to the Republican Army, the relevant passages read:

For officers who voluntarily lay down their arms without being guilty of the death of their fellows or other crimes, apart from being granted their lives, benevolence shall be exercised in proportion to the significance and efficiency of the services which at the last moments of the war they shall give to the cause of Spain, or in proportion to the smallness of their activity or malice [*haya sido menor su intervención o malicia*] in the war.[52]

Well might Casado conclude that the Insurgent 'concession' was an invitation to treachery and a reward to those who had dragged their feet during the war.

On 19 March, Franco agreed that two Republican officers could come to the Insurgent capital, Burgos, as spokesmen. Major Leopoldo Ortega and Lieutenant-Colonel Antonio Garijo, section heads on the GERC Staff, flew to Burgos on 23 March. Garijo was generally considered to be lukewarm in his Republican sentiments, though post-war accusations are not borne out by the record of the Burgos conversations.[53] At the first meeting, on 23 March, Garijo requested a clarification about the position of professional officers. The Nationalist representative, Colonel Hungría, pointed out that the presence of professionals in the Republican Army had strengthened it and so prolonged the war. Garijo countered that in his view the war had been lost precisely because the professionals had not been given a free hand. This was a bold statement, for it implied that the career officers had no influence merely because they were ignored, not because they were not loyal to the Republic.

No further concessions could be wrung from the Insurgent side. As Casado (*Last Days of Madrid*, 233) later wrote:

The obduracy of the Nationalists moved nearly all the Councillors to a state of great indignation ... the attitude of the Nationalists in denying us this had no precedent in history, especially as these negotiations were between compatriots.

A further meeting was arranged for 25 March. No attempt was made to gain further concessions but a document was handed over with the

51 CGG, L277, C12 and C18. See also Bouthelier and López-Mora, *Ocho días*, 146.

52 Casado, *Last Days of Madrid*, 213–14.

53 For the record of these see J. M. Martínez Bande, *Los cien últimos días de la República*, Barcelona, 1973, 228–32 and 246–50.

terms already granted. Since bad weather was closing in, the Republican Army officers were ordered to take off at once for Madrid.

This was effectively the end of the Spanish Civil War. As Casado, having failed to obtain more than minimum concessions from the enemy, flew from Madrid to Valencia, he saw troops leaving their positions and beginning to walk towards their homes. He gave formal instructions for surrender at 11 a.m. on the morning of 29 March 1939. As he wrote many years later, in words which would have been out of place in 1939: 'In this peaceful way, an army of 600,000 men and the civilian population of the Republican zone were handed over to the enemy.'[54] Unless, as the Insurgents sometimes thought, Casado was intentionally delaying to allow time for those in most danger to escape, it must be concluded that he failed. He did not gain the concessions that he thought he would, particularly for the professional officers.

Vicissitudes of the defeated

This is a major topic in itself, since it affected, to a greater or lesser degree, very large numbers of people, both men and women, who had lived in the Republican zone.[55] Future employment and all sorts of civil rights were often lost, and even people who had merely been in the Republican zone would have to report regularly to the police. Anyone who had had any sort of authority risked the death sentence or a very long term of imprisonment. Civil servants, teachers, journalists and professionals in general were, even after release from prison, prohibited from following their professions.

As for the men of the Republican Army, the charge against professional military men was military rebellion. For others it was 'aiding the rebellion' or *auxilio a la rebelión*. This was justice in reverse, because it was the Insurgents who has risen in rebellion. The victors, however, based their view on the Army constitutional law, which stated that the duty of the Army was to defend Spain against internal as well as external enemies. When the Insurgents assumed the direction of public life on 18 July 1936 they were obeying a concept which they saw as inherent in the Army's very reason for existence.

Treatment of prisoners of war followed the outlines of Franco's concessions, although anyone could be charged with political or other

[54] Casado, *Así cayó Madrid*, 185.

[55] See, for instance, Don Roque, the civil servant who lost his post merely because he was known have voted for the 'wrong' party, in Camilo José Cela's novel *La Colmena* (1951). For a close local study see Fuensanta Escudero Andújar, *Lo cuentan como lo han vivido: República, guerra y represión en Murcia*, Murcia, 2000.

offences. Widows, orphans and war-cripples were abandoned to their fate. The point was to rid the country of dangerous elements and to frighten and humiliate entire swathes of the population so that the circumstances which had encouraged the insurrection of 1936 would never occur again. The defeated had to know that they had been vanquished and to be convinced that they had been wrong.

Conscripts in the Republican Army were usually released after investigation, though the younger ones who had not already done their military service were reconscripted to complete it, while volunteers, men who had been promoted and particularly militia officers and commissars were sentenced to terms of imprisonment and many to execution. Such men, in the view of the victors' courts martial, would not have gained promotion in the 'Red' army had they not been leaders and known to be sympathetic to the Popular Front. When men went back to their home towns they might well be rearrested and charged with some political or 'social' offence, say, for example, having responsibility in or even having merely been present at a church-burning or a priest-killing, and this might result in execution or a long prison sentence. Anyone was liable to 'denunciation' for some activity judged nefarious.

Professional officers were in a special position. Many, if not most, of those who had not managed to leave Spain were conservative, often fervent Catholics, and, even if they had obtained a PCE membership card, had done so either for protection or because they shared communist views about the army and the way to fight the war. Furthermore, Franco's concessions made to Casado had granted their lives to officers who surrendered and furthermore had promised to graduate sentences according to how much they had contributed to the surrender and how little their '*malicia*' had been in the war, by which might have been meant how unenthusiastic they had been for the Republican cause and perhaps how much they had helped to sabotage it.

Those who had been responsible for the death of their comrades were liable to the death sentence. The offence was to have led attacks on barracks or to have sat on courts martial which had handed down death sentences to Insurgent officers who had been arrested in places where the uprising had failed. General Aranguren, head of the *Guardia Civil* in Catalonia, and Colonel Escobar, in a similar post in Barcelona, paid the price.[56] Escobar had been at least partially responsible for the failure of the insurrection in Barcelona and had 'tolerated' murders.[57] Aranguren

56 See García Fernández, *25 Militares*, which examines the courts martial of leading officers.

57 As reported by *The Times* of 17 April 1939.

had been a prosecution witness at the court martial which had sentenced the Insurgent generals Goded and Fernández Burriel in Barcelona in 1936, and in 1939 he courageously refused the offer of the protection of a Latin American embassy. Other death sentences were passed after the war on Cavalry Colonel Carlos Caballero and Lieutenant of the Legal Corps Pedro Rodríguez, who had been respectively examining magistrate and prosecutor against Goded and Fernández Burriel. Even Goded's defender, a retired Staff major, Antonio Aymat, received a 12-year prison sentence. The Army and Navy officers condemned by 1939 courts martial in, for example Cartagena, were accused, among other charges, of having given evidence against their comrades in 1936,[58] as had General Martínez Cabrera, commander in Cartagena at the outbreak of war,[59] where a large number of Insurgent naval officers had been assassinated by sailors who were out of control.

Officers who had a left-wing history would find it difficult to plead anything in mitigation. Miguel Gallo, for example, who had been involved in the pro-Republican uprising at Jaca in December 1930 and had been rewarded by a post in the Presidential military household, was a member of the PCE and one of the first commanders of a mixed brigade. Charged with military rebellion, his political responsibilities were investigated, after which he was shot.[60]

A close reading of the court martial of Major Urbano Orad de la Torre might reveal why this artillery officer, a member of UMRA and the PSOE, who shelled the Montaña barracks in Madrid and was indirectly responsible for the massacre of officers there, had his death sentence commuted. Could it be because his subsequent military career as a divisional commander was not distinguished and he was able to claim little '*malicia*'? Certainly he lost his rights as an officer, but he opened a very well-known and successful school in Seville to prepare boys for the entrance examination to the artillery academy. With the transition to democracy after Franco's death in 1975, Don Urbano, as he was widely known, gained his long-delayed promotion to Lieutenant-Colonel and the appropriate pension.[61] He was more fortunate than Joaquín Pérez Salas, commander of a corps in the Army of Extremadura, who faced the firing squad despite a report that he had protected people from revolutionary excesses and political persecution, a stance which had

[58] See Egea Bruno, 'La represión franquista'.
[59] *International Press Correspondence*, 13 May 1939. See also Ruiz, *Franco's Justice*, 4.
[60] *Boletín Oficial del Estado*, 27 October 1939.
[61] *ABC* (Seville), 18 September 1982. See also Paz Sánchez, *Militares masones*, under 'Orad de la Torre'.

brought the enmity of the communists on him.[62] He did, however, have political antecedents, having planned an uprising against Primo de Rivera in 1929, was involved in the Jaca conspiracy of 1930 and had been friendly with Azaña.[63] Furthermore, he could not claim that he was merely 'geographically loyal', because he had led a militia column against the rebellious garrison of Córdoba as early as 20 July 1936.[64] Nor could he claim to have helped to bring the war to a close, for he crushed a Fifth Column uprising in Cartagena on 6 March 1939.[65] In some ways he was one of the most original, if not eccentric, officers of the Republican Army. He was strongly anti-communist and rude to his Russian adviser, and reputed to be the originator of the *bon mot* 'We shall win the war in spite of the commissars'. Characteristically, he was rumoured to have defied the court martial which judged him.

The Insurgent concession to officers who had not distinguished themselves in long and faithful service to the Republican Army or by possessing heartfelt Republican convictions but who, on the other hand, contributed to bringing the war to a speedy end in 1939 was observed in the treatment of those who had collaborated with Casado's National Defence Council. Possibly one of the most compromised was Colonel Adolfo Prada, whose lot it was to surrender Madrid personally to the enemy on 28 March 1939. Prada had commanded in the north, Andalusia and Madrid. He had taken the membership card of the PCE. Yet he obeyed Casado's order to surrender the capital. He received death sentences on two counts which were commuted. In due course he was released, like most of the professional officers who were associated with Casado unless it was judged that their '*malicia*', to use the noun employed in the victors' concessions, was too great.

Yet even those who escaped the firing squad served terms of imprisonment, lost their careers and pensions and had when released to strive to remake their lives in the difficult circumstances of post-war Franco Spain. Manuel Matallana, for example, even though he served a relatively short term of imprisonment, had to support his family as a builders' foreman.[66] General Carlos Bernal died in prison at the age of 65.

[62] Information Section, CGG, 30 November 1937.
[63] As his brother, Jesús, also a Republican Army officer, wrote after the war (Pérez Salas, *Guerra en España*, 29, 41, 75).
[64] Arrarás, *Cruzada*, XXIII: 474.
[65] Luis Romero, *Desastre en Cartagena*, Barcelona, 1971, 248
[66] See Editorial Códex, *Crónica de la guerra española*, Buenos Aires, 1966, V: 388. This work habitually suggests that men who were not shot had few difficulties after the Franco victory ('*pasó sin dificultades por las purgas de la posguerra*'). See also Suero Roca, *Militares republicanos*, 189–90.

Others spent up to ten or more years before being released, among them Alejandro Sánchez Cabezudo. He had been an *africanista*, spending 15 years in Morocco. He was in the Montaña barracks when the officers rose in rebellion against the Government, but seems from his account to have played a delicate diplomatic game and to have been protected from murder by his own men when the barracks was stormed by the mob. During the war he rose from the rank of captain to lieutenant-colonel, in command of a division. Condemned to death by a post-war court martial, the Francoist General Varela interceded for him. His sentence was reduced to 30 years, then to 20, and he was released in 1945. Accused of plotting with other ex-Republican Army men he received a further sentence of seven years, which he served as a clerk in the Valle de los Caídos, which became Franco's mausoleum. He recounts that while a fellow *africanista*, General Millán Astray, visited him and brought him cigarettes, Franco ignored him on his visits ('of course, he didn't smoke').[67] Another officer of the Republican Army, who had been with Franco in the Infantry Academy and the General Military Academy at Zaragoza which Franco commanded between 1927 and 1931, was Eduardo Sáez de Aranaz. He rose to the rank of lieutenant-colonel during the Civil War. Since it was more or less obligatory to join a political party he became a member of the moderate, *prietista*, wing of the PSOE. He was sentenced to 30 years. He was released after serving four years. He worked in the offices of a mining company but was again arrested for activities concerned with appeals for releases of prisoners, and sentenced to eight years. He worked as a storekeeper in the Valle de los Caídos. Franco, knowing he was there, ignored him when he made his visits to what would be his place of burial. Sáez de Aranaz was released under supervision in 1950. He worked where he could, giving maths tuition and in an insurance company until he opened a bookshop.[68]

Some generals of the Republican Army, charged under the Law of Political Responsibilities, were deprived of their property *in absentia*. Hernández Saravia was fined 20 million pesetas (£155,000 at the 1939 exchange rate for the Nationalist peseta). Properties owned by him and his wife were auctioned off. General Masquelet likewise was fined, while General Asensio also lost all his property.[69]

Perhaps most unjust of all was the treatment of a number of officers who lived in Republican territory during the war but without

[67] This account is in D. Sueiro, *La verdadera historia del Valle de los Caídos*, Madrid, 1976, 90–100.
[68] *Ibid.*, 87–90.
[69] Navajas Zubeldia, *Leales y rebeldes*, 192–3.

serving at all in the Republican Army. On 30 March 1939, the victors announced that any professional officer would be subject to investigation, even if he had had no military role in the war.[70] Five out of six senior *Guardia Civil* officers, who had been removed from their posts during the war, were, nevertheless, sentenced to death.[71] Even, incomprehensibly, some officers, such as Major Emilio Sánchez Caballero, who from their posts undermined the efficiency of the Republican Army, received prison sentences, although in his case his sentence was under three years, which, at least in theory, meant that he was able to remain in the Army. Even more unfortunate was Major Manuel Albarrán Ordóñez, who was imprisoned in the Republican zone for Fifth Column activities, but on being freed in 1939 was sentenced to prison by the victors because at the beginning of the war he had led a column of militia. Like any other person condemned by a court martial for activities against the Glorious National Movement, he was judged again according to the Law of Political Responsibilities and heavily fined.[72] Because of the large number of career soldiers who lived in Madrid, they represented 27 per cent – 288 individuals – of those living in the capital punished under that law.[73]

To consider a simple private soldier, Esteve Mas Alsina was captured in January 1939 and sent to a prisoner of war camp in Galicia. His letters to his wife, Paquita, in Terrassa (Catalonia), are concerned with obtaining a certificate of 'good conduct' (that is, not having engaged in union activities) from the Banco Hispano Americano, in which he had been employed until he was conscripted in 1937. He was released, but died of bronchial pneumonia soon afterwards, leaving two young children.

As for those who succeeded in getting away, the General Staff and the officers of the Eastern Army Group, now in France, were joined by the 194 people taken on board HMS *Galatea* at Gandía. These included a substantial number of military men, including Casado himself and General Leopoldo Menéndez.[74] They would join the exiles in France, Great Britain and Latin America, only a few of whom would return to Spain. Generals Pozas, Llano de la Encomienda, Miaja, Asensio and

[70] Ruiz, *Franco's Justice*, 41.
[71] Navajas Zubeldia, *Leales y rebeldes*, 186–7.
[72] *Ibid.*, 71–2 and 158. [73] *Ibid.*, 157, table 4.1.
[74] See Luis Monferrer Catalán, *Odisea en Albión: los republicanos exiliados en Gran Bretaña, 1936–1977*, Madrid, 2007, who reproduces a list of 194 people. Mainar *et al.*, *Gandia*, 218–21, reproduce what appears to be the same list with descriptions of the passengers in English. The National Archives, ADM 116/3896 contains the report of the captain of the *Galatea*.

many other senior career officers died in exile, as did probably the oldest, General Riquelme, who died in Paris in January 1972 at the age of 91.[75] In the 1940s, the leading professionals in the Republican Army were scattered: Rojo in Bolivia, Asensio in New York, Sánchez Rodríguez in Puebla (Mexico), Martínez Monje, Parra (Azaña's aide-de-camp) and Francisco Galán in Buenos Aires, Fontán in Chile, Matilla in Costa Rica, Jurado in Montevideo. They went where could secure visas and obtain a suitable post. A few professional officers were among the 4,000 people who went to the Soviet Union. They included Antonio Cordón, Manuel Márquez, José María Galán and Francisco Ciutat.

Some were able to return. Rojo (see above) was amnestied, while Casado was investigated between 1963 and 1965 and finally all charges were dropped, but neither was able to regain even the rank he had in 1936 and thus draw a pension. Colonel Félix Muedra, even though his loyalty was suspected by many,[76] had to go into exile in Guinea. Returning to Spain he was seen by another senior officer, Aurelio Matilla, running a small shop.[77] Such was the fate of distinguished officers, who had fought honourably and were usually of conservative views. After terms of imprisonment, during which their families had to fend for themselves, they lived modestly and often in poverty. Not until long after Franco's death in late 1975 and the coming of democracy to Spain were they granted proper pensions according to their rank at the end of the Spanish Civil War.[78]

Probably less is known of the diverse vicissitudes of militia leaders and of commissars. Colonel Casado's National Council of Defence itself began the process of executions by shooting a commissar and Lieutenant-Colonel Luis Barceló, whose corps had resisted the Casado coup and who was judged responsible for the savage murders of three senior Staff officers and a commissar during the 'civil war within the civil war' in Madrid in March 1939. Several other communist leaders were detained. Many of these fell into Nationalist hands. Etelvino Vega, who had led the XII Corps of the Army of the Ebro, returned to Spain and was appointed military governor of Alicante. Captured when Alicante was occupied by Italian troops in Franco's service, the communist Vega, trained in the Frunze academy before the war, was executed.

[75] *Le Monde*, 1 February 1972.
[76] Thomas, *Spanish Civil War*, 894.
[77] Quoted in Rojo, *Vicente Rojo*, 409.
[78] By the Royal Decree Law of 6 March 1978, which granted retirement pensions to members of the military and of the Republican Public Order Forces, or to their heirs, who were fully qualified as professional before 18 July 1936.

Probably, communists, all other things being equal, were less likely to have their death sentences commuted than anarchists. One example might be that of Cipriano Mera, commander of the IV Corps, who was probably the best-known anarchist militant and senior commander to fall into Francoist hands. He was largely responsible for Colonel Casado's defeat of the communist divisions who did not accept his coup, so the commutation of his sentence has to be seen in that light. Extradited after many adventures from French Morocco in February 1942, but not tried until 26 April 1943, he received the death sentence, which was commuted on 28 July, together with 70 others. He was granted provisional release in 1946 and lived the rest of his life in France.

Within a few months of the end of the war partial commutations of sentences began. Yet if prisoners benefited from an amnesty, they were nevertheless always at risk of a further denunciation.

A circular order published on 25 January 1940 began the first significant reductions of sentence. Since the various levels of offence were carefully defined, it may be useful to describe this order fully as an example of the general principles of sentencing and commutation. Professional officers who had been 'notably outstanding' (*notablemente destacados*) for their Republican sympathies received no concession, but there were others who, though they had been 'the soul of the Marxist revolution' (*el alma de la revolución marxista*), had aided the people's militia to overthrow the Insurgent garrisons and had served in the Republican Army, had evidently not been so important as to merit the death sentence, which was now commuted to 30 years. Reduced to 20 years were sentences passed on those officers with Republican antecedents who had not served the Republic for long or in important posts. Further commutations to terms of between 12 and 20 years were granted to officers who had been sympathetic to the *Movimiento Nacional* (the name given to the military insurrection) before the war, that is, those who had held conservative views but yet had served the Republic for a long time. This was probably the clause which helped General Matallana. If such officers of conservative views had not served the 'Reds' for a long period, that is, if they had not put themselves forward to lead militias at the beginning of the war, their sentences were reduced to between 6 and 12 years. Shorter sentences still, in some cases bringing immediate release, were decreed for men of no political antecedents who had served in merely bureaucratic posts.

Yet even the last case meant imprisonment for, say, a retired conservative officer, who had spent the war, for example, in a recruitment office checking details of reservists. The sentences were passed and served at least partly. It was far distant from Casado's hope that officers of the Republican Army who had committed no common-law crime would have their ranks safeguarded.

On 4 June 1940, a decree was issued granting provisional liberty for those gaoled for under six years. Similar decrees in 1941 and 1943 applied to those serving under 20 years unless they had committed acts of cruelty, murder, rape, profanation or 'other acts repugnant to ordinary people'.[79] 'Provisional' or 'conditional' liberty meant that prisoners were released but had to live at least 250 km from their homes, which merely continued the punishment for their families. The *Patronato Central para la redención de penas por el trabajo*, an organisation which allowed for reduction of sentences by work, for poor wages and often accompanied by bad treatment and lack of medical care, announced in 1943 that of 50,877 cases examined, 47,234 were released and 3,640 refused, mostly because of poor reports from the mayor, *Guardia Civil* and *Falange* of their home towns.[80]

By decree in the *Boletín Oficial del Estado* of 2 March 1943, pensions were granted to military men, provided that loss of pension rights was not part of the original sentence. Such loss was, however, frequently the case. On the same date, release applications were invited even if the minimum part of the sentence had not been completed.

It may be stated tentatively that only a minority of those officers who were unable to leave Spain faced the firing squad, though sentence of death was commonly passed, and that only a few were serving sentences after 1945. Nevertheless, years were spent in hard conditions in gaol, families were left unprovided for, careers were destroyed and for many years after release officers and commissars of the Republican Army remained second-class citizens, obliged to report their comings and goings, watched for whom they spoke to and unable to defend themselves publicly. They had 'criminal' antecedents and lost whatever civil rights other Spaniards enjoyed until these were restored by decree in 1964. Not until 12 November 1966 did the *Boletín Oficial del Estado* remove all Civil War responsibilities from the list of offences. Yet it took until after the restoration of democracy for pensions to be granted to men and their descendants who had served in the Republican Army. The repression was long-lasting and harsh even for those least committed to the cause of the Republic and least proud of having served in the *Ejército Popular de la República*.

[79] *Boletín Oficial del Estado*, 4 June 1940, 11 April 1941, 30 March 1943 and see, for later decrees, 9 October 1945 and 4 November 1945.

[80] Patronato Central de Redención de Penas por el Trabajo, *La obra de la redención de penas*, Madrid, 1942.

Conclusions

Amid the plethora of impressions received after this study of the Republican Army in the Spanish Civil War, two main conclusions inevitably emerge: the continuous shortages and the constant interference of political tensions.

Although the arms depots in the territory which was retained by the Republic after the early days of the insurrection were as well stocked as those of the enemy, weapons shortage bedevilled the Republican Army at most times. This shortage, while clearly due to the effects of the international agreement not to supply arms to either side in Spain, and to Germany's and Italy's defiance of it, followed by the Soviet riposte, arose also because of the collapse of authority at the beginning of the war and the consequent difficulty in ensuring the efficient management of what was retained after the sacking of the arms depots and the abandoning of weapons by retreating militia. Nor was there sufficient and reliable production of arms or facilities for their repair in factories and workshops in the rear.

Nevertheless, the present state of research confirms that the supply of war material from Germany and Italy to Franco's Nationalist Insurgents was not only quantitatively greater than the resources purchased all over the arms market or supplied to the Republican Army by the Soviet Union, but also more appropriate at specific moments. This was particularly true as regards aircraft, where initial German and Italian machines were overtaken in quality by Soviet machines but where the latter were not replaced by better machines as the war progressed. It also seems that tanks and aircraft supplied by the USSR were much less under the control of the Republican Army command than the equivalent German and Italian material. The larger number of Soviet tanks, particularly the top-class ones sent, and the aircraft were of surprisingly little use to the Republican Army when they were most needed. However, neither side used tanks with sufficient skill in the Spanish Civil War for any conclusions to be drawn, although much was learnt by Russians and Germans about the sort of machine which was necessary and about the use of anti-tank guns.[1]

There can also be no doubt that the Republican Army suffered a severe shortage of professional officers and NCOs. There were few completely trusted officers left in the Republican zone after the insurrection had failed in Madrid, Barcelona, Valencia and other garrisons, and after the purge of the officer corps in general. A great many who had not taken part in the uprising were also distrusted, with the result that as the Republican Army developed into a force of a traditional kind, with brigades, divisions, army corps and armies, all requiring Staffs, commands were entrusted to men who were unfitted for them, either because of their low pre-war rank or their lack of combat experience. It was also found impossible to train sufficient new officers. The strongly political nature of the war meant that a great many of the natural leaders were elected or appointed by political parties or trade unions, though they had little if any military knowledge and skills, which in any case were often distrusted by the anarchist CNT and the POUM.[2] The success of their commands would depend on the extent to which they and their men were sufficiently able and willing to follow the instructions of the career officers and how far the latter were professionally competent, energetic and loyal. Moreover, the shortage of suitable young men coming forward to lead small units of the Republican Army was evident when compared to the much larger numbers of *alféreces provisionales* in the Insurgent army.

A corollary of this pattern of constant shortage was the extent of improvisation of units, officers and much of the structure of the Republican Army. By the time the administration had reached some closeness to professional level, say by late 1938, it was too late to be of use.

The pressure of politics and ideology was constant. This was evident in the ideological identity maintained and jealously preserved by many units until the end and in the memoirs written in exile. This came about because the Communist Party wished to preserve and expand its elite units, which reflected the politico-military doctrines about how to fight the war expressed in the early weeks by the Fifth Regiment. Similarly, anarchist fears of being swamped by the tide of communist influence were exacerbated by communist pressure and the prestige of the PCE among senior officers because communist and traditional military views

[1] S. Zaloga, *Spanish Civil War Tanks: The Proving Ground for Blitzkrieg*, Osprey, 2010.

[2] Mika Etchebéhère's memoirs *Ma guerre d'Espagne*, Paris, 1976) give vivid examples of this contempt for military methods in the POUM column which she came to command.

coincided. Nevertheless, in the light of the Casado coup and defeat of communist units in the central-south zone, communist influence seems to have been in general exaggerated. There were few communist units as such, except the Army of the Ebro. Largo Caballero and Prieto had made great efforts to counter the communist take-over of the Political Commissariat. In the counter-factual case of a victory of the Republican Army, the mass of conscripts would have gone home, while the professional officers would have returned to their conservative and in general apolitical stance. It seems unlikely that any of the communist militia leaders, none of whom were major political figures, would have been able to maintain any sort of significant influence even if two or three of them, such as Modesto or Líster, had remained as senior army officers. The para-military *Carabineros* were carefully shielded from communist influence. Soviet sources also show that Moscow wanted to keep its advisers at arm's length from the Republican Army. Nevertheless, politicisation of the Republican Army was inevitable in view of the fragmentation of the army in the Republican zone, the collapse of authority and its take-over by the trade unions and self-appointed committees. The Spanish Communist Party strove to counter this by emphasising the common struggle, not only of all left-wing forces, but also all forces which supported the liberal and parliamentary Republic against authoritarianism. This aspect of communist efforts to maintain a unified political conscience emerges clearly from commissars' reports. In any discussion of communism during the Spanish Civil War, the genuineness of the policy of the Popular Front has to be set against the intrigues and the outrages committed by the civilian agents of Moscow and the Comintern. The latter worked hard to strengthen communist power and to suppress dissident leftism, and this wore away the unity of purpose for which, contradictorily, the PCE was working. In view of the success of the Casado coup, the achievements of communist propaganda and political 'correctness' in the Republican Army should not be overestimated, but certainly the fear that rival organisations had of each other weakened the discipline and the common purpose, the cohesion and fighting power of the *Ejército Popular*. One would hope that, in the case of a Republican victory, the new Army of the Republic would have been one which, unlike the pre-war Army, was not the possession of a social or ideological group, nor one whose officers were bound by loyalty to each other and could thus describe officers loyal to the Republic as traitors, nor one which would see its role as above the State, entitled to declare the State of War if it alone judged that the country was going in the wrong direction.

This was what had happened in the Insurgent zone, where authority came from the army, to which politics was subordinated. General

Franco was first *Generalísimo*, and then not only Head of Government but Head of State also. The very nature of the attitude towards democratic politics among the Insurgents led to their suppressing political parties and compulsorily unifying the two major ideological movements, the *Falange* and the Traditionalists, under Franco's leadership. Thus no comparison between the two Spains is real. Could the military establishment in Republican Spain have taken power? In such a case, would there have been a single person, a Commander-in-Chief like Franco, who would have made strategic decisions? Certainly a military estate existed, and, when pushed to the limit of its tolerance by Negrín's insistence on an arguably unreal policy of resistance, it did establish a brief sort of dictatorship, aided by some politicians. When the central-south zone came under complete military rule at the end of the war, Negrín's authority as Prime Minister and Minister of National Defence was no longer respected. But at the beginning of the war the fact was that the officers of the Republican Army were, negatively, those who had not attempted a coup and had not brought their men out into the streets. They possessed only the authority that the militias would allow, which put them in the difficult position of being the servants of the situation rather than its masters and thus of having to fulfil their professional duties as far as they were allowed to or as far as their own sometimes hesitant loyalty permitted them to do.

One result of this was that professional officers took refuge in over-bureaucratisation and established a paper army. This was, in any case, natural to a great many of them, who had spent their lives as garrison bureaucrats. It contrasts strongly with the sense of urgency which typified in particular the early movements of the Insurgents. Thus imposing masses of paper were produced and the Republican Army used classic forms of organisation which modern military thinkers were already seeing as unsuitable even for armies which had fought the 1914–18 war, in which Spain had been neutral, and which were hard to apply to the manner of development of the Republican Army or its character.

This was the crux of the problem. The Republican Army was revolutionary in the sense that it was created out of chaos in a revolutionary situation and was obliged to improvise. Yet the other characteristics of revolutionary armies, the common will, the self-imposed discipline, a large proportion of volunteers and the audacity of command, were not present. Nor was the Republican Army fighting an enemy undermined by decadence. Insurgent officers were neither incompetent nor slothful. Despite the shocked reactions of Soviet advisers, it took a long time, probably longer than in Franco's army, to rid the Republican Army of some generals who did exhibit such qualities. While both armies were composed largely of conscripts, the Insurgents had professional troops and the framework of professional units into which volunteers and conscripts could be inserted. Most Insurgent officers were competent for the duties required for their ranks, so there seem to have been few panicky retreats. When attacks liable to suffer heavy casualties were to be made, it was the Legion or the Moors which were to carry them out. Thus while desertion from both sides was common, traffic from the Republican lines to the Nationalists was busier than the other way. In the Republican Army, on the other hand, absence of trust in leaders, at least at lower and intermediate levels, is evident from the repeated exhortations of the commissars to the men to trust the higher command and from officers' complaints of widespread insubordination. Conversations with ex-officers, commissars and men of the Republican Army, perusal of documents produced by the political organisations about their role in the army, comments by the Soviet advisers and study of memoir literature all build up an impression, if not of frequent and direct acts of insubordination, at least of an atmosphere where orders might or might not be obeyed, where people did what they liked on the sketchiest of authority, comments would be made in writing which would lead to instant court martial in any other army and relative nonentities could build up reputations because of a cult of personality.

It was felt, instinctively, that in the revolutionary situation, rigid military discipline was out of place. Possibly this was true, but the communists and many others, in the end even the anarchists, understood that it had to be replaced by the more severe self-discipline of the motivated soldier. For those who did not possess sufficient conviction to impose this discipline on themselves, the role of the commissars became one of political leadership rather than the original conception of a buffer between inspired volunteers and the distrusted remnants of the officer corps. In hindsight, the Republican Army was not ready for this freedom. Men for whom a large programme of literacy training, political education (some would call it politically correct indoctrination) and basic hygienic advice had to be prepared, circulated and imposed, could not be expected to act in a self-disciplined manner and fight successfully, with the added disadvantage of a lack of arms and leadership, against a comparatively efficient enemy. Some men could do so, and thus the Republican Army possessed its 11th and 26th Divisions, its V Corps and other units with a strong *esprit de corps*. But the mass of the Republican Army was conscripted and probably unwilling to such an extent that desertion and evasion of service, especially after the retreats of the spring of 1938, were widespread.

Perhaps it could be said that the creation of the formal, classic army failed, that the Spanish Civil War experience inspired the contrary view that guerrilla warfare in similar circumstances was more effective and that this experience was applied in the Second World War, though guerrillas in the Spanish war were not encouraged to do as much as they might have.

These were the inherent defects of the Republican Army. Given the political and social situation which had caused the war, they may have been inevitable. Yet, after the disappearance of the old Army in the Republican zone in 1936, the defection of most of the *Guardia Civil* at least in the rural areas and the strong anti-officer reaction of the unions and political organisations, the loyal officers of the Republic, beginning with the nucleus in the War Ministry and continuing under the leadership of José Asensio Torrado, Manuel Estrada and the new General Staff, built an army by summer 1937 which merited the name. It defended Madrid and fought off the enemy in the battles around the capital, and it would fight well at Teruel, Belchite and on the Ebro. It was undefeated on the central and southern fronts. But the proactive strategy of the battles of Brunete, Belchite, Teruel and the Ebro was incomplete because of insufficient air cover, without a logistics at least equal to that of the enemy and without sufficient and appropriate training of platoon, company and battalion commanders.

The Republican Army began the war with almost no knowledge or appreciation of the role of Military Intelligence. Throughout the conflict Major, later Colonel Manuel Estrada Manchón, led the Information Section of the General Staff with such energy that in general the Republican Army possessed Intelligence of high quality when it launched its attacks. This explains the initial successes of Brunete (July 1937), Belchite (August 1937), Teruel (December 1937) and the Ebro (July 1938). If these attacks were ultimately unsuccessful it was not for lack of military information. Elsewhere, it may have been the constant fear that Madrid was in danger that weakened the defensive efforts of the Republican Army, for example in Aragon in March and April 1938.[3]

Foreign influence in the Republican Army had been negligible. It is true that the International Brigades participated in some of the bloodiest fighting, but while the two half-formed and barely trained International battalions that came to Madrid in the critical second week of November

[3] For a general study of Republican Army Intelligence, see H. Rodríguez Velasco, *Una derrota prevista: el espionaje republicano en la Guerra Civil española (1936–1939)*, Granada, 2012.

1936 made a considerable propaganda contribution and suffered unparalleled losses, only the imagination of foreign journalists could say that they 'saved' Madrid. Nor were the 40,000 Internationals (there were no more than 15,000–20,000 in Spain at any one time) a significant proportion of the Republican Army. By late 1937, in any case, losses had been enormous and replacements were not arriving. Consequently, the International Brigades were becoming more and more Spanish in composition.

Again, foreign strategic and tactical guidance was no more than occasional. Soviet sources give the impression that the Russian advisers were inhibited, first by the instructions they had received not to tell the Spaniards what to do, though, contradictorily, to ensure that what the Soviets wanted was done, and second by the context of what was happening in the USSR, where a high proportion of senior officers of the Red Army was being liquidated. Specifically, Marshal Tukhachevsky, who was a proponent of deep advance with tanks used en masse, had been executed shortly before the battle of Brunete in July 1937, with the result that no Soviet adviser dared to suggest using the very up-to-date Soviet tanks which had been supplied to the Republican Army according to the new theories, known later as *Blitzkrieg*. Actually, Vicente Rojo knew the theory well, but the Chief of Staff of the Republican Army is unlikely to have judged the Republican Army capable of carrying out such a modern form of war.

Looking closely at the Soviet contribution to the Spanish Republic's war effort against Franco's Nationalist Insurgents in 1936–9, it is clear that, unlike Germany, the USSR did not develop a policy of constant reinforcement of its several hundred aircraft. When the Republican Army reached the level of organisation and efficiency which would have permitted it to carry out major strategic operations, it lacked the necessary air power. A few days before the successful crossing of the Ebro on 25–26 July 1938, when there was a definite possibility of victory, Rojo wrote to his friend Manuel Matallana, Chief of Staff of the GERC, complaining about the lack of air support and that the enemy was acting with 'insulting impunity'. Two days later, Rojo wrote to the Head of Operations of the Republican Air Force 'indignant that the Air Force did not take part in yesterday's nor today's operations'.[4] The reasons for this include the lack of machines but more than likely Soviet pressure on the high command of the Air Force. Yet a further and more fundamental question needs to be asked. How could an operation as important as that of the Ebro be planned without the planning procedures

[4] Quoted in Bahamonde and Cervera, *Así terminó*, 175–6.

including close liaison with the Air Force, whose role in covering the attack was indispensible, as the Italian defeat at Guadalajara should have shown? Even more so, how could the absence of the Air Force have been a surprise for the Chief of Staff? The answer is that neither side constructed a joint arms command, or a committee of the Chiefs of Staff of the Army, Navy and Air Force. However, it was more in the political interest of Germany and Italy to see that Franco was regularly supplied with up-to-date aircraft, while the Soviet Union had other concerns, both internal and external.

Some of the proactive operations of the Republican Army – Teruel and the Ebro are emblematic cases – give the impression of having been carried out, rather than for justified military reasons, to show the outside world that the Republic may not have been going to win the war but could halt Franco in his tracks and fight a war in a disciplined manner. Such decisions may have been appropriate politically, but pouring division after division into battles which began with dramatic successes but became like slogging matches had the effect of causing large loss of life. Brunete and the Ebro got bogged down, and created such a collapse in morale – whatever the communist self-convictions about the Ebro – that a disinterested observer might judge that the operations should have been stopped. However, the model of war that all the Republican Army leaders possessed in 1936–9 was the Great War, where despite huge losses of life and material, battles such as Verdun and the Somme were not stopped. As the battle of the Ebro was reaching its end, Rojo told Negrín on 8 November 1938 that:

> The best way of countering the plans of the enemy is to seize the initiative and, as at Teruel or on the Ebro, to create a critical position at a capital objective, which forces him to move most of his reserves to a war theatre far from the one to which he plans to launch his masses.[5]

Here, Rojo was explaining to Negrín that it was necessary to attract the enemy attacking forces away from the targets of Madrid or Valencia. The theory is correct, but in practice the observer might doubt whether applying it with such great losses of men, morale and material such as the Republican Army suffered at Teruel or on the Ebro was justified. In any cases, such strategy was purely diversionary and its importance lay in being to attract Franco's reserves in such a way as to leave his own fronts undermanned, thus allowing the Republican Army to launch a paralysing blow, which, however, never came. The best example of this manoeuvre never took place. This was Plan P, at the end of 1938.

[5] Quoted in Rojo, *Vicente Rojo*, 241.

There would be a beach landing at Motril (Granada), followed by a breakthrough of the enemy Front, from where many divisions had been moved to prepare for the Christmas Eve attack on Catalonia. It was hoped to reach as far as Seville and Badajoz, while from Madrid the Army of the Centre would cut enemy communications between the capital and Extremadura. D-Day would be 12 December 1938. Rojo telegraphed orders to Miaja, in supreme command of the Central Army Group (GERC), but Miaja refused to detach troops for the operation, maintaining that Admiral Buiza, in command of the Fleet, which would take part in the landings, agreed with him. Negrín decided to suspend the operation. Why Negrín did so, rather than dismissing Miaja, is unknown, but it may be assumed that, with or without the advice of the Soviet counsellors, fear of a tremendous catastrophe may have been one of the reasons. Had such decisions been concentrated in military hands and had the Chief of Staff, Rojo, held supreme command, the operation would have taken place.

The absolute aim of Republican strategy was the defence of Madrid. Until the end of the war, the Army of the Centre with its four corps ringed the capital. It was a force more than sufficient to dissuade Franco from trying to take the city. Miaja's unwillingness to detach some of his units and send them to other fronts is understandable in this context. So is the possible counsel of the Russians when Rojo – as Chief of Staff – ordered his superior in rank, Miaja, to detach the divisions needed. The question which arises, then, is not why Miaja refused to detach the units, but what was the political situation which allowed such a refusal to obey an order. During the battle of the Ebro, an interchange of messages between Rojo and Matallana illustrates, though does not explain, the problem: 'I request you [Rojo uses the familiar *tú*] to give the orders urgently so that the attack can take place.' Despite the 'I request you' ('*Te ruego*') Rojo indicates that the request is an order, so that Matallana was obliged to inform Miaja. But Rojo adds: 'I am not directing it to him nor do I express it as an order, so that he should not be annoyed.' ('*No se la dirijo a él ni empleo la forma de directiva para que no se ponga de mal humor.*')[6]

Furthermore, the authority of the Chief of Staff was questioned not only by Miaja, who admittedly had been a general when Rojo was only a recently promoted major, but also by Hernández Saravia, a lieutenant-colonel in 1936 and now general commanding the Eastern Army Group or GERO. Rojo wrote personally to his friend Matallana on 6 November 1938 that Hernández Saravia, 'despite my using all my

[6] *Ibid.*, 235–6.

tricks ['*maquievalismos*'] to stop him, goes against my will'.[7] In the light of these examples of lack of authority and decision among the leaders of the Republican Army, the roles of Negrín as Prime Minister and Minister of National Defence and of Antonio Cordón as Under-Secretary for the Army should perhaps be re-evaluated.

Given a fairer balance in the arms resources of the combatant armies of the Spanish Civil War, which would have reinforced confidence that the Republic could fight on in 1939 on terms approaching equality, the Republican Army might have been able to contain the great Francoist offensives in Aragon, on the Ebro and in Catalonia. It could not have won the war, if only because the Government had made strategic errors from the beginning of the conflict. Although the Republic's Fleet was undisciplined and commanded by low-ranking officers it would still have been capable of blocking the Strait of Gibraltar and preventing Franco bringing over the Legion and the Moroccan forces to overthrow the Republic. Although José Giral, Minister of the Navy, sent ships with orders to blockade the ports of Morocco, he failed to keep them there. A similar strategic error was made with the Air Force. Here the important principle which was not maintained was concentration of effort, for the aircraft were frittered away in the absence of a strategy. A further error, in August 1936, was to abandon Majorca to the Insurgents by not supporting the militia forces which tried to occupy the island. The consequences of allowing Palma to become a naval and air base of maximum importance in impeding sea traffic to Republican ports would be reflected in the large number of merchant ships sunk while making for the ports of Barcelona, Tarragona and Alicante.[8]

Other important decisions include what was possibly a mistake in the delay in employing officers who had not participated in the uprising. About 2,000 career officers, of the 16,094 (excluding generals) who appear on the active list in the *Anuario Militar de España* for 1936, served in the Republican Army. A large number of the rest, setting aside those who were with the Insurgents and those who had taken part in the failed uprising, must have been living in the Republican zone. There were also several thousand in retirement but of military age, who had left the Army, taking advantage of the offer of retirement on full pay granted by the reform of 1931. Yet, while career officers were used in the weeks in which a mixed brigade was being organised and trained, when the preparatory period was over it was usually a militia officer

[7] *Ibid.*, 236.

[8] On this see Alpert, *La guerra civil española en el mar.*

who took over command.[9] There may have been many reasons for this, but these may have been not so much political distrust as physical fitness, age and the ability of those officers to adapt their practices to a different kind of army.

Besides questions of strategy and organisation, tactics should be considered. The Insurgents, at least in the Legion and the Moroccan regiments, possessed units with experience and tradition, so that when new recruits enlisted they did so in a framework which was completely absent in a Republican Army brigade, where it would be rare to meet a professional military man. And what of the systems of training and particularly the tactical preparation which the junior commanders, the sergeants and provisional lieutenants received in Franco's army? The question is important in the light of the constant criticism by the senior Republican Army officers of the abilities of the junior commanders. Were company and platoon movements better taught in the Insurgent than the Republican Army? The inability of the junior commanders of the Republican Army to use their initiative and their waste of men and time in tackling secondary points of resistance were widely criticised. Once on their own and without concrete instructions 'it is obvious that they have nothing in them and lack self-confidence' ('*se les nota que no tienen nada dentro y carecen de confianza en sí mismos*'), commented Rojo.[10] Did this reflect insufficient training or perhaps the conservative attitudes of their professional leaders, who insisted on retaining absolute control, an authoritarianism shared by the communists, who stood for a formal and fully disciplined army? Nevertheless, the rhetoric of discipline was absent when it came to the necessary improvisation of a revolutionary-style army. When, for example, the Internationals found their Chauchat machine-guns unserviceable, they abandoned them.[11] The Insurgents recovered and used them after solving the problems.[12] Despite the tendentious nature of this comment it seems likely to reflect the truth. A comparison between the opposed navies in the Spanish Civil War shows that the Insurgents knew how to make the best of old ships in bad condition, while Republican navy ships spent excessive time in repair in dry dock.

Was the marked contrast between Franco's style of war and that of the Republican command due to the different characteristics of the

[9] This emerges clearly from Carlos Engel's *Historia de las brigadas mixtas del Ejército Popular de la República*, Madrid, 1999.

[10] Quoted in Rojo, *Vicente Rojo*, 226.

[11] As recalled by Gurney, *Crusade in Spain*, 78.

[12] According to A. Mortera, 'Armas para España, pese a Howson', *Historia Militar*, 9 (January 2001), 83–93 (specifically 91).

two armies? The commanders had attended the same military academies and not infrequently belonged to the same cohort of graduates. However, the Insurgent leaders were *africanistas* almost to a man, and had learnt their trade as young officers in the Riff wars of the 1920s, while the commanders of the Republican Army had drunk deeply from the wells of French strategic thought, considered near-perfect since 1918, and which in the 1930s was characterised by a highly defensive tone. Furthermore, the severe scarcity of professionals in the Republican Army led also to artillery, engineers and other officers commanding infantry divisions, corps and armies, while Franco's major commanders were all infantrymen.

An army is victorious because it is stronger than its adversary in commanders, numbers and quality, or because it handles its resources better than the enemy. Armies which lack resources tend to have recourse to irregular warfare and sabotage as a way of denying victory to the enemy. The Republican militias were neither of these two kinds of army. They did not make a real military revolution. Faced by the Insurgents' style of war, their better-trained and -led troops, and their Air Force, which learnt the techniques of air–ground cooperation, the Republican Army was simply out of date.

Nevertheless, given all its limitations, a balanced view of the Republican Army would conclude that it was in many aspects not only a fascinating and significant part of the contemporary history of Spain but also a phenomenon to be greatly admired for its long resistance when the circumstances against it were mostly unfavourable. Today, when it is evident that many conservative and Catholic officers saw serving the Republic as their duty, it enjoys at least the respectful consideration that its enemies denied it after its defeat.

Appendix 1: Unit establishments of the Republican Army

Mixed brigade in 1936

(According to Martínez Bande, *La marcha sobre Madrid*, 100n.)

four battalions of five infantry companies (four of rifles and one of machine-guns) plus a mortar section;

one motorised cavalry squadron;

four light batteries of 75 mm and 105 mm artillery;

one company of sappers;

ammunition column;

units of signals, supply and medical services.

Totals: 150 officers and 3,700 men.

Arms: 2,200 rifles, 96 automatic rifles, 96 light and 8 heavy mortars, 36 machine-guns, 16 artillery pieces.

With slight variations in the numbers of artillery pieces and machine-guns, the versions given by Vicente Rojo (*La defensa de Madrid*, 137) and Casado (*Last Days of Madrid*, 59) concur.

A more detailed establishment was laid down in November 1937 (DR, L474, C8):

four battalions of infantry with a total of 96 officers and 3,144 men;

a depot company;

a cavalry section;

an armoured-car section in one brigade in each division;

one battery of three pieces (the shortage of artillery is manifest);

ammunition column and signals, supply, medical and sappers units.

Total: 134 officers, 32 commissars and 4,029 men.

Battalion

(*Gaceta* 29 October 1936.)

headquarters and signals;

four rifle companies with rifles and some automatic weapons, machine-gun company with eight weapons;

mortar sections with four mortars.

Totals: 25 officers, 52 NCOs and 872 men.

Smaller units

three *escuadras* make a *pelotón* under a sergeant;
two *pelotones* make a *sección* under a lieutenant;
three *secciones* make a company under a captain.

(The *pelotón* is the British section; the *sección* is the British platoon. The establishments go into minute detail, stating which squad corporals were to carry rifles and which pistols, and which man was to carry grenades or Verey lights.)

Appendix 2: History of the 2nd Mixed Brigade

In October 1938 the mixed brigades were ordered to compose histories of their service. If this order was generally obeyed, which is doubtful in the chaotic conditions at the end of the war, very few such histories have survived. This one is the most complete, stretching from the foundation of the brigade until January 1939 (the source is DR, L1128, C6).

On 13 October 1936, Jesús Martínez de Aragón, heading a militia composed of railwaymen, was ordered to organise the 2nd Mixed Brigade in Ciudad Real, some hundred miles south of Madrid. Only one of the first battalion commanders was a military man, a sergeant just promoted to officer rank. As Chief of Staff the brigade had a major of the *Guardia de Asaltos* (*Asalto* officers were seconded from the Army). The sappers were commanded by an engineers lieutenant. The four battalions were composed of railwaymen and other militia groups as well as some units of the army which had been stationed in Madrid.

After fighting in the defence of Madrid, the brigade settled into the heavily fought over University City, at that time under construction. The Brigade History notes the appointments of political commissars and officers (none of whom appears in the 1936 Army List). The engineers lieutenant became Chief of Staff, although there is no indication that he attended even a short course in Staff work. The brigade remained in line until March 1937, when it was withdrawn for reorganisation. When its commander, Jesús Martínez de Aragón, was killed he was replaced by Juan José Gallego Pérez, an ex-regular NCO.

The brigade fought in the battle of Brunete in August 1937 under yet another Chief of Staff who was also a promoted ex-regular NCO. New commanding officers with the rank of *mayor*, equivalent to *comandante* (major), the highest to which militia officers could aspire, were appointed to the battalions. Gallego Pérez was given command of a division.

Until the end of 1937 the brigade was granted only five days' rest. In 1938 things became much quieter except for an attack towards Guadalajara, east of the capital. There were various command changes, but in no case was a professional officer appointed. In April 1938, after the Insurgent breakthrough to the Mediterranean Sea and the division of Republican territory in two, the brigade was transferred to the east of Spain and became part of the Army of Operations (*Ejército de Maniobras*). It suffered heavy losses, being reduced in size to two battalions. In summer 1938 the brigade was in constant movement in the defence of Valencia and underwent further reorganisation. On 10 July 1938 it received at last what the History calls a professional officer to command it, but his name does not figure in the 1936 Army List. He was thus either a promoted career NCO or had retired before the war.

From this time on the brigade remained in its depot near Teruel and later underwent training at Jamilena (Jaén), where the History ends.

The striking aspect of this not very interesting account is the constant change of officers who are not suited to their commands. If the Chiefs of Staff were, in turn, a lieutenant of engineers, various promoted ex-regular NCOs and possibly a retired officer, it is easy to understand how well-conceived plans for battles like Brunete went astray at the lower levels of command.

The other point that emerges is the unsatisfactory system of rotation and reliefs. This brigade was left in the line so long that complete reconstruction was required. The problem of continuity in command must have been serious, and the questions of health and hygiene, so often brought up by the commissars, are thrown into relief.

Appendix 3: Generals of the Spanish Army

The following are the generals of the Spanish Army according to the *Anuario Militar* of 1936, in order of rank and seniority. If a general was resident or stationed in the area where the uprising was successful and there is no information on his arrest, it is assumed that he supported the insurrection. Generals in the Republican zone and whose loyalty was doubted were put into *disponibilidad* (that is, they remained without posts) until their cases were examined. Dismissals were announced in the *Diario Oficial del Ministerio de la Guerra*. Dismissal may mean that the general in question was in prison, or had been killed or was in the Insurgent zone and had joined the insurrection, or merely that he was suspected of disloyalty.

Name	Age	Fate
LIEUTENANT-GENERALS		
López Pozas	65	Dismissed by Republic 26 August 1936. Shot
Castro Girona	61	Dismissed by Republic 26 October 1936
Rodríguez Casademunt	66	Dismissed by Republic 29 June 1938
GENERALS OF DIVISION		
López Ochoa	59	Murdered by mob in Madrid
M. Cabanellas	64	Insurgent
Rodríguez del Barrio	60	Died before uprising
La Cerda	64	Loyal
Goded	54	Insurgent. Shot in Republican zone
Losada Ortega	59	Dismissed by Republic 12 August 1936
Queipo de Llano	61	Insurgent
Gómez Morato	57	Arrested by Insurgents.
Villegas	61	Dismissed by Republic. Shot
De Salcedo	64	Loyal. Shot by Insurgents
Saliquet	61	Insurgent
Riquelme	56	Loyal
Núñez del Prado	56	Loyal. Shot by Insurgents
González Carrasco	59	Left Spain. Dismissed by Republic
Peña Abuín	64	Retired in Republican zone 18 November 1937
V. Cabanellas	63	Dismissed by Republic 3 November 1937

Name	Age	Fate
Sánchez Ocaña	62	Dismissed by Republic 12 August 1936
Batet	64	Loyal. Shot by Insurgents
García Gómez Caminero	65	Loyal. Died 14 December 1938
Villa-Abrille	58	Loyal. Gaoled by Insurgents.
Masquelet	65	Loyal. Retired 19 July 1937
Molero	66	Arrested by Insurgents
Franco	44	Insurgent
Fanjul	56	Insurgent. Shot
GENERALS OF BRIGADE		
Orgaz	55	Insurgent
Pozas	60	Loyal
Mola	49	Insurgent
Balmes	61	Accidentally killed 16 July 1936
González de Lara	62	Dismissed by Republic 26 August 1936. Shot
García Benítez	62	Insurgent
Patxot	60	Shot in Republican zone
Llanos Medina	63	Dismissed by Republic 7 August 1937
Benito Terraza	57	Insurgent
Urbano Palma	64	Placed on reserve in Republican zone
Bosch Bosch	63	Insurgent
Llano de la Encomienda	57	Loyal
Martínez Monje	62	Loyal
García Aldave	60	Shot in Republican zone 13 October 1936
Castelló	55	Loyal. Fled to France after breakdown. Dismissed
Romerales	61	Shot by Insurgents
Alvarez Arenas	54	Dismissed by Republic 12 August 1936
Mena Zueco	62	Arrested by Insurgents
García Antúnez	63	Died in Republican zone while under investigation
De Miguel Lacour	63	Shot in Republican zone
Miaja Menant	62	Loyal
López Pinto	60	Insurgent
De la Cruz Boullosa	62	Dismissed by Republic 29 June 1938
Fernández Burriel	57	Shot in Republican zone
Otero Cossío	63	Dismissed by Republic 3 November 1937
Iglesias Martínez	63	Dismissed by Nationalists
Morales Díaz	62	Retired by Nationalists
Rodríguez González	56	Dismissed by Republic 18 October 1937
Martínez Cabrera	62	Loyal
Gámir Ulíbarri	59	Loyal
Jiménez García	61	Dismissed by Republic 19 June 1938
López Gómez	62	Dismissed by Republic 19 June 1938
San Pedro Aymat	63	Loyal
Lon Laga	59	Dismissed by Republic 29 August 1938
García Alvarez	62	Insurgent

Name	Age	Fate
Cavanna del Val	61	Loyal
Barro García	57	Insurgent
Espinosa de los Monteros	56	Escaped to Insurgent zone
Avilés Melgar	60	Dismissed by Republic 29 June 1938
Moya Andino	62	Insurgent
Fernández Ampón	60	Shot in Republican zone
Caridad Pita	61	Shot by Insurgents
Carrasco Amilivia	61	Dismissed by Republic 12 August 1936
Ravassa Cuevas	62	Insurgent
López Viota	58	Arrested by Insurgents but also dismissed by Republic 12 August 1936
Martín-González	63	Insurgent
Capaz	42	Murdered by mob in Madrid
Bosch Atienza	64	Shot in Republican zone
Cardenal	63	Loyal
Legorburu	63	Shot in Republican zone
Rodríguez Ramírez	58	Dismissed by Republic 3 November 1937
Araujo Vergara	62	Shot in Republican zone
Barbero Saldaña	55	Arrested 28 February 1938 in Republican zone
Bernal	62	Loyal
Varela	45	Insurgent
Alcázar Leal	55	Placed in reserve by Republic
Campins	56	Shot by Insurgents
CIVIL GUARD		
Grijalvo (Valencia)	62	Shot in Republican zone
F. de la Cruz(Valladolid)	63	Insurgent
Salamero (Córdoba)	63	–
Santiago (Madrid)	63	–
Aranguren (Barcelona)	61	Loyal
CARABINEERS		
Bragulat	62	Escaped to Insurgent zone
Rodríguez Ocaña	60	–
SUPPLY (*INTENDENCIA*)		
Gallego Ramos	61	Dismissed by Republic
Jiménez Arenas	63	Dismissed by Republic
Meléndez	52	Dismissed by Republic 13 December 1937
Marcos Jiménez	62	Dismissed by Republic 29 June 1938
MEDICAL CORPS		
Castellví	65	Placed on reserve by Republic 3 September 1937
Del Buey	62	–
Potous	65	Dismissed by Republic 9 August 1937

Appendix 4: Biographies of significant officers and political commissars of the Republican Army

Santiago Aguado Calvo was a warrant officer (*brigada*) of *Carabineros*. Proceeding up the ladder of militia commands he led a battalion, the 9th Brigade and the 100th Brigade. Wounded in the battle of the Ebro, for the rest of the war he was an instructor at an officers' training school. After the war he attended the Frunze military academy in the Soviet Union and was later an adviser to Yugoslav anti-German guerrillas. He died in 1960.

Armando Alvarez was a major of infantry seconded to the *Guardia de Asalto*. He took part in the suppression of the disturbances in Barcelona in May 1937 and supported the Casado coup in March 1939.

José Alvarez Cerón was captain of artillery in 1936. In 1938 be became Sub-Inspector-General of Anti-Aircraft Services in the Eastern Army Group (GERO) with the rank of colonel. He lived in exile in Colombia.

Julio Alvarez Cerón, brother of the above, was an industrial engineer and a major of artillery in 1936, in charge of a motor-vehicle depot. He organised transport in the Madrid area, becoming Director-General of Transport for the Eastern Army Group in 1938. In Colombia after the war he had a distinguished career in the field of industrial engineering.

Aureliano Alvarez Coque was a colonel on the General Staff. He took part in the siege of the military academy in Toledo. Later he led one of the sectors defending Madrid. He was Chief of Staff in the Army of the Centre and temporarily chief of the General Staff, after which he was Director of Military Training. After the war he lived modestly in Mexico until his death in 1950.

Santiago Alvarez Gomez was born in 1913 in Orense. Since his teens he had been engaged in union and left-wing activities. When the war began he organised the *Milicias Gallegas* of Galicians living in Madrid. Later he was political commissar of the 1st Brigade, the 11th Division and the V Corps, all with his fellow Galician Enrique Líster as commander. He was ordered to stay with the Army of the Ebro when it was interned in France, rather than return to Spain. Later he went to the USSR, then to Latin America. Returning to Spain he was arrested in 1945, sentenced to a long prison term but freed in 1954. He went to Cuba. During the post-Franco epoch he was active in the PCE and wrote his memoirs. He died in 2002.

Emilio Alzugaray Goicoechea was a retired military engineer. He escaped from Morocco when the war began, rejoining the army. After commanding militia columns he led the 7th Division and the II Corps, and served in Staff posts. In France after the war he worked with British Intelligence but was captured by the Germans. He was killed when a German convoy in which he was travelling was blown up by the Resistance.

José María Anglada, a major in the mountain battalion stationed in Bilbao, was executed for passing information to the Insurgents.

Francisco Antón was an ex-railway official who became commissar-general on the Central Front probably through his PCE membership and his reputed friendship with 'La Pasionaria'. As he was of military age, the Prieto reform of the Commissariat required him to be enrolled in a brigade. When he refused he was dismissed from the Commissariat.

Modesto Aramberri Gallástegui was an infantry captain in command of the municipal police of Bilbao. He became head of the Operations Section of the Basque Army Staff. After the campaign in the North of Spain he did not return to Republican territory and was dismissed. Later he returned to Spain, where a post-war court martial sentenced him to three years' gaol. He was soon amnestied.

José Aranguren Roldán was a general of the *Guardia Nacional Republican* (ex-*Guardia Civil*). In Catalonia he was largely responsible for the suppression of the military uprising and hence the deaths of a large number of Insurgent officers, particularly the rebel Generals Goded and Fernández Burriel, at whose trials he gave evidence. He did not hold combat positions in the war, which he ended as military governor of Valencia. Scorning the protection of an embassy he surrendered, was court-martialled and executed by the victors.

José María Arbex was not on the active list in 1936 but had previously been a Staff captain. He became head of the Information Section of the Staff of the Basque Corps, going over to the Insurgents on the fall of Bilbao.

Abelardo Arce Mayoral was a 56-year-old lieutenant-colonel serving in a recruitment depot in 1936. He commanded a sector in the defence of Madrid and went on to lead the 42nd Brigade, the 6th, the 13th and later the 9th Divisions, after which he was retired and appointed to command an officers' training school.

Tomás Ardid Rey was a lieutenant-colonel of engineers highly praised for his work on fortifications in the defence on Madrid in 1936 and of Valencia in 1938. Casado appointed him inspector-general of fortifications.

Arturo Arellano was a retired infantry captain who helped train the Fifth Regiment, commanding its *compañías de acero*. He later commanded the 4th Mixed Brigade when it was formed. He was killed on 17 November 1936.

Gerardo Armentia Palacios was a major of artillery who was appointed commander of artillery in the Army of Andalusia. He was killed in the naval base of Cartagena during the suppression of the uprising there to support Casado in March 1939.

Alberto Arrando Garrido was a major in the *Guardia de Asalto* in Barcelona. Loyal to the Catalan Government, he was later in charge of public order in May 1937. He commanded the 30th Division at Teruel but was dismissed after the rout of April 1938.

Domingo Ascaso was a member of a well-known anarchist family. He was killed in the troubles of May 1937. His brother Francisco had been killed while suppressing the military uprising in Barcelona in July 1936, while his nephew, Joaquín, became president of the anarchist Council of Aragon and was arrested when that organisation was dissolved in August 1937.

Guillermo Ascanio Moreno, an industrial engineer from the Canaries, commanded the *Canarias Libre* battalion of the Fifth Regiment. He then commanded the 8th Division, refusing to accept the Casado take-over in March 1939. Imprisoned by Casado, he fell into enemy hands, was court-martialled and executed on 3 July 1941 despite an appeal by von Faupel, a previous German ambassador to Franco, who had been Ascanio's fellow student in Berlin.

José Asensio Torrado was almost at the head of the seniority list of the Staff Corps and an ex-*africanisa*. He had received his promotions to lieutenant-colonel and colonel by merit. After Asensio had won one of the few early victories of the militia – Peguerinos – on 30 August 1936, Largo Caballero promoted him general on 5 September 1936, giving him command in the Central War Theatre. He later became Under-Secretary for War, taking a major part in the creation of the first few mixed brigades. Flattered at first by the communists, his disagreements with them about the nature of the new army made him a target for their criticisms. He was charged with the responsibility for the constant retreats of the militia and finally for the loss of Málaga in early 1937. He defended his actions in his *El general Asensio: su lealtad a la República* (1938), written while he was in prison awaiting the enquiry into his responsibilities. The charges were quashed but Asensio held no further command. He was appointed military attaché in Washington in January 1939. After the war he lived in New York, occupying himself with teaching Spanish and with journalism until his death in 1961.

Patricio de Azcárate García de Lomas was a major of engineers who became colonel and inspector of the Corps. He went to Mexico after the war.

Gumersindo de Azcárate Gómez was commander of the cyclist battalion. He was sent to Bilbao as inspector of the Basque Army Corps. Captured by the Insurgents, he was shot.

José Balibrea Vera, major of infantry in Cartagena. He led forces attempting to retake Córdoba in August 1936 and later the XIII Corps at Teruel. Later he was on the Staff in the Army of the Levante. He died in Spain in 1970.

Luis Barceló Jover commanded the battalion guarding the Ministry of War. A member of UMRA and the PCE, he was first Inspector of Militias. Promoted to lieutenant-colonel, he took part in the siege of the Alcázar of Toledo and later commanded the 35th Mixed Brigade and the 2nd Division. Promoted to colonel he led the 1st Corps, and in March 1939 he led the counter-reaction to the Casado coup. Accused of responsibility in the murder of three pro-Casado Staff officers, he was in his turn executed.

Angel Barcia Galeote was a Madrid workman who took an active part in the assault on the Montana barracks and in organising the 1st Mixed Brigade. Later he was commissar of the 9th Brigade and of the 11th Division. He was killed in the battle of the Ebro, on 9 September 1938.

José del Barrio Navarro was a member of the PSUC. After leading the *Carlos Marx* column in Aragon he was made commander of the 27th Division and later of the XVIII Corps of the Army of the East. He was expelled from the PCE in 1943 but continued to be a militant but independent communist until his death in 1989.

Domingo Batet Mestres was in command of the Burgos Division. Refusing to support the military uprising he was executed after a lengthy process, despite personal appeals to Franco from other generals.

Albert Bayo Giroud was born in Cuba and educated for some time in the USA. He entered the Spanish Air Force and acquired a military pilot's qualification in 1915, but was forced to resign after a duel. In 1924 he joined the Spanish Legion, serving for some years in Morocco. Rejoining the Air Force he led the landing on Majorca in August 1936, when militia from Valencia tried to regain the island from the Insurgents. He spent most of the war in a backroom position. He went to Mexico after the war, where he taught flying. Later he advised guerrillas, first in Nicaragua and later in Cuba, where he became a close friend of Fidel Castro and Che Guevara. He died in 1967.

Antonio Beltrán Casaña ('El Esquinazao') was a native of Jaca (Huesca). Sent to live in the USA as a boy, he fought with Pancho Villa and then with the American Army in France in 1917–18, after which he returned to Spain to live in Canfranc. In 1930 he collaborated with the abortive Republican coup of Captains Galán and García Hernández. In the Spanish Civil War he formed militias in northern Aragon and became famous in command of the 43rd Division, which was isolated in 1938 for three months in the Pyrenees. He led the division in the battle of the Ebro and in the retreat through Catalonia in early 1939. He was one of the few militia commanders to be promoted to the rank of lieutenant-colonel. He was admitted to the USSR and spent some time at the Frunze military academy, after which he was active in organising guerrillas to infiltrate Franco's Spain. Breaking with the Communist Party, he was suspected of working for US Intelligence services. Refused political asylum in the United Kingdom, he went to Mexico, dying in 1960.

José Benedito Lleó had retired in 1931 as a lieutenant of artillery. Frequenting extreme left circles he was nominated as military secretary on the People's Executive

Committee in Valencia in 1936. In 1937 he was entrusted with the task of militarising the most recalcitrant of the anarchist columns, the *Columna de Hierro*.

Carlos Bernal García was a general of brigade of engineers. Briefly Under-Secretary for the Army in July 1936, he commanded a militia column and then was posted to the newly founded central depot for the Republican Army at Albacete, where he remained until 21 June 1937. Later he became Director-General of Rearguard Services and Transport, ending the war as commander of the naval base of Cartagena, where he was replaced by Francisco Galán in March 1939. Casado appointed Bernal military governor of Madrid. He died while in prison after the war.

Antonio Bertomeu Bisquert was a major of infantry. He commanded the VII Corps of the Army of Extremadura until transferred to a recruitment depot in 1938.

José Bertomeu Bisquert was not on the active list in 1936. He was Chief of Staff in the VII Corps.

Crescenciano Bilbao was a moderate socialist who was appointed sub-commissar-general in September 1936.

Mariano Bueno Ferrer was a retired officer who was briefly imprisoned at the outset of war. Released, he commanded the Catalan *Columna Pirenaica* in the Jaca zone and later the 130th Mixed Brigade. He was awarded the Medal of Valour in 1939.

Emilio Bueno Núñez de Prado was a retired infantry major with pronounced Republican sympathies who rejoined the army and took part in the defence of Madrid. He commanded the 41st Brigade, the 4th Division and then the II Corps. Casado replaced him with another officer. Though it seems unlikely, Nationalist Intelligence services suggested he was one of their agents. In fact his post-war court martial sentenced him to death, which was commuted to 30 years' imprisonment. He obtained 'restricted liberty' in 1943 and total amnesty in 1946. He was also heavily fined for his 'political responsibilities' and for having been a Freemason.

Ricardo Burillo Shtolle was an infantry major in command of the *Guardia de Asalto*, some of whose members assassinated the right-wing politician José Calvo Sotelo. A member of UMRA and the PCE, leading a militia column he took part in the attack on the Alcázar of Toledo and was then given overall command of *Asaltos* in Madrid. Later he commanded the 9th Division and then the III Corps of the Army of the Centre, followed by the Army of Extremadura until dismissed after grave loss of territory for which he was judged responsible. A member of the PCE, as Head of Security in Barcelona in June 1937 he had arrested members of the POUM. At the end of the war he was military governor of the port of Alicante. Captured by the enemy, he was executed after court martial.

Francisco Buzón Llanes was a *Guardia Civil* major. He commanded divisions and was head of the Information Section in the Army of the North.

A close friend of President Azaña, he was the author of an important report on the loss of the Basque Country, Santander and the Asturias.

Antonio Camacho Benítez, an officer in the Supply Corps, he served for a long time in Morocco conveying material and food to fighting columns. Camacho was trained as a pilot in 1915 and had a brilliant career. Head of *Escuadra* (Group) No. 1 at the military aerodrome of Getafe (Madrid), he defended it against the Insurgents and played an important part in rescuing many aircraft. Later Under-Secretary for Air, he ended the war as commander of the Air Force in the central zone. A supporter of the Casado coup, he accompanied Casado to London, then went to Mexico, where he lived until 1974.

Miguel Campins Aura, general of brigade, fellow legionary and colleague of Franco in the Zaragoza military academy, military governor of Granada, hesitated when called on to declare a State of War in 1936. Court-martialled by Insurgents, he was shot and at the same time dismissed by the Republic because he had delayed in dispatching troops. Franco tried in vain to persuade General Queipo de Llano, Insurgent commander of the division included which Granada, to spare Campins.

José del Campo was a mechanic who had been active in suborning troops during the Asturias revolution of October 1934. In the Civil War he was political commissar of the 46th Division. He went to the USSR, returning to Spain later to engage in clandestine activity.

José Cantero Ortega, colonel of the infantry regiment stationed at Badajoz, resisted the attack on the city by Insurgents and was court-martialled and executed on 14 August 1936, when the city was taken.

Manuel Cardenal Dominicis, general commanding the 1st Artillery Brigade, presided over the trials of Insurgent officers in Barcelona as well as Madrid. He commanded the artillery in Madrid and in 1938 was temporarily commander of the Army of the Centre. He was president of the *Junta Artística* and in charge of preserving art treasures.

Rogelio Caridad Pita, general of brigade and military governor of La Coruña, was executed by the Insurgents for opposing the Insurrection.

Saturnino Carod Lerín, a CNT militant, led a militia column in Aragon. Later he was commissar of the 118th Mixed Brigade and the 25th Division. Captured in Alicante at the end of the war, he escaped. He engaged in clandestine activities in Spain, where he was arrested, escaping the death sentence when a priest whose life he had saved spoke up for him. Freed in 1960 he continued to participate in illegal CNT activity. After working as a cinema usher he died in 1988.

Ernesto Carratalá Cernuda, a member of UMRA and commander of a sapper battalion in Madrid, was killed while opposing Insurgent officers, possibly when distributing weapons to the militia.

Segismundo Casado López led the uprising of professional officers against the Negrín Government on 5 March 1939, followed by surrender negotiations with the Insurgents. A cavalry officer, he took part in Republican plots in the 1920s. He was in command of the Presidential Escort. Acting as Chief of Staff of a militia column and then Head of Operations on the General Staff, he helped create brigades in Albacete. He replaced the commander of the XVIII Corps in the battle of Brunete. In May 1938 he was given command of the Army of the Centre. He was in contact with the clandestine *Falange* in Madrid from late 1938. When Negrín returned to Spain from France in February 1939 Casado planned his coup. He escaped from Gandía on a British naval vessel and was allowed to land in the United Kingdom, where he published a book in English justifying himself. He worked for the BBC during the war, after which he went to South America, returning to Spain in 1961. He was tried for his actions in the war, but though absolved in 1965 he was never granted his pension.

Fernando Casado Veiga, major of artillery, ADC to President Azaña, commander of artillery in the central zone and then inspector of artillery, was sentenced to death, reprieved and amnestied, after which he maintained his family with private tuition. He was the father of the actor Fernando Rey.

Victoriano Castán Guillén, a CNT militant, commanded the 118th Brigade of the 25th Division. Promoted to lieutenant-colonel in September 1938 he then commanded the 66th Division. Escaping from the prison camp near Alicante with his commissar **Saturnino Carod Lerín** he was active in the French Resistance and in Spain.

Luis Castelló Pantoja was a general commanding the 2nd Infantry Brigade at Badajoz. Summoned to lead the Madrid Division on 19 July 1936 he was made Minister of War. Suffering a nervous collapse because of the stress of the militia period and anxiety about his family in Badajoz, he sheltered in the French embassy and was evacuated to France, where he spent the war. The Germans handed him over to Franco. Tried and condemned to death he spent three years in prison until freed in 1946. He was granted his pension.

Enrique Castro Delgado, one of the leaders of the MAOC, was first commander of the Fifth Regiment, which he left (perhaps in a manoeuvre by 'La Pasionaria') in September 1936 to become Director-General of Agrarian Reform under the communist minister Vicente Uribe and inspector of commissars on the Central Front and later Secretary-General of the Commissariat. He left Spain for the USSR, where he was disillusioned, then Mexico, returning to Spain at the end of the 1950s, where he published books hostile to the Spanish communists.

Eduardo Cavanna del Val was an artillery general in command of the 3rd Artillery Brigade at Valencia. Under suspicion, he was exonerated of guilt in the insurrection but, after commanding briefly in Valencia, was not given posts in the Republican Army.

José Cerón González was a Staff officer of high ability. Though a practising Catholic he had defended the Republic, distributed arms to the militias and became Director-General of the Rearguard and of Transport and later Secretary to the International Committee for the Withdrawal of Foreign Volunteers.

José Cifuentes del Rey was an artillery major in the coastal artillery regiment at Cartagena when it rebelled against the Negrín Government in March 1939.

Francisco Ciutat de Miguel was an infantry lieutenant taking the Staff course in 1936. In September he became Head of Operations in the Staff of the Army of the North but had disagreements with the Basque President, Aguirre, perhaps because Ciutat was a communist and had little sympathy with Basque autonomy. After the defeat of the Republican Army in the north he became Head of Operations of the *Ejército de Maniobras* (Operations) with the rank of lieutenant-colonel. After the war he went to the USSR, where he studied and taught at the Voroshilov academy. He was an adviser in Cuba and Vietnam, and returned to Spain, dying in 1986.

José Coello de Portugal Maisonave was a retired reserve lieutenant. Described as '*muy rojo*' ('very Red') in Insurgent reports, he presented himself for service, was made a Staff captain and achieved rapid promotion to major and lieutenant-colonel, occupying Staff positions. He was involved in secret counter-espionage and guerrilla operations in the enemy rearguard. At the end of the war he was Deputy Chief of Staff in the Eastern Army Group (GERO) in Catalonia. He died in Uruguay in 1966.

Juan Colinas Guerra was a *Guardia Civil* officer who had helped to suppress the insurrection in Bilbao, where he was given charge of police. Suspected of treason he was later imprisoned in Barcelona. On 'liberation' after the Insurgents had occupied Barcelona on 26 January 1939 he was tried and executed for his activities in Bilbao.

Antonio Cordón García was a captain of artillery who had taken early retirement in 1931 after participating in conspiracies against Primo de Rivera. A member of the PCE, he returned to the army and was one of the officers striving to restore order to the Ministry of War in July and August 1936. He acted as Chief of Staff on several fronts and in early 1938 became Head of Operations on the General Staff. Negrín appointed him Under-Secretary for the Army. In this post he was largely responsible for the efficient reorganisation of the Republican Army after the routs of April 1938. Promoted to general on 1 March 1939, he left Spain when Colonel Casado mounted his coup. He went to the USSR and studied at the Voroshilov military academy. Later he was an adviser in communist Poland and lived in France. He taught Spanish literature in Prague, dying in Rome in 1969.

Manuel Cristóbal Errandonea was a communist militant from Irún, in the Basque Country. Having defended Irún and San Sebastián, he commanded a brigade and then a division of the Army of the North. Later he was commander of the XXI Corps of the Army of the Levante. In exile he was elected a member of the political bureau of the PCE.

Juan Cueto Ibáñez was lieutenant-colonel of *Carabineros* in President Azaña's military household. Sent to Bilbao, he trained Basque militias. When the city fell he was captured and executed.

Edmundo Cuevas de la Peña was a captain of infantry who commanded the 8th Division and then rose to command Barcelona police forces and became

Director-General of Security in that city. Returning to Spain after a period in France, he was tried but acquitted of charges.

Luis Delage had been in charge of PCE propaganda in the Madrid Provincial Committee. Highly competent, he became commissar successively of the 6th Mixed Brigade, the 4th Division, the V Corps and the Army of the Ebro. After the war he lived in Cuba, returning clandestinely to Spain in 1946 and then moving to Prague. He returned to Spain after the death of Franco, dying in 1991.

Felipe Díaz Sandino was an Air Force officer who had served with distinction in the Riff war. He was a Republican conspirator and founder-member of UMRA. In 1936 he commanded the 3rd Group stationed at El Prat (Barcelona), where he played an important part in suppressing the military insurrection and was appointed counsellor for Defence in the Catalan autonomous government, the *Generalitat*. Later he was sent to Paris as military attaché but returned in early 1938 to command the Air Force in Catalonia. After the war he lived in different Latin American countries.

Eleuterio Díaz-Tendero Merchán rose through the ranks and was a captain stationed in the Ministry of War. Founder of the UMRA, he tried in vain to warn the Prime Minister, Santiago Casares Quiroga, that there was a conspiracy among the officers of the Madrid garrison. He was one of the officers who worked to restore order to the Ministry after the failed coup of July 1936. He is best known for his work in classifying army officers as loyal, fascist or indifferent, and was for a time in charge of the *Gabinete de Información y Control,* which investigated officers living in the Republican zone. He rose to the rank of colonel. After the war he went to France, where he was handed over to the Gestapo, who imprisoned him in Dachau concentration camp, where he died, probably murdered, on 13 February 1945.

Gustavo Durán Martínez was a composer who worked for Paramount Films. In 1936 he joined the Fifth Regiment and for a short time was Chief of Staff of the 11th (International) Brigade. His military ability must have been considerable, because, with no background of leadership, he commanded the 69th Brigade and later a division. He was briefly in charge of the *Servicio de Investigación Militar.* Later he commanded the XX Corps. Though a communist, Durán accepted the Casado coup. He was evacuated from Gandía in 1939 and went to London, where he married an American citizen and went to the USA. There he worked in the Museum of Modern Art, became a US citizen and served in the diplomatic service in Buenos Aires. Accused of disloyalty by Senator McCarthy, he entered the service of the UN. He died in Crete in 1969. He is 'Manuel García' in André Malraux's novel *L'Espoir* (*Man's Hope*).

Buenaventura Durruti was a railway mechanic whose life was dedicated to the active and violent wing of Spanish anarchism. He led groups called *Los justicieros* and *Los solidarios* which undertook robberies and assassinations. During the 1920s he lived in Latin America. Returning to Spain with the Second Republic, he became an important influence in the CNT and the FAI. In July 1936 he took a leading part in the repression of the military uprising and a few days later led a column towards Zaragoza. The column became the largest militia column, rising to 6,000 people. In November 1936 he led half of his column to Madrid, where he was killed, probably by a stray bullet, on 24 November.

Manuel Eixea Vilar was an *africanista* who held the Staff diploma. A lieutenant-colonel in one of the infantry regiments in Valencia, he commanded the Eixea-Uribe column which went to defend Madrid, where he was wounded. He helped to organise the Fifth Regiment and joined the PCE. As colonel he was stationed on the Teruel Front as commander of the XIX Corps. Differences of opinion with the PCE and the Soviet advisers led to his losing his command and being posted as military commander of Castellón, where he became Head of Operations in the defence of the XYZ line protecting Valencia in June 1938. He was sent to Alicante in February 1939 to help in the evacuation, but abandoned by the PCE though he himself refused an offer from Miaja to enable him to leave. Captured, he was court-martialled and executed.

José María Enciso Madollel, an infantry captain, commanded a militia column, the Presidential Battalion, the 44th Mixed Brigade and the 10th Division at Brunete. He was captured by the enemy in 1938, court-martialled and executed.

Antonio Escobar Huerta, colonel of *Guardia Civil* in Barcelona, was in large part responsible for the loyalty of the *Guardia Civil* to the Republic and the defeat of the insurrection. He went to Madrid, where he commanded a sector and was wounded. In 1937 he was appointed Government representative for public order and again wounded during the 'May Days'. Promoted general he commanded the Army of Extremadura. He supported the Casado rebellion. Known as a conservative and Catholic, his responsibility for the failure of the military uprising in Barcelona led inexorably to his execution.

Federico Escofet Alsina was a cavalry captain, who had been commander of the Catalan rural police, the *Mossos d'Esquadra*. He was condemned to death but amnestied for his actions in October 1934 in favour of Catalan independence. In 1936 he was Commissioner for Public Order in Catalonia and as such played an important part in suppressing the insurrection in Barcelona and in trying to keep arms out of the hands of the CNT/FAI, for which reason he fled to France. Returning in 1937, he took part in the battles of Brunete and Belchite. After the war he lived in Brussels, returning to Spain in 1978.

Manuel Estrada Manchón was a Staff major in the War Ministry. An officer of great culture and liberal ideas (he was a Freemason and a socialist, with a UGT membership card and during the war joined the PCE), he spoke French and Arabic. Having done his best together with a small group of other officers in the chaotic conditions of the Ministry in the first weeks of war, he was made Head of Information in the reconstituted General Staff of October 1936 and later Chief of Staff, where he clashed with the Under-Secretary, Asensio, and the Minister, Largo Caballero. He took an important part in organising guerrillas and obtaining information about the enemy. Perhaps for political reasons he left the General Staff in March 1937 for a position on the Staff of the Army of the Centre, after which he was Chief of Staff of various large units. He returned to his post as Head of Information in the General Staff, which he would retain until the war's end. He reorganised the section and tried in vain to create a unified Intelligence service but came up against the objections of Vicente Rojo, the Chief of Staff. He crossed into France with 70 boxes of documents of the Information service, now in the Salamanca archive. After collaborating with the French Intelligence service, he eventually went to Mexico and lived with considerable economic difficulty. After many years his situation improved when he joined the university as a lecturer. He died in 1980, having recovered his civil rights and pension.

Anselmo Fantova Lausín was an officer of progressive views, expelled from the Army in 1935. Rejoining in February 1936, he was a major in the Tank Regiment. In June 1937 he became ADC to General Gámir in the Army of the North.

Manuel Fe Lloréns was a major of infantry with the Staff diploma. Stationed in Madrid, he had a history of conspiracy against the Primo de Rivera regime and association with the CNT. For some time he was Head of the Operations Section of the General Staff. After the war he lived in Mexico.

Antonio Fernández Bolaños was a retired lieutenant-colonel of engineers and a socialist parliamentary deputy for Málaga. He served abroad in arms purchase missions. He was Under-Secretary for the Army under Prieto from May 1937 until March 1938 and then military attaché in Paris.

Enrique Fernández de Heredia Gaztáñaga was an artillery major. He commanded the 3rd Division, then the IV Corps and the XVIII Corps at Brunete and Teruel.

José Fernández Navarro had participated in the Republican conspiracy of 1930. In 1936 he was an infantry major posted to Madrid. As soon as the insurrection in Madrid was crushed he was ordered to form one of the first five volunteer battalions.

Bibiano Fernández Ossorio y Tafall, a natural scientist of distinction and mayor of Pontevedra at a young age, was a member of the Galician regionalist party and of the Republican Left. He was Under-Secretary of the Interior at the time of the military insurrection. In 1938 he was appointed commissar-general. After the war he went to Mexico and worked in the service of the UN, ending as Special Representative of the Secretary-General in Cyprus.

Hilario Fernández Recio was a captain of *Carabineros*. He organised new units of the Corps and later commanded special *Asalto* groups. He led the 67th Division and supported Casado, who made him commander of the III Corps.

Arnoldo Fernández Urbano was a major holding the Staff diploma. He was promoted to lieutenant-colonel and joined the General Staff reconstituted by Caballero in October 1936. In November he was Head of the Organisation Section and served in the defence of Madrid. He remained in the same post in.

In 1939, a colonel, he was executed by anti-Casado forces during the Casado uprising.

José Fernández Villabrille Calívara was general of division in command of the Second Division at Seville. Unwilling to declare the State of War he was arrested. He was not tried until 1939, when he lost his rank and pension.

José Ferrer Bonet was a *Guardia Civil* lieutenant who was military adviser to the Ferrer-Carod column in Aragon.

José Fontán Palomo was Staff officer in the defence of Madrid. He lived in Chile after the war.

Manuel Fresno Urzáiz was a captain of *Carabineros* who commanded the 16th Division.

José Luis Fuentes Barrio took an active part in conspiracies against Primo de Rivera. He became Commander of Artillery in the Republican Army.

José Fusimaña was commissar of the 11th Division and then of the XV Corps in the Army of the Ebro. After the war he went to the Soviet Union, where he was killed in the Second World War while leading guerrillas against the Germans.

Francisco Galán Rodríguez was the brother of Fermín Galán, executed for his part in the Republican uprising in Jaca in 1930. He left the *Guardia Civil* in 1931, returning when the war began in July 1936 and leading a militia column. He led the 22nd Mixed Brigade and the 51st Division and XIV Corps in the north, followed by commands in various army corps in the Levante. On 4 March 1939 he was appointed military governor of Cartagena, one of a number of postings of communists to evacuation points. After the pro-Casado uprising he took refuge on a warship and left with the Fleet for Bizerta. After the war he lived in Buenos Aires.

José María Galán Rodríguez, brother of the above, was a lieutenant of *Carabineros* and one of the founders of the communist Fifth Regiment. After leading militias he was the first commander of the 3rd Mixed Brigade. During the war he led brigades and divisions, finally becoming commander of the XXIII Corps until the end of 1938. After the war he went to the Soviet Union and was admitted to the Voroshilov academy. He was military adviser to Fidel Castro.

Manuel Gallego Calatayud was an artillery captain who commanded the artillery at Teruel, and later the VI Corps.

Juan José Gallego Pérez, an ex-NCO, commanded the 2nd Mixed Brigade and the 69th Division. Casado appointed him to command the I Corps, replacing Barceló.

Miguel Gallo Martínez, an infantry captain involved in the 1930 Jaca insurrection, was a member of the PCE and an organiser of the Fifth Regiment. He was first commander of the 6th Mixed Brigade, the 24th Division at Brunete and the X Corps. His troops were forced to cross into France. He returned to Spain and briefly held commands in Extremadura. He may have been in Catalonia during the December 1938–January 1939 battles. After crossing into France he returned to Spain, was captured and abandoned by the *casadistas* in prison, where he was judged and executed by the victors.

Manuel Gámir Ulíbarri was a general of brigade of monarchist views, who was nevertheless loyal to the Republic. He had taught and headed the Toledo Infantry Academy. After coordinating the organisation of columns sent to Teruel, he was posted to the north in 1937, where he took charge of the Basque Corps and, when Bilbao fell, of the Army of the North until Santander was lost. He had little authority in Asturias and delegated command to Colonel Adolfo Prada. Later he was liaison officer with the International Committee for the Withdrawal of Foreign Volunteers and then in charge of military training. After living in France he returned to Spain without any action being taken against him and lived in retirement until his death in 1962.

Manuel Gancedo Sáenz was an infantry captain and a member of the UMRA in Barcelona. He commanded the 32nd Division in Aragon and Catalonia. During the Second World War he was active in the French Resistance.

Juan García Gómez Caminero was a general of division and inspector-general. He succeeded in escaping from the Insurgents and returning to Republican Spain through Portugal. Retiring in 1937, he died in 1938.

Alejandro García Val was a labour activist and Secretary of the Union of Clothing Workers. He was a civilian representative on the first of Largo Caballero's General Staffs and later Director-General of Transport.

Carlos García Vallejo was an infantry major who commanded militia columns fighting to retake Córdoba in 1936. He led the XVII Corps in Levante and supported the Casado coup.

José García Vayas was an infantry major, commanding the guard in the convict prison of Santoña (Santander). He helped suppress the insurrection of the officers of his battalion and then led the XV Corps in Santander province. After the loss of the north he commanded a recruiting depot and then was appointed inspector of recruitment depots. He died in France in 1962.

Miguel García Vivancos was a driver by profession and a CNT activist who took part in the suppression of the military insurrection in Barcelona. Fighting in the *Aguiluchos* column he was commander of the 126th Brigade and then of the 25th Division at Belchite and Teruel. He was an anarchist who saw the need for formal militarisation and tried to cooperate with the communists. In exile he lived in Paris and became a well-known painter.

Antonio Garijo Hernández was a Staff captain, rising to the rank of lieutenant-colonel and Head of the Information Section of the Army of the Centre and then the Central Army Group (GERC). Communist sources accuse him of treachery, but there is no indication of this in the record of his conversations on 23 March 1939 at the enemy *pourparlers* at Burgos. He was probably in contact with the Fifth Column in Madrid and a strong supporter of Colonel Casado. Nevertheless, he was imprisoned and expelled from the army by the victors.

Antonio Gil Otero was an infantry major stationed in Lérida. He held command in the PSUC column and later led the 109th Brigade and the XI Corps.

Rodrigo Gil Ruiz was one of the artillery officers at the centre of Republican conspiracies in the 1920s. He was a member of the UMRA and in charge of an arms deposit in Madrid. He distributed rifles to civilians who were combating the Insurgent officers. He was briefly Under-Secretary for War. He was evacuated from Gandía with Colonel Casado's party in the *Galatea*, spending some time in the United Kingdom.

Francisco Giménez (or **Jiménez) Orge** was a colonel who had organised a cell of the UMRA in the Ministry of War. He led militias and, briefly, a division, but was 60 years old and not successful in his command. He was appointed military governor of Ciudad Real. His brothers Alfredo and Evelino were also army officers who remained loyal to the Republic.

Alejandro Goicoechea Omar was a retired engineers officer who planned the 'Iron Belt' around Bilbao, with intentionally weak points which he betrayed to the enemy. After the war he invented the articulated 'Talgo' train. He died in 1984.

Ricardo Gómez García was a *Carabineros* lieutenant who commanded the 1st Basque Division and the 56th Division of the Republican Army.

Agustín Gómez Morato was a general of division and commander of all military forces in the Spanish zone of the Moroccan Protectorate. He was arrested by the Insurgents, tried much later and sentenced to a prison term. He died in 1952. Perhaps the relative mildness of his sentence was due to the fact that three of his sons were serving in the Insurgent army.

Valentín González ('El Campesino') was one of the best-known militia leaders because of his violent and unpredictable character. He came to international notice through his autobiography, *Listen Comrades*, published in the United Kingdom in 1952 at the height of the Cold War. He was one of the best-known communists to leave the party, which he had joined in 1929. He played an important part in suppressing the military insurrection in Madrid. Organising his own militias he was given the rank of *mayor de milicias*. He became commander of the 10th Mixed Brigade and then 46th Division at Brunete, Teruel and Belchite. He claims that the other communist leaders abandoned his division in Teruel. Modesto and Líster, accusing him of cowardice, dismissed him during the battle of the Ebro. He ended the war in a recruitment depot. He was rumoured to have been violent and careless of the lives of his men. It is very unlikely that Negrín would have thought of giving him an army command, as Casado alleges. For all his disagreements with the communist leaders, he was admitted to the Soviet Union and studied at the Frunze academy. Falling into disgrace he spent time in prison and succeeded in escaping. Having lived for many years in France, he died in Madrid in 1983.

Miguel González Inestal was a union secretary in San Sebastián. The CNT nominated him to be one of the four sub-commissar-generals. He occupied this post throughout the war, trying to persuade CNT militants of the importance of militarisation and at the same time defending CNT interests. After the war he lived in Chile, returning to Spain years later.

Serafín González Inestal, brother of the above, helped to organise mixed brigades in Albacete and was then commissar-inspector of the Army of Andalusia. He was imprisoned after the war.

Miguel González Pérez Caballero was an infantry lieutenant. He commanded the 8th Division. Sentenced to death by the victors, his penalty was commuted and he served three years.

Vicente Guarner Vivanco was an *africanista* and a military intellectual. He was Professor of Tactics in the Higher War School and held the Staff diploma. He observed the first British tank manoeuvres on Salisbury Plain. As Head of Public Order in the Catalan *Generalitat* he reorganised the *Guardia de Asalto*. A member of UMRA, he took a major part in the suppression of the military insurrection on 19 July 1936 in Barcelona. He was appointed Under-Secretary for Defence of the *Generalitat*. He became commander of the Aragon Front in 1937 and in May Chief of Staff of the Army of the East. In 1938 be became Director of the Staff Academy. Appointed consul in Tangiers, he tried in vain to stir up tension in the Spanish zone of the Moroccan Protectorate. He died in Mexico in 1981. He was fortunate to escape being handed over to the Gestapo by the Vichy authorities when he was in Casablanca in 1940. In Mexico he took Mexican nationality and was made a colonel in the Army.

Ernesto Güemes Ramos was an infantry captain. He commanded the 24th Mixed Brigade, a division and later the III and the XXI Corps. He died in 1970 in Spain.

Casiano Guerricaechevérría Usabel was an artillery captain. He commanded the *miñones de Vizcaya*, a rural police force. He became head of Basque artillery but deserted soon after the fall of Bilbao in June 1937.

Joaquín d'Harcourt Got was a captain in the Medical Corps, rising to head surgical services in the Republican Army. He went to Mexico.

Julián Henríquez Caubín held senior legal posts in public bodies. As a PCE member he organised the militias in the Fifth Regiment, later commanding the 37th Mixed Brigade. In the battle of the Ebro, on which he wrote an important book, he was Chief of Staff of the 35th Division, having obtained the Staff diploma. After the war he lived in Mexico.

Manuel Hernández Arteaga was an infantry major. He was imprisoned for responsibility in the loss of Málaga, but absolved. Later he became military governor of Alicante, where he was arrested at the end of the war and sentenced to death.

Angel Hernández del Castillo was an infantry captain in Gijón. Arrested by the Insurgents, he was released when the Simancas barracks was stormed. He commanded a division in the north.

Juan Hernández Saravia was a senior artillery officer who had been significant in the struggle in the 1920s between his corps and Primo de Rivera. Though a pious Catholic, he believed in separation of Church and State. A fervent Republican and member of UMRA, he was a close friend of Manuel Azaña, Minister of War, Prime Minister and later President of the Republic, and accompanied him till his death in Montauban in November 1940. He presided over Azaña's Military Cabinet but left the Army in 1934. He tried to warn Azaña about the danger of a military uprising and, in particular, about General Franco. Returning in 1936 in the chaos of the militia period he was active in the Ministry of War, organising the battalions of volunteers, and became Minister of War in August 1936. He held various commands and then was put in charge of anti-aircraft defence (*Defensa contra aeronaves*, DECA). Later he organised the Army of the Levante, which he led during the battle of Teruel from December 1937 until February 1938. Later, now a general, he commanded the Eastern Army Group (*Grupo de Ejércitos de la Región Oriental*) in Aragon and Catalonia until disagreements with Juan Modesto and General Rojo required his resignation. After the war he lived in France and later in Mexico, where he occupied high posts in Republican governments in exile until his death in 1962 (*see* Aroca Mohedano, *General Juan Hernández Saravia, el ayudante militar de Azaña*, 2006, in the Bibliography).

Jesús Hernández Tomás was a leader of the PCE and editor of the newspaper of the party. He became Minister of Education in Largo Caballero's Government of 4 September 1936, where he took an important part in developing education in the Republican Army. In early 1938 he helped to engineer the exit of Indalecio Prieto from the Ministry of Defence. From April 1938 he was commissar-general of the central-south zone until dismissed by the Casado coup. In exile he broke with the PCE and wrote an anti-communist book (*see* Bibliography).

Emilio Herrera Linares was lieutenant-colonel of engineers and Director of the Higher Aeronautical School. A specialist in aeronautics of international rank, he remained loyal to the Republic though a convinced monarchist. In the rank of general he was charged with responsibility for technical services and training schools for all aspects of the Air Force. In November 1938 he was appointed military attaché in Chile. From 1960 to 1962 he headed the Republican government in exile and continued his highly regarded scientific work.

Ignacio Hidalgo de Cisneros y López de Montenegro was a major in the Air Force, with a gallant record in the Riff war. After his marriage to the divorcee Constancia de la Mora, which scandalised conservative society, he was military attaché in Germany and Italy, 1933–5. In 1936 he was ADC to the Prime Minister, Santiago Casares Quiroga. In the war he ensured the loyalty of the air base at Getafe. After commanding I Group he supervised the arrival and distribution of the Soviet aircraft, which began to arrive in October 1936. At about this time he joined the PCE. Later he became Chief of Staff of the Republican Air Force. In September 1938 he was promoted general. In December 1938 he negotiated a further 108 million dollars' worth of war material from the Soviet leaders. In 1954 he was appointed member of the Central Committee of the PCE. He died in 1966 in Bucharest.

Juan Ibarrola Orueta was a captain in the *Guardia Civil*. He commanded the 50th Division in Asturias and the XXII Corps at Teruel. After the war he was sentenced to 30 years' imprisonment but was released under an amnesty.

Avelino de la Iglesia Martín was a lieutenant-colonel in charge of a recruiting depot. He was second in command of a sector in Andalusia.

Federico de la Iglesia Navarro was a major of the Staff Corps who served on the Madrid Staff in 1936, and was later Chief of Staff of the 34th Division, the V Corps and the Army of the Levante. He left Spain with Colonel Casado and spent some time in London.

Daniel Irezábal Goti was an infantry major commanding the recruitment depot in Bilbao. He commanded a division and was captured and executed by the Insurgents.

Carlos Jiménez Canito was an infantry major who had been the target of right-wing gunmen in the spring of 1936. He led militias and then the 23rd Division. At the end of the war he was military governor of Murcia. He was executed by the victors.

Gregorio Jover Cortés was a CNT militant who led a militia column into Aragon in August 1936. He commanded the 28th Division. He died in exile in Mexico.

Luis Jubert Salieti was an infantry captain in the Ortiz column in Aragon. He commanded the 25th Division until killed in action.

Enrique Jurado Barrio was an artillery major, stationed in Morocco but on leave in Spain when the war began. He commanded militia columns and the 1st Division, then the IV and the XVIII Corps. Later he was Inspector-General of Anti-Aircraft Defence and was promoted to general on 18 September 1938. In February 1939 he took over the command of the Eastern Army Group (GERO) from Hernández Saravia. Crossing into France he declined to return to what remained of Republican territory. He lived in Uruguay, directing official land valuations, dying in 1965.

Víctor Lacalle Seminario was a lieutenant-colonel of engineers. He was ordered to form one of five volunteer battalions on 19 July 1936. He commanded militia columns, the 50th Brigade and the 12th Division. For a time he led the Autonomous Cuenca Group but when it was formed into an army corps he was not given the command. He spent the rest of the war in administrative posts.

Pedro La Cerda y López Mollinedo was a general of division. He commanded the Burgos administrative division briefly. In February 1937 he took over in command in Valencia, retiring shortly afterwards.

Ernesto de la Fuente Torres was a Staff captain in Bilbao who became Chief of Staff of the Basque Army Corps. Captured, he was executed by the Insurgents in December 1937.

Angel Lamas Arroyo was an infantry captain with the Staff diploma. He was Chief of Staff of the VII Corps, then of the Basque Corps and then of the Army of the North. Captured, he wrote a long memorandum on the war in the north of Spain in which he claimed to have obstructed Staff work and to have hindered Republican resistance.

Jesús Larrañaga was a Basque communist metalworker who had been in the Soviet Union before the war. He was deputy in the *Cortes* for his province, Guipúzcoa. He led militias and occupied important civilian posts in the north. After the war he lived clandestinely in Spain, where he was captured and executed.

Domiciano Leal was a member of the JSU who led the 10th Brigade and replaced 'El Campesino' at the head of the 46th Division. He was killed in the battle of the Ebro.

Enrique Líster Forján, a member of the PCE, studied political and military matters in the Soviet Union. In 1936 in Spain he engaged in agitprop in the Army. During the war he led militias, was a leader of the Fifth Regiment and the 1st Mixed Brigade, later the 11th Division and the V Corps. He suppressed the anarchist communes in Aragon in 1937. He was the first militia officer to be promoted lieutenant-colonel and one of two to reach the rank of colonel. At the end of the war he crossed into France, returning to Spain in February 1939, only to leave with other leading communists when Colonel Casado mounted his coup. In Moscow he studied at the Frunze academy and took an important part in organising guerrillas in Spain in 1945 and 1946. He broke with the PCE over the Czech crisis of 1968 and was expelled. Returning to Madrid after Franco's death, he died in 1994 (*see* Bibliography and Chapter 6).

Justo López Mejías was an infantry lieutenant who had been involved in the Jaca anti-monarchist insurrection of 1930. He was involved in the formation of militias and later commanded the 20th Brigade and the 38th and 68th Divisions.

José López Otero was an engineers major posted to the Staff of the Army of the Centre. He was murdered by communist troops during the struggle between them and the *casadistas*.

Rafael López Tienda was an engineers captain who accompanied Captain Bayo on the failed expedition to recover Majorca for the Republic in August 1936. Afterwards he led a militia column and was killed in the battle for Madrid in November 1936.

Francisco Llano de la Encomienda had had two brilliant tours of duty in Morocco. In 1936, though only a general of brigade, the Popular Front Government made him commander of the Barcelona administrative division. He vacillated during the attempted uprising of 19 July 1936 and was dismissed from his command. In November, however, he was sent to take charge of the important Northern Front but was unable to impose his authority and was complained of by the Basque President, who considered him completely ineffective, as did other political leaders in the north. He was replaced by General Gámir in 1937. After occupying a number of posts, none of which included combat leadership, he went to Mexico after the war, dying there in 1963. (If he had surrendered to the victors in Spain he might have suffered the same death penalty as the *Guardia Civil* commanders Aranguren and Escobar, because he had given evidence at the trials of the Insurgent leaders.)

Virgilio Llanos Manteca had been a prompter in the theatre. He was political commissar in Captain Bayo's failed expedition to recover Majorca in August 1936 and in the López Tienda column in Madrid. Later he was commissar of the XII Corps in the Army of the Ebro and later commissar of the Army of the East. CNT authors accuse him of persecuting anarchists. He gave evidence against the leaders of the POUM. His last action in the war was to accompany the forces sent to crush the rebellion in Cartagena in March 1939.

Julio Mangada Rosenhorn had radical ideas and was considered eccentric as a vegetarian, Esperantist, spiritualist and nudist. He was also a Freemason. His service in Morocco was distinguished though he had no sympathy for the general *africanista* attitude. He took part in the abortive Republican plot in 1930. He created a scene in front of assembled troops when his superior, the later Insurgent Goded, refused to shout '*Viva la República!*' after a speech. Persecuted by his superiors, he left the Army in 1935, returning when the war began. In 1936 he led one of the first five volunteer battalions and later a sizeable militia column which elected him 'general' but had no important position in the Republican Army, being military governor of Albacete and colonel in charge of the recruitment depot in Ciudad Real. After the war he took ship to French North Africa and then to Mexico, where he was greatly aided by Esperantists worldwide.

José Ignacio Mantecón, a distinguished archivist, was a member of Azaña's *Izquierda Republicana* but entered the communist orbit during the war. Having been commissar of the 72nd Brigade he was appointed Government delegate in Aragon, where he oversaw the destruction of the anarchist Council of Aragon in summer 1937. He later became commissar of the Army of the East. In Mexico after the war he became a distinguished professor of bibliology and the specialised aspects of cataloguing.

Servando Marenco Reja was an officer in the Accounting Corps (*Cuerpo de Intervención Militar*). In 1930 he was intended to head the Republican insurrection in Lérida. In 1931 he was a candidate to the *Cortes* for the Radical-Socialist Party. When the Civil War began he was appointed Inspector-General of Militias and later of recruiting depots. At the end of the war he was in command of a machine-gun battalion covering the retreat through Catalonia.

Ernesto Marina Arias was a lieutenant-colonel of infantry, ordered to form one of the first volunteer battalions. He was later in charge of a recruitment depot.

Manuel Márquez Sánchez was an infantry captain who helped create the Fifth Regiment and commanded its *Primer Regimiento de Acero* in the sierra north of Madrid. He later led the 19th Brigade, the 18th Division and the VII Corps, achieving the rank of lieutenant-colonel. After the war he went to the Soviet Union, studied at the Voroshilov military academy, and later went to Yugoslavia and Czechoslovakia.

José Martín Blázquez was a captain in the Supply Corps stationed in Madrid. He worked in the embryonic General Staff in the Ministry of War in July and August 1936. He went to France and 1937 and did not return. He wrote a book about his experiences (*see* Bibliography).

Jesús Martínez de Aragón was a communist lawyer who led the 2nd Mixed Brigade. He was killed in April 1937 leading his troops in the Casa del Campo on the west side of Madrid.

Toribio Martínez Cabrera was a general of brigade of strong Republican sentiments. An instructor in the Higher Military School, he occupied important Staff posts. He crushed the 1936 insurrection in the Cartagena naval base. At the end of 1936 he was sent to the north as inspector-general to try to put some better order into the military situation. In November 1936 he became chief of the General Staff but was judged partially responsible for the loss of Málaga in February 1937. The communists and the Soviet advisers considered him at the least incompetent and possibly treacherous. He spent some months in detention during the enquiries into the Málaga disaster. The charges were dropped in May 1938. He became military governor of Madrid in December, a post of little responsibility. He favoured the Casado coup but was executed by the Nationalist victors, despite favourable evidence from important figures in the new regime, probably because of his responsibility in the failure of the insurrection and the courts martial and death sentences of Insurgent officers in 1936, as well as the murder of 150 naval officers in Cartagena, for which he denied responsibility.

Pedro Martínez Cartón was a communist deputy in the *Cortes*. He led militias in Extremadura and commanded the 16th Mixed Brigade. He succeeded in taking the Insurgent stronghold of Santa María de la Cabeza in 1937. Later he led the 64th Division. He opposed the Casado coup in March 1939 but was defeated. After the war he went to the Soviet Union.

Fernando Martínez Monje (or Monge) Restoy was a general of brigade who commanded the Valencia administrative division. He was a member of the committee organising the new army and played an important part in the creation of the new mixed brigades. Later he commanded the Army of the South but was disgraced because of the loss of Málaga in February 1937. After his delayed rehabilitation he occupied administrative posts, and lived in Buenos Aires after the war.

Angel Martínez Peñalver was an infantry colonel in Tarragona who commanded militias in Aragon in 1936.

Carlos Masquelet Lacaci was a general of division, a Freemason and a liberal Republican. A close friend of President Azaña, he was a distinguished specialist in fortifications. He was Minister of War in the Popular Front Government of February 1936. He was the author of a general plan of fortifications around Madrid, but occupied no other command during the war. He took refuge in France in 1939.

Manuel Matallana Gómez was a major with the Staff diploma. He was Head of the Information Section and later Chief of Staff in the Army of the Centre and then, as a general, Chief of Staff of the Central Army Group (GERC). In 1939 he was given the command of the GERC. He supported the Casado uprising, transmitting valuable information to the enemy. Given his background and his services to the Insurgent Nationalists, whom, he claimed, he had helped surreptitiously since 1937, he served a relatively short term of imprisonment, but lost his career and had to support his family as best he could, dying in 1956.

Pedro Mateo Merino was a mathematics student who commanded a battalion, then the 101st Mixed Brigade and the 35th Division on the Ebro. After the war he studied in the Frunze military academy and went to Yugoslavia and for some years to Cuba. He returned to Spain in 1972 and died in 2000 (*see* Bibliography).

Aurelio Matilla was a major in the Staff Corps, stationed in a post concerned with topography. He was Chief of Staff of the XIX Corps at Teruel. He rose to be Chief of Staff of the Eastern Army Group (GERO). He lived in France after the war but later in South America.

Eduardo Medrano Rivas was a retired artillery officer who returned to the army, serving as ADC to Colonel Villalba in command of militia in Aragon and later commanding the 33rd Division. He was captured and executed by the victors after the war.

Ernesto Melero Blanco was a 53-year-old infantry captain promoted from the ranks who played an important part in crushing the military insurrection in the Carabanchel barracks and later commanded the 6th Division.

Arturo Mena Roig was a retired lieutenant-colonel who led militias in Toledo and Madrid. He later led the 61st Division and the VII Corps. He was in his late fifties but looked much older. He was always accompanied by a pet monkey.

Julio Mena Zueco was general in command of the 11th Infantry Brigade at Burgos. Refusing to take part in the insurrection, he was arrested. Tried in 1937, he was declared innocent of the charges but nevertheless dismissed from the army.

Leopoldo Menéndez López had had a gallant career in Morocco, but his ideas were liberal. A cultured and intellectually curious officer, he attended courses at the Staff College. Disappointed with Primo de Rivera, he associated with Republican conspirators and was a founder member of the *Unión Militar Republicana*. He was an officer of the Presidential Guard from May 1936 onwards. The uprising led to the execution of his much more left-wing brother, Arturo, taken off a train on his way from Barcelona to Madrid. When Juan Hernández Saravia became Minister of War he appointed his fellow artillery officer Leopoldo Menéndez to be Under-Secretary (6 August 1936). Menéndez despised the militias. Of the militia commanders, Menéndez respected only Modesto. He was hostile to the communists but joined no political party. In 1937, Rojo proposed Menéndez as commander of the XX Corps. He led the struggle which led to the occupation of Teruel at Christmas 1937. Later he became commander of the Army of Operations (*Ejército de Maniobras*), succeeding in blocking the Insurgent advance on Valencia. He then took over the Army of the Levante. He was now a general. His support for the Casado coup was hesitant, but he saw it possibly as the lesser of two evils. He left Spain on the British warship *Galatea* on 29/30 March 1939. He stayed briefly in Great Britain, then went to France and finally to the military academy in Colombia, where he was offered a teaching post. Later he returned to France and then to Mexico, where he died in 1960.

Rafael Méndez, was a socialist pharmacologist who was very close to Negrín, who entrusted him with important posts, among them those of Under-Secretary of the Interior and Director General of *Carabineros*.

Francisco Menoyo Baños was an engineers captain and also a socialist deputy and sometime mayor of Granada. At the beginning of 1938 he was leading the IX Corps and at the end of the year he replaced Colonel Prada in command of the Army of Andalusia. The victors executed him in 1939.

Cipriano Mera Sanz was a trade union militant in the building industry, and a CNT leader who came to accept the militarisation of the militias. He had led militias which crushed the insurrection in July 1936 in the military centres of Alcalá de Henares and Guadalajara. He acted as political leader of the del Rosal column. Later he led the 14th Division and the IV Corps. He was one of the militia leaders to rise to the rank of lieutenant-colonel. He seems to have been deceived by Casado, whom he supported in crushing communist forces in Madrid. Condemned to death after the war, his sentence was commuted. Later he was amnestied and lived for the rest of his life in France, dying in 1975 (*see* Chapter 6).

José Miaja Menant, general of brigade, had had a career where garrison posts had alternated with postings in Morocco and in recruitment depots. In March 1936 he took command of the 1st Infantry Brigade in Madrid. He took over the entire Madrid administrative division and was briefly Minister of War in the short-lived Martínez Barrio Government of 19 July 1939, because he was considered a conservative. He led a failed attempt to retake Córdoba. His great moment came in November 1936, when he was placed at the head of the Defence Junta of Madrid. Later he was commander of the entire central zone. In April 1938 he became commander of the Central Army Group (GERC). He accepted the Casado coup and the post of President of the National Defence Council. He flew out of Spain and went to Mexico, dying in 1938 (*see* Chapter 6).

Juan Guilloto León, alias Modesto, occupied leading posts in communist militias before the war and was second commander of the Fifth Regiment. He led the 4th Division, the V Corps and, from the summer of 1938, the Army of the Ebro. He was one of the first militia officers to be promoted to lieutenant-colonel and the only one to become a general. After the war he attended the Frunze academy in the Soviet Union, dying in 1968 (*see* also Chapter 6).

Nicolás Molero Lobo was a general of division commanding the Valladolid administrative division in July 1936. Refusing to join the insurrection, he was gaoled until his release in 1940.

Alberto Montaud Noguerol was an engineers lieutenant-colonel who was Professor of Fortification in the Higher War School. Chief of Staff in the Basque Corps, he was dismissed shortly before the fall of Bilbao in June 1937. Since his whereabouts was unknown, he was dismissed from the Republican Army. He went to Latin America, returning to Spain in later years.

Gustavo Montaud Noguerol was a major of engineers who headed the Popular War School for engineer officers. He was awarded the Medal of Duty (*Medalla del Deber*) in 1938.

Domingo de Moriones y Larraga, the Marquis of Oroquieta, was an engineers lieutenant-colonel in the Railway Regiment. After participating in the suppression of the July 1936 military uprising in the capital he commanded militias and later the 2nd Division and the I Corps. In 1938 he took over the Army of Andalusia. He did not support the Casado coup and was dismissed from his command. After the war he was gaoled. He died in 1965.

José de los Mozos Muñoz, a major of engineers, supervised the placing of mines under the Alcázar of Toledo. In 1938 he held an important post in the inspection of engineers of the Army of the Ebro.

Félix Muedra Miñón was a captain of infantry who served on the Staff of the Army of the Centre and became Chief of Staff of the Central Army Group (GERC) at the end of the war. Communist writers accuse him of treachery. However, he does not seem to have profited from it. During the 1950s, after serving a term of imprisonment, he was running a little shop.

Bartolomé Muntané Cirici was an infantry captain who held the distinguished *Laureada* medal for gallantry in Morocco. When the war began he tried to counter the Insurgents in his Moroccan regiment, but failed and had to make his way back to Spain via the French zone. He commanded the 71st and 41st Divisions and the XI Corps of the Republican Army and was Head of the Operations Section of the Army of the East. He lived for many years in exile, returning to Spain in 1977.

Pablo Murga Ugarte was an engineers captain who led a spy ring in Bilbao, communicating military information to the enemy. He was executed by the Basque authorities in November 1936.

Antonio Naranjo Limón was a major in the *Guardia Civil* who took charge of the Organisation Section of the Basque Staff. He went to France, did not return to Spain and was dismissed from the Republican Army in March 1938.

Enrique Navarro Abuja, an infantry lieutenant-colonel, commanded the 2nd Division and then the Tank Brigade. In October 1937 he was Chief of Staff of the Armoured Division.

Miguel Núñez de Prado y Subsielas was a general of division in the Air Force. He had enjoyed a brilliant career in Morocco, gaining four merit promotions. He was sent to Zaragoza to try to convince the local army commander, General Miguel Cabanellas, not to rise in rebellion against the Republic. Arrested, he is assumed to have been executed though there is no documentary indication of this. There is some suspicion that he may have been assassinated.

Urbano Orad de la Torre was an artillery officer and a member of UMRA. After contributing to shelling the rebellious officers in the Montaña barracks, he distributed arms to the militias. Later he led the 20th Division and ended the war as military governor of Almería. He was condemned to death by the victors but his sentence was commuted and he profited from amnesties. He ran a preparatory academy for cadets and became a well-known and admired figure in Seville.

Antonio Ortega Gutiérrez was a long-term NCO of *Carabineros* who had recently been promoted to officer's rank. He took part in the combats around Irún and San Sebastián and commanded brigades on the Madrid Front. He joined the PCE and had particular responsibility in the crushing of the POUM after the Barcelona 'May Days'. Later he led the III Corps but tried to remain neutral in the struggle between the *casadistas* and communist-led units. Captured by the enemy, he was executed.

Daniel Ortega Martínez was a doctor, member of the PCE's Central Committee and *Cortes* deputy for Cádiz. He was a civilian adviser on Caballero's General Staff of 20 October 1936. On 29 July 1938 he became major of infantry – backdated to December 1936 – to be almost at once promoted to colonel. He was Head of Services in Madrid, where Colonel Casado arrested him. Captured by the enemy, he was tried in Cádiz and shot on 7 August 1941.

Antonio Ortiz Ramírez was a carpenter and CNT militant who led one of the first anarchist columns which marched into Aragon as soon as the military uprising was crushed in Barcelona. He was for some time commander of the 25th Division but dismissed because of tensions with the communists. He graduated from the Popular School for Staff officers. In France he was imprisoned in the Le Vernet camp and in North Africa, but served gallantly in the Free French forces. He organised a failed plot to kill Franco. He died in France.

Antonio Ortiz Roldán was a leader of the MAOC and member of the PCE in Espejo (Córdoba). He led militias and the 52nd, 73rd and 226th Mixed Brigades. Later he headed the 42nd Division and was one of the militia officers who rose to the rank of lieutenant-colonel. After the war he studied at the Frunze academy and then went to Yugoslavia.

Ossorio y Tafall, *see* **Fernández Ossorio y Tafall**.

Miguel Palacios Martínez was an Army doctor who had taken part in Republican conspiracies. He was on the Staff of the Uribarri column and commanded the 10th and the 39th Mixed Brigades and later the V Division. Finally he commanded the XVI Corps in the Levante. He contacted the Fifth Column in Madrid in 1939 and participated in the Casado coup. His brother was a member of the Fifth column and defended him at his court martial. His death sentence was commuted but he remained in prison until 1948.

Carlos Pedemonte Sabín was a Staff major who led militias in 1936, having managed to return to Republican territory from Río de Oro (Western Sahara), where he was local governor.

Primitivo Peire Cabaleiro was a lieutenant-colonel in charge of the machine-gun battalion stationed at Castellón. He commanded the 44th Division at Belchite. In 1938, when Republican forces were routed in Aragon, he was made head of a camp for regrouping scattered units and then military governor of Igualada (Barcelona).

Guillermo de la Peña Cusi was an infantry major heading a recruitment depot. He presided over the court martial which sentenced rebel Generals Goded and Fernández Burriel to death for their insurrection in Barcelona. He commanded the 1st Division of *L'Exèrcit de Catalunya*. When he and the members of the court martial were themselves tried in 1939, the deaths sentences imposed were all commuted.

Peñalver, *see* **Martínez Peñalver**.

Juan Perea Capulino was a retired infantry captain and Republican conspirator, who had close contacts with the CNT and was anti-communist. He commanded militias, the 5th Division and the IV and XXI Corps. On 30 March 1938 he was given command of the Army of the East. In exile he lived in Mexico.

Enrique Pérez Farrás was an artillery major who had commanded Catalan police during the failed revolution of 1934. He was amnestied when the Popular Front won the elections of 1936, becoming a military adviser to President

Companys. He accompanied the Durruti column into Aragon. After militarisation he was not given command of troops but became military governor of Tarragona and later of Gerona. He died in Mexico in 1949.

Augusto Pérez Garmendia was a Staff major and ADC to Colonel Aranda, who rebelled in Oviedo. On 18 July 1936 Pérez Garmendia was on leave in San Sebastián. He led Basque militias to try to retake Vitoria but was captured by the Insurgents and died of his wounds.

José Pérez Gazzolo was an infantry major and ADC to General Miaja at the outset of war. He became Chief of Staff of the Army of the South and then deputy Chief of Staff in Madrid, where he stayed until the Casado uprising, when he was murdered by communist forces in the minor civil war that took place in the city in March 1939.

José Pérez Martínez was a major in the *Guardia de Asalto*. He became ADC to General Miaja. He supported Casado, but his responsibility in the crushing of the military insurrection in July 1936 made it advisable for him to leave. He was in the French Foreign Legion but later returned to Spain, where he received the death sentence, which was commuted.

Jesús Pérez Salas had conspired against Primo de Rivera and had been for a time in Azaña's Military Cabinet. He left Spain because of his involvement in the failed uprising of 1934, returning with the Popular Front victory in February 1936. He led the Macià-Companys militia and commanded it when it became the 30th Division. In March 1938 he became for a brief time Under-Secretary for the Army. After the war he went to Mexico. In his book he reflects the views of the professional officers who could not adjust to the new 'Popular' army (*see* Bibliography).

Joaquín Pérez Salas, brother of Jesús, had also been a Republican conspirator. In 1936 he was a major of artillery with a high professional reputation. Briefly he led the Army of the South. He commanded the Artillery of the Army of Operations and several corps, ending the war in command of the VIII Corps in the Army of Andalusia. He crushed the pro-surrender uprising in Cartagena in March 1939, which probably led to his death sentence. Despite being well known as anti-communist and having protected many people in danger because of their political views, the sentence was carried out. He was said to have courageously insulted the court-martial judges, telling them that they, not he, were the rebels. Yet he was also known for having refused to wear the new officers' insignia of the Republican Army.

Manuel Pérez Salas was another brother in the same family as the preceding two officers (a further one was in Franco's army). He was a lieutenant-colonel of infantry in Valencia. He directed one of the Popular War Schools for training new officers. Because of his role in repressing the July 1936 insurrection he received the death penalty.

Vicente Pertegás Martínez was a primary school teacher and member of the PCE who commanded the 9th Division.

Sebastián Pozas Perea was a cavalry general of brigade with no history of political activity, and an *africanista* who believed in the absolute authority of civilian rule. As judge in courts martial for the failed Catalan uprising of 1934 he insisted that the Republic had suspended the *Generalitat* from its functions and thus that the officers who had supported the bid for Catalan independence were guilty of military rebellion. As inspector-general of the *Guardia Civil* in February 1936 he had rejected Franco's suggestion to bring out the *Guardia* to reject the Popular Front victory in the elections. During the war he maintained the loyalty of the *Guardia Civil* in Madrid, although many units of the *Guardia Civil* hesitated and joined the Insurgents. Pozas was successively Minister of the Interior, held command on the Central Front and in the Army of the East. However, was not able to weld disparate forces together and lead them with determination. He was replaced at the head of the Army of the East by Colonel **Juan Perea** and occupied the posts of military governor of Gerona and Figueras during the fighting retreat of the Republican Army through Catalonia. In exile he lived in Mexico.

Adolfo Prada Vaquero had taken early retirement in 1931. In 1936 he led militias, the 7th Division and the VI Corps on the Madrid Front. Then he commanded the XIV Corps in the north, where he remained until the fall of Gijón in October 1937, escaping by ship. For a short time in 1938 he led the Army of Andalusia and later the Army of Extremadura. Colonel Casado entrusted him with the Army of the Centre in March 1939 and as such he officially surrendered Madrid to the Nationalist Insurgents. Death sentences were imposed on him but commuted. He later served several years in gaol. After release he died in 1962.

José Riquelme y López-Bago was a general of division, an *africanista* and expert Arabist. He was also of deep Republican sympathies. Replaced in command of the Madrid administrative division in September 1936 after several failures, he spent the rest of the war in honorary positions, ending as military governor of Barcelona. After the war he lived in France, where he died in 1972 at the age of 91.

Ambrosio Ristori de la Cuadra was a major of marine infantry who was ADC to José Giral when the latter was Prime Minister between 20 August and 4 September 1936. He was killed in action that autumn.

Vicente Rojo Lluch was a recently promoted major who rose to the rank of lieutenant-general. He had been the highly respected Professor of Tactics at the Toledo Military Academy. He was on Caballero's Staff, heading it by October 1936, and during the defence of Madrid, rising to be Chief of Staff of the entire army and as such planning all the great offensives of the Civil War. After entering France he considered that it was pointless to continue the war. He spent his exile mostly in Bolivia as a professor at the military college. He returned to Spain in 1957, was tried, sentenced and amnestied, but never recovered his rank nor was granted his military pension.

Carlos Romero Giménez was a highly decorated *africanista* who had spent much time in gaol for his Republican sympathies. He took early retirement according to the Azaña decree of May 1931. He was also a scholarly writer on military subjects and an inventor. Returning to the army when the war began he was promoted to major and led the 4th Mixed Brigade, taking part in the defence of Madrid. He then led the 6th Division and the II Corps at Brunete. He subsequently led the XIII Corps of the Army of the Levante. After the Civil War he took part in the French Resistance based at Bordeaux, sabotaging German war production in France. He was arrested and tortured by the Gestapo. Managing to escape, he finally reached Mexico, where he edited a military journal, dying there aged 87.

Francisco del Rosal Rico was an infantry lieutenant-colonel who had conspired against Primo de Rivera. He commanded CNT militias in the central zone, but did not obtain combat commands, ending the war as military governor of Tarragona. He died in Nicaragua in 1945.

José Rovira Canals was a leader of the POUM who led the Lenin column and then the 29th Division. After this unit was disbanded in 1937 Rovira was arrested. Freed by the intervention of the War Minister, Indalecio Prieto, during the Second World War Rovira led a unit responsible for maintaining contacts across the Pyrenees with London via Portugal.

Esteban Rovira Pacheco was a lieutenant of *Carabineros* who led the 42nd Brigade and the 12th, 15th and 17th Divisions. Captured by the enemy and sentenced to death, he escaped and died in Latin America.

Antonio Rubert de la Iglesia was an infantry captain who commanded various units in Madrid. Later he led the 49th and the 9th Divisions, and finally, as a lieutenant-colonel, the VII Corps. He managed to board a ship leaving Alicante in March 1939.

Niceto Rubio García was a major in the Air Force and a hero of long-distance flights in the 1920's. In 1936 he commanded troops in the sierras north of Madrid. He left Spain for unknown reasons.

Fernando Sabio Dutoit was a retired captain of the Supply Corps who led militias at the beginning of the war. He was made an honorary leader of the Fifth Regiment and commanded the 5th Mixed Brigade but had no further important combat commands. He led *Carabineros* in Catalonia and at the end of 1938 was on the Staff of the Army Group of the East (GERO).

Rafael Sabio Dutoit was a major of engineers and rose to be principal commander of engineers in the Madrid area.

Eduardo Sáez Aranaz was an infantry captain who was for some time Chief of Staff of the Army of the Levante. Later he occupied the same post in the Army of Extremadura despite the opposition of the Information and Control Office. Later he was on the Staff of the GERC. He spent several years after the war doing forced labour in the Valle de los Caídos.

Mario Salafranca Barrio was a colonel in charge of the Ciudad Real recruitment depot. He commanded militia columns and then a sector in Andalusia. At the end of 1938 he became Deputy Chief of Staff of the Army of Andalusia.

Fernando Salavera Camps was an infantry major. He was the military adviser of the Ortiz column in Aragon and later led the 18th Brigade and the 43rd Division and lastly the XIII Corps. He was arrested in France and murdered in Dachau concentration camp.

Enrique de Salcedo Molinuevo was general in command of the La Coruña administrative division. Indecisive at first and then opposed to the uprising, he was arrested and executed by the Insurgents.

Narciso Sánchez Aparicio was an infantry major who was ordered on 19 July 1936 to organise a battalion of volunteers. Later he was Chief of Staff of the XXIII Corps.

Rafael Sánchez Paredes was an infantry lieutenant-colonel commanding one of the tank regiments. In the war he commanded the Tank base at Archeria (Murcia).

Pedro Sánchez Plaza was lieutenant-colonel of cavalry attached to the *Guardia de Asalto*. He helped to crush the military uprising at Vicálvaro barracks (Madrid). In 1937 he led the XII Corps at Belchite and in 1938 was put in charge of the recovery of disorganised units fleeing through Gandesa. At the end of 1938 he became Head of the Organisation Section of the Staff of the Army of the Ebro.

Angel de San Pedro Aymat was the general commanding the 7th Brigade in Barcelona. Arrested by the Insurgents in July 1936, he was freed when the former were defeated, but was given no command in the Republican Army. A post-war court martial sentenced him to 12 years' imprisonment.

Eusebio Sanz Asensio was a CNT militant who rose to command the 70th Mixed Brigade and later the 25th and the 22nd Divisions.

Ricardo Sanz was a CNT militant who was second in command of the Durruti column in Madrid and its leader after Durruti's death in November 1936 and later when it became the 26th Division. He was deported to North Africa by the French in 1940, returning after 1944, when he remained in France until returning to Spain in 1979 (*see* Bibliography).

Cándido Saseta Echevarría was a captain in the Supply Corps who served as an adviser to the Basque Defence Junta. He was killed in the struggle for Oviedo.

Manuel Tagüeña Lacorte was a mathematics and physics student who had militated in the Students' Union, the FUE. He participated in the early struggles around Madrid and, having had some military training in the university cadet corps (*milicias universitarias*), he led the militia battalion called *Octubre No. 1* and later the 30th Mixed Brigade and the 3rd Division. In 1938 he was transferred to the Eastern Front and given the XV Corps, which he led – at the age of 25 – in the battle of the Ebro and the fighting retreat through Catalonia and into internment in France. He returned to Republican territory but was given no post. When Colonel Casado rebelled against the Negrín Government, Tagüeña left Spain with the other communist leaders and attended the Frunze military academy in the Soviet Union. However, he became disillusioned with communism and went to Czechoslovakia, where he completed his medical training, and then to Mexico, where he worked in medical laboratories until his death in 1971.

Nilamón Toral Azcona was a young boxing instructor who was doing his military service. He led militias and the 32nd Brigade at Brunete. By the end of 1937, he was commanding the 70th Division. He was promoted to lieutenant-colonel and took part in the late, though successful, attack in Extremadura in January. He was imprisoned until 1944 by the victors, released but arrested again for communist guerrilla activity. Sentenced to death, he spent three years in solitary confinement.

Manuel Uribarri Barutell was a *Guardia Civil* captain stationed in Valencia who played an important role in organising militias. He took part in the expedition to try to recover Majorca from the Insurgents. He commanded the *Fantasma* column and later the 46th Brigade, rising to the rank of lieutenant-colonel. He led a guerrilla group and was also at the head of the *Servicio de Investigación Militar*, where his task was, as he later confessed, to pass information over to the Soviets. Dismissed, he went to France and later to Cuba and to Mexico, writing several self-justificatory books (*see* Bibliography).

Manuel Uribeecheverría was a retired artillery officer who headed a section of the Basque Staff.

José Valcázar Crespo was an artillery major who commanded a mountain group in Oviedo. He rose to command the artillery of the Army of Extremadura. His death sentence was commuted by the victors.

Etelvino Vega Martínez was a PCE agitprop expert in the army. He studied for some time in the USSR at the Frunze military academy. He commanded militia battalions and brigades, the 34th Division and the XII Corps of the Army of the Ebro. In the final round of his decrees Negrín made him military governor of the port of Alicante, where he was captured and executed by the victors.

Antonio Verardini, an engineer and militant, was Chief of Staff in the IV Corps. In late December 1936 he was involved in the affair of the fictitious 'Embassy of Siam', which was a trick to identify hidden right-wingers. Verardini was linked to the Special Services section of the Ministry of War.

Joaquín Vidal Munárriz was the commander of the mountain battalion stationed in Bilbao. He later led the 2nd Basque Division and the XIV Corps, which fought in Santander. After the loss of the north he commanded the XIX Corps in the Levante.

Vittorio Vidali, alias 'Carlos Contreras', was a communist from Trieste who had lived in exile from Fascism. He was in Spain under cover of a mission for

International Red Aid. He became the commissar for the Fifth Regiment and editor of its paper, *Milicia Popular*. After the dissolution of the Fifth Regiment he occupied various posts in the Commissariat and the Soviet NKVD, eliminating anti-Stalinist communists and staying in Spain until the loss of Catalonia. He later went to Mexico, where he was the lover of the artist Tina Modotti. After the Second World War he became a Senator for Trieste, dying in 1983.

Villabrille, *see* **Fernández Villabrille**.

José Villalba Rubio was an Africanist colonel who in 1936 was in command of the half mountain brigade garrison at Barbastro in Aragon. He did not join the insurrection in July 1936, though he had been expected to. He acted as military adviser to a militia column, then a division and was given the difficult talk of defending Málaga, where hardly any appropriate preparation had been made. When the city was lost Villalba was imprisoned awaiting court martial for some time. In 1938 he was exonerated. In 1949 he returned voluntarily to Spain from France and received the relatively mild sentence of 12 years in prison, being immediately amnestied. His many brothers fought with Franco.

Matías Yagüe, a member of the PCE who commanded the 9th Mixed Brigade, was killed during the battle of the Ebro.

Miguel Yoldi Benoy was a CNT militant who led the 24th Division.

Sebastián Zamora was an infantry captain not on the 1936 active list. He led one of the earliest militia columns in Aragon, then the 29th Division and the 16th Division. He was on the Staff of the Army of the East and led a division on the Ebro.

Joaquín de Zulueta Isasi was a reserve officer of cavalry who had been expelled from the Army by the right-wing Government of 1935. He rejoined when the war began and led militia columns and the 2nd and 38th Mixed Brigades. Later he headed the 7th Division until Colonel Casado made him commander of the II Corps in March 1939.

Bibliography

OFFICIAL PUBLICATIONS

Anuario Militar de España 1936, Ministry of War, Madrid.

Boletín Oficial del Estado, Burgos, later Madrid. Consulted from October 1939.

Boletín Oficial de la Junta de Defensa de Madrid, 17 December 1936–24 April 1937.

Diario Oficial del Consejo Nacional de Defensa, Madrid, 15–28 March 1939.

Diario Oficial del ministerio de la Guerra, later *de Defensa Nacional*, Madrid, Valencia, Barcelona, 1936–9.

Documents on German Foreign Policy 1918–1945, series D, vol. III, *The Spanish Civil War*, HMSO, 1951.

Gaceta de Madrid, later *Gaceta de la República*, Madrid, Valencia, Barcelona, 1936–9.

ARCHIVES

Servicio Histórico Militar, Archivo de la Guerra de Liberación (Madrid):

Cuartel General del Generalísimo

Documentación Nacional

Documentación Roja.

The National Archives, Kew (UK):

Archives of the British Foreign Office, Series FO 371.

PRIMARY AND SECONDARY SOURCES

(All works cited in notes are listed as well as some others which have been consulted. The editions cited are those used.)

Abad de Santillán, *Por qué perdimos la guerra*, Buenos Aires, 1940.

Abrahamson, P. and Abrahamson, A., *Mosaico Roto*, Madrid, 1994.

Academy of Sciences of the USSR, Soviet War Veterans' Committee, *International Solidarity with the Spanish Republic*, Moscow, 1975.

Acier, M., *From Spanish Trenches*, Cresset Press, 1939.

Aguilar Olivencia, M., *El ejército español durante la Segunda República*, Madrid, 1986.

Alcófar Nassaes, J. L., *Los asesores soviéticos en la guerra civil española*, Barcelona, 1971.

Allan, T. and Gordon, S., *The Scalpel, the Sword: The Story of Dr. Norman Bethune*, Boston, 1952.

Alpert, M., 'The Clash of Spanish Armies: Contrasting Ways of War in Spain 1936–1939', *War and History*, 6, 3 (1999), 331–51.

'Los enigmas de la rendición de Casado', *Historia 16*, 16, 185 (September 1991), 8–16.

La guerra civil española en el mar, Madrid, 1987 (rev. edn Barcelona, 2008).

'Negrín y el Ejército', in *Juan Negrín, médico y jefe del Gobierno, 1892–1956*, Madrid, 2006, 181–8.

A New International History of the Spanish Civil War, Palgrave Macmillan, 1994 (rev. edn 2004).

La reforma militar de Azaña, Madrid, 1982 (2nd edn Granada, 2008).

'Soldiers, Politics and War', in P. Preston, ed., *Revolution and War in Spain, 1931–1939*, Methuen, 1984, 202–24.

'"Una trompeta lejana". Las Brigadas Internacionales en la guerra de España: una reconsideración sesenta años después', *Espacio, Tiempo y Forma*, series 5, *Historia Contemporánea*, 12 (1999), 225–38.

Alonso Báquer, M., *El Ejército en la sociedad española*, Madrid, 1971.

Alvarez, Santiago, *Memorias II. La guerra civil de 1936–1939. Los comisarios políticos en el Ejército Popular de la República*, La Coruña, 1986.

Alvarez del Vayo, J., *Freedom's Battle*, Heinemann, 1940.

Amilibia, M. de, *Los batallones de Euskadi*, San Sebastián, 1978.

Anonymous, *El pueblo vasco frente a la cruzada franquista*, Toulouse, 1966.

Aralar, J. de, *La rebelión militar española y el pueblo vasco*, Buenos Aires, 1937.

Araquistáin, L. 'The Communists and the Spanish Civil War', at www.whatnextjournal.co.uk/Pages/history/Araquist.html.

Aroca, J. M. *Los republicanos que no se exiliaron*, Barcelona, 1969.

Aroca Mohedano, M., *General Juan Hernández Saravia, el ayudante militar de Azaña*, Madrid, 2006.

Aróstegui, J and Martínez, J., *La Junta de Defensa de Madrid*, Madrid, 1984.

Arrarás, J., *Francisco Franco*, Valladolid, 1939.

Historia de la Segunda República española, Madrid, 1956.

Arrarás, J., ed., *Historia de la Cruzada española*, 8 vols., Madrid, 1939–43.

Artís-Gener, A., *556 Brigada Mixta*, Mexico City, 1946.

Asensio, J., *El general Asensio: su lealtad a la República*, Barcelona, 1938.

Atholl, K., *Searchlight on Spain*, Penguin Books, 1938.

Azaña, Manuel, *Obras Completas*, 4 vols., Mexico City, 1966–8.

Aznar, M., *Historia militar de la guerra de España*, 3 vols., Madrid, 1958–63.

Bahamonde A., and Cervera, J., *Así terminó la guerra de España*, Madrid, 2000.

Bajatierra, M., *Crónicas de la guerra*, Valencia, 1937.

La guerra en las trincheras de Madrid, Barcelona, n.d.

Balfour, Sebastian, *Deadly Embrace: Morocco and the Road to the Spanish Civil War*, Oxford University Press, 2002.

Barea, A., *La forja de un rebelde*, Buenos Aires, 1951.

La ruta, Buenos Aires, 1951.

Bauer, E., *Impressions et expériences de la guerre d'Espagne*, Lausanne, 1938.

Baxell, Richard, *British Volunteers in the Spanish Civil War: The British Battalion in the International Brigades, 1936–1939*, Warren and Pell, 2007.
Bayo, A., *Mi desembarco en Mallorca*, Guadalajara (Mexico), 1944.
Bazal, L., *¡Ay de los vencidos!*, Toulouse, 1966.
Benavides, M. (Domingo), *Guerra y revolución en Cataluña*, Mexico City, 1946.
Bertrán y Musitú, J., *Experiencias de los servicios de información del nordeste de España (SIFNE) durante la guerra*, Madrid, 1940.
Bibliotecas del frente y de la retaguardia en la España republicana, Barcelona, 1938.
Bloch, J.-R., *España en armas*, Santiago de Chile, 1937.
Bolloten, B., *The Grand Camouflage*, Hollis and Carter, 1961.
The Spanish Revolution: The Left and the Struggle for Power during the Civil War, Chapel Hill, NC, 1979.
Borkenau, F., *The Spanish Cockpit*, Faber and Faber, 1937.
Bouthelier, A., and López-Mora, J., *Ocho días: la revuelta comunista*, Madrid, 1940.
Boyd, C., *Praetorian Politics in Liberal Spain*, Chapel Hill, NC, 1979.
Brenan, G., *The Spanish Labyrinth*, Cambridge University Press, 1943.
Broggi, M., *Memòries de un cirurgià 1908–1945*, Barcelona, 2001.
Broué, P. and Témime, E., *La révolution et la guerre d'Espagne*, Paris, 1961.
Buckley, H., *Life and Death of the Spanish Republic*, Hamish Hamilton, 1940.
Bullón de Mendoza, A. and de Diego, A., *Historias orales de la guerra civil, I*, Barcelona, 2000.
Busquets, J., *El militar de carrera en España*, Barcelona, 1967.
Cabezas, J. A., *Asturias: catorce meses de guerra civil*, Madrid 1975.
Campanario, J. M., 'Los ascensos y nombramientos de militares comunistas en marzo de 1939', at www2.uah.es/jmc/an40.pdf.
Campanario, J. M., Díez Hernando, C. and Cervera Gil, J., 'El enigma del general republicano Manuel Mantallana Gómez', at www2.uah.es/jmc/matallanacongresogce.pdf.
Camps, J. and Olcina, E., *Les milicies catalanes al front d'Aragó*, Barcelona, 2006.
Cardona, G., *El poder militar en la España contemporánea hasta la guerra civil*, Madrid, 1983.
Cardozo, H., *March of a Nation*, Eyre and Spottiswoode, 1937.
Carr, R., *Spain 1808–1939*, Clarendon Press, 1966.
Casado, S., *Así cayó Madrid*, Madrid, 1968.
The Last Days of Madrid, trans. R. Croft-Cooke, Peter Davies, 1939.
Casas de la Vega, R., *Brunete*, Madrid, 1967.
Teruel, Barcelona, 1973.
Castro Delgado, E., *Hombres 'Made in Moscú'*, Barcelona, 1965.
Cattell, D., *Communism and the Spanish Civil War*, Berkeley, CA, 1965.
Celeiro, Purificación and López Ochoa, Libertad, *Memoria familiar: memorias de un soldado*, with introduction and notes by Michael Alpert, Barcelona, 2007.
Cervera, J., *Madrid en guerra: la ciudad clandestina 1936–1939*, Madrid, 1998.

Cierva, R. de la, *Los documentos de la primavera trágica*, Madrid, 1967.
'Feliciano Martín Villoria, el hombre que justificó la Quinta Columna', *Historia y Vida*, 3 (June 1968), 56–65.
Historia de la guerra civil española, vol. I, Madrid, 1969.
Historia ilustrada de la guerra civil española, Madrid, 1970.
Cimorra, C., *España en las trincheras*, Madrid, 1938.
Cirre, J., *De Espejo a Madrid*, Granada, 1938.
Ciutat, F., *Relatos y reflexiones sobre la guerra de España*, Madrid, 1978.
Cleugh, J., *Spanish Fury*, Harrap, 1962.
Cobb, C., *Los milicianos de la cultura*, Bilbao, 1995.
Colodny, R., *The Struggle for Madrid*, New York, 1958.
Colvin, Ian, *Canaris, Chief of Intelligence*, Pan Books, 1957.
Comín, Colomer E., *Historia secreta de la Segunda República*, Madrid, 1954.
La República en el exilio, Barcelona, 1959.
Coni, N., *Medicine and Warfare: Spain 1936–1939*, Routledge, 2008.
Cordón, A., *Trayectoria: recuerdos de un artillero*, Paris, 1971.
Córdova Itúrburu, C., *España bajo el comando de pueblo*, Buenos Aires, 1938.
Corral, Pedro, *Desertores: la guerra civil que nadie quiere contar*, Madrid, 2006.
Cox, Geoffrey, *Defence of Madrid*, Gollancz, 1937.
Cruells, M., *L'expedició a Mallorca*, Barcelona, 1971.
Els fets de maig, Barcelona, 1970.
Cuesta Monereo, J., 'La guerra en los frentes del sur', in *La guerra de Liberación Nacional*, Zaragoza, 1961, 193–258.
Cueto, J, *Mi segunda vuelta*, Bilbao, 1937.
Cuevas, E., *Recuerdos de la guerra de España*, Montauban, 1940.
Díaz, J., *Tres años de lucha*, Barcelona, 1939.
Duval, M., *Les Espagnols et la guerre d'Espagne*, Paris, 1939.
Les leçons de la guerre d'Espagne, Paris, 1938.
Editorial Codex, *Crónica de la guerra española*, Buenos Aires, 1966.
Egea Bruno, Pedro M., 'La represión franquista en Cartagena (1939–1945)', unpublished manuscript, Murcia, 1987.
Ehrenburg, I., *Men, Years, Life*, vol. IV, *Eve of War*, MacGibbon and Kee, 1963.
Elorza, A., and Bizcarrondo, B., *Queridos compañeros: la Internacional Comunista y España 1919–1939*, Barcelona, 1999.
Endériz, *Teruel*, Barcelona, 1938.
Engel, Carlos, *Historia de las brigadas mixtas del Ejército Popular de la República*, Madrid, 1999.
Escudero Andújar, Fuensanta, *Lo cuentan como lo han vivido: República, guerra y represión en Murcia*, Murcia, 2000.
Etchebéhère, Mika, *Ma guerre d'Espagne à moi*, Paris, 1976.
Falcón, C., *Madrid*, Madrid, 1938.
Fischer, L., *Men and Politics*, Cape, 1941.
Flores Pazos, C. and Recio Cardona, R., *Uniformes y pertrechos: Ejército Popular Republicano 1936–1939*, Madrid, 1997.
Fontana, J. M., *Los catalanes en la guerra de España*, Madrid, 1956.

Foquet i Boreu, C., 'Cultura y teatro en las trincheras: la 31a división del Ejército Republicano', *Teatro*, 13–14 (1998–2001), 137–72.
Franco-Salgado Yaraujo, F., *Mis conversaciones con Franco*, Barcelona, 1972.
Fraser, R., *Blood of Spain: The Experience of Civil War 1936–1939*, Allen Lane, 1979.
Frutos, V. de, *Los que no perdieron la guerra*, Buenos Aires, 1967.
Gabriel, J., *La vida y la muerte en Aragón*, Buenos Aires, 1968.
Galíndez, J. de, *Los vascos en el Madrid sitiado*, Buenos Aires, 1945.
Galland, Adolf, *The First and the Last*, Collins, 1955.
Gámir Ulíbarri, M., *De mis memorias*, Paris, 1939.
Gárate, J. M. *Tenientes en campaña*, Madrid, 1976.
García, J., *Ispania Narodnova Fronta*, Moscow, 1957.
García Escudero, J. M., *El pensamiento de 'El Debate'*, Madrid, 1983.
García Fernández, J., ed., *25 militares de la República*, Ministry of Defence, Madrid, 2011.
García Lacalle, A., *Mitos y verdades: la aviación de caza en la guerra civil española*, Mexico City, 1973.
García Morato, J., *Guerra en el aire*, Madrid, 1950.
García Pradas, J., *Como terminó la guerra de España*, Buenos Aires, 1940.
García Valiño, R. 'La campaña del norte', in *La guerra de liberación nacional*, Zaragoza, 1961, 259–314.
García Venero, M., *Falange en la guerra de España*, Madrid 1967.
Historia de los internacionales en España, Madrid 1957.
Historia del nacionalismo catalán, Madrid, 1967.
García Vivancos, M., *'Memorias'*, unpublished manuscript [1971?].
Garder, M., *History of the Soviet Army*, Pall Mall Press, 1966.
Gil Robles, J. M., *No fue posible la paz*, Barcelona, 1968.
Goded, M., *Un faccioso cien por cien*, Zaragoza, 1938.
González, V. ('El Campesino'), *Comunista en España*, Mexico City, 1952; English trans., *Listen Comrades: Life and Death in the Soviet Union*, Heinemann, 1952.
González Quintana, A., 'Justicia militar en la España republicana durante la guerra civil española (1936–1939)', in *Justicia en Guerra*, Archivo Histórico Nacional, Sección de la Guerra Civil, Salamanca, November, 1987, Madrid, 1990, 171–89.
Graham, Helen, *The Spanish Republic at War, 1936–1939*, Cambridge University Press, 2002.
Guarner, V., *Cataluña en la guerra de España*, Madrid, 1975.
'Memorándum', unpublished manuscript.
Gurney, J., *Crusade in Spain*, Faber, 1974.
Guzmán, E. de, *Madrid rojo y negro*, Barcelona, 1938.
Halperine-Kaminski, E., *Ceux de Barcelone*, Paris, 1937.
Hanighen, F., ed., *Nothing but Danger: Thrilling Adventures of Ten Newspaper Correspondents in the Spanish War*, Harrap, 1940.
Henríquez Caubín, J., *La batalla del Ebro: maniobras de una una división*, Mexico City, 1944.
Hermet, G., *Les communistes en Espagne*, Paris, 1971.

Hernández, J., *La grande trahison*, Paris, 1971.
Hidalgo, Diego, *Cómo y por qué fui lanzado del ministerio de la Guerra*, Madrid, 1934.
Hidalgo de Cisneros, I., *Cambio de Rumbo: Memorias*, Bucharest, 1964.
Hinojosa Durán, J., *Tropas en un frente olvidado: el ejército republicano en Extremadura durante la guerra civil*, Mérida, 2009.
Hopkins, J., *Into the Heart of the Fire: The British in the Spanish Civil War*, Stanford, CA, 1998.
Howson, G., *Aircraft of the Spanish Civil War*, New York, 1990.
Arms for Spain: The Untold Story of the Spanish Civil War, John Murray, 1998.
Ibárruri, D., *El único camino*, Paris, 1962.
En la lucha, Moscow, 1968.
Ibárruri, D., Azcárate, M., Balaguer, L., Cordón, A., Falcón, I. and Sandoval, J., *Guerra y Revolución en España*, 3 vols., Moscow, 1966.
Izcaray, J. *et al.*, *Madrid es nuestro*, Madrid, 1938.
Jackson, G., *The Spanish Republic and the Civil War*, Princeton, NJ, 1965.
Jellinek, F., *The Civil War in Spain*, Gollancz, 1938.
Julià, S., ed., *Víctimas de la guerra civil*, Madrid, 1999.
Kelsey, U., 'Fuentes del Ebro', *Military Modelling* (December 1994), 45–7 and 58–60.
Klotz, H., *Les leçons militaires de la guerre d'Espagne*, Paris, 1937.
Koltsov, M., *Diario de la guerra de España*, Paris, 1963.
Kowalsky, D., *La Unión Soviética y la guerra civil española, una revisión crítica*, Barcelona, 2004.
Krivitsky, W., *I was Stalin's Agent*, Hamish Hamilton, 1939.
Lacruz, F., *El alzamiento, la revolución y el terror en Barcelona*, Barcelona, 1943.
Langdon-Davies, J., *Behind the Spanish Barricades*, Secker and Warburg, 1936.
Lamas, Angel, *Unos ... y otros*, Barcelona, 1972.
Largo Caballero, F., *Mis memorias*, Mexico City, 1954.
Last, J., *The Spanish Tragedy*, Routledge, 1939.
Liddell Hart, B., *Defence of the West*, New York, 1950.
The Other Side of the Hill: Germany's Generals, Their Rise and Fall, with Their Own Account of Military Events, 1939–1945, Cassell, 1951.
Lines, L., 'Female Combatants in the Spanish Civil War: *Milicianas* on the Front Lines and in the Rearguard', *Journal of International Women's Studies*, 10, 4 (May 2009), 168–87.
Líster, E., *Nuestra guerra*, Paris, 1966.
Liubarskii, C., *Nekotorie operativno-takticheskie vivodi iz opita voini v Ispanii*, Moscow, 1939.
Lizarra, A. de [Manuel de Irujo], *Los vascos y la República española*, Buenos Aires, 1944.
Llordés, J., *Al dejar el fusil*, Barcelona, 1968.
Llovera, F., *La columna Uribarri*, Valencia, n.d.
Lojendio, L. de, *Operaciones militares de la guerra de España*, Barcelona, 1940.

López J., *Una misión sin importancia*, Madrid, 1972.
López Fernández, A., *General Miaja, defensor de Madrid*, Madrid, 1975.
Maidanik, K., *Ispanskii proletariat b nationalisno-revolutionnoi voine*, Moscow, 1960.
Mainar, E., Santacreu, J. M. and Llopis, R., *Gandia i el seu port, marc 1939*, Gandía, 2010.
Maiskii, I., *Spanish Notebooks*, Hutchinson, 1966.
Malinovski, R., Voronov, N., Kuznetsov, N., Batov, P., Rodimtsev, A., Krivoshein, S., Yakushin M. and Prokofiev, G., *Bajo la bandera de la España republicana*, Introduction by Dolores Ibárruri, Moscow, n.d. [1968?].
Manual del miliciano, Barcelona, 1937.
Manzanera, E., *The Iron Column: Testament of a Revolutionary*, Kate Sharpley Library, 2006.
Martín Blázquez, J., *I Helped to Build an Army*, trans. F. Borkenau, Secker and Warburg, 1939.
Martínez Bande, J. M., *La batalla de Teruel*, Madrid, 1974.
La batalla del Ebro, Madrid, 1978.
La campaña de Andalucía, Madrid, 1969.
La campaña de Cataluña, Madrid, 1979.
Los cien últimos días de la República, Barcelona, 1973.
El final de la guerra civil, Madrid, 1985.
El final del frente norte, Madrid, 1973.
La gran ofensiva sobre Zaragoza, Madrid, 1973.
La guerra en el norte, Madrid, 1969.
La intervención comunista en la guerra de España, Madrid, 1965.
La invasión de Aragón y el desembarco en Mallorca, Madrid, 1970.
La llegada al mar, Madrid, 1975.
La lucha en torno a Madrid, Madrid, 1968.
La marcha sobre Madrid, Madrid, 1968.
La ofensiva sobre Segovia y la batalla de Brunete, Madrid, 1972.
La ofensiva sobre Valencia, Madrid, 1977.
Vizcaya, Madrid, 1971.
Martínez Paricio, J., Aspizua Turrión, J., Ramón, J., Urbina, B. and Molina Benayas, J., eds., *Los papeles del general Rojo*, Madrid, 1989.
Martínez Reverte, J., *La batalla del Ebro*, Barcelona, 2003.
Mas Alsina, E. and Anglada, Paquita, *En aquesta carta hi ha tabac: epistolari d'un soldat de l'exércit republicá*, Valls, 2010.
Mateo Merino, P., *Por vuestra libertad y la nuestra*, Madrid, 1986.
Matthews, J., 'Conscripts in the Republican Popular Army and the Nationalist Army in the Spanish Civil War (1936–1939). A Comparative Study of the Armies of the Central Region', unpublished doctoral thesis, University of Oxford, 2008. Published as *Reluctant Warriors*, Oxford University Press, 2012.
Mejías Correa, María de la Luz, *Así fue pasando el tiempo: memorias de una miliciana extremeña*, Seville, 2006.
Mera, C., *Guerra, exilio y cárcel de un anarcosindicalista*, Paris, 1976.
Mezquida, L., *La batalla del Ebro*, 3 vols., Tarragona, 1963–70.
La batalla del Segre, Tarragona, 1972.

Mira, E., *Psychiatry in War*, New York, 1943.
Miralles Bravo, R., *Memorias de un comandante Rojo*, Madrid, 1975.
Ministry of Justice, *La causa general*, 4th edn, Madrid, 1961.
Modesto, J. *Soy del Quinto Regimiento*, Paris, 1969.
Mola, E., *Obras Completas*, Valladolid, 1940.
Monferrer Catalán, L., *Odisea en Albión: los republicanos exiliados en Gran Bretaña, 1936–1977*, Madrid, 2007.
Montero, A., *Historia de la persecución religiosa en España*, Madrid, 1961.
Montero, S., *Brunete*, Madrid, 2009.
Montseny, Federica, *In Memoriam of Comrade Durruti*, Barcelona, 1937.
Moradiellos, E., *El reñidero de Europa: las dimensiones internacionales de la guerra civil española*, Barcelona, 2001.
Mortera, A., 'Armas para España, pese a Howson', *Historia Militar*, 9 (January 2001), 83–93.
Moyano, I., 'La batalla del Ebro: la acción de la artillería', *Ejército*, 23 (December 1941), 18–27.
Nash, M., *Rojas, las mujeres republicanas en la guerra civil*, Madrid, 1999.
Navajas Zubeldia, C., *Leales y rebeldes: la tragedia de los militares republicanos*, Madrid, 2011.
Nelken, Margarita, *Por qué hicimos la revolución*, Madrid, 1936.
Nenni, P., *La guerra de España*, Mexico City, 1964.
Neves, M., *La matanza de Badajoz*, Mérida, 2007.
Orwell, G., *Homage to Catalonia*, Penguin Books, 1966.
Pagés, P., *Cataluña en guerra y en revolución (1936–1939)*, Seville, 2007.
Pastor Petit, D., *Los dossiers secretos de la guerra civil*, Barcelona, 1978.
Patronato Central de Redención de Penas por el Trabajo, *La obra de redención de penas*, Madrid, 1942.
Payne, S., *Politics and the Military in Modern* Spain, Stanford, CA, 1967.
The Spanish Revolution, Weidenfeld and Nicolson, 1970
Unión Soviética, comunismo y revolución en España (1931–1939), Barcelona, 2003.
Paz, Abel, *Buenaventura Durruti 1896–1936*, Paris, 2000.
Paz Sánchez, Manuel de, *Militares masones en España. Diccionario biográfico del siglo XX*, Valencia, 2004.
Peirats, J., *Los anarquistas en la crisis política española*, Buenos Aires, 1964.
La CNT en la revolución española, Toulouse, 3 vols., 1951–3; Paris 1971 (English edn Meltzer Press, 2001–6).
Perea Capulino, J., *Los culpables. Recuerdos de la guerra 1936–1939*, Barcelona, 2007.
Pérez López, M., *A Guerrilla Diary of the Spanish Civil War*, André Deutsch, 1972.
Pérez Salas, J., *Guerra en España 1936–1939*, Mexico City, 1947.
Preston, P., *Franco: A Biography*, HarperCollins, 1993.
The Spanish Holocaust, Christie Books, 2011.
Prieto, I., *Cómo y por qué salí del Ministerio de Defensa Nacional: intrigas de los rusos en España*, Mexico City, 1940.
Convulsiones de España, Mexico City, 1968.
'Epistolario Prieto–Negrín', *Indice*, 263/4 (February 1970).

Puig Casas, L., *Personal Memories of the Days of the Spanish Civil War, in Catalan and English*, ed. and annotated Idoya Puig, Edwin Mellen Press, 1999.
Radosh, S., Habeck, M. and Sevostianov, G., eds., *Spain Betrayed: The Soviet Union in the Spanish Civil War*, New Haven, CT, 2001.
Regler, G., *The Great Crusade*, New York, 1940.
Reparaz, G. de, *Diario de nuestra guerra*, Barcelona, n.d.
Richards, V., *Lessons of the Spanish Revolution*, Freedom Press, 1953.
'Rieger, Max' [Wenceslao Roces], *Espionnage en Espagne*, Paris, 1938.
Rodríguez Velasco, H., *Una derrota prevista: el espionaje republicano en la Guerra Civil española (1936–1939)*, Granada, 2012.
'Las guerrillas en el Ejército Popular de la República (1936–1939)', *Cuadernos de Historia Contemporánea*, 33 (2011), 235–54.
Rojo, J. A., 'Rojo, el estratega de la República', *La Aventura de la Historia*, 94 (August 2006), 34–9.
Vicente Rojo, retrato de un general republicano, Barcelona, 2006.
Rojo, V., *¡Alerta los pueblos!*, Buenos Aires, 1939.
Así fue la defensa de Madrid, Mexico City, 1967.
España heroica, Buenos Aires, 1942.
Romero, L., *Desastre en Cartagena*, Barcelona, 1971.
El final de la guerra, Barcelona, 1976.
Tres días de julio, Barcelona, 1967.
Romero Basart, L., *Impresiones de un militar republicano*, Barcelona, 1937.
Romilly, E., *Boadilla*, Hamish Hamilton, 1937.
Ruiz, J., *Franco's Justice: Repression in Madrid after the Spanish Civil War*, Clarendon Press, 2005.
Runacre, W., 'Portrait of an Anarchist General: Major-General Miguel García Vivancos', at http://flag.blackened.net/revolt/spain/general_vivancos.html.
Rybalkin, Y., *Stalin y España: la ayuda militar soviética a la República*, Madrid, 2007 (originally published Moscow, 2000).
Salas Larrazábal, J., *La guerra desde el aire*, Barcelona, 1966.
La intervención extranjera en la guerra de España, Madrid, 1974.
Salas Larrazábal, R., *Los datos exactos de la guerra civil*, Madrid, 1980.
'The Growth and Role of the Republican Army', in R. Carr, ed., *The Republic and the Civil War in* Spain, Macmillan, 1971, 158–87.
Historia del Ejército Popular de la República, 4 vols, Madrid, 1973.
Sánchez del Arco, M, *El sur de España en la reconquista de Madrid*, Seville, 1937.
Sanz, R. *Los que fuimos a Madrid*, Toulouse, 1969.
Schwartz, F., *La internacionalización de la guerra civil española*, Barcelona, 1971.
Seaton, A. and Seaton, J., *The Soviet Army, 1918 to the Present*, The Bodley Head, 1986.
Seco Serrano, C., *Militarismo y civilismo en la España contemporánea*, Madrid, 1984.
Seidman, M., *Republic of Egos: A Social History of the Spanish Civil War*, Madison, WI, 2002.
Skoutelsky, R., *L'espoir guidait leurs pas: les volontaires français dans les Brigades Internationales*, Paris, 1998.

Novedad en el frente: las brigadas internacionales en la guerra civil española, Madrid, 2006.

Soler, J., *La guerra en el frente de Aragón: junto a la línea de fuego*, Barcelona, 1937.

Southworth, H. R., *El mito de la cruzada de Franco*, Paris, 1963.

Somoza, L., *El general Miaja*, Mexico City, 1944.

Steer, G., *The Tree of Gernika*, Hodder and Stoughton, 1938.

Strong, A. L., *Spain at Arms*, New York, 1937.

Sueiro, D., *La verdadera historia del Valle de los Caídos*, Madrid, 1976.

Suero Roca, M. T., *Militares republicanos de la guerra de España*, Barcelona, 1981.

Tagüeña, M., *Testimonio de dos guerras*, Mexico City, 1973.

Téry, S., *Front de la liberté: Espagne 1937–1938*, Paris, 1938.

Thomas, H., *The Spanish Civil War*, 3rd edn, Penguin Books, 1977.

Torres, E., *La batalla de l'Ebre*, Barcelona, 1971.

Torriente-Brau, Pablo de la, *Peleando con los milicianos*, Mexico City, 1938.

Trueta, J., *Treatment of War Wounds and Fractures with Special Reference to the Closed Method as Used in the War in Spain, etc.*, Hamish Hamilton, 1939.

United Editorial, *Spain at War* [later *The Voice of Spain*], London, 1938–9, No. 11 (May 1938).

Uribarri, M., *El SIM de la República*, Havana, 1943.

Uribe Gallejones, F., *Un miliciano de la UGT*, Bilbao, 2007.

Vidali, V., *Il Quinto Reggimento*, Milan, 1973.

Vilanova, A., *La defensa del Alcázar de Toledo*, Mexico City, 1963.

Los olvidados, Paris, 1969.

Viñas, A., 'The Financing of the Spanish Civil War', in Paul Preston, ed., *Revolution and War in Spain*, Methuen, 1984, 246–84.

El oro de Moscú: alfa y omega de un mito franquista, Barcelona, 1979.

El oro español en la guerra civil, Madrid, 1976.

Viñas, A. and Hernández Sánchez, F., *El desplome de la República*, Barcelona, 2010.

Wintringham, T., *English Captain*, Penguin Books, 1941.

New Ways of War, Penguin Books, 1940.

Worsley, T., *Behind the Battle*, Robert Hale, 1939.

Zaloga, S.J., 'Soviet Tank Operations in the Spanish Civil War', at http://bobrowen.com/nymas/soviet_tank_operations_in_the_sp.htm.

Spanish Civil War Tanks: The Proving Ground for Blitzkrieg, Osprey, 2010.

Zaragoza, C., *Ejército Popular y militares de la República*, Barcelona, 1983.

Zugazagoitia, J., *Guerra y vicisitudes de los españoles*, Paris, 1968.

CONTEMPORARY PAMPHLETS AND ARTICLES

(Mostly kept in the Biblioteca Nacional Madrid. Many have no date or place of publication.)

Published by army units

124th Battalion, Fragmento del *Código de Justicia Militar*, n.p., 1938.

'Joven Guardia' Battalion, *Para fortalecer la disciplina: leyes penales*, Madrid, n.d.
42nd Brigade, *Instrucciones generales para oficiales*, n.p., n.d.
44th Brigade, *Escuela de cabos y sargentos*, Madrid, 1937.
3rd Division, *Libro del Oficial*, n.p., n.d.
8th Division, *Programa de la escuela de cabos*, n.p., n.d.
11th Division, *Once División en Aragón*, Caspe, 1937.
12th Division, *Academia militar popular*, Madrid, 1937.
Sanidad en campaña, n.p., 1937.
14th Division, *Programa de la escuela divisionaria de oficiales*, n.p., n.d.
18th Division, *A los jefes, oficiales, clases y soldados de esta División*, n.p., n.d.
26th Division, *Indice biográfico de la 26 división*, n.p., 1938.
III Army Corps, *Normas tácticas para la infantería*, Madrid, n.d.
XIX Army Corps, *Sargentos: guión de materias para alumnos y aspirantes*, n.p., 1938.
XXI Army Corps, *Programa de Instrucción: batallón*, Valencia, 1937.
Army of the Centre, *Primer curso de jefes de brigada*, Madrid, 1938.
Instrucción reservada no. 172 para el funcionamiento de los Estados Mayores de este Ejército, Madrid, 1938.
Army of the Centre, General War Commissariat, *Orientaciones a los comisarios sobre el trabajo político en relación a las evasions*, n.p., 1939.
Army of the North, *Instrucción general No. 1. Organización de los Estados Mayores en el cuerpo de ejército, en la división de infantería y en la brigada mixta*, n.p., 1937.
Memoria del batallón de instrucción, Noreña, 1937.
Obligaciones por las que han de regirse los oficiales y clases afectos a esta escuela, Noreña, 1937
Army of the South (Insurgent), III Corps, Justice Section, *Colección de órdenes*, n.p., n.d.
Armoured Forces Group, *Nuestras armas: sus averías, entorpecimientos e interrupciones*, n.p., 1938.
Comandancia Militar de Milicias, *Un esfuerzo en 1936*, Madrid, 1937.

Publications of the Political Commissariat and other military departments

Comisariado de guerra, *Datos sobre utilización de la infantería en el combate*, Guadalajara, 1937.
Comisariado de guerra, 48th Division, *Guiones del trabajo del comisario*, n.p., n.d.
Comisariado de guerra, 105th Brigade, *Instrucciones para el trabajo de nuestros activistas*, n.p., 1938.
Comisariado de guerra, I Cuerpo de Ejército, *Recopilación de las disposiciones más importantes sobre el Comisariado General de Guerra*, Madrid, 1938.
Comisariado de las Brigadas Internacionales, *Libro de táctica militar para nuestros combatientes*, Madrid, 1937.
Comisariado del Grupo de Ejércitos de la Zona Central, *Instrucciones a los delegados de compañía respecto a su misión en período de combate*, Valencia, 1938.
Comisariado general de guerra, *ABC del Comisariado*, Madrid, n.d.

Camarada soldado, Valencia, 1937.
Delitos y faltas militares; instrucciones a los comisarios para su extinción, n.p., 1938.
Comisariado general de guerra, Ejército del Centro, *Orientaciones a los comisarios sobre el trabajo político en relación a las evasions*, n.p., 1939.
Comisariado general del Ejército de Tierra, *Instrucciones a todos los comisarios a fin de dar aplicación concreta a las tareas del momento*, n.p., 1938.
Normas para la intervención de los vocales comisarios en los tribunales militares permanentes, n.p., 1938.
El comisario, sus métodos y formas de trabajo en el seno del Ejército Popular, Madrid, 1938.
Subcomisariado de agitación, prensa y propaganda del comisariado general de guerra, *Escritos de soldados*, n.p., n.d.
Las relaciones del Comisariado con el mando militar, n.p., n.d.
Intendencia militar de Santander, *Instrucciones por las que han de regirse todos los cuerpos y unidades armados para la reclamación de devengos*, Santander, 1937.
Sanidad de guerra, *The Achievement of the Socorro Rojo Internacional*, Valencia, n.d.

Named authors and organisations

Altmaier, J., *Sur le front de la liberté*, Paris, 1938.
Andrés, T., *Indicaciones para la organización de las bibliotecas de frentes, cuarteles y hospitales*, Valencia, 1938.
Antón, F. *El comisariado en el Ejército Popular*, n.p., n.d.
Madrid, orgullo de la España antifascista, Valencia, 1937.
Asensio, J., *Movilización general: algunos de sus aspectos*, Barcelona, 1938.
Astro, Dr, *Consejos a los milicianos*, Barcelona, n.d.
Casado, S., 'The Republican Command in the Spanish Civil War', *National Review* (London), July 1939.
Castro Delgado, E., *Las relaciones del Comisariado con el mando militar*, n.p., 1938.
Charlton, L., *The Military Situation in Spain after Teruel*, United Editorial, 1938.
Cimorra, C. *Crónicas de guerra*, Valencia, 1937.
Clavego, P., *El trabajo de los comisarios políticos*, Barcelona, n.d.
Colmegna, H., *Diario de un médico argentino en la guerra civil española*, Buenos Aires, 1941.
Comité Militar PSU-UGT, *Como luchar para vencer*, Nos. 1–7, Barcelona, 1937.
Confederación Nacional del Trabajo, *Durruti: en memoriam*, Barcelona, 1937.
De julio a julio: un año de lucha, Barcelona, 1937.
Contreras, C., *Problemas del Ejército Popular*, Caspe, 1937.
Durán Jordà, F., *Service of Blood Transfusion at the Front*, Barcelona, 1937.
Fernández Aldana, B, *La guerra de Aragón, como fue*, Barcelona, n.d.
Fuente Hita, Dr F., *Salud del combatiente*, Madrid, n.d.

Gobierno Autónomo de Euzkadi, *Report on the Administration of Justice in the Basque Country during the Civil War*, Paris, 1938.
González Inestal, M., *La toma de Teruel*, Barcelona, 1938.
Julián, Narciso, *Como funcionan los trenes blindados*, Madrid, n.d.
López de la Fuente, J., *Ideas generales para soldados y cabos*, Madrid, 1937.
Madinaveitia, J. *Higiene del soldado en campaña*, Barcelona, 1938.
Martí-Ibáñez, Dr F., *Mensaje eugénico a los trabajadores*, n.p., n.d.
Partido comunista de Euzkadi, *Instrucciones a los comisarios políticos, mandos militares y milicianos en general*, Bilbao, 1937.
Rust, W., 'The Spanish People's Army', *Labour Monthly*, August 1938.
Stowe, L., 'Spain's Shirt-Sleeved Heroes', *The Nation* (New York), April 1938.

MILITARY PRESS

(This list is a sample of the large number of unit newspapers which have been consulted. Some existed for most of the war, others for some time or intermittently. Few series are complete.)

Battalion

Cultura en el frente	4th Battalion	66th Brigade	Weekly

Brigade

¡A Vencer!	39th Brigade	Fortnightly
Avanzadilla	36th Brigade	Irregular
El Combate	2nd FAI column	Alternate days
En Marcha	22nd Brigade	Irregular

Division

El Frente	26th Division	Irregular
Kriss	5th Division	Monthly
Pasaremos	11th Division	Weekly
La Trinchera	27th Division	Irregular
Triunfaremos	48th Division	Irregular
Veinticinco División	25th Division	Weekly

Army corps

Acero	V Corps	Monthly
Diana	X Corps	Irregular
España	III Corps	Monthly
Superación	XX Corps	Irregular
Tchapaieff	XIV Corps	Weekly

Army

Diario Sur	Army of Andalusia	Irregular
El Ejército Popular	Army of the East	Monthly
El Frente	Army of Extremadura	Daily

Specialised Arms

¡A sus puestos!	Artillery of the Army of the Centre	Monthly
Democracia Artillera	Artillery of I Corps	Fortnightly
Nuestras Armas	Engineers of the Army of the Centre	Irregular
Transmisiones	Signals of the Army of the Centre	Irregular

Index

Please also refer to the biographies in Appendix 4.